CONTRADICTION OF ENLIGHTENMENT

Dedicated to Sue

Contradiction of Enlightenment

Hegel and the Broken Middle

NIGEL TUBBS
School of Education
King Alfred's
Winchester

Ashgate

Aldershot · Brookfield USA · Singapore · Sydney

Published by
Ashgate Publishing Ltd
Gower House
Croft Road
Aldershot
Hants GU11 3HR
England

Ashgate Publishing Company
Old Post Road
Brookfield
Vermont 05036
USA

British Library Cataloguing in Publication Data

Tubbs, Nigel
    Contradiction of enlightenment : Hegel and the broken
    middle. - (Avebury series in philosophy)
    1.Hegel, Georg Wilhelm Friedrich, 1770-1831 2.Enlightenment
    3.Philosophy, British
    I. Title
    190

Library of Congress Catalog Card Number: 97-73407

ISBN 1 84014 109 3

Printed in Great Britain by The Ipswich Book Company, Suffolk.

Contents

Acknowledgements

I am especially grateful to Sheila Roche for her advice and comments, to Anne Judd and to Cherry for her work on the text.

Preface

The aim of this book is to read social and educational relations against each other in order to develop a comprehensive notion of education.

It follows on from work begun by Gillian Rose in her book *Hegel Contra Sociology*. Through her reading of Hegel she argued that illusion is implicitly contained within and unavoidably reproduced by bourgeois social relations. She showed how sociological critique repeats those illusions and how it fails to comprehend that repetition in any substantial way. Like other such cultures, sociology is torn apart by the aporias (the irresolvable dilemmas) which it generates by its own reasoning and self-reflection. It is driven by the desire to know these aporias in a way which will overcome its contradictions and heal its divisions. But, despondent and exhausted at the repetition of aporias, caught in the impasse of dualisms of object/subject, structure/agency, and individual/collective, sociology despairs at its eternal failing to overcome and to heal.

The significance of Rose's work is that it comprehends the fate and repetition of such cultures as an educational movement and development. Contra sociology, Rose protests against despair and against the overcoming of despair. Her protest is comprehensive. It includes itself within that which must be protested against. In this sense, what Rose offers is protest as contra-diction and contradiction. In speaking against, protest also and at the same time opposes itself. This is the contradictory self-relation of 'contra' for Rose. *Contradiction of Enlightenment* seeks to extend this insight regarding protest to educational categories and educational theorising. Contra enlightenment and critique, it argues that illusion is implicitly contained within and unavoidably reproduced by educational relations, particularly those determined around its categories of 'knowledge' and 'the teacher'. Educational critique, like sociological critique, fails to comprehend its repetition of illusion and its aporetic reasoning in any substantial way. As Rose did for sociology so, now, *Contradiction of Enlightenment* shows how education can achieve a comprehensive understanding of its contradictory self-relation and can come to experience protest as the development and education of its own philosophical consciousness. Put differently, it shows how, in protest, education becomes itself.

The educational significance of Rose's work is contained in her notion of 'the broken middle'. It is an idea which contains oppositions and contradictions, seeking not to resolve them, but to risk their negativity and to learn from it. The broken middle holds within itself both our despair at the impasse of repetition, and the education which is implicit in these negative (self) experiences. In the broken middle, illusion is formative, the negative is substantial, and learning, or the education of our philosophical consciousness, is self-determinative. Above all, the broken middle holds the positive and the negative together and apart, learning from the experience of contradiction and the contradiction of experience.

One of the key aspects of the broken middle is that it is constitutive of and is constituted by the ambivalence of our experience of identity, that is, our experience of who or what we are. In *Love's Work*, Rose writes that 'you may be weaker than the whole world but you are always stronger than yourself' (1995, p. 69). In terms of social and educational relations, this translates into experiencing ourselves as both less than the identity of person and teacher, less than independent, but also as more than the non-identity of slave or student, more than merely dependent. The broken middle is this gap. The experience of this gap in and for itself is set out abstractly in the Introduction. The determination of this experience in social and educational relations is explored in the rest of the book. It is in drawing out the educational work contained within the broken middle of social relations, and in drawing out the social or public work contained within the broken middle of educational relations, that this book continues and develops the work begun in Rose's *Hegel Contra Sociology*.

Such a broken middle is contained in this Preface (and in the Conclusion). This is the beginning of the book yet it is written at the end of the book. It is written as the beginning with the hindsight gained from the end. This position at the beginning is therefore illusory and unstable. It is not what it appears to be. It announces that which has already happened yet also that which is yet to come. As such the Preface is already contra itself, already a protest against its own statements. It contains its own contradictory self-relation, its own self-opposition, its instability, for its truth lies in its development and that development lies elsewhere than in the Preface. This is the difficulty of the 'speculative proposition' in Hegelian philosophy. This Preface, with its apparently definitive statements, commends that it be read as you, the reader, experience it, i.e. as definitive statements whose certainty you protest against. It is in that experience where what is abstract becomes *for* consciousness, where certainties are negated, and where, in the relation of certainty and protest, the content of the Preface becomes actual.

Actuality is the whole as it is lived and experienced. It is the whole of the broken middle of social and educational relations. But presuppositions of reason, of enlightenment, of overcoming, of the positive and the negative, and of repetition dominate actuality and avoid its difficulties, its risks and its circles of certainty and uncertainty, and of uncertainty and certainty. Such presuppositions are a domination of life as it is lived and experienced. Rose's reading of Hegel takes the comedy of actuality seriously. This means taking the comedy of contradiction seriously, risking its negative implications and having faith in the risk when the results are less than were hoped for. Above all, it means recognising the educational life and soul of philosophical consciousness, a recognition which is formative, and in which, as Nietzsche's Zarathustra demands, we become what we are. In risking the experience or misrecognition of illusion by itself, Rose has exposed, for us, the broken middle as (our) self-experience, and recognised our illusory being as the formative process which is self-relation. When the broken middle of the culture of reason (*Verstand*) is known as self-determinative, then philosophical consciousness has returned to itself, the same but different, changed by the education of the return. The repetition of culture is empty and the work of experience is blind until what returns, in itself and for itself, is philosophical consciousness.

The misrecognition implicit within this return of philosophical consciousness to itself determines the ways in which the return is interpreted. Put another way, illusion already determines how illusion is comprehended. As Rose argues in *Hegel Contra Sociology*, this can be interpreted as the end of philosophical consciousness in two senses. One is end in the sense of *telos*, where return implies end as completion, or as 'the definitive political experience' (1981, p. 209). Such an interpretation gives rise to the interpretation that return in Hegel's philosophy is announcing the 'end of history'. The other interpretation of return is the end of philosophy in the sense of *finis*. Here, such cultures are held to have exhausted their capacity for knowing their own misrecognition (within, for example, bourgeois property forms) in a way which is substantial or self-determining. Whereas *telos* implies meaning and purpose, *finis* invokes meaninglessness and despair. But return in Hegel, as in Nietzsche, carries both meanings. To take sides 'for' or 'against' return, or to posit that the positive and the negative can or cannot be known, or, above all, to side for or against the absolute, are all repetitions of the misrecognition of illusion, by itself, within social relations. Such presuppositions or positings enable sociological and educational critique, at their most crucial moments of despair, to side-step, positively or negatively, the educational and philosophical significance of their aporias or dilemmas. These presuppositions are necessary in order to avoid the impasse of the contradiction produced by critique under the continuing domination of bourgeois property law. They are, however, presuppositions which are themselves grounded in another, even more fundamental, presupposition. They are dependent upon the presupposition that the totality of the educational self-relation is known as 'enlightenment'. Critique reveals its own presupposition of enlightenment each time it judges that contradiction and return have or have not been overcome. Such pronouncements are another experience for us of repetition and contradiction. Hegel, Nietzsche and Rose do not presuppose educational self-relations positively or negatively, and do not therefore side-step the difficulties posed by the aporias of our rational consciousness. On the contrary, they employ them in their own work as the movement and risk which constitute the ambivalence of their own subjectivity. It is with the contradiction of return, a contradiction implicit within judgments of overcoming (*telos*) or repetition (*finis*), that *Contradiction of Enlightenment* begins.

The terms education and enlightenment are often used interchangeably. However, it is necessary to distinguish between them if the social relations implicit within educational theorising and educational categories are to appear. Enlightenment is always abstract and always personification; it is always a repetition of (the freedom of) the bourgeois person. Education, on the other hand, is comprehensive, and is the broken middle or self-relation of (its own) self-activity and self-result. Education is the comprehensive whole of which enlightenment, contradiction and return are constituent parts. They are all contained within the term 'education relation'. Enlightenment presupposes education as result, and this result is always presupposed as a knowledge of something, even when, as with Adorno, its result is presupposed as the knowledge of no-result. Knowledge 'of' is a category of domination over its object and is based on exactly the same principle of independence and sovereignty that the free person enjoys in its property rights over objects, the same misrecognition of relation and non-relation. Reason and the bourgeois person are the same presupposition of independence. Private property law and enlightenment are the repetition of that presupposition, although they appear to be merely the principle of independence expressed in its universality. There is also an ambiguity in the term 'educational relations' which is used throughout the work. By educational relations I mean both relations which one finds in the world of education, for example, teacher and student, and the way in which those relations found in education come to be educational. In many cases in the text the use of the term 'educational relations' refers specifically to the first case, and implies the second case as a development which their uneasy relationship commends.

This misrecognition of relation and non-relation (dependence and independence, learning and knowledge, student and teacher) in social and educational relations is explored as the broken middle which they share and which they repeat as their own self-determination. This repetition is examined in Chapter 1 in regard to critics who accuse teachers of reproducing, consciously or otherwise, relations of domination which are implicit within bourgeois social relations. This knowledge of these teachers, a knowledge which belongs to the critics, is revealed as the latter's own personification and enlightenment, or their own repetition of the very relations which they criticise. A series of such repetitions (of enlightenment) or personifications is followed through the experience of (this) 'despairing teacher' who finds every attempt at reform contradicts his own intentions. The despairing teacher finds no relief from this dilemma, encountering critical educational and pedagogical theory stuck in an impasse which it can only ever repeat, even when it holds that, in its enlightenment about (i.e. of) repetition, it has overcome it. Every enlightenment, even about repetition, still contains and repeats the illusions with which it is forced to begin and end its critical activity.

Chapter 2 moves this despairing teacher out of educational theory and into social theory. However, even here in the examination of Rousseau, Marx and Durkheim, the despairing teacher finds the educational relation presupposed as enlightenment, a presupposition which is repeated in the personification of these three teachers of critique. Finally, in Chapter 3, the despairing teacher seeks a solution to the impasse of personification in Foucault's de-personification of the subject, which Foucault reveals to be merely a network of power relations. But a knowledge of power relations as power/knowledge is equally repetitious of the broken middle of social and educational relations. In Foucault, however, there is no one left to learn from the experience or the despair.

Part II examines this experience of the contradiction of the teacher and the critic as the dialectic of enlightenment. It begins by introducing Hegel's understanding of the relation between natural consciousness and philosophical consciousness and applying this relation to the development of its self-certainty as reason as described in his *Phenomenology of Spirit*. The instability of this certainty is then explored through the work of Adorno and Horkheimer as the dialectic of enlightenment. This dialectic is held apart in two of its three constituent moments by, on the one hand, Habermas' theory of communicative action and, on the other, Adorno's theory of negative dialectics, before that tension speaks its own word as actuality or the broken middle. Here a speculative exposition of enlightenment is offered as self-light, or as the triune relationship of light, dark and shadow. The phrase 'shining for others' is intended to capture this *ménage-à-trois* and is returned to in Part IV with regard to Nietzsche's Zarathustra.

Part III explores the broken middle in detail in Hegelian philosophy, in terms of both social and educational relations. In terms of the former, the broken middle emerges in Chapter 6 out of a close reading of the master/slave relation in the *Phenomenology* which is then applied to Hegel's idea of ethical life and to his critique of bourgeois property relations. The broken middle of social relations is then transposed to the broken middle of educational relations in Chapter 7 and in particular the critique of bourgeois property relations is read, now, as a critique of rational knowledge relations. The master/slave relationship is applied to the teacher/student relationship, offering the despairing teacher his own self-relation, his own philosophical consciousness, as teacher and student.

Part IV sees the return of the despairing teacher but this time able to comprehend the whole of his educational relation through the contradictions which constitute his life and experience. The contradiction of enlightenment, its broken middle, is lived out in the story of Nietzsche's Zarathustra. Part IV offers a close reading of this text, which relates particular events in Zarathustra's life to the whole of the story of his life. It is often the case that readers dip in and out of *Thus Spake Zarathustra* to extract some of his teachings regardless of at what stage of his development they occur. Such asset-stripping is a violation of the integrity of the whole. The book concerns the continuing education of Zarathustra, an education which runs the whole length of the book. It must be read to the end in order to understand the truth and falsity of all that went before. Zarathustra, the despairing teacher, follows a similar path of despair to that outlined in Parts I, II and III. By the end of the book, Zarathustra no longer merely teaches protest, for he has become in himself the contradictory self-relation of protest; he has become what he is – the contradiction of enlightenment. What Rose's reading of Hegel opens up, among other things, is how Nietzsche and Hegel share an understanding of the determinate negation which is (eternal) return, and that return, released from the presupposition of enlightenment as positive or negative, is what is actual. In the totality which is the eternal return of will-to-power as Zarathustra, and in the totality which is the system in Hegel, both realise and work with and as, the self-relation which is the absolute. What in Nietzsche is the substantive but contradictory relation of shining for others is, in Hegel, the actuality of comprehensive education.

This project was originally intended to be limited to an Hegelian critique of the presuppositions of education as enlightenment. But the labour of the notion, as Hegel puts it, once begun, achieves a mind of its own. 'Speak your word and break', says the silence to Zarathustra. *Hegel Contra Sociology* enjoyed the same fate. Its first chapter is the (Hegelian) critique of sociology by itself. In speaking of itself as contradiction, or self-relation, it breaks itself and becomes for itself what it already was. Having spoken in Chapter 1 of *Hegel Contra Sociology*, the notion is then ripe to become itself, and it achieves a mind of its own in the rest of the book. So, too, I had not expected the notion to force itself so strongly upon education as the self-relation of what education is. It speaks its word and breaks with regard to critique and enlightenment in Parts I and II. It enjoys a mind of its own in Parts III and IV. It imposes itself as the philosophical system which is the comprehensive education and relation of the teacher and the student, and as the comprehensive (state) education which is our ethical life. Above all, it recognises the educational work of the philosophical consciousness of those who teach and learn, a work which has its truth as (public) service, and its actuality for us as contradiction. As such, Hegel, Nietzsche and Rose, between them, offer us the self-relation of education and philosophy, wherein critique is social, political and spiritual.

Two comments are appropriate finally regarding the use of language. The first concerns specialist Hegelian terminology. Mindful of an audience in education who are not acquainted with Hegel or with concepts in critical theory, it is clearly important to ensure that specialist terms are explained. Equally, however, it runs counter to the argument presented in the book to resolve difficulties in cases where the difficulties themselves are the work which form the substance of our education. The strategy adopted, sometimes successfully and sometimes not, is to try and ensure that the meaning of specialist terms emerges from the way they are being used in the argument. 'Definitions' of terms are not given. Concepts in Hegelian philosophy protest against merely abstract definitions which take no account of the self-contradictions which they already contain. If the reader thinks that, for example, they have not completely grasped what Hegel means by 'positing', then the risk and the failure of comprehension and of education continues. Where a concept is introduced but not in a context where its meaning is part of the work being carried out, reference is given to those parts of the book where such a context can be found. Capital letters for Hegelian terms have been retained only where they appear in cited quotations.

The same strategy applies in Part IV with regard to Zarathustra. Here there is a complete shift of specialist terminology, but again meanings have been related to the context and events of Zarathustra's life rather than to abstracted definitions. The intention throughout is to hear the voice of the despairing teacher and to follow his experiences. By the time we reach Part IV, that voice has become something other than mere despair and, through the story of Zarathustra, is able to speak its own word (and break), to keep its 'mind in hell, and despair not' (Rose, 1995, p. 98).

A note is also appropriate here on the use of gendered terms. I began by not using gender-specific language, using plurals where possible. However, in discussing, for example, the master/slave relation, plurals became clumsy and inappropriate. In addition, I came to realise that, in a book about the experience of opposition and contradiction, to 'hide' gender contradictions, oppositions and relations through neutral language was an even greater deceit and/or domination. If some readers feel themselves 'not included' within discussions in the text because I have used 'he' and not 'he/she', or 'they', then I think that is appropriate. Gender will be only one of many reasons for the experience of this text as for the reader, or of its being a part of and apart from the reader. The whole question of inclusion and exclusion, in itself and for another, is exactly the philosophical education with which the text is working. It would be a nonsense, therefore, to write as if readers could be known as included or excluded, or for me to legislate for your experience, your contradictions, or our formative opposition. I have therefore resorted to the use of 'he' in most chapters, keeping open the experience of identity and non-identity as a dilemma and as part of the content of (our) contradictory, self-formative educational experience.

'Whoever is a teacher through and through takes all things seriously only in relation to his students.' (Nietzsche, 1968, p. 269)

But

'The danger of those who always give is that they lose their sense of shame.' (Nietzsche, 1982, p. 218)

Therefore

'Where better to hide a book than in a library... If chanced upon it will be expelled or gain an ally who, recognising the gesture, will return it to its obscurity. So the book, on being sent out, retains some of the aspects of prayer.' (Roche, 1987)

Introduction

The broken middle

Gillian Rose has bequeathed a philosophical idea which 'is its own time apprehended in thoughts' (Hegel, 1967, p. 11). This idea is the broken middle. It is an idea which is philosophical and autobiographical, and which expresses the broken middle of the self, or of self-relation. The autobiographies examined in this book are of the teacher and the person. This introduction offers a philosophical statement regarding the logic of the broken middle or self-relation.

A middle is an indeterminate universal. It is a whole. It has nothing lying outside of it upon which it is dependent. It is a complete and independent identity. It is not a relation of one thing to another, nor is it constituted by 'parts' within it. A middle is not differentiated from itself and is in relation to nothing. Its independence, therefore, and its identity is its being a non-relation. It is a universal which is wholly and completely itself.

Such a middle is not a self-relation, for no such middle can survive the logic of self-relation. A middle, as independent non-relation, is indeterminate. It is indeterminate because it is not known. It is a universal which is for no one, not even itself. Nothing which is known can remain indeterminate, for indeterminateness is a quality which cannot survive its being known. When a universal is known, it has already fallen within the logic of self-relation. It is already a determinate existence. It has to be determinate if, as a middle, it is to be something. To be, is already to be differentiated from universality, or from itself. It is to be particular. The previous paragraph, therefore, did not in fact describe the thing it was talking about. What it was describing has been lost. That middle, now, in being known, is something. The logic of self-relation demands that what is related to itself is not itself. As a universality, or a whole, it separates itself from itself, differentiates itself from itself, and becomes known, determinate, something. A middle, therefore, is never itself. It is always a broken middle.

1

How, then, can a self-relation or a broken middle know itself? It cannot know itself immediately, for that immediacy has already divided itself in being something that can be known. The knowing is already the division, and each knowing repeats the division. The answer appears to be, therefore, that a self-relation can never know itself in its pure unity as a middle, or as pure self-relation, but can only know itself in its divided state or as a broken middle. This is true in two senses. It is true in the sense that knowing is separation. But it is also true that, as a broken middle, the middle is knowing itself, and is the absolute truth of self-relation. In Hegel's *Science of Logic*, this self-relation of self-relation is the notion. It is the self-relation of relation and non-relation known by itself, a relation which is only achieved in and through division and separation. It is as the broken middle that self-relation knows itself. In knowing itself, it is for itself, and actually to be for itself is the truth of self-relation. It is self-relation doing itself, and becoming what it is.

But how is this self-relation or broken middle present in and for the consciousness which is doing the knowing? In seeking to know self-relation as universality, consciousness is faced with an insurmountable contradiction, or aporia. Each time it knows the object, its knowing is already the division of the object. It can never overcome the divisive action of knowing, it can never see the middle 'in itself'. This experience is formative for consciousness, for it is in this experience that it learns about knowing, and comes to comprehend the absolute unity of determinate self-relation.

The logic of self-relation for the individual self-consciousness is the experience of contradiction. It has several constituent moments. First, consciousness cannot begin with the middle. When consciousness comes on the scene, the middle is a broken middle, and consciousness is a part which has been separated from it. But consciousness does not see that it is part of that (now broken) middle. Consciousness, too, is determinate, a something. It is a particular individual in relation to the universal, or otherness *per se*. But it does not see itself as the result of a divided middle, and so does not see itself as the result of its relation to or struggle with the other. It simply takes itself as it finds itself. It does not appear to it to be a result at all. Thus the first effect of the broken middle is the appearance that each knowing consciousness is not in relation to anything. It is merely itself. It is independent, it is a non-relation, and therefore it believes that it is in itself the principle of self-relation or of identity. This principle is called the person. It is given objectivity in property rights, for property rights are the legal guarantee of independence from and non-relation to others. Relation is something which belongs to slaves and objects, not persons.

This misrecognition of self-relation as independence is also the misrecognition of law as universality. The person is already the absence of the middle or universality. The contradiction of law is that it is put there to do the job of the middle, but simply bears witness to the absence of the middle. The need for law is already the loss of the self-relation which it would express.

2

The second moment of the logic of self-relation is this contradictory experience for consciousness of the particular and the universal. Each is only a misrecognition of the broken middle which each repeats, but does not see. The person and the law are in eternal conflict. The law expresses the universality of a self-relation which is whole and self-contained in the independent person. The law also contradicts that independence, for independence becomes dependent upon its being recognised in and protected by the law, or by 'others'. Between person and law there is always the contradiction of non-relation and relation, or of independence and dependence. Their confrontation is always implicitly that of the truth of self-relation as the broken middle, but the experience in which that relation of the relation appears, a contradictory one, is always resolved into another law, another misrecognition of self-relation as identity, or non-relation.

There is a third stage or moment to the logic of self-relation. In the experience that universality contradicts the appearance of self-relation as independence, consciousness is forced back into itself. Here it develops its awareness of subjectivity. This self-relation appears to be determinate in a way in which the person was not. The person was mere being-for-self, determinate because alive and 'independent'. The subject is the return to being-for-self from universality (the law) in its experience of contradiction, an experience in which it realises that the universal does not express the identity of the person. It is returned to itself as the awareness of its universality as its own. In the experience of non-relation as contradiction, consciousness takes its own relation to itself, its self-reflection, as the (new) principle of self-relation. As a subject it is responsible for its own universality, and its law becomes something internal to itself, for example, its conscience, a law which is another misrecognition. The subject takes its own self-awareness as its essence, and as the truth of self-relation.

In the fourth stage of the logic of self-relation, that contradictory experience of particular and universal, person and law, becomes educational for the subject, and marks the self-determination of (absolute) self-relation. The education involves the re-cognition of misrecognition, or the formative experience of illusion. Illusion is the presence of the universal in the particular where the particular takes itself to be the principle which is universality. So far, the broken middle has created a host of illusions, in which things have appeared to be natural and substantial. In fact, these appearances are the results of events and struggles which have disappeared and been forgotten. The appearance of consciousness as a self-relation is an illusion, for this appearance is itself in relation to universality. Consciousness is determinate, and only a something. The independence of the person is an illusion, for its non-relation is already the result of its (life and death) meeting with others. Now, the subject is also an illusion, for its self-relation is the result of its experience of having universality (law) contradict its own independence or non-relation.

Just as consciousness and the person cannot begin with their immediate appearance, as if that were pure self-relation, nor can the subject. The subject, too, must pass through an experience in which it becomes determinate. This involves the negation of its immediate appearance as self-relation. We already know that subjectivity is not independent, for it is dependent upon social relations for the experience of itself. But self-consciousness, 'to begin with', has this experience, or its own development, behind it and 'forgotten'.

Subjectivity, taking (its) reflection as (its) essence, is only illusory being. It is only an appearance of self-relation, or of a determinate middle. It is merely an illusory self-relation. It is only an insubstantial shining of itself for itself. It is where what is reflected to itself as itself, and what is known as itself, is, in fact, nothing at all. It is a shining which is a wholly internal affair, and one which is not yet aware of itself as the result of its relation to others. It is identity, or non-relation, or independence, appearing as 'itself' for itself, an appearance or an illusion which it takes to be its own self-determination. But this is merely a positing, or a presupposition that what appears as self-relation is an identity. This is the status of merely illusory being. The only thing that 'exists' is the presupposition itself. Positing is all that illusory being is. It is still indeterminate, unknown by itself because it is not yet an illusion or shining for itself, something which it is only when it is for another.

This illusory universality or middle is embarrassed when, as a being in the world, it is forced to realise that this being is not universal. The universality which it took as itself is called into question when it meets other universalities. What follows is an experience for each illusory being of determinate negation, an experience in which the illusion comes to be known in its true shape, as an illusion.

The illusory self-certainty has its meeting with others as a negative experience. It is a contradictory experience. It finds that its own certainty as universality is contradicted by all other such universalities, and that it is only one of the universalities. This negative experience, therefore, is that it is not universal. To be not universal is to be merely particular. This proves to be a formative experience for the illusory self. On the one hand, the negation of the illusion now means that the illusion, finally, is known, or is determinate. What is known is the presupposition as presupposition. Illusory being is realised to be merely a positing, an empty reflection. In being known it is no longer an empty reflection, and it no longer consists only in being posited. It is no longer a presupposed shining, for now the shining is known as the nothing which it always was. But the consciousness which knows that it is only an illusion, knows itself as illusion. The negative experience is therefore determinative, for now nothing is known, and what knows it is something. Illusion, for itself, is no longer empty. Now it is a self-relation. The negative experience of the loss of (illusory) certainty is a positive self-determination of the subject. The subject is a self-relation, for it is illusory being now known by itself, or (illusory) non-relation now related to itself. The subject, in this one-sided presentation, is now the determinate non-relation.

But, and on the other hand, this self-relation is not something which illusory being is able to bring about on its own. The determinate negation was the result of an experience of other. The negation of illusory being, its being known, is

4

therefore dependent upon, or is itself only possible in relation to, its experience of other. To have its own negative self-determination is to be in relation to the universal. It is in relation to the universal that the particular learns of itself. Its self-relation is itself in relation. The subject is not therefore an independent self-relation at all. It is itself only because of its dependence upon, or relation to, or difference from the universal.

Two things have happened here which are, in fact, the same thing. On the one side, the subject has achieved for itself its own self-relation or independence. It has become a non-relation. On the other side, it has done so only negatively, i.e. in relation to, or in-dependence of that which it is not. This produces the contradiction that non-relation is achieved only in relation. However, these two moments are the whole of a self-determinate self-relation, or a broken middle which relates itself to itself and so becomes itself. The two moments of subject and universal substance are one (contradictory) self-relation. The middle is divided into universal and particular. But universal and particular are now in the same self-relation, for non-relation is in relation, and to be in relation is also to be non-relation. This is determinate self-relation. It can now be known that the truth of non-relation, or the middle, is achieved only by being in relation (to itself), or by being determinate. The negation of each is the truth of each in and as its opposite, or as the other. Together, they are the absolute self-determination of self-relation, or the self-determination of the middle as the broken middle.

This is not the middle in the form in which it was referred to in the second paragraph of this Introduction. That was an indeterminate middle. This is now a determinate middle, for it is a middle which is known by itself. It is the truth of self-relation, a self which is in relation to itself, and not an empty presupposition which lacks all the moments described above. This absolute is not an immediate universality. This absolute is the truth of self-relation, or self-determined universality. It is the relation of itself to itself, for itself. Put another way, the truth of self-relation is that it is the relation of relation and non-relation, or the relation (opposition) of subject and substance. Their relation to each other is their opposition. It is not an opposition which can be overcome, for their opposition is the (self-) determination of the universal or middle wherein each has its own truth in the other.

Looked at from this point of view, the relation of relation and non-relation is not accurately described as a middle at all. The relation to self has to be performed, a performance which requires that it divide itself from itself in order that a relation to self becomes possible. A middle is only an abstract universal. A broken middle is a self-determining and therefore absolute self-relation.

To sum up, the logic of self-relation is its self-determination in and as the broken middle. Within its self-determination lies the moments of separation and return, moments which together constitute its whole. This logic is not a law of recognition, nor of unification, nor of overcoming, nor in any sense a healing of the broken middle. It is the 'law' and the logic of the broken middle as misrecognition and as illusion, and of (the re-cognition of) the broken middle as

5

self-determination in and through contradiction. As such, it contains self-contradiction and illusion as its own substance. It also therefore contains our misrecognition of it. Law implies the middle, but is only ever a broken middle.

One further point requires to be made in relation to self-relation. Our consciousness is already within the broken middle. It arrives on the scene too late not to have law before it as the misrecognition of the middle. Law is the misrecognition of the social relation, or of mutual recognition. Equally, consciousness arrives on the scene too late not to have knowledge before it as the misrecognition of the absolute. In the same way that law is the misrecognition of social self-relation, so knowledge is the misrecognition of experience or the educational self-relation. The experience of this misrecognition within property and knowledge relations is contradictory for us. But it is in that experience of contradiction that we lose the certainty of ourselves, and are returned to ourselves aware of our determination. We become educated with regard to that which lies behind us, and to that which will be repeated ahead of us. We learn that our appearance has a past and a future, that it is determined, and that its determination is our vocation. In this eternal return of the experience of individuality and law, subject and substance, independence and dependence, and self and negation, lies our education that what we are is already that which we have become and will lose again. The experience of contradiction, of the loss of self to comprehend the self, is the education of what Hegel calls actuality. It is where the whole of the broken middle is present, but where its presence depends upon our risking the broken middle as the question of the self, or the question of the teacher and the person.

Part I
THE DESPAIRING TEACHER

Part I follows the despair of the teacher who, in attempting to 'enlighten' his students, finds that he only repeats his domination over them. In particular, it explores the plight of the radical or critical teacher who seeks to enable his students to see through, transform and overcome prevailing social relations characterised by oppression, inequality and alienation. The attempts described here within educational theory, social theory and a representative of post-modern theory, succeed only in repeating the very conditions they seek to change, a repetition which progressively deepens the despair of the teacher and the theorist as they are forced to face the aporetic nature of their reasoning, their theorising and their practice.

1 Critiques of the teacher

This chapter describes various ways in which the practice of teachers has been criticised by theorists and educators. It does not attempt a comprehensive range of such critiques. Its purpose, rather, is where such critiques have been accompanied by alternative forms of pedagogy, to read these alternatives against the same critiques made by their authors. What emerges in so doing is the return of the teacher, a return in which attempts to overcome domination and abstraction in the names of freedom, emancipation and self-determination merely repeat those same dominations and abstractions. Theorists have attacked the identity of the teacher, but such an identity also returns in the person of the critic. Theorists often criticise the abstract knowledge of the teacher, but such abstractions return in their knowledge of those abstractions. What emerges from the return of the teacher is a despairing teacher, one who finds all attempts to educate for liberation and freedom self-defeating and contradictory. This despair is, at times in what follows, related to bourgeois social relations and abstract rational knowledge relations, and to the broken middle. All of these ideas are returned to in more detail in later chapters. This chapter is concerned to open up the space in which the despair of the teacher is recognised, returned to, and not overcome. It is within such spaces that the deeper self-relation of what it is to be a teacher can then be explored.

The tin god

A. S. Neill's work on the school he founded, called *Summerhill*, is one of the best known and most widely read attempts to create a model of education which replaces domination with freedom. As such, it provides a powerful critique of the identity of the teacher. (I refer in this section only to the Summerhill that is described by Neill himself.) His educational philosophy, and his school, are centred around the idea of the free development of the child according to its own interests and desires, and without external intervention or manipulation by the teacher.

> I believe that to impose anything by authority is wrong. The child should not do anything until he comes to the opinion – his own opinion – that it should be done. The curse of humanity is the external compulsion, whether it comes from the Pope or the state or the teacher or the parent. It is fascism *in toto* (Neill, 1961, p. 111, emphasis removed).

His goal for the school and for education was 'to make the school fit the child, instead of making the child fit the school' (1961, p. 20). Therefore, in the Summerhill that Neill describes, the students are free to do what they like. There are no dress codes, lessons are not compulsory, and a teacher will never tell students what they ought to be doing. 'It is the idea of *non-interference* with the growth of the child and non-pressure on the child that has made the school what it is' (1961, p. 91, my emphasis).

Neill is describing a negative or non-interventionist role for the teacher, one where the duty of the teacher is to do nothing, and to leave the child to develop freely and naturally. At Summerhill no one teaches students anything unless the students specifically ask for that teaching. Lessons are voluntary, and it is possible that a student could leave Summerhill without ever having attended a lesson, although Neill does not think this is likely.

Neill, therefore, is critical of the teacher as an identity or an authority in itself. He gives little attention to pedagogy, believing that the teaching of subjects is one of the least important parts of a teacher's job. Inevitably a teacher of subjects becomes an authority over the students. With schools as they are, he says, 'what can a teacher do but teach something and come to believe that teaching, in itself, matters most of all?' (1961, p. 40). Such a view of teaching is an obstacle to freedom and has no place in Neill's Summerhill. Indeed, Neill states 'We have no new methods of teaching, because we do not consider that teaching in itself matters very much' (1961, p. 20). When, in 1949, HMI visited Summerhill they criticised the old-fashioned and formal teaching methods which were used when students did attend lessons. Neill dismisses such criticism as merely 'academic preoccupations' (1961, p. 88). A good teacher in Summerhill is one who is not the teacher. The students dislike most the 'earnest teacher, who wants to see their drawing and written work. The most welcome visitor is the one who has good tales to tell...' (1961, p. 26). Neill records that on his frequent visits to lecture student teachers he finds them being trained to become enlightened, knowledgeable, and therefore personally authoritative. They are, in effect, being trained out of the possibility of freedom and into their role as dominators.

> They have been taught to *know*, but have not been allowed to feel... Their textbooks do not deal with human character, or with love, or with freedom, or with self-determination. And so the system goes on, aiming only at

standards of book learning – goes on separating the head from the heart (Neill, 1961, p. 38).

At Summerhill Neill believes that the teacher is not an authority figure. Everyone, adults and children, has equal rights, and consequently the fear and domination which characterises most teacher/student relationships does not appear. Neill notes with pride that visitors to the school 'cannot tell who is staff and who is pupil... There is no deference to a teacher as a teacher. Staff and pupils have the same food and have to obey the same community laws' (1961, p. 26). The key to freedom at Summerhill is that authority and discipline have been replaced by self-regulation and self-government. All matters to do with the school, including rules and punishments for offences, are dealt with at a Saturday night meeting. Everyone's vote at the meeting counts the same, head, staff, and students. Neill states:

> At Summerhill we have proved, I believe, that self-government works. In fact, the school that has no self-government should not be called a progressive school. It is a compromise school. You cannot have freedom unless children feel completely free to govern their own social life. When there is a boss, there is no real freedom. This applies even more to the benevolent boss than to the disciplinarian. The child of spirit can rebel against the hard boss, but the soft boss makes the child impotently soft and unsure of his real feelings (1961, p. 59).

Neill's critique of the teacher is that intervention is domination. If the teacher disciplines a child then this prevents self-regulation. If a teacher takes knowledge to a child who does not seek this knowledge, then this is an imposition based on force, not on consensus. If a teacher teaches a child morality then this replaces the natural development of reason. 'A child will learn what is right and wrong in good time – provided he is not pressurised' (1961, p. 224, emphasis removed). All such interventions by the teacher are justified by the view that the teacher is the enlightened person, best able to make decisions on behalf of children, regardless of what the children themselves think. It is a justification based on and grounded in the teacher's possession of knowledge. What the teacher knows about the child, which it is presumed that the child does not know for itself, gives the teacher the authority to work for, and sometimes use force against, the children in their own best interests. Such knowledgeable and enlightened teachers

> make it a business to influence children because they think they know what children ought to have, ought to learn, ought to be. I disagree. I never attempt to get children to share my beliefs or my prejudices... I put my trust in the power of freedom... (Neill, 1961, p. 224).

11

However, Neill's assertions about freedom, non-intervention, non-domination and self-determination are all based on the positing or presupposing of his idea of freedom as an immediate self-relation. They are removed from the contradiction that Neill's philosophy of non-intervention is already based on his own personal enlightenment and is a personal intervention by him into their lives. The positing of 'real' freedom is itself only a reflection of the enlightenment of the teacher regarding what 'real' freedom is, as opposed, for example, to its merely illusory appearances in other forms of education. Such an enlightenment becomes the basis for intervention, and is always again the return of the authority of the teacher, and of the domination of the non-enlightened pupils. In Neill's particular case, the positing is grounded in the laws of psychology. The school in which the authority of the teacher is 'overcome' is also the school in which the teacher returns. Neill, an opponent of intervention, justifies the need for him to intervene with his pupils at a psychological level in order to counteract the effects of previous parental intervention. Neill offered his students 'private lessons', given by himself, to put right that which parents, society and other schools have distorted. But in the relationship of therapist to patient, the knowledge relation is itself one-sided. Even if in the therapy an attempt is made to achieve a 'discourse' between the participants where the 'validity' of the treatment is grounded in the patient and not the analyst, nevertheless the structure of the meeting and the form in which its truth is judged are both decided upon in advance by the therapist in the light of his own 'enlightenment'. In analysis, as in liberationist or emancipatory education, the teacher and the therapist repeat themselves and their own 'enlightenment' as their authority and their identity for others. In Neill's private lessons, it is the laws of psychology which provide advance knowledge of the truth of the pupils. The experience of the pupil which is professed to be self-development is already a knowledge of self-development held by the teacher, a personal enlightenment which has already structured the teacher (therapist)/student (patient) relationship.

Sometimes, says Neill,

> A case of stealing is brought up at the General School Meeting... Often children will come to me and say, 'John stole coins from David. Is this a case for psychology, or shall we bring it up?'
> If I consider it a case for psychology, requiring individual attention, I tell them to leave it to me (1961, p. 56).

This 'me' is already the return of the teacher in Summerhill as the personification of enlightenment regarding (universal) psychological knowledge. Neill refuses to be classified as a teacher. 'Think', he says, 'what a tin god a teacher really is. He is the centre of the picture; he commands and he is obeyed; he metes out justice; he does nearly all the talking' (Neill, 1992, p. 101). Yet the refusal is self-contradictory. The tin god is not overcome. It is repeated in the method which is employed to overcome it. The tin god returns as the teacher who is the

12

personification of the laws of psychology, and of enlightenment regarding 'real' freedom. Neill's attempts to overcome the dominating teacher, and domination in education in general, require him to become the very thing he was opposed to. He is forced to intervene in the name of non-intervention. His idea of freedom is constructed within psychological laws which justify that intervention. The pattern and possibility of student self-determination are themselves already determined beforehand, and are ideas to which his students will conform if they are to qualify as being free and self-determined. The difficulties posed by the return of the teacher who tries to overcome the teacher are not addressed by Neill. Those difficulties are left to the consciousness of the despairing teacher who experiences such attempts to educate for freedom as contradictory and self-defeating.

The subject(ed)

This despair of the teacher who, in seeking to teach for freedom experiences only contradiction and the return of himself as a domination of freedom, is expressed by the Marxist theorist, Louis Althusser. Althusser argues that bourgeois social relations fetishise the subject, masking the class relations which constitute the real work of history, and which are the true identity of subjects. Fetishised man, or the subject, is the ideological form in which all individuals are forced to appear. This is because both the identity of a subject and the practice or action of a subject are always positioned within the ideological state apparatus. All subjects live a material existence, one which is pre-defined for them by the current shape of the class struggle. Life as it appears for them is already ideological, including the appearance of themselves as subjects. This gives ideology what Althusser calls 'a mirror structure' (1984, p. 54) such that not only are social relations fetishised into individual subjects, but also the relation of subjects to that process appears in an ideological form. The subject sees neither their own shape as ideological, nor the work of ideology as their own (i.e. social) work. In the ideological appearance of the (social) person, the person knows the social only in an ideological form.

The power of ideology in maintaining this mirror structure, and in reflecting itself as the truth of the person, and of the personal as the truth of the social, is due to its having established for itself a material base. This material existence is constituted by the rituals of practice which define and determine the ideas and actions of subjects within different ideological apparatuses. The subject, already ideological, becomes ideological in itself when placed within apparatuses which define its own ideas, concepts and beliefs. Within the ideological state apparatus the subject becomes subject to the world as it appears; the subject becomes that which it already is. The negative relation of a person in a social relation becomes real or positive within 'the material existence of an ideological apparatus' (Althusser, 1984, p. 42, emphasis removed). The real life of a person is already ideological. Each of us is already a subject, and subject to the rituals and practices of ideological state apparatuses.

13

With regard to the first point, Althusser explains that 'all ideology has the function (which defines it) of "constituting" concrete individuals as subjects' (1984, p. 45, emphasis removed). On the second point, this constituting is real or material because the ideas of a subject 'are his material actions inserted into material practices governed by material rituals which are themselves defined by the material ideological apparatus from which derive the ideas of that subject' (1984, p. 43, emphasis removed). Ideology is thus circular, self-sustaining and total; 'there is no practice except by and in an ideology' (1984, p. 44), and there is no ideology apart from 'its functioning in the material forms of existence of that functioning' (1984, p. 45). Ideology 'interpellates' or hails individuals as subjects, for it is in ideology that each of us comes to know and recognise our own selves. Ideology functions to name each subject, which at the same time subjects them to the apparatus and provides their concrete and real material existence. It also enables one subject to recognise another. Taken together, the material existence of ideology amounts to a water-tight case that what appears so, is so. The result is that:

> The subjects 'work', they 'work by themselves' in the vast majority of cases, with the exception of the 'bad subjects' who on occasion provoke the intervention of one of the detachments of the (repressive) State apparatus. But the vast majority of (good) subjects work all right 'all by themselves', i.e. by ideology... (1984, p. 55).

With regard to teachers, Althusser sees them as occupying a central role in the ideological state apparatus, a role which, even if they work against it, is nevertheless already an interpellation of the teacher as subject to and a subject within the rituals and practice of educational institutions. The power of Althusser's critique of the teacher is twofold. Not only is it an indictment of the teacher as a bearer of bourgeois ideology, but for the radical teacher it is an insight into the experience of the contradictory nature of resistance and of forms of education which seek to overcome ideology.

On the first of these points, Althusser argues that teachers, practising their rituals in the material existence of education, train children for their different, specialised roles which the capitalist division of labour demands. Children learn at school a number of useful techniques 'which are directly useful in the different jobs in production (one instruction for manual workers, another for technicians, a third for engineers, a final one for higher management etc.)' (1984, p. 6). Teachers also serve the ideological function of producing in children a set of values, a moral belief system, necessary to ensure the stability of bourgeois relations. The teacher is charged with inculcating bourgeois values, morality and standards of behaviour into the consciousness of the working class so that they can become 'good subjects', able to work by themselves in a world which they accept as being 'as it should be'. The children learn to be subjects, and to be subjected to ideology as to the truth. They learn

14

the 'rules' of good behaviour, i.e. the attitude that should be observed by every agent in the division of labour, according to the job he is 'destined' for: rules of morality, civic and professional conscience, which actually means rules of respect for the socio-technical division of labour and ultimately the rules of the order established by class domination (1984, p. 6).

Schools, for Althusser, have become the most important institution within the ideological state apparatus, replacing the Church. The priest has been replaced by the teacher as the central agent of ideology, able to ensure the subject-ing of (bad) pupils to 'suitable methods of punishment, expulsion, selection etc.' (1984, p. 19). It is an ideological function from which the teacher can find no emancipation. The good teacher is in this sense the good subject. The good subject is the one who accepts his interpellation in and by the material existence of education, and who becomes the subject. Teachers, like all 'agents of production, exploitation and repression... must in one way or another be "steeped" in this ideology in order to perform their tasks "conscientiously"...' (1984, p. 7). Indeed, the more conscientious teachers are in their work, the more care they take nurturing their charges, the more effectively they become subjects, and the more effectively they reproduce their pupils as subjects.

Critical or radical teachers are offered no relief by Althusser from the totality of their subjection to and within the ideological state apparatus. Teachers who understand their subjection are still subjects and in practising the ritual of teaching are still oppressors, even if what they teach, and how they teach, are in opposition to bourgeois ideology. The teacher is already ideological, and teaching is only possible as ideology, for the teacher as subject precedes the radical, the critical, or the revolutionary teacher. The teacher, for Althusser, is determined within social relations. If those relations become an object for the teacher, that is only a further material existence of the teacher as subject. Althusser offers the despairing teacher no comfort.

I ask the pardon of those teachers who, in dreadful conditions, attempt to turn the few weapons they can find in the history and learning they 'teach' against the ideology, the system and the practices in which they are trapped... their own devotion contributes to the maintenance and nourishment of this ideological representation of the School, which makes the School today as 'natural', indispensable-useful and even beneficial for our contemporaries as the Church was... for our ancestors (1984, p. 31).

Althusser presents bourgeois property relations in the full light of their all encompassing totality. Subjects are persons who have their determination hidden from them by and in a world which presents itself as the truth of the subject. However, the world as it appears is also a reflection of the truth of the person, a truth which is authenticated in a world which interpellates the person and 'recognises' its independence. Althusser sees that in bourgeois legal relations, social relations are not social (see 1984, p. 84) and are merely abstract relations between persons, and that the social relation is 'conjured away' (1984, p. 84). Equally, Althusser shares an Hegelian insight in comprehending that the implications of a life in which 'individuals are always-already subjects' (1984, p. 50, emphasis removed) makes the investigation of this ideology (Althusser, not Hegel) something which lacks a beginning. Althusser, on a logical reading, points out that:

> One thing is certain: one cannot *begin* with man, because that would be to begin with a bourgeois idea of 'man', and because the idea of *beginning with* man, in other words the idea of an absolute point of departure (= of an 'essence') belongs to bourgeois philosophy… 'Man' is a myth (1984, p. 85).

Althusser, however, in a less logical and more positing frame of mind, continues the same paragraph with the (1984, p. 85, emphasis removed). He says:

> These men are thus the *point of arrival* of an analysis which starts from the social relations of the existing mode of production, from class relations, and from the class struggle. These men are quite different from the 'man' of bourgeois ideology (1984, p. 85).

What is at issue is how these men are different. When Althusser is talking to teachers, he argues that one cannot but begin with person, because the 'individual' is already a concrete and material existence working 'independently' within the ideological state apparatus. When Althusser talks of his own writing he acknowledges that it too is performing an ideological ritual (see 1984, p. 47), and that we the readers have no choice but to begin with Althusser as subject. All of this he claims as part of a theory of ideologies, i.e. of the material existence of subjects, something which is not optional or voluntary, but totalitarian and inescapable.

However, when Althusser moves from ideologies to a science of ideology in general he is forced to posit a subjectless discourse; 'we have to outline a discourse which tries to break with ideology, in order to dare to be at the beginning of a scientific (i.e. a subjectless) discourse on ideology' (1984, p. 47). The substance of Althusser's critique of the teacher is that no beginning is possible except as a subject. The presupposition of Althusser's science of this critique is that a beginning is possible which is not a subject. In this presupposition he is able to posit 'real men', or 'class struggle', or 'social relations', or 'social individuals' (1984, p. 134) as an immediate self-relation of particular and universal, and thus as the beginning from which critique proceeds, and as the end in which critique is grounded. To 'start' with class relations is to

16

presuppose a knowledge of class relations which is known in and for itself. Upon this positing he is able to claim to know, and thereafter to teach us, of a history without a subject, i.e. that 'History is a process and a process without a subject' (1984, p. 83, emphasis removed). This knowledge of process and of activity is a claim to knowledge of self-determination by that which is also forced to claim itself as such a self-determination. What is being claimed is that the non-subject knows itself. Yet since it did not have itself to begin with, on what grounds is this self-determination, this knowledge, to be based? The impossibility of beginning does not lend itself to becoming a self-sufficient ending, since precisely what is absent at the start is the criterion upon which the judgment of self-determination can be made. Knowing 'real men' is a knowledge which is only available to us as bourgeois subjects. It is, therefore, a knowledge of real men, posited by that which is (still) not one.

In order to sustain the totality of his critique, Althusser is forced to remove science from the knowledge relation (see Chapter 7). The removal, however, like everything else in Althusserian critique, is always already an ideological ritual performed within the material presupposition of enlightenment as result. The removal of the science of ideology from the knowledge relation is the immediate return of that science to the knowledge relation, such that its posited real men are realised as presupposed. This return is determinative of the despairing teacher.

Put another way, the critique of the teacher returns upon a despairing Althusser and contradicts its own insight and truth. Althusser is right to observe that teachers can only teach as an ideological practice, and that the form of the subject is imposed upon all individuals. He is not, however, rigorous in recognising this truth, as contradiction, to be equally the case for science (critique), for knowledge and for enlightenment. Nor, therefore, does he pursue the universality of the contradiction of bourgeois social relations as science, i.e. as philosophical science (see Part II). Althusser's critique of property relations is based upon an abstract presupposition of the knowledge relation. To this extent his critique is a teaching, but not a self-education. It is an experience of being subject(ed) which is not comprehended as self-relation. Here, as so often, it is a case of teacher, teach thyself.

The narrator

The despairing teacher is offered some relief by recent critical theory of education which seeks to define a critical pedagogy wherein an emancipatory education and a non-oppressive relationship between teacher and student become possible. The work was begun in the now seminal study *Pedagogy of the Oppressed* by Paulo Freire, one of the few books in education to attempt to define a (scientific) philosophical structure to the teacher/student relationship, and to the substance and subject of education as activity and result.

17

In *Pedagogy of the Oppressed* Freire argues that the teacher/student relationship is characteristic of 'the fundamental theme of our epoch' (1972, p. 75), that is, of domination. It always involves 'a narrating Subject (the teacher) and patient, listening objects (the students)' (1972, p. 45). The task of the teacher, says Freire, 'is to "fill" the students with the content of his narration' (1972, p. 45), a form of domination in which the pupils are treated as 'containers' or receptacles to be filled by the teacher. 'The more completely he fills the receptacles, the better a teacher he is. The more meekly the receptacles permit themselves to be filled, the better students they are' (1972, p. 45). The process described here is referred to by Freire as the 'banking' system of education. It is a critique of the teachers and of the educational activity which they perform.

> Education thus becomes an act of depositing, in which the students are the depositories and the teacher is the depositor. Instead of communicating, the teacher issues communiqués and 'makes deposits' which the students patiently receive, memorise and repeat. This is the 'banking' concept of education, in which the scope of action allowed to the students extends only as far as receiving, filing and storing the deposits (1972, pp. 45–6).

In the banking system of education, knowledge is personified in the teacher who is separated from the pupils by his knowledge and their ignorance. Equally, the teacher is abstracted from the knowledge relation, and appears as an independent person who is the result of education, i.e. who is enlightened. This abstraction, this identity, is his authority over the pupils and is what defines the teacher/student relationship. Freire writes:

> In the banking concept of education, knowledge is a gift bestowed by those who consider themselves knowledgeable upon those whom they consider to know nothing. Projecting an absolute ignorance onto others, a characteristic of the ideology of oppression, negates education and knowledge as processes of inquiry. The teacher presents himself to his students as their necessary opposite; by considering their ignorance absolute, he justifies his own existence (1972, p. 46).

The banking system is Freire's description of education determined in and by bourgeois property relations. The teacher 'owns' knowledge, that is his identity. Equally, therefore, knowledge is a thing, an object, which can be passed on as property. In education, then, not only is the identity of the teacher fixed as the personification of knowledge (as property), but equally knowledge itself is determined abstractly as a fixed identity. This knowledge is already the result or the end product of the process of learning, not the process itself. The teacher's knowledge of the world, therefore, only contains that learning, or the process of the education of the teacher, negatively, as something over and done with or completed. The teacher is already the master, for he is the person with something to teach. The determination of the teacher as this identity (his learning) is no longer visible, leaving the teacher to appear independent and self-sufficient (i.e. educated). The teacher's narration 'talks about reality as if it were motionless, static, compartmentalised and predictable' (1972, p. 45), and its contents, therefore, are 'detached from reality, disconnected from the totality that engendered them and could give them significance' (1972, p. 45). This educated teacher appears for the pupils as only personally authoritative, that is, as a domination of them, and as separate from them or as 'other'. But the students' negative experience here finds no authentication, for this is not the teacher's experience. Freire's work has always been aimed at the teachers who experience their own identity as existing within this contradiction, as within the knowledge relation, in order to develop a critical pedagogy that can unite this negative experience of the pupil and the teacher, the same experience, into one critical, dialectical, non-dominating education or relationship. The critical teacher knows that his identity is abstract, experiences this contradiction as his enlightenment regarding his determination, and thus shares the same view as the student. 'Education,' says Freire, 'must begin with the solution of the teacher–student contradiction, by reconciling the poles of the contradiction so that both are simultaneously teachers and students' (1972, p. 46).

It is to enable teachers to lose their ideological identity, and to understand themselves as dominators of pupils, that Freire develops the method of teaching known as 'conscientisation'. In the experience of themselves as masters, they, like their pupils, have the master as object, and in this education the masters are able to see themselves as they appear for their pupils. Only now are these 'new teachers' ready to accept the pupils' view of the world as legitimate, to authenticate their experiences and to hear their voices. In this new pedagogical relationship, 'The teacher is no longer merely the-one-who-teaches, but one who is himself taught in a dialogue with the students, who in their turn while being taught also teach. They become jointly responsible for a process in which all grow' (1972, p. 53).

Freire points out that this pedagogy is not another 'gift' from teacher to student, for the knowledge which is created and authenticated is not the teacher's to give. The learning which is realised in this critical pedagogy 'expresses the consciousness of the students themselves' (1972, p. 44). It does so through the 'problem posing' method which, says Freire, 'rejects communiqués and embodies communication' (1972, p. 52). It does not allow teachers to name the world for their students. Rather, it treats the world as a question and seeks answers from all of those involved in the investigation. The teacher no longer regards the world 'as his private property, but as the object of reflection by himself and the students' (1972, p. 54). Freire continues:

> In this way, the problem posing educator constantly re-forms his reflections in the reflection of the students. The students – no longer docile listeners – are now critical co-investigators in dialogue with the teacher. The teacher

presents the material to the students for their consideration, and re-examines his earlier considerations as the students express their own (1972, p. 54).

The result of this *praxis* is a renaming of the world as it is understood by the students, not as it is merely narrated by the teacher. For example, within this method, schools were renamed culture circles in recognition that they were not merely passive, teachers became co-ordinators, lectures became dialogues, and pupils became group practitioners (see Freire, 1974, p. 42).

Recently Freire has sought to make clear that even in dialogical, critical, radical pedagogy, the progressive teacher does not divest himself of authority. Both the teachers and the students are subjects of education, but, respectively, as teacher and student. Both are required if the relationship is to be educational. He states that 'the authority of the teacher does not diminish the freedom of the student. One has to grow up through the contradiction of one with the other' (1995, p. 21). Expressed in 1993, the idea is consistent with that expressed in *Pedagogy of the Oppressed* some 23 years earlier. It is not that a teacher ceases to be a teacher in the problem posing pedagogy, or that a student ceases to be student. What is vital is that the one does not become merely the object of the other, but that both understand themselves to be the subjects of education. In *Pedagogy of the Oppressed* Freire stated 'Teachers and students... co-intent on reality, are both Subjects, not only in the task of unveiling that reality, and thereby coming to know it critically, but in the task of recreating that knowledge' (1972, p. 44).

Freire, then, offers a critique of the teacher whose identity is formed abstractly within the property relation, and a critique of the knowledge which teachers own as property. Together they represent the personification of enlightenment and the domination of the process of learning. The great advance that Freire made in his work on pedagogy was the understanding that critique in education is educational for the teacher because it is based in experience, and further that it is the experience of contradiction. A critical teacher is one whose experience of self is as the contradiction of particular and universal. Such a teacher comes to see his particularity, his personification, as a domination of the universal because, as a teacher, the universal is already claimed as a result, or as enlightened knowledge, a result which is embodied in the identity of the teacher.

However, having identified the knowledge relation as the substance and subject of a teacher's self-education, this is then abstracted by Freire into a pedagogy or a method. The pedagogy of the oppressed is experience turned into result, and the critical teacher (the non-identity) returned merely to the teacher (the identity) again. Freire also turns the contradictory experience of the knowledge relation into a knowledge of the relation. Contradiction becomes an object, a result, and the experience is therein posited as the self-relation or immediate identity of enlightenment. It is this presupposition of knowledge of contradiction as knowledge *per se* on which Freire grounds his claims for the liberating and emancipatory power of critical pedagogy. As the teacher of the contradiction, and of the personification of dialectical knowledge, Freire has contradiction as his object, as his property, and as his gift to us. He teaches us the truth of our contradiction. He is still a teacher, this time identified by his knowledge of the truth of his students, a knowledge which they have yet to achieve.

Similarly, as the teacher of the contradiction, he is making claims to know experience in itself. This is manifested in his teaching that 'Education must begin with the solution of the teacher–student contradiction, by reconciling the poles of the contradiction...' (1972, p. 46). But a beginning is only possible for a teacher who personifies experience as result, and has it as 'property' or knowledge. A solution of the contradiction can only be posited, that is, can only be based upon the presupposition that what overcomes the contradiction is itself free of it. Its 'poles' can only be reconciled in a consciousness which claims to have knowledge of contradiction yet, at the same time, not to have this knowledge as another object or as property. But any knowledge of is already (the return of) the same contradiction. A similar positing lies behind Freirean teaching that critical pedagogy produces 'authentic liberation' (1972, p. 52), that education is 'the practice of freedom' (1972, p. 54), and that such *praxis* produces 'the constant transformation of reality' (1974, p. 115). Authenticity, freedom and overcoming are all experienced as objects, or for us, and therefore as merely particular identities. The experience of such identities as negative is not, for the teacher, contained within the identities themselves. Indeed, overcoming such negation or doubts is what notions of authenticity are judged against. But each presentation by the teacher of an authenticity is, at the same time, the negation of that authenticity and its personification (as the teacher) for the students. It is in the repeated crisis and despair of teaching authenticity, freedom and overcoming, that Freire becomes the repetition of the teacher of whom he is so critical. He is our teacher when he tells us, his pupils, that we 'must confront reality critically' (1972, p. 28), that we 'must re-examine (ourselves) constantly' (1972, p. 36), that we 'must reject the banking concept' (1972, p. 52) and 'must abandon the educational goal of deposit-making' (1972, p. 52). This 'must', this *Sollen*, is just such a deposit, and just the kind of teaching that Freire is critical of. It does not matter that in this case the must is tied to emancipation and liberation instead of tyranny and domination. The teacher is still abstracted from the truth about which he is teaching, and is still the personification of that truth, is still an object and a re-experience of the knowledge relation for us, his pupils, and is still only a particular who owns truth as a vanished universality (i.e. as an object or commodity). It is not enough for Freire to assure us that he is still a subject of education, for in the assurance itself he presupposes knowledge of such contradictions as a result or as his own property. Contradiction, however, requires that Freire also recognise that assurance as misrecognition, to lose the assurance itself to contradiction, and to comprehend the actuality of the teacher as the relation of the relation. The despairing teacher who turns to Freire for a method of teaching which will not repeat the domination of the teacher over his pupils finds that Freire is already the teacher. His pedagogy, as Hegel might say, comes on the scene too late to change reality, for it is already the repetition of that reality, and of the broken middle of the knowledge relation in which our education is self-determined.

The pedagogue

The work of Henry Giroux has been and continues to be much influenced by that of Freire. What Freire seeks to achieve through renaming, Giroux has incorporated into a body of theorising which has, at its centre, the idea of critical pedagogy. Recently he defined critical pedagogy as 'a project whose intent is to mobilise knowledge and desires that may lead to significantly minimising the degree of oppression in people's lives' (1994, p. 65).

At the heart of Giroux's project has always been the idea that the relationship between teacher and student can be transformed from one between master and slave to a mutual relationship wherein the conditions for 'equality, liberty and justice' (1994, p. 65) can be created. This project, for Giroux, is embodied in critical theory. In 1983, in *Theory and Resistance in Education*, he employed the Frankfurt School as a guide to the sort of dialectical critique which he hoped to embody in his radical pedagogy. 'Within the theoretical legacy of critical theorists such as Adorno, Horkheimer, and Marcuse, there is a sustained attempt to develop a theory and mode of critique that aims at both revealing and breaking with the existing structures of domination' (1983, p. 4). Teachers using this critique as their method of teaching, as their pedagogy, could enable their students to become conscious of themselves as subjects who had been constructed within a world (or, for the later Giroux, worlds) which was already formed in the vested interests of powerful groups. Identities of things, of subjects, of institutions, which appeared natural, given and unchangeable now, in critique, become merely socially determined and historically contingent constructions, embodying the values of particular interests. In the light of such critique, Giroux argued for a critical and radical pedagogy for teachers based upon the dialectical approaches of Frankfurt School critical theory.

> Drawing on Adorno's notion of negative dialectics, a theory of dialectical critique begins with a rejection of the 'official' representation of reality. Its guiding assumption is that critical reflection is formed out of the principles of negativity, contradiction and mediation. In short, negativity refers to a thorough questioning of all universals, an interrogation of those 'received' truths and social practices that go unquestioned in schools because they are dressed in the discourse of objectivity and neutrality. Negativity in this case represents a mode of critical engagement with the dominant culture, the purpose of which is to see through its ideological justifications and explode its reifications and myths (Giroux, 1983, p. 64).

22

But Giroux was never content to rest with critical engagement as merely negative. He refused the abyss of a deconstruction which became nothing more than 'a form of refusal' (1983, p. 65), something of which he has more recently accused cultural studies (see Giroux, 1994). He has consistently argued that the point of critical pedagogy was political engagement and its transformative potential. The real achievement of the Frankfurt School was, he argued, to rename 'the very notion of rationality… [which] now became the nexus of thought and action in the interest of liberating the community or society as a whole. As a higher rationality it [critique] contained a transcendent project in which individual freedom merged with social freedom' (1983, p. 22).

This result of critique is the basis of his own criticisms of Marxist theory in education which simply offered an analysis of the repetition of bourgeois social relations without the prospect or possibility that they could be overcome. He lists the work of Althusser, Bowles and Gintis, Bernstein and Bourdieu as all surrendering 'to a version of domination in which the cycle of reproduction appears unbreakable' (1983, p. 98). He argues that it represents a pessimism which is itself the result of relations of domination, and something, again, to be overcome.

Radical pedagogy develops in Giroux's work into a form of critique in which the identity of the teacher, and the lack of voice given to the students, are both posed as problems. In Giroux's version of the pedagogy of the oppressed,

> Teachers must promote pedagogical conditions in their classrooms that provide spaces for different student voices. The critical pedagogy being proposed here is fundamentally concerned with student experience; it takes the problems and needs of the students themselves as its starting point. This suggests both confirming and legitimating the knowledge and experience through which students give meaning to their lives. Most obviously, this entails replacing the authoritative discourse of imposition and recitation with a voice capable of speaking in one's own terms, a voice capable of listening, retelling and challenging the very grounds of knowledge and power (1989, p. 165).

For the coherence of radical pedagogy, it is important that Giroux be able to distinguish between different types of teacher authority. He is opposed to all forms of banking education, to all forms of conservative, functional or reproductive teaching, and to all curricula where knowledge is abstract and undialectical. Yet he consistently acknowledges through his work that radical pedagogy does require the teacher. But their authority is not merely authoritarian when it is used to create democracy in the classroom, to authenticate student voices and experiences, and to challenge existing forms of domination, including that of the teacher over the student. Giroux argues that to see conservative teacher authority as being on a par with radical teacher authority is 'shameful and perfectly appropriate for those who have become fully integrated into the ideological dynamics of higher education' (1989, p. 70). Radical pedagogy does not privilege the knowledge of the teacher; indeed, it becomes a target for immediate critique. It is point repeated by Giroux more recently in *Disturbing Pleasures*. Asked about whether his concept of 'emancipatory authority' (see 1989, p. 89) escapes charges of 'authoritarianism in the traditional sense' (1994, p. 162), Giroux again makes clear his distinction between uncritical authoritarianism and radical and self-critical authority. He reminds his interviewer that the authority of the teacher involves a 'double movement' (1994, p. 162). On the one hand, 'to give up authority is to renounce the responsibility of politics, struggle and commitment as educational projects' (1994, p. 162). Thus teachers have to take responsibility for 'establishing conditions for students to be able to theorise...' (1994, p. 162). On the other hand, this authority is itself only authoritative when it is itself 'subject to debate, recognise[s] its own partiality and [is] open to change' (1994, p. 162). Thus, says Giroux, the radical teacher is not conservative precisely because he recognises himself, in the very act of teaching, to be another content for critique. Giroux says of his own teaching, 'I situate myself not within a discourse in which my authority is taken for granted and therefore uncontestable but, in fact, is rendered visible as an ethical, political and social construct' (1994, p. 163).

In *Border Crossings* Giroux broadens the idea of radical pedagogy to encompass the work of all cultural workers, including those in law, social work, architecture, medicine, theology and literature. In attempting these border crossings, Giroux tries to ensure that the political project which lies at the heart of his critical pedagogy remains. In all of these cultural areas the rationale of pedagogy is still to 'disrupt the ideological, cultural and political systems that both inscribe and contain' the logic of domination (1992, p. 222). Above all, it is to enable the voices of opposed groups to rename realities (1992, p. 156) in relationships of mutuality and non-domination which are 'transformative and emancipatory' (1992, p. 29).

For all cultural workers, then, Giroux advocates a 'border pedagogy' which can be used to try and ensure that these workers do not merely reproduce oppressive social relations in their work, nor reproduce culture as knowledge in a banking system of communication. He tries to bring to these areas the idea of emancipatory authority, that is 'a notion of authority rooted in a political project that ties education to the broader struggle for public life...' (1992, p. 137). His vision of these border crossings is that it 'is not an abandonment of critique as much as it is an extension of its possibilities' (1992, p. 30).

However, two years later there is evidence that Giroux's hopes have remained unfulfilled. He is himself forced to make a critique of the post-structuralist tendencies in cultural studies which repeatedly fails to link 'any of the problems and possibilities of pedagogy to a viable, democratic political project' (1994, p. 123). He laments that, in his view, it has become increasingly difficult to assess what cultural studies are 'either as a political project or as post-disciplinary practice' (1994, p. 127). Finally, he laments 'the current lacunae in cultural studies regarding the theoretical and political importance of pedagogy as a founding movement in its legacy' (1994, p. 128). To explain this implicit conservatism in cultural studies, Giroux discerns a difference between a pedagogy of theory and a pedagogy of theorising. In the first, teachers often teach theory as a body of knowledge, repeating the relations of the banking system of education. They have abstracted themselves from the theory which they are 'positing' (1994, p. 117) as the truth which has to be learned by the students. What these teachers are not, therefore, practising is a pedagogy of theorising in which the students themselves actually do the theorising, including putting the teachers' authority into question. Giroux is accusing post-structuralist teaching of overlooking the relations of power and domination which are implicit in its pedagogy of theory. It is not practising the self-reflective critique in which it, too, becomes a question for the students. It has not made the authority of its own teachers 'the subject of an ongoing debate' (1994, p. 119) and is not, therefore, 'a politically engaged pedagogy' (1994, p. 121). It is not at all clear, then, that the border crossings have been successful. The political involvement of critical pedagogy rests upon a 'constant vigilance regarding teacher authority coupled with a respect for student knowledge' (1994, p. 121), and it is not an involvement Giroux finds easy to locate in the pedagogy of theory in cultural studies.

What Giroux has highlighted in his critique of cultural studies is the broken middle of the knowledge relation. The teacher who teaches theory has knowledge as a result, and is the personification of that enlightenment, the owner of the knowledge. His relationship to non-owners is therefore already one of power and domination. Giroux is sufficiently open and honest to admit that the broken middle also characterises his own practice. Of recent teaching experiences he writes:

> It became clear to me very quickly that in spite of my use of oppositional material and the seminar format of the class, I was reproducing a set of pedagogical relations that did not decenter authority, undermined my attempts both to provide students with an opportunity to speak in a safe space and to appropriate power in the class in order to deconstruct the texts, and engage in a collective self-criticism and a critique of the politics of my own location as a teacher (1994, p. 134).

He explains the contradiction of this broken middle as him 'being theoretically or politically accurate and pedagogically wrong at the same time' (1994, p. 169). He says, 'I reproduced the binarism of being politically enlightened in my theorising and pedagogically wrong in my organisation of concrete class relations' (1994, p. 135).

The broken middle of Giroux's teaching is the same knowledge relation that he finds repeated in cultural studies. His own political enlightenment is itself merely a positing of critique as self-determination, and is immediate self-relation. It is upon this presupposition that he seeks to build his classroom relationships, yet is it precisely because of this presupposition that he must always fail. He seeks to

25

begin with the problems and needs of the students themselves, to begin with their voices and experiences so that his own authority may be negated. Yet this is not a beginning. It is still the conservative authority of a teacher whose agenda is brought into the classroom as the defining reality. To say to the students that the curriculum will be their agenda is still to define what the curriculum will be. The students, therefore, do not need to become critical of the teacher. For them, the teacher is always already in charge, no matter how critical or benevolent the message. The inescapable aporia of the radical teacher is that he is still the teacher, the personification of the particular enlightenment which he has as the truth and justification for his intervention. If this 'theoretically and politically accurate' enlightenment is that of emancipatory authority, then that 'truth' can only appear for the student as a result possessed by the teacher. The experience of the student is not that of self-determination, but of self-determination as dominated in and by the particularity of the teacher.

Giroux's critique is based upon a positing of self-determination as the immediate self-relation of result and activity, or of knowledge and experience. For Giroux, the experience of the property relation as contradiction overcomes the contradiction, such that a theoretically and politically accurate enlightenment, or authentic self-determination, is the result. Critical theorists, both in general and in education, hold this result to be an enlightenment regarding the abstract appearance of the person, and of knowledge, an enlightenment which is itself not abstract. They take truth here to be the experience or negation of identity and a true self-determination, an enlightenment realised in the activity of critique and producing its own substantial (self) result. But this knowledge can only be posited as a self-relation because it is already another object for us, already abstracted from the work, the experience, in which it was produced and which is posited, now, as a result. Critique only re-presents the broken middle of the knowledge relation, and is available for the subject only as the separation of knowledge from experience, even when the work is known as the work of consciousness.

In the classroom, Giroux finds that as the teacher he is already the personification of the knowledge relation. He is already the determination of enlightenment within bourgeois social relations, he is already the abstraction of (radical and critical) knowledge. He can be nothing else than a contradiction as an emancipatory teacher. He can only repeat the relation of himself to his students, he cannot overcome it. His response to this aporia, to the fact that he is always already an abstract domination, reveals the posited view of political enlightenment which is his own self-defeat. In response to the broken middle of education he says, 'I relinquished all claims to objectivity' (1994, p. 136). This is the despair of the teacher who, unable to avoid the abstraction of emancipatory authority, and its repetition as mere authority, relinquishes the implicitly educational nature of the dilemma of the political project, a relinquishing which risks not freedom but scepticism, cynicism and resignation. Also, Giroux says that he got the students to subject his authority to extensive critique in their essays and debates. But there is no solace to be gained for the master in using the experience of his students as his

26

own political education. They cannot think for him, nor can he become solely dependent upon their work. Giroux, taking this option, ignores his own instinct to 'always be mindful of our obligation not to run away from authority' (1992, p. 157). On the other hand, and in more positive mood, Giroux states that he tried 'to work through and resist the negative effects of my own authority as a teacher' (1994, p. 135). Yet to resist the negative is precisely to resist the movement which is the self-education of the teacher within the broken middle of the knowledge relation. To resist the negative is to posit substance as grounds and legitimacy for being a teacher and for having 'authority'. The authority which Giroux seeks is precisely the 'negative effects' of the teacher. Giroux has, for 20 years or so, been caught within the repetition of the dialectic of enlightenment, a dialectic which is the substance of a tradition of critical thought with which he began, but which has become increasingly overlooked in his work. It is, however, the substance and the tradition to which, as the teacher, he has inevitably and already returned.

The interest

Although Giroux does not link his own work to the form of critique which lies at the heart of Habermas's theory of 'communicative action', they share the presupposition that enlightened knowledge is where knowledge and interest, or teacher and pupil, are unified in self-relation. Wilfred Carr and Stephen Kemmis, and Robert Young, have been explicit in their attempts to mount a critique of the teacher using Habermas's notion of the emancipatory knowledge-constitutive interest, and its successor, communicative action.

In *Knowledge and Human Interests*, Habermas distinguishes between the technical, practical and emancipatory knowledge-constitutive interests. Empirical-analytical enquiry has as its basis the technical interest which is concerned to dominate nature and is characterised by measurement and calculation, not by intersubjective relations. In it, 'action is... reduced to the solitary act of the purposive-rational utilisation of means. And individuated experience is eliminated in favour of the repeatable experience of the results of instrumental action' (Habermas, 1987a, p. 193).

The practical knowledge-constitutive interest is reflective, and acknowledges the aspect of social determination which lies behind any enquiry. Whereas the interest in technical control dominates the object, the practical interest 'constitutes itself in a self-formative process' (Habermas, 1987a, p. 195), and because of this, it has an increased practical import.

These two knowledge-constitutive interests determine much of the research carried out in education and many of the perspectives found in the sociology of education. Carr and Kemmis point out how the technical interest underpins the natural scientific view of educational theory and practice, and state that 'this kind of research will always be biased towards prevailing educational arrangements and its theories will be structured in favour of the "*status quo*"' (1986, p. 79). For

Young, this interest is the cause of a modern educational crisis which has led to a view of pedagogy as manipulation and intervention, and where the 'older view of pedagogy as a moral/ethical and practical art was abandoned' (1989, p. 20). Carr and Kemmis, and Young, see the practical interest in educational research as unable, in Young's words, to 'penetrate behind the facade of the existing culture' (1989, p. 33), and, in the words of Carr and Kemmis, as 'always predisposed towards the idea of reconciling people to their existing social reality' (1986, p. 98). The technical and practical knowledge-constitutive interests, although different, both share the same uncritical attitude towards social reality. In both, therefore, the teacher and/or the researcher is merely the uncritical transmitter of prevailing social values.

Young, Carr and Kemmis find the emancipatory interest to be the substance of radical critique, and to lie at the heart of Habermas's theory of communicative action. In communicative action the intersubjective substance of all (social) knowledge is not only understood, it is realised (i.e. brought about) in the activity of dialogue which, between consenting participants, aims at the truth. This mutual critique acknowledges its own determination, but does so as an act of self-determination. It is here that critique as the self-relation of enlightenment is found. Translated into critical educational science (Carr and Kemmis) or critical theory of education (Young), this critique, or communicative action can be used to produce:

> A form a practice in which the 'enlightenment' of actors comes to bear directly in their transformed social action. This requires an integration of theory and practice as reflective and practical moments in a dialectical process of reflection, enlightenment and political struggle carried out by groups for the purpose of their own emancipation (Carr and Kemmis, 1986, p. 144).

Carr and Kemmis employ communicative action as their proposal for a self-formative critique of the teacher by the teacher in action research. They argue that involvement in this type of research not only enables teachers to see through the ideological distortions of educational and social reality, and of their own practice, but at the same time to be immanently involved with the transformation of that reality and practice. It is to be seen as 'a form of self-reflective enquiry undertaken by participants in social situations in order to improve the rationality and justice of their own practices, their understanding of these practices, and the situations in which these practices are carried out' (Carr and Kemmis, 1986, p. 162). The result is intended to be the enlightenment of teachers regarding the way technical interest in particular distorts educational theory and practice, and prevents rational discourse and transformation of social relations. This self-critical community of action researchers:

...creates conditions under which its own practice will come into conflict with irrational, unjust and unfulfilling educational and social practices in the institutional context in which the action research is carried out.

The organisation of enlightenment in action research thus gives rise to conditions under which the organisation of action can take place as an attempt to replace one distorted set of practices with another, undistorted set of practices (Carr and Kemmis, 1986, p. 197).

Action research in education, organised in this way and grounded in critique as communicative action is therefore a unification of knowledge and interest, where the technical knowledge-constitutive interest is seen through and overcome by rational, open, democratic, communicative, self-critical groups of self-enlightening teachers and professionals. This is critique as 'political action' (Carr and Kemmis, 1986, p. 197) because 'it creates a model for a rational and democratic social order' (Carr and Kemmis, 1986, p. 200).

Young is more cautious about action research, but offers a model of Habermasian critical theory of education which shares the same objectives. He places Habermas at the end of a development of critical theory in education in Germany. He notes how an originally Marxist project was replaced by a hermeneutic insight in educational research leading to a criticism of positivist epistemology in research by both left and right. Against those who argued that a critical theory of education could proceed only negatively, Young states that a 'positive moment was needed' (1989, p. 57) and was provided by the positive theory of communicative action developed by Habermas. Young notes, 'The lack of a clear normative basis for educational construction was finally overcome when Habermas' later work on language and validity, including normative validity, pointed the way to procedural resolution of the normative problem' (1989, p. 59).

The most important potential of Habermasian critique, argues Young, is its ability to enable practitioners to see through knowledge which is presented as 'a matter of fact' (1989, p. 71) as determined in and by the technical knowledge-constitutive interest. The aim is to reveal to teachers that their own identity, the curriculum they teach, and the methods they employ are all determined in accordance with the interest which seeks to control, to explain, to legitimate the 'official' view of reality and to possess knowledge as property. He gives the example of the typical question and answer routine between teacher and student where the child's frame of reference, their knowledge, is recontextualised from lay vocabulary to technical vocabulary, and from personal vocabulary to textbook vocabulary. Critique will enable teachers to see how the technical interest is often mirrored in their own assumptions about knowledge, which tends towards a greater or lesser degree of objectivism 'with little awareness of questions of reflectivity and problems of the social independence or dependence of knowledge formation' (1989, p. 95).

Like Giroux, Young is keen to introduce critique to teachers as democratic (or radical) pedagogy. Young formulates what he calls the 'ideal pedagogical speech situation', which he sees as a way of reforming, through practice, the relationship between teacher and student. As Giroux sought to provide for the space in which student voices could be heard, and their worlds given recognition, so Young argues that communicative action provides for classroom discourse in which all are involved in rational speech acts. One way in which this could be achieved is for the teacher and student to discuss the mutual constraints which determine both of them in an educational institution, thus raising the construction and determination of student and teacher to a self-conscious and critical level. 'By speaking about the speech roles of participants, and about how breaches of protocol are recognised, felt and dealt with, it is possible to recognise and change these patterns... by the introduction of specific structures designed to implement new "rules"' (1989, p. 113).

This critique is seen by Young as emancipatory in the sense that the participants become enlightened with regard to the impregnation of knowledge, identity and truth by the technical knowledge-constitutive interest. It is transformative because the new knowledge, mutually produced in communicative actions which seek rational agreement, becomes the new understanding of self and of the world, one which enables and encourages different forms of knowledge and of activity. It is, for Young, 'an activity in which the human species looks at itself' (1989, p. 145), re-forms itself, and creates new forms of association and social relations. For teachers, then, self-critique of their own determination in and by the technical knowledge-constitutive interest is an overcoming of that determination, an overcoming 'which realises itself immanently as changed social practices' (1989, p. 129).

What Carr and Kemmis and Young seek, like all radical educators, is an authority from which to criticise authority. They seek to teach about teachers and to criticise the domination of the teacher over the student in the property relation, where knowledge is owned as a thing. They are all critical of the teacher as owner, as the personification of enlightenment, and they all seek to expose the teacher as this abstract identity. Yet to do this is to teach the teachers. Aware of this contradiction, critical teachers have sought to find a different form of authority which will justify their intervention without repeating the relations of domination which are the object of their critique. For Freire, the new authority was conscientisation, for Neill it was freedom, for Giroux it was emancipatory authority, for Althusser it was class struggle, and now for Habermasian critical theory of education it is the authority of communicative action. In each case the new authority is a positing of the experience of contradiction, that is, of the knowledge relation, as an immediate self-relation in which activity and result, critique and enlightenment are united. This presupposition of unification is then taken to be the ground for a non-dominating intervention which aims to teach the teachers. In Habermas' case, for reasons discussed later (see Chapter 5), it is a particularly seductive presupposition, for it appears to find in the dialectic of enlightenment a positive intersubjective life-world upon which even the experience of the knowledge relation itself is grounded. But, as in each of the new authorities examined in this chapter which seek to offer a critique of the teacher, such presuppositions only return the teacher to the contradiction implicit within the knowledge relation. All teachers, even radical teachers, are always already teachers, having the truth of their new authority as another abstract domination. The truth of the new authority, its self-relation, cannot survive its being known, neither can it survive its being taught without repeating the relations of domination it would claim to have overcome.

The logic of pedagogic reproduction

An ambitious attempt to categorise the component parts of the way pedagogy reproduces social relations, and to explain the interrelationship of those parts, can be found in Bourdieu and Passeron's book, *Reproduction in Education, Society and Culture*. Part 1 of the book sets out a theory of the symbolic violence which pedagogy reproduces. Part 2 examines some of the ways in which this symbolic violence can be observed in schooling and in classrooms as methods employed in the task of 'keeping order'. Their work serves equally well as an analysis of the despairing teacher and the contradiction of enlightenment.

In terms of the teacher/student relationship, and in particular its mediation through language, Bourdieu and Passeron are clear regarding its inequality, and its role in transmitting cultural values from the former to the latter. All teaching not only 'imposes a social definition... of what merits transmission' (1977, p. 109), but carries within it decisions already made regarding

> the code in which the message is to be transmitted, the persons entitled to transmit it, or, better, impose its reception, the persons worthy of receiving it and consequently obliged to receive it and, finally, the mode of imposition and inculcation of the message which confers on the information transmitted its legitimacy and thereby its full meaning (1977, p. 109).

The lecturer, in particular, finds that the 'authority' inherent in the teacher/student relationship is given a material existence in the structure of the lecture, and in the academic language used therein. The lecturer at the front is:

> Elevated and enclosed in the space which crowns him orator, separated from his audience, if numbers permit, by a few empty rows which materially mark the distance the laity fearfully keep before the *mana* of the Word and which at all events are only ever occupied by the most seasoned zealots, pious ministers of the magisterial utterance... (1977, p. 109).

31

These 'symbolic conditions' (1977, p. 109) govern and determine the inequality of this teacher/student relationship 'so rigorously that efforts to set up a dialogue immediately turn into fiction or farce' (1977, p. 109), and students are subjected to a role which demands no more than 'responses' (1977, p. 109). Worse still, the teacher often employs a language or terminology which is deliberately designed to mystify and obscure his message, for much of his status as master depends upon his not being completely understood. Bourdieu and Passeron remark that 'Students are the less inclined to interrupt the professional monologue when they do not understand it, because status resignation to approximate understanding is both the product and the condition of their adaptation to the university system...' (1977, p. 112). This adaptation involves a duty on the part of the students and teachers 'to over-estimate the quantity of information which really circulates in pedagogic communication' (1977, p. 113). If a teacher, against this duty, did try to explain clearly and without mystification in regard to his discoveries, then this would entail damaging the symbolic mystique of his own identity; 'he would be liable to appear even to his own students as an elementary school teacher who had strayed into higher education' (1977, p. 113). This echoes Froebel's despair when he lamented 'Enough! the Universities paid no heed to the simple schoolmaster' (Michaelis and Keatley Moore, 1915, p. 117).

In short, Bourdieu and Passeron point out that the 'performance' of education which the teacher and student must adhere to is constructed in such a way that the teacher can 'deflect the authority of the institution onto his own person' (1977, p. 124), while the student ought to be 'none other than his "being-for-the-teacher"' (1977, p. 111). Both work within and reproduce 'the context of authority the institution sets up for them' (1977, p. 125). But what makes Bourdieu and Passeron's analysis of this context so interesting is that they seek to show how pedagogy itself contains within it a logic of domination. To comprehend this logic, or this system of pedagogy, requires a close reading of Part 1 of their book, and familiarity with a number of specialist terms which they employ.

Axiomatic to their study is the argument that:

> Every power which manages to impose meanings and to impose them as legitimate by concealing the power relations which are the basis of its force, adds its own specifically symbolic force to those relations (1977, p. 4).

Pedagogy is just such a form or power. It places its own representation of power on top of pre-existing power relations. In so doing, 'pedagogic action' not only hides the power relations or social relations which are its grounding, but it reproduces those relations in a changed and symbolic way. If social relations have 'the objective truth of those relations as power relations' (1977, p. 5), then pedagogy represents those power relations in a symbolic form. This representation, because it is power (relations), even though it may not appear so,

32

is a form of symbolic violence. It imposes power relations through its own practices, but in ways which mask or 'neutralise' that violence.

All pedagogic action, all symbolic representation of social relations, is the imposition of 'a cultural arbitrary' (1977, p. 5). For Bourdieu and Passeron, a cultural arbitrary is a meaning or value which, although attached to a class or culture, 'cannot be deduced from any universal principle, whether physical, biological or spiritual' (1977, p. 8). A social system is constituted by such cultural arbitraries, but those cultural arbitraries which enjoy a dominant position are those which most fully but always indirectly express 'the objective interests (material and symbolic) of the dominant group or classes' (1977, p. 9). Pedagogic action takes place within the power relations which have defined the relation of pedagogical communication. Those power relations are the precondition 'for the imposition and inculcation of a cultural arbitrary by an arbitrary mode of imposition and inculcation (education)' (1977, p. 6).

Therefore, in Section 1 of Bourdieu and Passeron's system, the case is made that pedagogy is a form of action whose structures are predetermined by the social relations which define not only the (arbitrary) values which are to be transmitted, but also the relation between transmitter and receiver. In addition, it is the case that the arbitrary value is made to appear grounded and objective, and that arbitrary power is made to appear legitimate and authoritative. Thus can pedagogical actions reproduce, legitimise and mask the power relations which are their basis, and whose violence they symbolise and represent. This is the argument presented in Section 2 of their book. Because the arbitrary power which makes pedagogical action possible 'is never seen in its full truth' (1977, p. 11), and because 'the arbitrariness of the content inculcated is never seen in its full truth' (1977, p. 11), therefore 'pedagogic action necessarily implies, as a social condition of its exercise, pedagogic authority and the relative autonomy of the agency commissioned to exercise it' (1977, pp. 11–12, emphasis removed).

One example of how pedagogic action reproduces misrecognition of the objective truth of social relations, i.e. of how it masks its own reproduction of violence, can be found in the application of pedagogy as self-critique. Bourdieu and Passeron explain that even in identifying 'the objective truth of pedagogic action as violence' (1977, p. 12), this pedagogic action still reproduces that violence. Pedagogic action is only possible as pedagogic authority, where the latter is the legitimacy of the former. 'The idea of a pedagogic action exercised without pedagogic authority is a logical contradiction and a sociological impossibility' (1977, p. 12). Pedagogic action is already violence manifested as pedagogic authority, even or especially in its critique of being so. Such a critique is experienced by us as a contradiction between the objective truth of social relations that is being expressed, and the reproduction of those social relations which is achieved in the exposure. Our seeing of the truth of social relations, and of pedagogic action, 'objectively manifests the misrecognition of that truth' (1977, p. 12). Thus, Bourdieu and Passeron note that 'a pedagogic action which aimed to unveil, in its very exercise, its objective reality of violence and thereby to destroy the basis of the agents pedagogic authority, would be self-destructive' (1977, p. 12). Critical pedagogy, like all forms of pedagogic action, is entwined in the contradiction 'that every pedagogic action requires as the condition of its exercise the social misrecognition of the objective truth of pedagogic action' (1977, p. 12). Pedagogic action is already that misrecognition, even when the object of its enquiry is such misrecognition. The despairing teacher is faced here by a most vicious circle: the means to liberation are already part of the weaponry employed to ensure oppression. It is critical pedagogy, indeed, which 'evades' this despair by promoting its own intervention as 'necessary' or 'natural' (1977, p. 13), an evasion which 'reinforces the arbitrary power which establishes it and which it conceals' (1977, p. 13). Bourdieu and Passeron argue that such misrecognition or reproduction is not 'psychological'. The totality of pedagogic action and pedagogic authority lies in its being 'the currency' (1977, p. 13) in and by which such reproduction is produced, criticised and reproduced. They dismiss 'radical challenges' (1977, p. 16) to this currency as Utopian, as a desire for a pedagogy without arbitrariness, a pedagogy which is not predetermined as symbolic violence.

> All these Utopias constitute an instrument of ideological struggle for groups who seek, through denunciation of a pedagogic legitimacy, to secure for themselves the monopoly of the legitimate mode of imposition... The idea of a 'culturally free' pedagogic action, exempt from arbitrariness in both the content and the manner of its imposition, presupposes a misrecognition of the objective truth of pedagogic action in which there is still expressed the objective truth of a violence whose specificity lies in the fact that it generates the illusion that it is not violence (1977, pp. 16–17).

Symbolic violence is not psychological, nor is it personal. Pedagogic communication is preceded by and has its genesis in 'the power relations between the groups or classes making up a social formation' (1977, p. 6). This 'arbitrary power' is the precondition of pedagogic communication. Therefore pedagogic communication is not reducible 'to a pure and simple relation of communication' or to some sort of 'primordial relation' (1977, p. 19) between pre-social individuals. On the contrary, pedagogic communication is always already determined solely with a view to reproducing itself, that is, to reproducing in its pedagogic action the pedagogic authority which is the symbolic violence of the cultural arbitrary. The players within the relation of pedagogic communication are transmitters and receivers of these cultural arbitraries. The pedagogic communication is not dependent upon 'the degree of technical or charismatic qualification of the transmitter' (1977, p. 21) or the teacher. Pedagogic authority avoids the need for any

> pre-sociological illusion of crediting the person of the transmitter with the technical competence or personal authority which is, in reality,

automatically conferred on every pedagogic transmitter by the traditionally and institutionally guaranteed position he occupies in a relation of pedagogic communication (1977, p. 21).

Personalising the relation of transmitter and receiver into one of 'master' and 'disciple' is, for Bourdieu and Passeron, a misrecognition of the objective conditions in which they work, a misrecognition of the predetermination of pedagogic communication by the pedagogic authority inherent in pedagogic action. Teaching is always the imposition of a cultural arbitrary. To personalise this action is to increase its pedagogic efficacy as the imposition of a cultural arbitrary. This efficacy lies precisely in 'concealment of the fact that it is not a simple relation of communication' (1977, p. 23). Further, naturalising the teacher/student relationship makes it necessary to talk about the natural 'needs' of the receivers, the students. Teachers are then able to justify their pedagogic action on the grounds that it is in the interests of their students that they be taught what the teacher thinks they need. This assumes that such needs in some way pre-exist 'the social and pedagogic conditions of [their] production' (1977, p. 23), and increase the efficacy of the pedagogic act by further reproducing symbolic violence as misrecognition. Symbolic violence successfully imposes itself in direct proportion to the degree to which it imposes misrecognition of that violence. Pedagogic action, seen as merely a pedagogic communication between the individuals, serves only to increase the misrecognition of the 'objective truth' (1977, p. 25), and therefore to reproduce its violence further.

Above and beyond the psychological and the personal, misrecognition also operates at a cultural level. Violence is not only reproduced as the misrecognition of pedagogic communication, but also in the relation between cultural values and social groups and classes. Pedagogic action, because it is recognised as a legitimate agency of imposition, also tends 'to produce recognition of the cultural arbitrary it inculcates as legitimate culture' (1977, p. 22). The mere fact that a cultural arbitrary is transmitted, or taught, designates that arbitrary as worthy of being taught. What is arbitrary is misrecognised as being what is legitimate, a misrecognition reproduced by the form in which such arbitraries are 'communicated' to us. Thus:

> In any given social formation, legitimate culture, i.e. the culture endowed with the dominant legitimacy, is nothing other than the dominant cultural arbitrary insofar as it is misrecognised in its objective truth as a cultural arbitrary and as the dominant cultural arbitrary (1977, p. 23).

The same contradictions appear here, when seeking liberation from the dominant culture, as appeared when seeking to free pedagogic action from pedagogic authority. It is a 'blindness' in regard to 'what the legitimate culture and the dominant culture owe to the structure of their symbolic relations' (1977, p. 23). This blindness 'inspires on the one hand the "culture for the masses" programme of "liberating" the dominated classes by giving them the means of appropriating legitimate culture...' (1977, pp. 23–4). While on the other hand it seeks to criticise such culture as dominating by 'canonising it as "popular culture"' (1977, p. 24). This, argue Bourdieu and Passeron, expresses the antinomy of a sense of unworthiness on the part of the oppressed, and a depreciation of the culture of the oppressors, which 'can outlive the social conditions which produce it' (1977, p. 24). Every pedagogic action, even if it is on behalf of, or in the name of, the dominated classes, 'presupposes a delegation of authority' (1977, p. 25). The symbolic actions or interventions of these pedagogies 'can work only to the extent that they encounter and reinforce predispositions' (1977, p. 25). The reproduction of violence is inevitable whether the pedagogic action be that of protest or self-realisation, for violence is implicit in any pedagogic activity 'which succeeds in imposing itself' (1977, p. 25). The success of any pedagogic action 'cannot be deduced from the intrinsic properties of the message' (1977, p. 26) because every message, every pedagogic intervention, can only 'add its own specifically symbolic strength to the pre-existing power relations...' (1977, p. 26). Bourdieu and Passeron sum up this antinomy of cultural critique with an observation similar to that regarding the reproduction of neutral pedagogic communication as misrecognition. A pedagogic action, whether imposing a cultural arbitrary or in its delimitation of what it imposes, commands its own pedagogic authority 'within the limits laid down by that cultural arbitrary' (1977, p. 26). For the despairing teacher, then, not only the hope of transformative educational relations but now also the liberatory cultural programmes fall within the same pernicious reproductive circle, that all radical and transformative pedagogical intervention 'reproduces the fundamental principles of the cultural arbitrary' (1977, p. 26) which it seeks to overcome.

Bourdieu and Passeron make two further points regarding the logic of domination inherent in pedagogic action. Pedagogic action occurs in time, and over time, as 'habitus', and is an action given concrete or objective form within institutionalised 'educational systems'. In order that pedagogic action continues and is perpetuated even when the action itself has ceased, it is necessary that it must continue to work on, or to influence, its receivers. Thus, pedagogic action 'entails pedagogic work, a process of inculcation which must last long enough to produce a durable training, i.e. a habitus' (1977, p. 31). This habitus is formed by the successful internalisation of the principles of a cultural arbitrary, an internalisation which then performs its own pedagogic work without the need for the constant presence of the transmitters. Bourdieu says elsewhere of habitus that it is 'the system of structured, structuring dispositions' (1990, p. 52). Habitus does not require people to think through or calculate for themselves the ends which are aimed at by their dispositions. 'The practical world that is constituted in the relationship with the habitus, acting as a system of cognitive and motivating structures, is a world of already realised ends – procedures to follow, paths to take...' (1990, p. 53). The despairing teacher realises, in the idea of habitus, that their symbolic violence is always present, even when the teachers themselves are not in a direct face-to-face relation with their students. What is reproduced here is the teacher himself. Pedagogic work turns the student into the teacher. Habitus, or pedagogic work, reproduces 'the conditions in which the reproducers were produced, i.e. the conditions of its own reproduction' (1977, p. 32). Habitus is no less than the reproduction of the whole system by itself according to itself and in its own image. Bourdieu and Passeron draw a biological analogy:

> Education, considered as the process through which a cultural arbitrary is historically reproduced through the medium of the production of the habitus productive of practices conforming with that cultural arbitrary... is the equivalent, in the cultural order, of the transmission of genetic capital in the biological order (1977, p. 32).

Pedagogic work is measured according to the criterion of reproduction. It is successful to the extent that it reproduces the conditions of the production of a cultural arbitrary, the extent to which that reproduction is durable and is sustained over time, its being able to achieve that reproduction in an ever greater number of different fields, and, finally, the extent to which its (self-) reproduction is exhaustive. The power of pedagogic work lies in its reproduction of the criteria against which culture (i.e. being cultured) is measured while masking its arbitrary and dominating nature. Pedagogic work is able to define the length of time necessary to achieve recognition as a cultured or cultivated person, a definition which is its own self-reproduction. Whether imposing or protesting against this definition, it is in both cases the definition which is reproduced. Bourdieu and Passeron explore this later in regard to schooling and examination certificates. These have become the currency of cultural capital, the means by which the teachers, and their symbolic violence, are reproduced, and the violence by which culture can be seen to have been achieved. The pedagogic work or habitus is not only the reproduction of this violence, it is the imposition of this violence as the currency by which culture is represented, the value by which such culture is measured and against which human beings have no choice but to measure themselves. In later work, this currency is explored as *homo academicus* (see Bourdieu, 1984).

In the work under discussion here, Bourdieu and Passeron note that this currency operates a principle of inclusion and exclusion as regards what is to count as 'education'. They remark that:

> One of the least noticed effects of compulsory schooling is that it succeeds in obtaining from the dominated classes a recognition of legitimate knowledge and know-how (e.g. in law, medicine, technology, entertainment or art), entailing the devaluation of the knowledge and know-how they effectively command (e.g. customary law, home medicine, craft techniques, folk art and language...) [thus] providing a market for material and especially symbolic products of which the means of

37

production (not least higher education) are virtually monopolised by the dominant classes...' (1977, p. 42).

This divisive currency of legitimate and illegitimate culture gains its neutral appearance in the separation of theory and practice. It subordinates practical mastery to 'symbolic mastery of that practice' (1977, p. 44) or practice by teaching. This is a concrete example of how a seemingly neutral pedagogic communication between apprentice and teacher is one which enjoys the pedagogic authority of pre-existing power relations, relations which are themselves reproduced in and as the currency with which this pedagogic action is pedagogic work. The mere fact

> of using theoretic discourse to make explicit the principles of techniques of which working-class children have practical mastery is sufficient to cast the knacks and tricks of the trade into the illegitimacy of makeshift approximation, just as 'general education' reduces their language to jargon, slang or jibberish (1977, p. 50).

The result is a cultural currency which 'sets an unbridgeable gulf between the holder of the principles (e.g. the engineer) and the mere practitioner (e.g. the technician)' (1977, p. 50). The cost of a lack of cultural capital is exclusion from the dominant class, for reasons which, on the surface, seem purely meritocratic, but which, objectively, are pre-determined by a habitus which reproduces a dominant cultural arbitrary.

As with ideological state apparatus in the work of Althusser, pedagogic work or habitus enables the dominant class to reproduce 'its intellectual and moral integration (of the dominated classes) without resorting to external repression or, in particular, physical coercion' (1977, p. 36). The more successful it is in this, the more pedagogic action masks the pedagogic authority or power relations which lie behind it, and the more it masks that authority, the greater is its reproduction of the cultural arbitrary. Habitus is an important constituent in the vicious circle of reproduction referred to earlier. Those who would intervene in cultural domination to effect a transformation can only do so from within the habitus. Pedagogic work is the cultural agenda upon which critique is founded. Habitus, or pedagogic work, given its durability and transposability, 'produces more and more fully the objective conditions for misrecognition of cultural arbitrariness' (1977, p. 37). Bourdieu and Passeron argue that anyone 'who deliberates on his culture is already cultivated and the questions of the man who thinks he is questioning the principles of his upbringing still have their roots in his upbringing' (1977, p. 37). At its most powerful, habitus ensures that our subjective experience of domination holds itself to be 'natural', that is, that our critique is not predetermined and is not mere repetition, but is, rather, a form of natural or innate reason. It is this reason, and not pedagogic authority, which is then taken to be the natural beginning, a beginning which is the posited grounding of critique and enlightenment (this is explored in Part II). Bourdieu and Passeron refer to such natural reason as one more 'magical solution' (1977, p. 37) to the circle of pedagogic authority. It is merely 'a retrospective illusion' (1977, p. 37), one which fails to see its own predetermination within the habitus, and its own misrecognition of pedagogic authority in pedagogic work. Habitus, as the work of pedagogic authority or power relations, is not merely a vicious circle. It is more sophisticated than that. The pedagogic authority 'commanded by every pedagogic action that is exercised breaks the pedagogic circle to which any pedagogic action without pedagogic authority would be condemned, only to lock the recipient of the pedagogic work thus made possible ever more firmly' in their cultural circle (1977, p. 37). It is in knowing pedagogic authority that its illusion, its misrecognition, is at its strongest, for it is in the gap in this circle that we presuppose natural reason; a gap, however, which only binds us captive within the circle ever more effectively. The more exhaustive is pedagogic work, the more all-encompassing is habitus, and, conversely, the more we think we know about this predetermination the more powerful our illusion of critique becomes, and the greater is the growth in our 'genesis amnesia' (1977, p. 38). As such, habitus is seen by the despairing teacher as cause for ever greater despondency.

If habitus is the currency of inculcation of a cultural arbitrary, educational systems are the sites or institutional conditions where such inculcation becomes possible. Such systems not only provide the conditions for producing a habitus, but also ensure, at the same time, the 'misrecognition of those conditions' (1977, p. 54). One such system of regulated pedagogic work is the 'work of schooling'. The work of schooling is a cultural practice in which the habitus defines who a teacher is, and the limits within which he can be active. Teachers are, in Bourdieu and Passeron's words, 'a permanent corps of specialised agents, equipped with the homogenous training and standardising instruments which are the precondition for the exercise of a specific, regulated process of pedagogic work, i.e. the work of schooling' (1977, p. 57). These agents are prevented by the system from 'any practice incompatible with the function of reproducing the intellectual and moral integration of the legitimate addressees' (1977, p. 57). Such teachers are faced with the 'routine' which provides the 'disposition' for all decision-making. Our despairing teacher now finds himself not only reproducing pedagogic authority in his work, and that his work is a reproduction of habitus, but also that his practice constitutes the work of schooling, and that, as such, it cannot 'escape bearing the mark of the institutional conditions of its exercise' (1977, p. 58). The degree to which this 'agent' performs a standardised routine of educational work can be measured by the ease with which each agent can be replaced by another, or by texts which also reproduce their functions, i.e. transmit their cultural arbitraries. What is required is merely another teacher, another agent or manual which can ensure the durability of the reproduction of pedagogic work and the misrecognition of pedagogic authority. Regardless of the message, 'all work of schooling generates a discourse... in accordance with a logic which primarily obeys the requirements of the institutionalisation of apprenticeship' (1977, p. 59).

The educational system, in order to maintain itself as habitus, and to ensure duration and durability, 'necessarily monopolises the production of the agents appointed to reproduce it' (1977, p. 60). The identity of 'a teacher' is itself predetermined within the habitus and according to the needs of the dominant cultural arbitrary. If a teacher is to reproduce pedagogic authority through pedagogic work, then not only must he bring this about for others, he must also have been produced in the same way. When the teacher teaches, he is reproducing himself in others. The successful student, i.e. the cultivated student, is the receiver who has fully received the messages, integrated them into himself, and becomes them. This receiver is then equipped to be a transmitter, and thus the durability of the reproductive cycle is ensured. Teachers, therefore, are 'equipped with the durable training which enables them to perform the work of schooling tending to reproduce the same training in new reproducers [which] therefore contains a tendency towards perfect self-reproduction (inertia)' (1977, p. 60).

The circular nature of pedagogic work is raised to the level of consciousness each time the 'authority' of the teacher to teach is called into question. But 'personal' pedagogic authority is institutionalised as school authority, and this prevents 'agents of the institution from having endlessly to win and confirm their pedagogic authority' (1977, p. 63). The legitimacy of the teacher is raised in each pedagogic action. But pedagogic action, as seen earlier, raises this question only the more forcefully to ensure the misrecognition of the power relations which lie behind it. In the same way that pedagogic action reproduces misrecognition of its legitimacy, so schools are also able to ensure the misrecognition of their (arbitrary) legitimacy as pedagogic institutions. The teacher is able to shelter behind the legitimacy of schooling when crises of authority are invoked, for his position and his authority (which are the same pedagogic authority) are 'guaranteed by the institution [and are] socially objectified and symbolised in the institutional procedures and rules defining his training, the diplomas which sanction it, and the legitimate conduct of his profession' (1977, p. 63). Any belief that the school or the teacher can work independently of pedagogic authority, and are not directly reproductive of the dominant cultural arbitrary, is only further illusion and misrecognition. The power of such illusions, in the guise of neutrality, is the production of ever greater 'dependence through independence' (1977, p. 67).

What Bourdieu and Passeron have attempted here is a comprehensive analysis of the power relations which inhere in all pedagogic action, whether the aims of that action be radical or conservative. The themes which they raise are returned to in Part III when pedagogy is again analysed, this time within Hegelian philosophy. Two brief points can be made here, however, with regard to Bourdieu and Passeron's work.

First, the courtroom in which the authors make their judgments is itself drawn into the circle of reproduction. Their intervention is just such another pedagogic action, locked even more firmly within the circle by its drawing our attention to it. Their intervention is further evidence of how such breaks in the circle are self-defeating. The status of their intervention, of their pedagogic action, is thus itself called into question. Their text is yet another reproduction of the learned teacher and his apprentices. Their assertions regarding the objective conditions of power relations and pedagogic authority fall prey to their own observations regarding misrecognition. The belief that objectivity can be known is only another illusion regarding the innate reason that is believed to be able to see through misrecognition without, at the same time, falling victim to it. Ultimately, Bourdieu and Passeron's system falls victim to itself. Either the system is comprehensive, in which case their observations are all illusory, or their observations are somehow above the system, in which case the system itself is not as comprehensive as they are describing. Either way, our experience of their system is one of repetition and reproduction.

The second point to be made is that while Bourdieu and Passeron employ their system as a methodological tool for analysis and research (see Part 2, 1977), they do not pursue this experience of the totality of the system as itself a comprehensive education. They are right to point out that misrecognition is total in the sense that it even implicates itself. They are among the few theorists in education to reveal how misrecognition and repetition are inextricably linked to the dialectic of independence and dependence. There is a fundamental truth to the observation that misrecognition produces ever greater dependence, but it is not a truth which Bourdieu and Passeron explore. Misrecognition never experiences itself in their work, never becomes its own illusory being, is never explored as the educational and comprehensive self-experience of our philosophical consciousness. The self-determination of illusion and misrecognition remains implicit within Bourdieu and Passeron's work, but unexplicated. As such, reproduction in education, society and culture remains precisely that, never risking the opportunities presented by the authors to learn, in a substantive way, from the contradictions which they repeat, never risking the experience of the contradiction of subjectivity as a theory of the self-determination of subjectivity. This risk is taken up in Parts II, III and IV of this book.

Return of the teacher

What those performing a critique of the teacher have in common is the view that the teacher dominates. For Neill, the teacher dominates the potentially free pupil; for Althusser, the teacher is the material domination of the pupil and of the curriculum; for Freire, the teacher dominates the naming of the world, or controls knowledge *per se*; for Giroux, the teacher dominates the voices and experiences of the pupils; for Habermasian critical theorists, the teacher dominates the intersubjective by ensuring the transmission of technical and abstract knowledge; and for Bourdieu and Passeron, the teacher embodies the domination inherent in pedagogic authority.

Equally, however, what all these critiques have in common is that the critique of the teacher as dominator is, at one and the same time, the return of the teacher as dominator. The idea of return, here, is explored in detail in Parts III and IV. By way of announcing the argument which lies ahead, it can be said of the experiences described earlier that the teacher, whose sovereignty is his (critical or enlightened) knowledge, misunderstands his own determination as another abstract result of the knowledge relation. The teacher is produced as a person because and when knowledge is defined as an object. But knowledge must always be defined as an object within the rational knowledge relation (see Chapter 7), because that relation has already determined knowledge in its own image. Knowledge comes to the educational process predetermined as identity, as object, a thing to be collected and owned. It is a reflection of the sovereignty of the person, and the person itself comes to knowledge predetermined as identity, a result. Knowledge confirms the independence of the teacher as property confirms the independence of the person. (This is dealt with in detail in Chapter 7.) Even when the person comes to knowledge seeking to be critical of its objectification, and arguing for a relation between knower and knowledge which does not simply repeat the owning of the latter by the former, it is still the case that the relation itself is an object for the person. The person cannot choose a 'time' to know the relation which is before or after his own separation from it. He cannot approach knowledge as a non-person, either in the sense that he is yet to be affected by the relation, nor in the sense that he has overcome it. His approach to knowledge is already defined by his independence from it. In the face of this separation, critique takes knowledge of separation to be a reunification of knower and known, a reunification which is posited as enlightenment, and where knowing (the activity) and what is known (the result) are one and the same. Thus, for Neill, the self-work and result of education is the child, for Althusser it is the real men at the end of critique, for Freire, educational self-work is the pupils' own renaming of the world, for Giroux, it is student voice and student experience, and for Habermasians, it is communicative action.

The critique of the teacher as dominator is inevitably the return of the teacher as dominator. The truth which he seeks to reveal is the relation of knower and knowledge, that is, to restore to visibility the relations which are masked by bourgeois social relations. The work of overcoming illusion is presupposed as the work which establishes the relation of knower and knowledge as self-activity and result. No longer the illusion of abstract education, no longer the sovereign independence of the teacher, but now the teacher and the student together in a relation of mutual interdependence.

But the very activity of these teachers in seeking such ends is self-defeating, and cannot but repeat the separation of the knowledge relation and its consequent relations of domination. Critique may well be generated by the experience of contradiction, but when it becomes the expression or method of that experience for others, it is already a knowledge separated from the process of its becoming. The relation of knower and knowledge in experience can only exist for a consciousness. Thus it is never a self-relation, it is always a relation of object to other. Taken as a result in which the relation can be maintained, 'The latter appears at first sight to be merely the reflection of consciousness into itself' (Hegel, 1977, p. 55). This misrecognition allows the critical teacher to believe that such critique is self-work, generated not by abstractions from without, but moved and moving solely by that which lies within, i.e., that it is immanent critique, and self-sufficient experience. There is a self-sufficient experience here, but it is not that which critical teachers posit it to be.

The experience which is self-sufficient, and which includes this positing, is the experience not of overcoming the teacher but of the return of the teacher, not of the depersonification of enlightenment, but of the re-personification of enlightenment. The teacher, in possession of this experience, is in possession of the experience as knowledge, and as knowledge, it is property. But there is no other way in which something can be known except as the repetition of the teacher as person and as the personification of enlightenment. The teacher, therefore, is part of the truth which is the contradiction that they would teach about. But in their critical teaching they are always already the embodiment of that contradiction as knowledge. There is no experience available to us which is not already such a result, and similarly there is no teacher who is not already personification of enlightenment as result, as owner.

The teacher is as much a content to be comprehended as are the objects which he would teach about. However, the teacher has not been a popular choice of content through which to examine the contradictions of bourgeois social and legal relations, nor rational knowledge relations. This is primarily because the contradiction of the teacher, the return of the teacher, is pervasive to all forms of critique, not only in education but in social theory generally. The negative implications of return are often seen as too horrifying, too abysmal, and too self-defeating to be worked with. Instead, solutions to return are posited on which more positive theories can be erected. The concern in this book is the way in which enlightenment and education are posited as just such a solution. It will be shown how the despairing teacher, who refuses to abandon his negative experiences simply because what they teach him is unexpected, unwelcome and painfully unsatisfactory, is closest to the truth of education, or in regard to what education is. In the philosophical consciousness of the despairing teacher, where despair is the philosophical consciousness, there the separation of knower and known, teacher and student, can be known as self-work and self-result. When the despairing teacher becomes the content of his own philosophical consciousness, then the self-relation of enlightenment can be known.

In knowing himself as this content, the despairing teacher has before him his self-relation within comprehensive education. But to realise this, teachers have to refuse the solutions of radical and critical educators. The subject and substance of the teacher as philosophical content is to be found not with those who posit unity and repeat separation, but with those who live and teach in the actuality of separation and unity, as the truth which is return, or as the broken middle (see

43

also the Introduction and Chapter 5 onwards); that is, with those who are teachers not only of, but as philosophical activity. It is by losing the identity of the teacher that the truth of the return of the teacher, and the self-relation of enlightenment, can be realised. That loss has begun in this chapter, for the despairing teacher has not been saved from despair, nor has the knowledge of the despairing teacher overcome the causes of that despair. Rather, the despair has deepened. In the depth of that loss he is now able to form a deeper relationship to himself as a teacher. The recognition of that deeper relationship will not be found in writings which are merely abstract definitions and dominations of education, nor in those which are merely abstract statements of the philosophical, shot, as it were, from a pistol. On the contrary, the despairing teacher will find his deepening self-relation in work which is philosophical because it is educational and which is educational because it is philosophical, i.e. in work which knows itself to be their contradictory relation. Put more simply, the depth of educational experience which is the return of the teacher is to be found in those teachers who have lived and taught as the contradiction of their return, or who have been, for their students, what they are.

Chapter 2 moves away from education by taking the despairing teacher to sociology and social theory. This move deepens and repeats the contradictions and negations which characterise the despairing teacher, and which (will) determine his return to education.

2 Teachers of critique

One of the overriding interests of the critical sociological tradition has been to reveal the social determination and the social nature of the single individual. Theorists in this tradition have not been satisfied with the individual as he appears in society, as the person, and have sought to discover the truth of what lies behind the person. The sociological imagination has therefore always been our own critical reflection on ourselves, driven by the desire for true knowledge about what we really are. It is a desire Hegel describes in the section on essence in his *Science of Logic*.

> Since knowing has for its goal knowledge of the true, knowledge of what being is in and for itself, it does not stop at the immediate and its determinations, but penetrates it on the supposition that at the back of this being there is something else, something other than being itself, that this background constitutes the truth of being (Hegel, 1969, p. 389).

Sociology has put itself forward as the perspective in which this something else becomes visible. In the full glare of sociological enquiry, our historical contingency and our social determination have been revealed as the real conditions upon which our true selves are based. The social is revealed as the truth of the individual, determination becomes the truth of freedom, independence is seen to be dependence, and the collective is seen to be the truth behind the merely single individual. This chapter briefly explores three theorists who offer different critiques of the person and different versions of the truth which lies behind the person.

The three theorists, however, have also been selected for another reason. Among sociologists and social theorists, Rousseau, Marx and Durkheim stand apart as employing their critiques of the person as an education of the person wherein, at one and the same time, each of us will come to know ourselves differently, and to know ourselves as we really are. Their use of critique as enlightenment reveals their interest not only in analysis but also in diagnosis. The illness that each believes us to be suffering from is a false life, filled by false needs and giving rise to false opinions and values. The remedy for this is our education regarding the mere appearance of the person, so that we come to see through and behind our false life to a more genuine existence, one based on genuine needs and ethical relations with others. Education, for these theorists, is the means by which the ethical relations of solitary persons who treat each other merely as means to personal ends, relations which characterise Western societies, can be replaced with mutual ethical relations wherein all individuals share a genuinely communal and social existence. The critique of the person aims to overcome the merely civil, bourgeois or individual person, and to put in its place the genuinely social human being. The degree of success which each enjoys in their respective critical projects is assessed at the end of this chapter.

The civil person

In the *Discourse on the Origin of Inequality*, Rousseau links the origin of the person in society to the establishing of property relations. 'The first man who, having enclosed a piece of ground, bethought himself of saying "This is mine", and found people simple enough to believe him, was the real founder of civil society' (Rousseau, 1973, p. 84).

Private property for Rousseau was merely a false or inauthentic expression of the instinct for self-preservation which characterised 'natural man'. It was this desire for self-preservation which led natural man to the understanding that co-operation with others aided self-preservation. The selfishness of natural man was mutual, and therefore brought about self-motivated co-operative forms of living. Such a union was a natural union, for it was based solely upon the desire for the self-preservation of each individual. For Rousseau, such a union is not yet a social union, and natural man who co-operates with other such men is not yet a person.

The natural union becomes a social union through the influence of the common life which natural man begins to lead. What was formed in order to best preserve the independence of natural man now turns against its original purpose and creates all of the social customs to which the individual loses his independence. These include speech, feelings of love, the family, leisure time and most importantly, public esteem. 'Each one began to consider the rest, and to wish to be considered in turn; and thus a value came to be attached to public esteem' (1973, p. 90). In the leisure time brought about through the efficiency of co-operation, natural man came to judge himself in comparison with others around him. As a result, natural self-preservation was turned into social self-interest. Independence ceased to be natural. Now man was preserved not only through self-preservation of the body, but also in addition his identity was preserved through and by the good opinion held of him by others. In these social relations of dependency, for Rousseau, lay the origin of property and inequality:

46

...so long as they undertook only what a single person could accomplish, and confined themselves to such arts as did not require the joint labour of several hands, they lived free, healthy, honest, and happy lives... But from the moment one man began to stand in need of the help of another; from the moment it appeared advantageous to any one man to have enough provision for two, equality disappeared, property was introduced, work became indispensable... (1973, p. 92).

In this social situation, it was no longer the case that man worked for himself and in the interests of pure self-preservation. Now, through property, it became possible for some not to have to work at all, while others had absolutely no choice but to work for those who had 'provision for two'. Rousseau notes that 'In this state of affairs, equality might have been sustained, had the talents of individuals been equal' (1973, p. 94). However, with the disappearance of the independence of natural man, and his dependence upon others, there was now nothing to prevent the natural inequality between men unfolding, and becoming a social inequality. Strength, skill and ingenuity made equal work into unequal reward, one man gaining 'a great deal by his work, while the other could hardly support himself' (1973, pp. 94–5).

This social inequality, made possible by the division of labour and private property, gave rise to a whole new way of life which Rousseau terms 'civil society'. It became in the interests of men to secure co-operation with others in order to gain advantage over them, to make someone work not for the benefit of himself, but for another. To this end civil man invented new strategies to ensure his own success at the expense of others.

> Insatiable ambition, the thirst of raising their respective fortunes, not so much from real want as from the desire to surpass others, inspired all men with a vile propensity to injure one another, and with a secret jealousy, which is the more dangerous, as it puts on a mask of benevolence, to carry its point with greater security. In a word, there arose rivalry and competition on the one hand, and conflicting interests on the other, together with a secret desire on both of profiting at the expense of others. All these evils were the first effects of property, and the inseparable attendants of growing inequality' (1973, p. 96).

Property therefore gave rise to a society where each was at war with the other, a war masked by the pretence of 'civility'. So often seen as the natural state of man, for Rousseau this war of all against all was a corruption of natural man, a corruption inevitably brought about when one man co-operated with another for reasons other than his own self-preservation. To be able to have more than was necessary for self-preservation, and to see the advantages over others of doing so, were the beginnings of the evils of civil society. The *coup de grâce* was achieved

47

when the right to inequality was enshrined in the universal right of private property. Rousseau argues that the rich realised quickly that the force by which they had appropriated their riches was a force that others could use against them. To secure themselves from such usurpation, the rich 'conceived at length the profoundest plan that ever entered the mind of man' (1973, p. 98). Masking the benefit which such a plan gave the rich, they argued to all those who had less and were a threat:

> Let us join... to guard the weak from oppression, to restrain the ambitious, and secure to every man the possession of what belongs to him: let us institute rules of justice and peace, to which all without exception may be obliged to conform; rules that may in some measure make amends for the caprices of fortune, by subjecting equally the powerful and the weak to the observance of reciprocal obligations (1973, p. 98).

The ruse was successful, for the weak were also busy trying to gain rewards for themselves, and saw in political institutions at least some advantage to their attempts. What they did not see was how the law served to ensure that social inequality was preserved, and mitigated against their own attempts for riches. 'All ran headlong to their chains...' (1973, p. 99), unable to see through the mask of political equality how law enshrined social inequality. Rousseau concludes on the origin of civil society that it:

> ...bound new fetters on the poor, and gave new powers to the rich; which irretrievably destroyed natural liberty, eternally fixed the law of property and inequality, converted clever usurpation into unalterable right, and, for the advantage of a few ambitious individuals, subjected all mankind to perpetual labour, slavery, and wretchedness (1973, p. 99).

In the social relation of private property the natural need that each has of the other is distorted into the need of one to exploit the other. The strength of the independent natural man is overcome in civil society by the weakness of dependent man who seeks to exploit that need. The honesty of self-preservation is replaced by the deceit of self-interest. Natural man is replaced by social man, or by the property-owning person, and all the inequalities which are maintained in his name.

This person is related to other persons by way of exploitation. Because each person is potentially a way of another gaining self-advantage, personal relations are characterised by falsity and by deceit. In civil society it became in the interests of men 'to appear what they really were not. To be and to seem became two totally different things' (Rousseau, 1973, p. 95). In social relations the person becomes a mere illusion of 'sociability', for public life is a pretence, and is wholly artificial. Behind the civility lies the selfishness and greed of the person who works solely for his own self-interest. But the mask is useful, for, like the law, it hides the real inequality behind the merely formal assurances of equality. Rousseau writes that before civil society, 'men found their security in the ease with which they could see through one another' (1973, p. 6). In civil society, enjoying social relations based upon private property, that transparency has vanished, and every person is now merely a false show and an appearance.

> We no longer dare seem what we really are, but lie under a perpetual restraint... we never know with whom we have to deal... What a train of vices must attend this uncertainty! Sincere friendship, real esteem, and perfect confidence are banished from among men. Jealousy, suspicion, fear, coldness, reserve, hate and fraud lie constantly concealed under that uniform and deceitful veil of politeness (1973, pp. 6–7).

The falsity of the person is what Rousseau calls *amour-propre*, a self-interest which is fed through the degree to which another can exploited, be it in terms of material riches or personal aggrandisement. The open transparency of natural man Rousseau calls *amour-de-soi*, 'a natural feeling which leads every animal to look to its own preservation, and which, guided in man by reason and modified by compassion, creates humanity and virtue' (1973, p. 73, footnote). The formal equality of civil society masks the fact that natural inequalities have been institutionalised. The formal relationship of one person to another masks the fact that each is out to get from the other as much advantage as it can. In the market-place advantage is sought by exploiting the needs of others, yet giving the appearance of fairness. In social relations advantage is secured by constructing an appearance of civility and compassion which will gain social favour. In both relations, the person is forced to behave in a deceitful and hypocritical way. Rousseau sees *amour-propre* as the embodiment of the fall of natural man from self-preservation to self-interest. The cause of the fall is not man's nature, but the nature of society. It is the social relation which has turned man from an honest and open human being to a cunning and artificial person.

Rousseau turns his critique of civil society into a programme for the realisation of a more genuine society in his book *Emile*. The goal of *Emile* is an educational programme which will not repeat the evils of civil society, but will instead produce a society where the relations between individuals are again based on self-preservation modified by reason and compassion. In this community, people will be not be educated to become slaves to false and artificial needs, but to recognise their real needs and pursue them openly with each other. Rousseau's educational formula for achieving this community is a negative one. To guard against children becoming infected with social and artificial requirements, his advice to teachers is that they do nothing, and allow natural needs to develop instead.

Emile is not merely an educational philosophy, it is an educational philosophy which results from a critique of the origin of inequality, of civil man and of private property. It seeks to employ this critique to construct a different type of person, albeit within a social situation. Rousseau does not advocate a 'return' to natural man, rather a progression to a more enlightened and less artificial social man.

As Rousseau sees the 'civil' to be a corrupting of *amour-de-soi*, so he sees the teacher as a corrupter of the child's natural instincts, drives and needs. His challenge to the teacher, therefore, is this: 'Forced to combat either nature or society, you must make your choice between the man and the citizen, you cannot train both' (1974, p. 7). If the teacher chooses the former then the pedagogical maxim which Rousseau advocates is 'reverse the usual practice and you will almost always do right' (1974, p. 58). All that is required of the teacher is that they teach 'without doing anything at all' (1974, p. 84). Above all they must not intervene between what the child wants to do and what the child is able to do, for this will affect in a 'social' way the natural education which the child is to receive. A natural education is a self-education, for in it children have come to terms with what their strength and abilities enable them to do, and, moreover, modify their desires solely to that which they can satisfy on their own. 'True happiness', says Rousseau, 'consists in decreasing the difference between our desires and our powers, in establishing a perfect equilibrium between the power and the will' (1974, p. 44). This is a definition not only of a child's natural education, but also of the principle behind the social contract. The teacher, like the future rational citizen, must not 'kick against the stern law of necessity' (1974, p. 47), but learn to judge the usefulness of things (and laws) in relation to genuine and real needs.

Rousseau concludes that 'man is truly free who desires what he is able to perform, and does what he desires. This is my fundamental maxim. Apply it to childhood, and all the rules of education spring from it' (1974, p. 48). Civil society negates *amour-de-soi*; a natural education will, in return, negate the influence of civil society. A positive natural education is a negative social education. The most important thing for the teacher 'is to prevent anything being done' (1974, p. 9).

The result of this socially negative and therefore natural education in Emile is an individual who grows up rationally because an equilibrium has developed between his power and his will. He has grown up to know his own genuine needs because his needs have had to be determined by his own capability of fulfilling them. When he grows up and meets other such individuals, then there will be no need for exploitation or artifice between them for the needs of each will be in balance with the ability of each to fulfil them. Prior to private property, amour-de-soi led each man to observe conformities between himself and others based on them acting solely according to real needs. Rousseau hopes that the same will be the case for Emile and his companions who have all received a socially negative education:

> Finding that they all behaved as he himself would have done in like
> circumstances, he naturally inferred that their manner of thinking and

acting was altogether in conformity with his own. This important truth, once deeply impressed on his mind, must have induced him, from an intuitive feeling more certain and much more rapid than any kind of reasoning, to pursue the rules of conduct, which he had best observe towards them, for his own security and advantage (1973, p. 86).

For Rousseau, in modern society these rules of conduct would have form as the social contract, a contract which is only rational if it is based upon the natural development of *amour-de-soi* outlined in *Emile*. Emile's education at first is natural. His tutor tells him nothing, offers him no books (save *Robinson Crusoe*), keeps him from attending school and protects him from that which civil society offers him. 'Compelled to learn for himself, he uses his own reason not that of others, for there must be no submission to authority if you would have no submission to convention' (1974, p. 169). Emile learns to use his own reason because his education is natural, self-determined and undistorted. He learns for himself the restrictions and obligations which nature places upon him when he seeks to exert his will over it. He is 'naturally' educated into restricting his desires. This natural education in *amour-de-soi* or self-preservation looks to civil man to be a merely selfish education. But for Rousseau, qualities of selfishness and greed are not natural but social. They stem from the advantages made possible by private property. Emile will have no need for selfishness or greed, for nature will have limited his desires and needs to those which are possible for him to achieve alone. In this way, he will 'base his judgments on the true relations of things' (1974, p. 147) because he will judge relations on their usefulness in satisfying his already controlled needs. Such judgments form the basis of the education of his will, and the judgments themselves are grounded in intelligence. This, for Rousseau, is when instinct is overcome by reason, but a reason based around no other influence than its own natural development. Emile learns to judge relations not selfishly but mutually. Thus he develops pity, sincerity, kindness and sympathy for suffering because he is able to know his own suffering as the same suffering in others. His social relations are rational because they are mutual, and they are mutual because they are natural and undistorted by the self-interest of civil reason. Citizens who share self-love will act out of genuine need, and judge mutual interests accordingly. Persons who live only for self-interest will act out of false needs, and all co-operation will be inevitably exploitative. Reasoning is Emile's own activity, not based upon the opinions of others, and not corrupted into securing his own advantage over and against others in the gratification of false needs. Rousseau advocates that teachers 'fit a man's education to his real self, not to what is no part of him' (1974, p. 157).

The will of each, when this will knows *itself* and is not what it has become in *amour-propre*, is the basis of the general will. The general will is only infallible when it is general, and it is general not as 'a sum of particular wills' (Rousseau, 1973, p. 203) but as the will of each becomes common. What is at stake for Rousseau is that the general will is not the will of all civil persons put together.

That would be merely the will of all persons seeking advantage over each other. A will based on any particular or personal need would not be (natural, rational) mutual dependence, and thus not general. The general will is that 'in which each alone, while uniting himself with all, may still obey himself alone, and remain as free as before' (1973, p. 191). The general will is based upon the free will of each person who understands his real needs because he has modified his own desires to match his ability to satisfy them. Each attends to the general will in this spirit of harmony and balance, obeying himself only. Each is independent, and therefore true and genuine mutuality is possible. Where some are only dependent, then the general will would reflect not universality but particularity, not genuine needs but merely civil and exploitative interests. In the genuine expression of mutual dependency, based on the pure rationality of mutual (independent) self-preservation, 'each man, in giving himself to all, gives himself to nobody; and as there is no associate over which he does not acquire the same rights as he yields others over himself, he gains an equivalent for everything he loses' (1973, p. 192). Social (civil) needs, as opposed to natural needs, corrupt the general will because they seek advantage and power over others. The general will is the expression of mutuality in which (natural) independence is the prerequisite of social dependence. The former is itself dependent upon a natural and an anti-social education in which each individual is determined in relation to himself before he then begins (equal and mutual) relations with others.

The bourgeois person

Like Rousseau, Marx argued for the possibility of seeing through the ideological distortions of the 'personification' of human social relations to the genuinely communal relations which lay behind it. What in Rousseau was a critique of civil society, in Marx is a critique of capitalist society, its division of labour and its mode of commodity production. As Rousseau saw a genuine 'nature' lying behind the mask of social relations, so Marx sees a genuine human species lying behind the illusions of commodity fetishism, and of individual workers. Marx was concerned to show how, at the heart of many forms of thinking and analysis, lay the presupposition (the positing) of the person. The person is the legal category upon which the whole edifice of private property rests. It is the presupposed unit or worker in (political) economics; it is the independent civil man of political studies; above all, it is the 'free' individual of social and political analysis. Each of these forms of thought is ideological for Marx, because they presuppose the person as a free, substantial and independent individual, as if the person was a 'natural' manifestation, outside of its determination within history, forms of production, or law.

In the *Early Writings* Marx mounted a four-point attack upon the determination of the person within bourgeois social relations. The person is the 'member of civil society, the *egoistic, independent* individual' (Marx, 1975, p. 234) which is presupposed as the natural state of man, and universalised in the political state. Just such a person, the private man, is also presupposed in the science of political economy, most notably as the wage labourer, the worker.

> Political economy proceeds from the fact of private property. It does not explain it. It grasps the material process of private property, the process through which it actually passes, in general and abstract formulae which it then takes as laws. It does not comprehend these laws, i.e. it does not show how they arise from the nature of private property (Marx, 1975, p. 322, emphasis removed).

Therefore, in presenting a critique of the person, Marx begins with the person as 'a present-day economic fact' (1975, p. 323), not merely as a posited 'natural' fact.

He exposes the person in political economy to be the estranged worker, estranged from what is made, from the making of it, from life or species activity, i.e. from essence, and from the human community in general. Civil society is the expression of that estrangement, yet it constitutes the world as it is presented to our consciousness, and is the world in which we find ourselves. The estranged worker and civil society are the same presupposition of the private person. Both are the embodiment of estrangement and its determination. Unlike political economists, Marx does not begin with private property and define persons accordingly. Rather he arrives at an understanding of private property as the result of estrangement and, reciprocally, as the means of realising this estrangement. This latter fact Marx refers to as the 'secret' of private property (1975, p. 332). He means that while estrangement and its manifestation as private property appear as reality, behind that reality lies the cause of the estrangement and of private property, labour itself. Labour (which is really social), when it is seen as an attribute of the single person, the estranged worker, loses its social character and has that character transferred to the life of the objects which are produced. This is the basis of Marx's critique of the fetishism of commodities. The value of the commodity expresses the social relations between workers which, by nature, belong to them. Labour does not appear to them as a social relationship because they are alienated from themselves, from the object, from labour, and from the collective human essence, in commodity production. It is through this alienated labour that workers create their relations to each other as relations between things. It is hardly a social relation at all, since in their estrangement all the workers know is their isolation, their independence and freedom from each other. The social nature of labour is expressed only in the exchange-value of the commodities which they make. It is the commodity which enjoys the social relation denied to the worker.

The commodity therefore has a phantasmagoric form different to that of its natural appearance which political economy presupposes. Rose argues that 'phantasmagoric' is the appropriate term here, for it conveys not only a strange and shadowy world but also one in which what is unclear is the person. 'The epithet "phantasmagoric" stresses the personifications as well as the strangeness of the form in which the relations between men appear' (Rose, 1978, p. 31). When men take on a relation between themselves as between things, and when the things enjoy the social relation, not only is social labour personified, but also commodities are 'socialised'.

The commonality that commodities enjoy which workers do not is embodied as value. All commodities contain the individual labour of different workers, yet the labour of each different worker is collectively expressed as value. Even though the labour performed is different, in its exchange-value it is able to be treated homogeneously as if it were just one substance. This substance is human labour. But now it belongs not to the producers but to the commodities. The commodity 'reflects the social relation of the producers to the sum total of labour as a social relation between objects' (Marx, 1976, p. 165). This, then, is the phantasmagoria: a 'misty realm' (1976, p. 165) in which men appear as less than themselves, but at the same time achieve this illusory appearance in relation to that which they have themselves produced. What Marx calls the fetishism of commodities expresses a relation between the person and the commodity, a relation which is itself an illusion. The presupposing of the commodity as having value as a natural attribute is the same presupposition of labour as merely 'personal'. Both are the separation of subject and substance, and both are therefore the misrecognition of labour by itself, or a broken middle. The actual significance of the relationship between work and illusion is explored in Part III. For now, it is important to note that the essence of human beings, collective human labour, is estranged from them in the personal (and free) labour which each private person or worker performs in commodity production. The commodity, in this sense, contains the true social relation which rightfully belongs to the human species. The complication is that although commodity production presupposes the person or the individual worker, nevertheless it is a presupposition which each of us repeats for ourselves as if it were our own truth. To see through the phantasmagoria, and to clear the mist so that the (illusory) relation can appear as the true human relation, is the goal of Marx's critique.

The *Grundrisse* and *Capital* take up the challenge of seeing behind the abstract concepts of political economy and revealing the human activity which creates them, but which, then, is also dominated by them. Marx notes that 'Reflection begins *post-festum*' (1976, p. 168) with the totality of commodity production already established. Even a critique which sees into the secret of their origin 'by no means banishes the semblance of objectivity possessed by the social characteristics of labour' (1976, p. 167). The worker produces a commodity in which human social relations are present as exchange-value. This exchange-value, already the estrangement of the worker, realises its universality in the form of money, for money is the 'common measure' of all values (1976, p. 188). It is not money that makes objects valuable, it is money by which their (exchange-) value is expressed. Given, therefore, that money is the universal commodity, and that the commodity appears as the social relationship which workers are estranged from, then, says Marx, 'The individual carries his social power, as well as his bond with society, in his pocket' (1973, p. 157). Money ensures that relations between persons reproduce the relations of commodity production, where what they have in common (money) at the same time ensures that they have nothing in common with each other. Money, not human labour, is the (social) relation of one person to another, and they are brought together as buyers and sellers through money. Thus, 'In exchange-value, the social connection between persons is transformed into a social relation between things' (1973, p. 157) which is then made concrete in the market-place.

However, like all relations between particular and universal, money is a contradiction. As a universal it is the commodity of all values, it is the medium of their exchange. But, in this exchange, it is also the particular representation of the value of each commodity. Money is only the abstraction of 'all money', or wealth, and yet at the same time is the negation of that universality when it is thrown into circulation. In circulation, money is merely the particular of general wealth. It is the negation of wealth when it is being spent. 'It pretends to be the general commodity, but because of its natural particularity it is again a particular commodity' (1973, p. 234). Thus money faces the problem that it is both the universal and the particular.

> If negated as the mere general form of wealth, it must then realise itself in the particular substances of real wealth; but in the process of proving itself really to be the material representative of the totality of wealth, it must at the same time preserve itself as the general form. Its very entry into circulation must be a moment of its staying at home, and its staying at home must be an entry into circulation (1973, p. 234, emphasis removed).

The relationship of exchange-value to money is the same as that of the worker to the commodity. In both cases the latter is only an illusory form of the self-relation which is the former, but it is an illusion which determines also the former's relation to the latter. The phantasmagoria of the fetishism of commodities is the same confusion of exchange-value in circulation as money. Marx calls the result of the contradiction of exchange-value as money, capital. He writes,

> As soon as money is posited as an exchange-value which not only becomes independent of circulation, but which also maintains itself through it, then there is no longer money, for this as such does not go beyond the negative aspect, but is capital (1973, p. 259).

Capital is therefore 'speculative', for it is a result which can only be achieved through contradictory or negative activity. Money has to be risked in circulation in order to realise its true self-relation as capital. In being risked it is also, at the same time, returned to itself. The actuality of capital is return, or profit. But the whole self-relation of capital is the contradictory activity of speculation, the negation or risk of itself in circulation as exchange-value.

Marx employs an Hegelian determinate negation in the Grundrisse to argue this point (determinate negation is explored in Chapters 5, 6 and 7). He argues that capital is the presupposition of exchange-value as exchange-value, a reference to illusory being posited as illusory being in Hegel's *Science of Logic*. The logic of capital therefore becomes the same as the structure of the notion in Hegel. Both are a self-realisation of themselves as the relation in which loss is return and return is loss.

What is missing in Marx, but not in Hegel, is the same speculative logic employed to comprehend the other parts involved in the illusion of the phantasmagoria of commodity fetishism. Marx comprehends the relation of the value of commodities with itself (as capital) but not the self-relation of the person to the illusory relation between itself and the fetishism of commodities. It is as if the truth of an illusory social relationship, as loss and return, belongs only to commodities. They are allowed to know their contradiction as their truth. We, on the other hand, are not allowed to know ours. But commodities are only one half of the broken middle of the relation which is commodity fetishism. The other half, the person, also experiences that relation as loss and return, as their own illusory being posited as illusory being. They, too, have a return, which is actual as (the contradiction of) the subject. But the subject is denied this actuality in Marx's work. Only commodities are allowed to experience the return of their own illusory appearance. Marx has a higher goal for us, not repetition but transformation. But in pursuing this goal, our self-determination in and as the illusory phantasmagoria of commodity production is denied to us as self-knowledge. The person is disallowed from positing itself as itself. We are not allowed to know ourselves as we are; instead we are posited as we ought to be, that is, an ought which is itself removed from the self-determining relation of commodity fetishism, and therefore of bourgeois social relations.

Rose, describing this point, argues that

> Marx's failure to understand Hegel's actuality meant that he did not develop any notion of subjectivity. Subjects are merely 'bearers' of economic functions... This accounts for the weakness in Marx's concept of ideology (1981, pp. 216–17).

The aim of Marx's critique of bourgeois ideology is the same as that of his critique of political economy, to reveal its presupposition of a particular form of natural individual as a historical and social determination. Just as his critique of political economy sees the secret of capitalist production to be estranged human social labour, so, in his critique of ideology, he repeats the same argument to show that the secret of ideas is that they, too, are human activity but determined within the illusion of bourgeois social relations. Just as commodities appear to the worker as if they have a life of their own, so ideas appear to the person as if they, too, have an objective and autonomous existence. In each case, the relation of object to person is self-determining for both parties; i.e. illusion becomes concrete as object and person. 'Reality' is always the result of social relations, even though the result appears to be independent of social relations. So Marx is able to state that 'life is not determined by consciousness but consciousness by life' (1970, p. 47). For example, the independence of the person is determined within the illusion of the property relation, and all ideas relating to the person, whether in political economy, religion, metaphysics, morals or philosophy, simply reproduce the illusion. Since 'individuals are now ruled by abstractions' (1973, p. 164), the only understanding available to man about himself is that in which he is abstracted from the social relations which determine that abstraction. We can only know ourselves as we are determined within the illusion. Just as with Hegel, where the property relation repeats itself even in the knowing of itself because the work is already a self-determination of the property relation, so in Marx all ideological thought is also already a reproduction of abstraction. However, whereas in Hegel actuality expresses and contains this determination as known, and in Marx profit is the actuality of that self-reproduction of exchange-value, with regard to consciousness, determination is never actually known, for it is presupposed as overcome. In other words, in Marx it is never the subject in the relation of commodity fetishism which experiences determinate negation, it is always 'collective social labour' which realises itself. But collective labour has to be posited beforehand if it is to find itself doing its own work. It is never therefore the illusory worker of commodity fetishism which posits itself. It is denied a self-relation and an actuality. Marx does not begin with the posited person, he begins by assuming that positing is being done by social labour, which then, magically, finds itself. It is in this presupposition, and not in the illusory determination of the worker, that the secret of the property relation as human activity becomes for Marx the enlightenment and the secret instrument by which to overcome the illusion and domination of abstraction.

In the light of this knowledge of illusion, Marx is able to proceed upon the assumption that in labour which is not estranged labour, individuals are no longer related through property, but naturally as mutual labourers who are able to reproduce both themselves and their human relations to others:

> Just as society itself produces man as man, so it is produced by him. Activity and consumption, both in their content and in their mode of existence, are social activity and social consumption. The human essence of nature exists only for social man (1975, p. 349, emphasis removed).

The secret of the property relation, then, is that it is *social* activity. This, for Marx, is its fundamental contradiction, a contradiction which renders unstable the forces of production and the relations of production. When a class is formed which sees itself as a class, working together for example in factories or mines, and not as isolated individuals, then property relations no longer serve as the reality of that class, and 'these relations turn into their fetters. Then begins an era of social revolution' (1975, pp. 425–6). The secret of the contradiction of private property is also here revealed to the bourgeoisie who, unknown to themselves, have created the conditions whereby the contradiction becomes revolutionary.

> The advance of industry, whose involuntary promoter is the bourgeoisie, replaces the isolation of the labourers, due to competition, by their revolutionary combination, due to association. The development of Modern Industry, therefore, cuts from under its feet the very foundation on which the bourgeoisie produces and appropriates products. What the bourgeoisie, therefore, produces, above all, is its own grave-diggers (1967, pp. 93–4).

It is in critique, then, that the social nature of labour and the social relations of human workers are revealed to Marx. This he takes to be an enlightenment of (social) man by and in his own social activity about his truth as social man. Whereas value did not overcome its contradiction, but was realised in it, man, in realising the contradiction as his own work, does overcome and is transformed into a new truth, one which has seen through the illusions. (This presupposition of the identity of enlightenment is examined in Part II.) Even in the activity of critique, claims Marx, an activity mostly isolated from others, 'I am still socially active because I am active as a man' (1975, p. 350). However, although for Marx the contradiction between (private) relations of production and class consciousness raising forces of production can be known through critique, it cannot be overcome in critique for, like capital, that would amount only to its repetition. It is not the circulation of ideas which Marx requires for the workers, it is the transformation of them. However, his ideas are already, like capital, a return from circulation. Holding revolutionary class consciousness above such circulation enables Marx to argue that what lies ahead for the proletariat, in realising itself as the universal class of producers, is to overthrow the conditions which determine the world of commodities and bourgeois ideologies which, in turn, have determined them in their estrangement and abstraction. It is a task for the proletariat because, precisely, the work of determination is theirs already. Reality 'is only a product of the preceding intercourse of individuals themselves' (1970, p. 86). The ideas which men have of that reality are also a product of the same. Therefore consciousness will change as the social relations of productions are realised, and the cause of their abstraction, private property, is overcome. The universal class of mutual producers can only be a class in and for itself in and by revolutionary activity.

> Both for the production on a mass scale of this communist consciousness, and for the success of the cause itself, the alteration of men on a mass scale is necessary, an alteration which can only take place in a practical movement, a *revolution* (1970, pp. 94–5).

58

For Marx, these genuinely mutual relations are now no longer characterised by estrangement because human labour no longer reproduces separation from object and from other human beings. Now human labour reproduces the dependence of workers upon each other in nature, in material production, a mutual relation which expresses the universal social existence of labourers, not their particular and isolated existence. 'The standpoint of the old materialism is civil society; the standpoint of the new is human society or social humanity' (1970, p. 123).

The individual person

Durkheim's sociology is also a critique of the person. Like Rousseau and Marx, Durkheim is concerned to highlight the property relation as the misrecognition of mutual social relations. As with Rousseau and Marx also, one of his major concerns is how the independence of the person in modern societies (characterised by a division of labour) can be known to be dependent upon the social. For Durkheim it is the property relation which separates one person from another, giving the appearance that each, alone, is independent of the other. Yet the law itself is social and part of the collective conscience which results from the division of labour.

The contradiction between the universal (the social) and the particular (the person) raises for Durkheim the question of the identity of the person. In the Introduction to *The Division of Labour in Society* he asks, 'Is it our duty to seek to become a rounded, complete creature, a whole sufficient unto itself or, on the contrary, to be only a part of the whole, an organ of the organism...? Two opposing tendencies confront one another' (Durkheim, 1984, p. 3). It is precisely to the division of labour that Durkheim looks to resolve the antinomy (see 1984, p. xxx) of autonomous individuals and social solidarity.

Law for Durkheim is the external symbol of inner social solidarity, and takes different forms according to the type of solidarity it is reflecting. He characterises laws according to their sanctions, arguing that repressive sanctions represent 'mechanical' solidarity and restitutive sanctions represent 'organic' solidarity. The former are acts of collective sentiment against individuals who transgress the beliefs and sentiments which constitute the social identity of all its members. The latter are acts which do not punish in the name of the collective, but rather restore a former situation on behalf of the person. A crime in the former is punished, a crime in the latter is put right.

Durkheim argues that mechanical solidarity is based on the similarity and resemblance which each member has to another. But this is not a 'recognition' of similarities, it is only total indistinctiveness, or the non-recognition of differences. Nor, in a sense, is it misrecognition, for, at its most pure, it is prior to the person.

> The solidarity that derives from similarities is at its maximum when the collective consciousness completely envelops our total consciousness,

coinciding with it at every point. At that moment our individuality is zero. That individuality cannot arise until the community fills us less completely (1984, p. 84).

Durkheim uses the term mechanical to suggest the lack of 'will' which is present in this form of solidarity. He likens the 'relation' of the individual to the collective as like the relation of a thing to a person. The thing exerts no will in the relation, but is wholly dependent upon the owner's will. As the thing is at the disposal of the owner, so, in mechanical solidarity, the individual 'is literally a thing at the disposal of society' (1984, p. 85). However, the analogy is not a good one. If the individual is 'owned' by society then a relation does exist, and the individual is already separated from society. What Durkheim is really trying to show is that the individual has no existence, not even as a thing, but is wholly and completely encompassed within the social. The failure of the analogy lies in the impossibility of property being anything other than a relation. Mechanical solidarity is trying to suggest an unmediated relation, i.e. an immediate existence of the 'we' in which there is no 'I'. Mechanical solidarity is the absence of difference and relation, whereas property is already a relation.

Durkheim sees property as part of another type of solidarity, organic solidarity. Here it is not the similarity and resemblance of each which constitutes the collective conscience, it is precisely their differences. Mechanical solidarity is a very weak form of cohesion because it cannot survive the inevitable changes brought about by the increasing population of a society. The larger a society grows, the greater are the number of functions it requires, and the greater therefore grows the differentiation between the people who perform these different functions. Mechanical solidarity cannot survive the division of labour because with the division of labour the personal sphere outgrows the collective. Reflective thinking seeks to apply the universal to particular cases, and individuality becomes the dominant force in 'social' life. The development of individualism, like the division of labour, is 'an iron law... against which it would be absurd to revolt' (1984, p. 122). Durkheim uses the term 'moral density' to describe the extent to which, with the division of labour, individuals have ever increasing opportunities to act with one another. The greater the moral density, the greater the number of social relationships, and the greater the number of social relationships, the greater the degree to which the sphere of the personal develops. Evidence of this fragmentation of the collective was everywhere to be seen; the decline of religion, the separation from the religious sphere of the political, the economic and the scientific, the division of philosophy into 'special disciplines, each having its purpose, method and ethos' (1984, p. 2), and most influential, the differentiation of labour into ever increasing specialist tasks. Whereas in mechanical solidarity the substance of socialisation was similarity, in organic solidarity the substance of socialisation is difference.

More and more we deem it necessary not to subject all children to a uniform culture, as if all were destined to lead the same life, but to train them differently according to the various functions they will be called upon to fulfil (1984, p. 4).

With organic solidarity, then, comes the development of the person, and of the type of law which reflects the individual rights of the person. However, Durkheim sees property law as a form a misrecognition of the social bond. It is, he says, a merely negative form of solidarity and gives the impression that there are no common ends at which to aim, only personal ends. Ownership, or the property relation, is simply a relation between the person and the thing. No third party is required to secure the bond between property and owner, they are sufficient unto themselves in the relationship. Private property, for Durkheim, links things to persons, but not persons to other persons, thus a form of 'misrecognition' occurs here between those who recognise each other only as the owners of things. They have the social body only as a vanishing and a negative moment. Such a society:

> ...will resemble a huge constellation in which each star moves in its orbit without disturbing the motion of neighbouring stars. Such a solidarity thus does not shape from the elements drawn together an entity capable of acting in unison. It contributes nothing to the unity of the body social (1984, p. 73).

Thus, the property relation negates the social relation which it seeks to ensure. It does not bind men together, it separates them and keeps them apart. A contract is only the 'law' between the will of two or more persons, it has no authority to those outside of its particular sphere. Property disputes, or any dispute in the realm of 'real' rights which concern those things over which the person has mastery, health, honour, reputation, material goods, derive 'no active co-operation, no consensus' (Durkheim, 1984, p. 73, emphasis removed) between the persons involved. Thus Durkheim concludes,

> The rules relating to 'real' rights and personal relationships that are established by virtue of them form a definite system whose function is not to link together the different parts of society, but on the contrary to detach them from one another, and mark out clearly the barriers separating them (1984, p. 75).

This negative solidarity, however, is only the merely negative appearance of a positive solidarity which lies behind it and is, in fact, that upon which negative solidarity is itself dependent. 'Negative solidarity is only possible where another kind is present, positive in nature, of which it is both the result and the condition' (1984, p. 75). Durkheim acknowledges that the property relation is unstable, especially when defining relations between societies, and that it is insufficient to make society itself possible. A contract is not possible as a particular case of the law of contract unless the law as universal, as common to all, exists in the first place. 'If a contract has binding force, it is society which confers that force' (1984, p. 71). The legal relationships between persons, although particular to them, are social in nature. 'It is society that declares what the law is' (1984, p. 70). Private property law expresses that upon which it is itself dependent, the positive solidarity of common life, of co-operation, of resemblance, of common purpose, or, succinctly, of social life itself.

> In fact, for a man to acknowledge that others have rights, not only as a matter of logic, but as one of daily living, he must have agreed to limit his own. Consequently this mutual limitation was only realisable in a spirit of understanding and harmony (1984, p. 76).

If private property law is only negative solidarity, it is because it fails to recognise the mutual social bond which it presupposes but masks. The person, for Durkheim, is already dependent upon the universal for its being particular. This universal, in modern societies, is what Durkheim calls organic solidarity, and arises specifically from the division of labour. Co-operative law, for example, domestic law, contractual law, constitutional law, are positive because they define the roles and functions that each 'particular'. needs to fulfil in relation to the whole. These laws do not separate, they bring together; they do not establish barriers, but break them down by enabling each particular to see clearly its relationship to, and membership of, the whole. The strength of organic solidarity is therefore the weakness of mechanical solidarity. In the latter, solidarity was based on similarity and threatened by difference. In the former, solidarity is based on difference 'and is only possible if each one of us has a sphere of social action that is peculiarly our own, and consequently a personality' (1984, p. 85). Modern society consists of individuals who have 'thrown off the yoke of the common consciousness' (1984, p. 118). 'It is the division of labour that is increasingly fulfilling the role that once fell to the common consciousness' (1984, p. 123).

At the heart of Durkheim's sociology, then, is the contradiction between universal (social) and particular (person). In mechanical solidarity there is no real contradiction, because the latter is wholly absorbed into the former. But the contradiction becomes apparent with an increase in moral density when the particular sees itself as only related to the universal, but not therefore as absolutely lost within it. They key problem for modern societies, therefore, is how to ensure positive solidarity where persons relate to the universal as their own truth, and overcome negative solidarity where persons relate only to themselves and to things. Within a society characterised by the division of labour where each person has a specialised, i.e. non-universal, function, it becomes essential to ensure that the role of each particular action within the universal is plainly visible. Only the knowledge of the relation and contribution of each part to the universal can ensure social solidarity in modern societies.

Durkheim rejects the Rousseauian idea that this universal can consist of a contract. A contract for Durkheim is optional, whereas the social (universal) is not. To agree on a social contract in the first place presupposes that individuals are already universal; 'when society is making the contract... if assent is unanimous the thoughts of every consciousness are identical' (1984, p. 150). But contracts, as seen earlier, are only the expression of individual interests. The universal, for Durkheim, cannot be found in any relationship based upon particular interests, for the bond which such personal interests creates is merely an external one. This is the centre of Durkheim's critique of the person. 'In the fact of exchange the various agents involved remain apart from one another and once the operation is over, each one finds himself again "reassuming his self" in its entirety' (1984, p. 152). The 'civil society' that arises from the 'relations' of persons is one characterised by self-interest and is wholly unstable. 'Today it is useful for me to unite with you; tomorrow the same reason will make me your enemy. Thus such a cause can give rise only to transitory links and associations of a fleeting kind' (1984, p. 152).

The universal social bond (organic solidarity) is therefore not merely the sum of particular wills. For Durkheim the universal exists as a social not a personal fact. The universal is itself because it is the whole of which a person is only a part: 'even where society rests wholly upon the division of labour, it does not resolve itself into a myriad of atoms juxtaposed together... The members are linked by ties that extend well beyond the very brief moment when the act of exchange is being accomplished' (1984, p. 173). The property relation hides the social bonds which make any form of contract legal and binding. It is the realm of duties, laws and functions which all particular associations depend upon, and according to which they are determined.

On the one hand the division of labour separates individuals and provides them with the sense of their particularity. On the other hand, 'the division of labour unites at the same time as it sets at odds; it causes the activities that it differentiates to converge; it brings closer those that it separates' (1984, p. 217). The contradiction between universal and particular is therefore overcome because each particular finds its truth in the universal, which already exists, expressing in terms of laws and duties the social dependence which all persons will experience throughout their lives. Through self-reflection (and for Durkheim this self-reflection was the science of sociology) the person comes to understand that morality is the concrete existence of this dependence, a 'solidly linked system' (1984, p. 173) or a 'network of obligations' (1984, p. 173) which become the state and which have an existence over and above each person, or *sui generis*.

What is crucial for Durkheim in resolving the contradiction of universal and particular is that the former, although containing the latter, is not itself dependent upon it. Rather, society is the concrete existence of the dependence of each particular upon another. From the point of view of any one particular, it is something other, perhaps external. But from the scientific point of view, from the perspective of the social itself, although at first it appears external, it is in fact absolutely the truth of all particulars. The appearance of the independence of the person is overcome when such persons come to understand that they are not self-sufficient and, further, when they understand this negative to have positive expression in and as law, duty and morality. Mutuality arises only through the direct experience of association, an association in which personal relations 'become something else' (1974, p. 26), namely, society experienced as morality.

However, Durkheim's sociology also reveals how this synthesis, in the modern division of labour, has not produced the sort of social solidarity that such association demands. At the end of *The Division of Labour in Society*, he explains that the division of labour has produced abnormal forms of collective sentiment which threaten the stability of society and can be a cause of disintegration, the exact opposite of its true expression. He cites three main types of abnormality. The first is the negation of organic solidarity caused by industrial and commercial crises, particularly bankruptcies. The second is the (class) struggle between labour and capital due, in part, 'to the fact that the working classes do not really desire the status assigned to them and too often accept it only under constraint and force' (1984, p. 293). The third is the increasing specialisation of scientific work which divides the study of the universal into the study of particulars. The effect of each of these is to lose the 'spontaneity' (1984, p. 312) which Durkheim sees as a crucial component of the division of labour. Spontaneity does not characterise abnormal forms of the division of labour because in it, social inequalities are not a reflection of natural inequalities, and workers do not do the jobs to which they are most naturally suited.

Modern societies are distinguished by 'the state of legal and moral anomie in which economic life exists at the present time' (1984, pp. xxxi–xxxii). In such a condition, 'the entire sphere of collective life is for the most part removed from the moderating action of any rules' (1984, p. xxxii). Overall, in an anomic state, one side of the division of labour dominates the other. Whereas normally it separates and unites, currently it only separates:

> A state of anomie is impossible wherever organs solidly linked to one another are in sufficient contact, and in sufficiently lengthy contact. Indeed, being adjacent to one another, they are easily alerted in every situation to the need for one another and consequently they experience a keen, continuous feeling of their mutual dependence (1984, p. 304).

However, the density of modern societies is not sufficiently strong to ensure this type of contact between producers and consumers, or between employers and workers. Consumers are dispersed across whole nations and therefore the need which producers must satisfy is virtually unlimited and unrealisable. Workers are reduced to the role of a machine, cut off from family, from other workers, and from their employers.

Every day he repeats the same movements with monotonous regularity, but without having any interest or understanding of them. He is no longer the living cell of a living organism, moved continually by contact with neighbouring cells, which acts upon them and responds in turn to their action, extends itself, contracts, yields and is transformed according to the needs and circumstances (1984, p. 306).

Thus, with regard to economic crises, to employer/worker relations and to science itself, that which requires to be spontaneously universal and to reveal that which each person has in common disintegrates into the particularity of each person, who now has the universal, the social, the common, as something over and against them and to which they do not feel that they belong. The 'common' problem shared by each is the lack of regulation which would express the mutual bond (hence *anomie, a-nomos*: without a law; see Rose, 1992, p. xiii). What is prevalent is the separation of the division of labour, what is missing is the *sui generis* synthesis of these differences into the whole which is the expression of the truth, i.e. social life. Durkheim argues for greater regulation in the form of codes of professional ethics and systems of rules within institutions to try and resolve the first two types of abnormality. However, he gives greatest attention to the third type of abnormality, that found within the scientific (i.e. academic) community, and argues at length that a more scientific, i.e. social (or sociological) education, would enable the contradiction (the abnormal form of solidarity) between universal and particular to be overcome.

In a manner very similar to that of Rousseau, Durkheim argues that the key to the problem is to negate the deformities which produce the abnormalities by leaving the universal to present itself without 'interference' in order to reveal its own truth. Durkheim is not in favour, for example, of a liberal education which, although widening the mental horizons of the worker, leaves his working life atomised and separated. What resolves the contradiction between universal and particular is an education in and by the division of labour, or organic solidarity itself.

> For it to be able to develop without having so disastrous an influence on the human consciousness, there is no need to mitigate it by means of its opposite. It is necessary and sufficient for it to be itself, for nothing to come from outside to deform its nature (1984, p. 307).

Thus, in the workplace, or more especially for Durkheim in the classroom, the division of labour ensures that the worker or student 'far from remaining bent over his task, does not lose sight of those co-operating with him, but acts upon them and is acted upon by them' (1984, p. 308).

Durkheim's sociology of education is no less than a strategy for overcoming the abnormalities of the modern division of labour. It works on two levels. One is the unification of the universal and the particular in the division of labour. The other is the resolution of the contradiction between universal and particular as science itself. Durkheim takes the principles of science to the classroom to allow differentiation the opportunity for its synthesis into the *sui generis* collective realm of ideas, beliefs and sentiments.

> Society can survive only if there exists among its members a sufficient degree of homogeneity; education perpetuates and reinforces this homogeneity by fixing in the child, from the beginning, the essential similarities that collective life demands. But on the other hand, without a certain diversity all co-operation would be impossible; education assures the persistence of this necessary diversity by being itself diversified and specialised (1956, pp. 70–1).

The contradiction of universal and particular is resolved because both of its moments are present, mutuality and differentiation. Thus Durkheim advocates that education must train children 'differently according to the varying functions they will be called upon to fulfil' (1984, p. 4). The maxim of such an education – its categorical imperative, (1984, p. 4) is 'equip yourself to fulfil usefully a specific function' (Durkheim, 1984, p. 4). This is in keeping with the spontaneity which the division of labour demands, where the occupation that each child is drawn to results from natural abilities and not social inequalities. Thus the division of labour will express part of itself in both curricula and pedagogy, ensuring differentiation according to specialisation, and the forms of knowledge, ideas and practices which are required for particular occupations. Critics of this view (see e.g. Sharp, 1980, p. 33) seldom refer to the other half of the division of labour, which Durkheim sees as equally if not more important. Differentiation for Durkheim is that which reveals mutuality, because it reveals clearly the part which each particular plays in the whole, a whole which provides the overall meaning.

The second moment of the division of labour, that of organic solidarity (the universal) is present in Durkheim's sociology of education because it is also a moral education. In schools, law or social regulation is expressed as discipline, which in turn is seen as a precursor to duty.

> Too often, it is true, people conceive of school discipline so as to preclude endowing it with such an important moral function. Some see in it a simple way of guaranteeing superficial peace and order in the classroom... In reality, however, the nature and function of school discipline is something altogether different... It is the morality of the classroom, just as the discipline of the social body is morality properly speaking (1961, p. 148).

66

Through discipline the child learns self-restraint, control of desire, the need for co-operation, and comes to respect rules and laws as the truth of this non-individual existence: 'education sets out precisely with the object of creating a social being' (1982, p. 54), at first through the imposition of authority by teachers, but only with the long-term aim of replacing that external imposition with an internalised self-discipline, or morality.

> To be free is not to do what one pleases; it is to be master of oneself, it is to know how to act with reason and to do one's duty. Now, it is precisely to endow the child with this self-mastery that the authority of the teacher should be employed (1956, pp. 89–90).

The abnormalities which express themselves as the contradiction between universal and particular are overcome when the division of labour is given free expression in the classroom, and both of its moments, difference and mutuality, emerge unfettered. At a more general level, Durkheim sees science itself (sociology in particular) as fulfilling the same educational function. Science, appearing only in its specialised roles, cannot reveal the whole of which it is the expression. Thus science also requires to be approached and taught in such a way that both moments, the person and the law, can be seen as constituting the whole which is the division of labour. This revelation comes about through the education which science, properly understood, is able to provide. Science enables the whole to present itself as the whole, from the perspective of the collective itself. This, and this alone, makes possible action/legislation which will eradicate and not exacerbate abnormalities.

In essence, science is Durkheim's critique of the person through revealing the social that lies behind it. In science, the collective meets itself, and becomes 'more and better aware of itself' (1974, p. 66). It is the synthesis of particulars known to itself, but as something no longer particular. 'Science is not an individual; it is a social thing, pre-eminently impersonal' (1974, p. 66). Science forces man 'to step outside himself' (1977, p. 215); it enables him to learn that he is 'dependent upon something other than himself' (1977, p. 215) and to 'feel this dependence' (1977, p. 215). Science is the realm of mutuality *sui generis*, knowable as social facts, and practised as sociology and moral education. In science, mutual dependence is not illusory being, except to those who study and rely on individual consciousness. The universal and the particular appear contradictory only when elements which are already synthesised are reduced again to mere elements. The whole cannot become the parts for it is not the parts, it is something else entirely. 'The states of the collective consciousness are of a different nature from the states of the individual consciousness; they are representations of another kind' (1982, p. 40); a kind which can only appear in science, as science. Access, therefore, to mutuality can only be gained by an act of sacrifice on the part of persons. Man has to 'renounce the unlimited power over the social order that for so long he ascribed to himself' (1982, p. 46), in order that he may then realise his own limited freedom within its dominion. Society imposes science upon its members as a duty, for in its self-reflection co-operation becomes visible. In this education the goal is to create 'a new being' (1956, p. 72), one which overcomes the freedom of the person in the realisation that 'man is man, in fact, only because he lives in society' (1956, p. 76).

Contradiction of critique

Rousseau, Marx and Durkheim, although offering distinctively different forms of critique, share various common characteristics. First, each produces a critique of the mere appearance of the person in (civil) society. Rousseau sees persons as forced to become what they are not, and to live a social life based on pretence and dissemblance. Marx sees individual workers to be merely an abstraction of their true existence as social labour, and therefore alienated from their true species activity. Durkheim sees the individual in the division of labour to have lost a sense of the overall meaning and purpose of life within the whole of a society characterised by organic solidarity. In each critique, what is realised is that the person is only a false appearance.

Second, Rousseau, Marx and Durkheim seek to realise a society in which our true identity can be achieved. The general will, class consciousness and the collective conscience are the conditions wherein that true identity can appear, and where genuine social relations replace the purely instrumental and personal (social) relations which dominate in civil society.

Third, the tool by which these new social relations are to be brought about is the education of the person. For Rousseau, the general will relies on a natural education so that each person learns to be independent, which in turn ensures that their relations with others will be based on genuine and self-determined needs, and not false, civil needs. For Marx, class consciousness has its basis in the education of the workers to see through the bourgeois values and laws which determine their isolated existence, and in which they come to see their own mutuality with other workers in and as the human labouring species. For Durkheim, the role of education is much more explicit, for it is in the classroom that the individual learns to become a social being.

Fourth, it can be said that what is at stake in these and similar critiques is a knowledge of the universal essence of human beings. Rousseau, Marx and Durkheim are all prepared to state what they believe to be the essence, or the universality that is common to all and which defines the true existence of human beings. At root, then, these theorists are arguing that in civil society, the 'I', or the person, is only a false appearance, and that the 'we' or the collective is the true existence or essence. Each person is separated from or alienated from that essence, and it is the goal of Rousseau, Marx and Durkheim to overcome that separation and to unite the 'I' with the 'we'.

68

Fifth, each implicates private property relations as at least partly responsible for this alienation and estrangement. Rousseau sees the instigation of private property as the fixing in law of inequalities. While these inequalities remained 'natural', then natural man remained strong and self-sufficient. But fixed in the law of private property, these inequalities became social, forcing each to treat others as merely a means to gaining advantage. For Rousseau, property is the beginning of the evils of civil society. Marx highlights private property as the precondition of estrangement and of the capitalist mode of production. The bourgeois individual is the private person. Political and economic theory then accepts the person as if it were our natural state, whereas for Marx this is only an appearance, one determined in and by relations of private property. These relations pre-empt our self-consciousness, and determine beforehand our separation from universal human labour. Durkheim sees private property as contrary to the aims of the collective conscience, for it highlights only that which is particular to each person, thus masking the universal interests which are common to all. The property relation, for Durkheim, is not a social relation, and therefore can contribute to the abnormalities of organic solidarity within the division of labour.

Finally, what Rousseau, Marx and Durkheim also have in common is that their critique contradicts the aims they set for it. Their attempts to unite the 'I' and the 'we', the particular and the universal, fail in the sense that each attempt merely repeats the separation of the 'I' and the 'we', the particular and the universal. The reasons for this repetition will be examined shortly. What can be said at this stage is that the critique of the person is itself an education of the theorists which creates another separation between the particular and the universal. This time the education of the theorist, who has essence or universality as his knowledge, separates him from the universality which he is claiming as the immanent truth of the 'we', and therefore from his own truth. Just as the property relation is contradictory (this is examined in Chapter 6) so this new relation in education, the knowledge relation, is also contradictory (examined in Chapter 7).

In Rousseau's social theory, nature is the essence of man and is realised when the corruption of nature in civil society is avoided. The essence is known to the teacher but not at first to the pupils. It is therefore the task of the teacher to protect the pupil from civil influences, in order that they may grow up in harmony with nature, aware of their real needs, and forming genuine rather than artificial associations to meet these needs. When the pupils have reached the age where, through their own reasoning, they have come to understand nature and natural needs as their essence and as the foundation of the general will, then they are able to shape their own lives in keeping with the principles which nature has taught them. They will be able to judge for themselves 'the action and re-action of self-interest in civil society' (Rousseau, 1974, p. 212).

Rousseau acknowledges that in teaching Emile in this way the teacher is placed in a relation of domination. However, the limitation of *Emile* is that although it recognises this, it does not include this experience of teacher as dominator within it as an educational experience. It is true that Rousseau admits that he is the master, and that all of this mastery has not been admitted to, but the experience of repetition, although found in Emile, is not what the work is about. In seeking to overcome the opposition between self and community, the 'I' and the 'we', the teacher has to take the place of reason until the child has this capacity for itself. The teacher reasons on behalf of the child, and this involves preventing the 'civilising' process from affecting its natural development. Thus the teacher, in order to ensure a negative civil influence, has to maintain a positive intervention. Rousseau is acknowledging that the state of nature cannot be reproduced in civil society, and that therefore the teacher must try to prevent society from influencing the child's natural development. The need for the teacher is itself evidence that a natural development is no longer possible. In acting on behalf of nature, Rousseau is arguing that the teacher also reproduces nature. When Rousseau says that the pupil is 'nature's pupil' (1974, p. 83) and that the teacher's role 'is to prevent anything being done' (1974, p. 9), he is aware that this can only seem to be the case. In fact, like everything else in civil society, education appears as something which it is not, and the teacher, like the person, is forced to practise a deceit on behalf of the pupils. Rousseau reminds teachers that the art of teaching 'consists in controlling events' (1974, p. 209) in such a way that the pupil does not realise that they are being controlled: 'Let him always think he is master while you are really master' (1974, p. 84). The pupil can seem to be in control, just as the teacher can seem not to be in control, but as Rousseau himself admits, as a tutor of a young child 'I succeeded during the short time I was with him in getting him to do everything I wanted' (1974, p. 89). The whole point of Rousseau's social theory and teaching is to reveal how, in civil society, 'the mask is not the man' (1974, p. 198). Yet precisely to prevent the mask from being worn by his pupils he, as the teacher, is forced to wear one himself. Rousseau understands himself as a teacher determined within the broken middle of social relations, but does not pursue this education of himself. His book *Emile* is an education of the student, but not of the teacher. Indeed, while the student is left to his own natural development, Rousseau is laying down maxims and methods for the teacher to follow. The teacher, as the personification of the knowledge of nature, is merely a repetition of the contradiction that negative intervention is deception. But Rousseau does not pursue this experience with regard to experience or to the contradiction of education and teaching, or, lastly, with regard to his being a teacher of teachers.

Knowing that mutuality is negated in civil society, by creating false needs rather than mutual needs, and creating thereby a society of private property and inequality, is not, in itself, also the overcoming of civil society. Rousseau is still a member of civil society, even as its critic, and even as the teacher who would realise its downfall. The society which he seeks to replace has determined his relation to that solution, just as it determines his relation to other persons and to his pupils. Rousseau's knowledge of nature, and of the mutuality of self-preservation, is not also the creation of nature and self-preservation as reality. Rousseau has a relation to nature, but not a natural one. He is not nature, nor self-preservation in itself. The truth which Rousseau's critique arrives at is, again, another negative in relation to the substance or knowledge it claims for itself. This knowledge has no being except as being not-Rousseau, which is really the beginning of *Emile* as regards a book about the education of the teacher. Wearing a mask in order to overcome the need to wear a mask is a contradiction which is determinative of the teacher.

Equally, when Rousseau seeks to act on behalf of nature as a teacher he cannot overcome his repetition of the contradiction between universal and particular. To his pupils, he (the particular) has knowledge of mutuality (nature) but he is not himself the truth which he professes to represent. For his pupils, also, the truth which the teacher seeks to teach is only another negative experience for them. The being of the teacher is precisely not the being of mutuality, he is merely the personification of the knowledge of it. Admitting this relation of domination, which Rousseau does, cannot nullify its being experienced by his pupils as a negation of the (natural) authority which it claims.

Marx faces a similar problem. His critique of and enlightenment regarding the illusions of bourgeois social and legal relations repeats those same relations but denies that the subject is actual as that relation. This is the empty return of his attempts to overcome those relations. As a natural education was for Rousseau, so critical education, and its result as critical consciousness, are seen by Marx as immanent self-transformation.

Whereas for Rousseau the person came to know the truth of his freedom naturally, for Marx the process is historical and dialectical. Increasingly the bourgeoisie will come to see their true existence as precisely that from which, as persons, they are denied, i.e. the human or social community of producers. This recognition of the person as misrecognition is at the same time the recognition of the truth of the worker to be the mutuality expressed in the class consciousness of the proletariat. This consciousness is taught by nothing other than itself and its own development in its relation to the bourgeoisie. The theorist of the universal consciousness, Marx himself, admits that his consciousness is only the theoretical form of 'that whose *living* form is the *real* community' (Marx, 1975, p. 350), i.e. the proletariat. No 'intervention' by the communist theorist is required in order to establish this truth for the proletariat. On the contrary,

> The theoretical conclusions of the Communists are in no way based on ideas or principles that have been invented, or discovered, by this or that would-be universal reformer.
> They merely express, in general terms, actual relations springing from an existing class struggle, from a historical movement going on under our very eyes (1967, pp. 95–6).

The truth of communism is theoretical in Marx and Marxism, and 'real' in the consciousness of the proletariat. However, as was argued earlier, the truth of the critical subject is never actual because its actual being is already determined for it.

Whereas commodities, or exchange-value, are seen to have an inescapable actuality as capital – their contradictory return from circulation – the revolutionary subject is granted immunity from return and circulation, an immunity precisely from the dilemma of the return of the person within (the circulation which is) bourgeois property relations. Avoiding this dilemma, and avoiding therefore the contradiction into which even revolutionary consciousness must fall, the task of the communist becomes that of representing the truth of the proletariat to the proletariat, on their behalf, until their consciousness achieves in reality what the communists have achieved in theory. But this relationship is necessarily one of domination, repeating for the workers the experience of their separation from the universal, not their unity with it. For the worker, the universal can be experienced (again) but only negatively, or positively (again) as merely the person or a worker. 'It is above all necessary', wrote Marx, 'to avoid once more establishing "society" as an abstraction over against the individual' (1975, p. 350). Yet even in the sentences which follow this thought, this is precisely what Marx does. 'Man's individual and species-life are not two distinct things' (1975, p. 350, emphasis removed). For the person this is precisely a domination of real experience, where species-life, and even the critique of the person, are known (experienced) as a contradiction, i.e. as separated. This experience of return, unlike the experience of value as return, is never given a treatment in which it is allowed to appear as both of its moments. For persons, species-activity only reinforces them as what they are not, and repeats their personal relation to the universal.

Just as Rousseau was forced into a contradictory position between himself and the truth of the freedom about which he wished to teach, so Marx, Marxists and Marxism face the same problem. The truth of mutuality is still contradictory, even when the person is negated, for mutuality in theory, or as knowledge, still reproduces a negative relation between itself and the consciousness of each person whose truth it claims to be. Those who seek to represent the universal can only appear as over and against the person, dominating the person, and reinforcing that abstract independence which they sought to overcome.

In Durkheim's sociology the contradiction of universal and particular, law and person, is overcome when the two moments of the division of labour, differentiation and unification, are allowed to appear at the same time, and unaffected by the abnormalities within society. Without law as the social regulation and collective truth of each person, there is *anomie*. Without the comprehension in each person of the self-discipline required for moral (social) relationships, there is only individualism. In a society with a true division of labour, the law is only that which self-discipline demands, or duty. With the association of persons comes the recognition of co-operation between persons, i.e. of mutual dependence. It is a recognition which is possible only because of differentiation, and yet at the same time one which (already) transcends its own differences and stands over and above each person as the truth of (their) differentiation.

Whereas Rousseau acknowledges that teaching for the understanding of mutuality forces the teacher into a relation of domination over the pupil, Durkheim is more concerned to establish the moral validity of the teacher, not as a person, but as one imbued with the authority of the collective. Rousseau acknowledges but does not pursue how the teacher is already the resolution of the contradiction between universal and particular, and in seeking to prevent the pupil from having to face the same contradiction, is a domination of and a resolution of the pupils' experience. Durkheim faces the same problem, but, like Marx, presents the resolution of the contradiction in terms which do not acknowledge the return of the teacher.

Since, for Durkheim, the teacher is the representative of the collective, working on its behalf, then the teacher's work is at the level of science. The teacher has no individual authority at all, and any overt individuality on the part of the teacher threatens moral legitimacy. Durkheim warns against the ease with which teachers can assume personal authority. 'When one is continually in relationships with subjects to whom he is morally and intellectually superior, how can he avoid developing an exaggerated self-conception...?' (1961, p. 194). He notes that discipline, understood scientifically, is a duty for pupil and teacher, and that in some cases, 'certain steps are indispensable to protect the freedom of the child' (1961, p. 144) against individual excesses by the teacher. The teacher must learn to 'resist himself, his own inclinations' (1961, p. 153). Teachers working at this scientific level are not working as individuals at all. It is their job to 'radiate authority' (1961, p. 154) to the child, an authority which works through them, and thus is moral, but which is not their own, not personal. Discipline works against itself when it is merely imposed, for children do not come to respect it as their own truth, nor to internalise it, nor therefore to understand association as self-discipline. 'The child must come to feel himself what there is in a rule which determines that he should abide by it willingly' (1961, p. 154). This requires that teachers embody and exhibit the social authority of their role, that they be true representatives of the social bond. Durkheim describes the unity of the teacher and society in terms the relationships between a priest and God. Only as a vocation, as a calling, can the sacrifice of the person be sufficient to exhibit for others the truth which lies behind the person.

> It is not from the outside, from the fear he inspires, that the teacher should gain his authority; it is from himself. This cannot come to him except from his innermost being. He must believe, not perhaps in himself or in the superior quality of his intelligence or will, but in his task and the greatness of that task. It is the priest's lofty conception of his mission that gives him the authority... (to speak) in the name of a God, who he feels in himself and to whom he feels himself much closer than the layman in the crowds he addresses. So, the lay teacher can and should have something of this same feeling. He also is an instrument of a great moral reality which

surpasses him and with which he communicates more directly than does the child...

In this authority, which derives from a quite impersonal source, nothing of arrogance, vanity, or pedantry must enter. It is entirely brought about through the teacher's respect for his role or, if one may put it this way, for his ministry (1961, pp. 154–5).

Durkheim, however, does not examine the experience of the (return of the) teacher in this self-sacrifice. The knowledge that the person is overcome when his obligation to the social is recognised becomes something which is known only by the person. The teacher, even in the selflessness of a powerful calling or vocation, is still only in relation to science, to the universal, and still has it as something other than his own determinate being. It, the universal, is still what teacher is not, and it is still therefore in relation to the teacher. In the same way, the teacher who seeks to represent the universal to his pupils is still in a relation of authority over them, and they see the teacher merely in a relation to that authority but not the authority in itself. In both cases, the relation is of the determinate person to the truth of association as what each person is not.

For teachers, mutuality is something which, even if they believe it to be their true existence, is still experienced as not their own determinate being. The knowledge of the mutual is still only a relation between the knower (person) and the object (community), and is thus a repetition of the person in the relation. The contradiction is not overcome, it is experienced. This experience is precisely of the non-overcoming of the contradiction, that is, of its repetition. But for Durkheim this experience of the teacher is not acknowledged, and no examination is made of the teacher beyond his (now) abstract unification with the collective. Even though Durkheim acknowledges that for the teacher moral law 'imposes itself on him' (1961, p. 156), that the teacher, like the pupils, is 'constrained' (1961, p. 156) by it, and that 'it dominates him and obliges him as it obliges them' (1961, p. 156), nevertheless this experience of domination is, for Durkheim, precisely the moment when the person becomes something else. What Durkheim makes into a science is half of the experience of contradiction. It consists of the realisation that the person is already in relation to the social, but it does not also include the realisation that science is already in relation to the person. Durkheim identifies the contradiction, but does not work with the experience of that knowledge, only with and at the level of that knowledge itself, a level to which the person has no immediate access, but from which it is constantly returned to itself as a person.

The critiques of Rousseau, Marx and Durkheim, then, in trying to unite the universal and the particular only repeat, again, their separation from each other. The theorist becomes the particular who has the universal as object or property. To own an object, whether as knowledge or property (they are one and the same relation) is to be separated from that object. The two have not become united as one, the I is not the we. Chapters 6 and 7 will explore the property relation and the knowledge relation as the same broken middle. For now, it can be said that the work of critique produces three outcomes.

First, as our self-critical reflection upon ourselves, it reveals that our immediate appearance in the world is not our truth. We come to know ourselves as determined, and we come to realise that the single individual is always already in relation to a universality which it is only a part of, but also apart from. Reflective critique, in the first instance, is therefore negative, for it is a dissolving of the independent appearance of the person within the context in which it is determined, shaped and formed.

Second, however, in seeing through this appearance of independence to the truth of our mutual dependence, for example, the general will, class consciousness and collective conscience, what results is not unification but a repetition of our separation from that mutuality. The negation of the person is not replaced by a positive reidentification of the individual as at one with this universal. On the contrary, the knowledge of the universal is a reidentification of the owner of the knowledge, and the owner is another single, particular person. The critical negation of the person in relation to a genuine universal essence creates a return to the person who is again separated from the universal, this time in and through its knowledge. The result of critique, here, is the personification of the universal, and the most common appearance of this personification of the universal as knowledge (or enlightenment) is *the teacher.*

Thirdly, it can be seen that the result of critique is not what was originally intended. The attempted unification of universal and particular has in fact resulted only in the repetition of their separation. This result is itself known in the experience of critique. The experience is of contradiction. The universal and the particular are known in the experience of their opposition and their separation. This experience belongs to the same person who began the critique for, in the experience, each is returned to the self from the universal. In this failure to grasp the universal as anything other than a particular knowledge, it is no longer the person who is negated, but the universal itself. It slips from our grasp, and the attempted unification fails, a failure in which our own particularity as persons is reaffirmed.

It can be said, then, that what really happens in reflective critique is that the independence of the person is negated by and in the realisation of its relation to the universal. In this realisation, the person is returned to its particular existence through the new relation it now has to the universal, that of a knowledge of the universal. The knowledge of the universal opposes and contradicts the knower ever becoming at one with the universal. The result of critique, therefore, is contradiction, separation and return, not at all what was intended. Rousseau, Marx and Durkheim are returned from their knowledge of the universal to become only the personification of that universality. They become our teachers, and a teacher, for us, is only another particular assertion of the universal, or, more exactly, another domination of it and us.

What, then, is critique? This question is best approached at this stage by examining what it is that critique thinks it can do. For Rousseau, Marx and Durkheim the achievement of critique is the same. In the negation of the person is the overcoming of the separation of particular and universal. The universal, by definition, is not particular. Therefore in negating the person this (not) particular and the universal are one and the same. Neither Rousseau, nor Marx, nor Durkheim claim that their critique is sufficient suddenly to realise this unification in the world. But what they do claim in their theorising is that critique can both negate the person and know the universal as the truth of this non-person. The work which critique performs is a self-negation, for self-consciousness is reflecting upon itself. Equally, its realisation of its relation to the universal is achieved in and as the same negation. To know that the person is not-universal is also, at the same time, to have realised its relation to the universal. Therefore, negative self-critique has a positive outcome for self-consciousness; its truth as the general will, class consciousness and the collective conscience.

This is what critique claims it can do. But it has been shown that this is not at all what results from critique. What in fact critique achieves is not a unification at all, but a new separation. The result of critique is not immanent negation and overcoming, it is immanent re-separation and return to particularity. At its most fundamental level, critique is the presupposition that its activity (negation) and its result (overcoming and transformation), i.e. its self-relation, are the identity of enlightenment. In other words, critique presupposes itself to be the truth of enlightenment. What it does not see, and why it becomes return, is that enlightenment, like the person, is already determined within and as a (property) relation which renders its work and its identity contradictory. This is examined in Parts II and III. The critique of social relations employs enlightenment as its immanent method. But critique is only immanent in the experience of that method as a broken middle. That experience is the substance of the following chapters, and constitutes the re-education of critical theorists and critical teachers which lies at the heart of this book.

3 Critique of the subject

Foucault presents the despairing teacher, at least on the surface, with a very different set of problems. Whereas those theorists examined earlier have identified the domination of the student by the teacher as a merely negative phenomena, Foucault insists that such subjection, both of student and teacher, is also positive. The teacher, in Foucault, is challenged not simply to change from being a repressive master to an emancipatory master, but rather to lose the teacher as a person altogether in a network of power relations.

Foucault's work moves from 'archaeological' investigations to 'genealogical' investigations. In each of these stages there is either implicitly or explicitly a critique of the teacher. Unlike those theorists considered thus far, however, the despairing teacher will not find in Foucault suggestions for a pedagogy which can negate the structure of power which inheres in the teacher/student relationship. On the contrary, the despairing teacher can find in Foucault that the despair is both deepened by the loss of the person as a sovereign subject altogether, and alleviated by this loss.

Archaeology – into the light

Foucault's concern in his early archaeological works is to reveal the underlying rules upon which scientific discourses were based, the rules upon which something could be expressed as true or false, 'the rules which come into play in the very existence of such a discourse' (Foucault, 1970, p. xiv). He is clear that such archaeology operates neither at the level of subjective consciousness nor at the level of structures, seeing both of these as made possible only within, and therefore as the result of, the rule of particular discourses. Each discourse operates as a silent ordering of things, an ordering which is only heard, or seen, or known, through the material practices, techniques and values which are its 'coherence'. 'Man', for Foucault, is just such an ordering, produced as the discourse in which

77

language orders differences rather than similarities. That which we understand as 'man' is a concept only made possible in a discourse of designation and of naming, a discourse which enables the seeing of things previously unseen. Being himself only the result of a particular discourse, 'man' will disappear when that discourse dissolves, when man will no longer be seen, or named or exist. Man is 'the effect of a change in the fundamental arrangement of knowledge... If those arrangements were to disappear as they appeared... man would be erased' (1970, p. 387).

On a more concrete level, Foucault offers examples of how new 'visibilities' constitute new discourses. The turn of the 19th century saw doctors beginning to see things which previously had been invisible to them, for example, diseases. That which was named was separated from that in which previously it was undifferentiated. Disease was no longer a 'unity' of interior and exterior; now it was the patient who was the subject of the disease, the one therefore being differentiated from the other. 'If one wishes to know the illness from which he is suffering, one must subtract the individual, with his particular qualities' (1973, p. 14). Thus the discourse of medicine moves from that which is said (a linguistic unity of illness and person) to that which is seen (a linguistic separation and differentiation between objects). Just as 'man' represents a new visibility, so too does disease. For both, 'The eye becomes the depository and source of clarity... [the] sovereign power of the empirical gaze' (1973, p. xiii).

This archaeological investigation of truth and scientificity at the level of discourse makes it possible for Foucault to explain how the hospital becomes a material pedagogical practice. Since the gaze was now the instrument which provided the truth of this 'newly perceived order' (1970, p. xxi), and by which the disease could be 'entirely stated in its truth' (1973, p. 95), then practices had to be established which enabled, created and facilitated the production of truth:

> The clinic was to undergo a sudden, radical restructuring: detached from the theoretical context in which it was born, it was to be given a field of application that was no longer confined to that in which knowledge was *said*, but which was co-extensive with that in which it was born, put to the test, and fulfilled itself: it was to be identified with the *whole* of medical experience. For this, it had to be armed with new powers, detached from the language on the basis of which it had been offered as a lesson, and freed for the movement of discovery (1973, p. 62).

In this way the clinic became a field designed to enable visibility in order to ensure that what was hidden could be brought out into the gaze by being placed before the eye. Patients had to be made accessible to this 'examination'. The architecture and layout of clinics, even of wards themselves, were a material realisation of this new truth of the gaze. In addition, Foucault notes that 'At the end of the 18th century, as at the beginning of the Renaissance, education was given a positive value as enlightenment: to train was a way of bringing to light, and therefore of discovering' (1973, p. 64). The clinic, in embodying visibility and the bringing of, for example, diseases to light, also therefore became a material pedagogy. It was designed around this new view of enlightenment, for in securing for the gaze a sovereignty, it is implicitly a training ground, an educational practice of bringing to light. Previously, 'the clinic was concerned only with the instruction, in the narrow sense of the word, that is given by a master to his pupils. It was not in itself an experience, but a condensed version, for the use of others, of previous experience' (1973, pp. 60–1). Now, in the new clinic, teaching is no longer provided by saying but by seeing for oneself within 'the concrete field of experience' (1973, p. 68) which the hospital provides. The gaze replaces the master/pupil relationship. The hierarchy of what is said and passed from one to the other is supplanted by an equality before that which the gaze reveals:

> Medical experience now has a collective subject; it is no longer divided between those who know and those who do not; it is made up, as one entity, of those who unmask and those before whom one unmasks. The statement is the same; the disease speaks the same language to both (1973, p. 110).

Thus the hospital becomes a domain in which 'truth teaches itself, and… offers itself to the gaze of both the experienced observer and the naïve apprentice; for both, there is only one language: the hospital, in which the series of patients examined is itself a school' (1973, p. 68). This Foucault calls the lesson of the hospitals (1973, pp. 64–87), lessons not only for those within them, but also for the archaeologist who sees how the gaze not only brought things to light, but created for itself a field of operations in which it could practise. Clinics, in this example, are the space in which the gaze is realised. Visibility is the discourse within which the clinic and clinical practice is formed. But it is this discourse of visibility itself which is the hardest of all to see. It infuses itself into reality such that it becomes unremarkable and even passed off as common sense. What is seen is what anyone would have expected to have seen, provided that their view was not obscured by prejudice or myth.

> What was fundamentally invisible is suddenly offered to the brightness of the gaze, in a movement of appearance so simple, so immediate that it seems to be the natural consequence of a more highly developed experience (1973, p. 195).

It is as if, Foucault says, at last people were able to approach the object 'with the purity of an unprejudiced gaze' (1973, p. 195). However, the situation is really the reverse. The experience (of objectivity) is the result of the gaze (the ordering of things), not the gaze and its knowledge a result of experience or consciousness or reason.

One other point can be drawn out from the birth of the clinic which will have relevance for the teacher, a point which is a major and continuous theme throughout Foucault's work. The gaze makes disease visible in order to destroy it. Disease has to be granted life before it can be overcome and vanquished. It is named in order to be killed. It is given an individual and differentiated identity in order that it can become the same as all other medical knowledge. As with discipline, punishment, confinement, madness and sexuality, disease is made expressible and brought into the exterior only so that it can all the more successfully and effectively be negated and pushed into the interior. That which is repressed requires first to be expressed. The two, positive and negative, co-exist and are mutually dependent.

Foucault attempts to explicate the implications of archaeology in *The Archaeology of Knowledge*. One of the most central implications is that the process of bringing to light, of expressing, of naming, of identifying, of rendering visible through knowledge, is not the prerogative of a sovereign subject or consciousness. An archaeology of knowledge does not accept the subject as the author of knowledge, nor consciousness as the originator of what is known. Archaeology sees the subject and consciousness as merely another effect of the discourse which is expressed materially and in practice by those effects. The 'enunciative' function (the making of statements) is not the property of consciousness. Rather, consciousness is itself already an expression (a reality) of that function. The subject is not 'the cause, origin, or starting-point of the phenomenon of the written or spoken articulation of a sentence... It is a particular, vacant place that may in fact be filled by different individuals' (1972, p. 95). The statement makes the subject possible by defining what position the subject can have within it. A discourse, for Foucault, is merely a 'group of statements that belong to a single system of formation' (1972, p. 107) and there are multifarious systems of formation which archaeology can uncover. Thus, as well as the loss of the sovereign subject in Foucault, archaeology also signals the impossibility of historical continuities based in and around sovereign subjects of history. For archaeology, neither the 'I' nor the 'we' are determinative. They are merely the effects of networks of particular discourses. To those in search of an author, Foucault says, 'Do not ask me who I am and do not ask me to remain the same' (1972, p. 17). Foucault states that the 'enunciative domain refers neither to an individual subject, nor to some kind of collective consciousness, nor to a transcendental subjectivity... The analysis of statements operates therefore without reference to a cogito' (1972, p. 122). Archaeology, then, undermines the idea of the subject of consciousness as determinative or in any way sovereign. The subject is the result of discourses. Discourses themselves are not formed by ideas, rather, ideas are formed within the spaces that discourses create. The subject, single or collective, is visible because it is within particular discourses and, at the same time, external to others. It is this process of distribution which the archaeologist examines, an examination at the level of discourses, not at the level of what are merely their expressions. Archaeology is not interested in what is

80

made visible, or made exterior, as much as it is interested in the selection procedure of why some things become visible while others do not. In regard to philosophy, Foucault remarks that the breakdown of subjectivity 'is not the end of philosophy, but rather, the end of the philosopher as the sovereign and primary form of philosophical language' (1977a, p. 42). It could also be argued from this that the breakdown of subjectivity is also not the end of education *per se*, but the end of the teacher as its central form or its personification.

This is not a teacher

The breakdown of the teacher as sovereign subject within the enunciative function can be illustrated in Foucault's 1968 work entitled *This is not a Pipe*, a reference to the painting by Magritte of the same name. A teacher stands before this painting and announces to the class, 'this is a pipe'. But the statement, like the painting, is not a pipe. One is only a sentence about the pipe, the other only a drawing of it. So the teacher corrects himself, and says 'this is not a pipe, it is only a drawing of a pipe; this is not a pipe but a sentence saying that this is not a pipe'. Foucault points out that the teacher cannot be sovereign in this discourse precisely because the space in which he is 'the teacher' is not the space that is the truth of the discourse. The story continues with the teacher desperately trying to explain 'In the sentence "this is not a pipe"; *this* is not a pipe: the painting, written sentence, drawing of a pipe – all this is not a pipe' (Foucault, 1983, p. 29). For the teacher there is no pipe. The teacher is within a discourse, a set of statements formed around the separation of the teacher, the statement and the painting from the pipe. 'No longer can anything pass between them save the decree of divorce... Nowhere is there a pipe' (1983, p. 29).

For the archaeologist, everything in the classroom, like the painting of a pipe, 'is solidly anchored within a pedagogic space' (1983, p. 29). That space is formed where that which is to be made visible, the pipe, is forced into exteriority. By being made visible, in statement or drawing, it is able to appear only as an object which is not itself. In being made visible it is also made invisible. Every positive show is a negation and a disappearance. The teacher's sovereignty here is equally elusive. The teacher cannot, in the discourse of the lesson, overcome the rules by which his own performance and discourse are determined. Each true statement the teacher makes is, in being made, equally untrue, and each attempt to correct the statement simply repeats the rules of formation and does not establish the subjective mastery of the teacher.

Foucault completes the story by referring to Magritte's second version of *This is not a Pipe*, where a second pipe appears over and above the first one which is now clearly only a drawing. Foucault describes the teacher stuttering and stammering his way through the infinity of negations which the discourse effects, his voice becoming increasingly confused and choked.

The baffled master lowers his extended pointer, turns his back to the board, regards the uproarious students, and does not realise that they laugh so loudly because above the blackboard and his stammered denials, a vapour has just risen, little by little taking shape and now creating, precisely and without doubt, a pipe. 'A pipe, a pipe,' cry the students, stamping away while the teacher, his voice sinking ever lower, murmurs always with the same obstinacy though no one is listening, 'And yet it is not a pipe' (1983, p. 30).

For the archaeologist, teaching is an effect and practice of a discourse. Its statements form the activity of the teacher, and in this sense the discourse is a pedagogy in which the teacher and the whole of the classroom are situated. Pedagogy ceases to be an objective strategy. On the contrary, the teacher becomes a strategy of the pedagogy which is discourse as material practice. The lesson no longer belongs to the teacher. Even the second pipe, the one which appears above the teacher, is not a pipe. There is no pipe. There is also therefore no lesson, for the teacher who would be master is like the pipe. There is no pipe, and there is no teacher. 'The commonplace... everyday lesson – has disappeared' says Foucault (1983, p. 31), disappeared because the lesson is already performed within the discourse of enunciative function. It is the discourse, and not the teacher, which 'form[s] the objects of which they speak' (1972, p. 49). The pipe, like the lesson and the teacher, is defined by the discourse. There is no pipe, no lesson, no teacher. There are only effects and results of discourse. This disappearance is examined later.

In archaeology, then, the teacher, like the subject, vanishes. Foucault does not offer this as a critique of the personification of enlightenment, of knowledge as personal property, yet it could be seen to be one. However, what archaeology does not do is examine the vanishing of the subject as an experience in and for that subject. Teachers, despairing of their personification and their return, find in archaeology that they have been dispersed into effects and functions of pedagogical spaces over which they are not masters. They find that the subject is deprived 'of its role as originator' (1991, p. 118) and becomes 'a variable and complex function of discourse' (1991, p. 118). But equally they do not find anything further with regard to their experience of this deconstruction of themselves, i.e. of their subjectivity as the teacher and its negation. It was to speak to this issue in particular that Foucault moved his attentions from archaeology to genealogy, to speak not only of the breakdown and the negation, but equally of the creation and positivity of the subject. For this, Foucault turned his attention increasingly away from the order of things in which subjects are only a 'wrinkle in our knowledge' (1970, p. xxiii), towards power/knowledge in which subjects are themselves more the subject of and a subjection to the enquiry than they appeared to be in archaeology.

Genealogy – subject and subjection

In many respects this genealogical examination of the subject (as subject to and as subjection) is carried out by examinations of the body and the processes of domination and power which leave their mark upon it. Genealogy is still not, however, enquiry at the level of consciousness. One still has to:

> ...dispense with the constituent subject, to get rid of the subject itself, that's to say, to arrive at an analysis which can account for the constitution of the subject within a historical framework. And this is what I would call genealogy, that is, a form of history which can account for the constitution of knowledges, discourses, domains of objects etc., without having to make reference to a subject which is either transcendental in relation to the field of events or runs in its empty sameness throughout the course of history (Foucault, 1980, p. 117).

Genealogy is rather enquiry at the level of 'war'. Moreover, this descent into power struggles is not one prefaced upon the presupposition of a 'closed field' (1991, p. 84) upon which all the combatants are 'equal'. Foucault is scathing of the theorists of sovereign power who see 'war' as a struggle among those already bound in social and juridical relationships. Those relationships are themselves a product of war and cannot be fixed as the origin, the truth, or the 'place' upon which all wars are fought. There is no 'universal agreement' upon war as a strategy. 'Universal agreement', the legal system, is itself only a strategy of war. Foucault remarks that:

> It would be false to think that total war exhausts itself in its own contradictions and ends by renouncing violence and submitting to civil laws. On the contrary, the law is a calculated and relentless pleasure, delight in the promised blood... The desire for peace, the serenity of compromise, and the tacit acceptance of the law, far from representing a major moral conversion or a utilitarian calculation that gave rise to the law, are but its result and, in point of fact, its perversion (1991, p. 85).

Quoting Nietzsche, Foucault makes the case that law extracts obligations from its subjects. It, too, is a domination 'saturated in blood' (see Nietzsche, 1968, p. 501). Law is not an end to war, it is the continuation of war by other means.

Thus, Foucault's descent into power relations is one which examines power not at the level of personal or sovereign property, either that of an 'I' or a 'we', but at the level of surveillance and discipline where power is manifest in material practices. This is argued particularly in *Discipline and Punish*, which begins by revealing how sovereign power has been replaced. No longer is it necessary for the sovereign to appear personally for his power to be represented, nor for the gallows to stand as a representation of that power in his (personal) absence. The war of power relations now has a new and far more effective method of domination. Now power is not possessed, it is 'exercised' (Foucault, 1977b, p. 26). Power is distributed and realised in practices which provide for economies of scale and yet ever increasing efficiency. Schools and prisons are just such economic sites.

What is key to a genealogical understanding of both is that domination is no longer practised by a sovereign over his subjects. Now it is realised through, and most importantly as, the subjects themselves. Domination becomes material as the subject. The word 'subject' carries this meaning, for a subject is also subject to something which is over it. The subject is therefore the fixing of subjection as an identity. Through the techniques of surveillance and discipline, subjects are able to become themselves, that is, to become subjection. When they achieve this they carry within them surveillance, discipline and supervision as their own selves. They have become the masters of their own slavery.

Schools became a mechanism of power, having a hold over what the bodies of its subjects might do, how they may do it, and the efficiency and performance expected. The classroom defined an individual space for each pupil and for the teacher, thus disciplining the body to accept its place. A timetable of exercises was drawn up to ensure that the body conformed to the activities demanded of it at particular times, and to ensure that time itself was not a property of the pupil or the teacher. Pupils were differentiated in terms of the exercises they were to perform, but in being subject to this discipline they were all made to conform, all to be the same. Finally, the bodies were all subjected to the discipline of surveillance and examination. They were placed within an economy of power relations where they could be watched, measured, judged, placed, 'normalised' and examined without the sovereign power of an individual in whose name the 'education' was to be carried out. The genealogy of power relations within the school reveals discipline and punishment not to be a personal prerogative, but a function which is realised in the practice of all concerned and in the identities of its personnel. What is done to teachers and pupils is done by them, for what they do is what they are. Their own 'subjectivities' are an effect of the distribution of power relations which is the school. They are formed within an economy of power in which their very being is already defined for them in terms of subject as subjection. In the economy of schools, power is discipline and discipline is the 'self'. When the body conforms to the power/knowledge of the school, or any disciplinary instruction, then through (the control of) the body comes the formation of the 'self'. The self is truly subject when it and discipline are indistinguishable, or put bluntly, when it performs as it is supposed to.

It would be a mistake, however, to see discipline as personal in any other sense than as subjection. No one owns the discipline, no one person has the school or any disciplinary institution as his own sovereign territory. Discipline is not personal power, but it is the power to define and shape what is to count as 'a person'. It is this 'impersonal' sense of power which often seems the most chilling aspect of Foucault's theorising. He states,

> One doesn't have a power which is wholly in the hands of one person who can exercise it alone and totally over the others. It's a machine in which everyone is caught, those who exercise power just as much as those over whom it is exercised... Power is no longer substantially identified with an individual who possesses or exercises it by right of birth; it becomes a machinery that no one owns (1980, p. 156).

For the despairing teacher, it might appear that there are two general directions in which genealogy points. The first does not appear very optimistic, and easily seems to deepen the despair. Within a genealogical approach, the teacher, placed within the power relations of the school, becomes an effect of discipline, a part of the machine which continues the war of subject and subjection in ever more effective but increasingly impersonal ways. It is no good the teacher asking 'in whose interests am I being made to operate as a functionary of this discipline?', or 'whose war am I fighting?', because the question misunderstands how the teacher is already a form and shape in which the war is being fought. There is not, within disciplinary power, a centre or a sovereign. 'Ultimately, what presides over all these mechanisms is not the unitary functioning of an apparatus or an institution, but the necessity of combat and the rules of strategy' (1977b, p. 308). To wish to re-personalise power relations is to seek to explain discipline in terms of a sovereign again, whereas the school, like the prison, is not a field of battle, it is the war itself: 'non-sovereign power... is disciplinary power' (1980, p. 105). Its form of war has replaced the sovereign and his subjects. Teachers can no longer look to take sides, for the war is no longer 'them and us', now it is power as us. The teacher is a manifestation of power. There are no sides, there is only the machine which the teacher helps to operate.

As an operator, the teacher in Foucault becomes the technologist of the souls of the pupils, the technician of time and space, the instructor of exercises, the gaze of surveillance, the inflictor of punishment, the enforcer of conformity, the imposer of difference, the examiner and, as Foucault expresses later in Volume 1 of the *History of Sexuality*, the extractor of confessions. The teacher practises the discipline in which information is extracted from the pupils such that each becomes a 'case', and therefore becomes calculable, measurable and objectified. With regard to the self, the teacher is also within and subject to the disciplinary power which is the school. Teachers' authority is not their own. Indeed, like all individuals, the teacher 'is an effect of power, and... is the element of its articulation. The individual which power has constituted is at the same time its vehicle' (1980, p. 98).

However, Foucault's genealogical enquiries have another side to them, a side which provides continuity with a major theme begun early in his archaeology. Thus far it appears that power in the form of discipline is a merely negative and repressive force. It appears to signal the domination of the pupil by the teacher, who functions as the vehicle of 'normalisation', judgment and examination. The gaze has its materiality through the teacher, they are 'the element[s] of its articulation' (1980, p. 98). Their function is to ensure that 'There is no need for arms, physical violence, material constraints. Just a gaze...' (1980, p. 155). Further, discipline operates also as a domination of teachers in the ways that it sites them within a network of power relations, a network which creates the space in which their 'subjectivity' is defined, created and made real. Genealogy paints a wholly repressive picture of teacher and pupils depersonalised, and subjected without choice, autonomy or control to a web of power. The situation is even more repressive to the extent that the subjectivities are none other than the materiality of this web. They are its reality. It is no longer the case that the subject will see the web of power relations and seek to transform or overcome them, for the power relations are already interiorised into and are the body of that subject. Not surprisingly, given Foucault's links with Althusser, the view expressed here condemns those same teachers referred to by Althusser who are 'interpellated' by ideological practices and whose devoted work contributes to, maintains and is the material reality of the ideological state apparatus (see Chapter 1). As Althusser himself said of Foucault,

> He was a pupil of mine, and 'something' from my own writings has passed into his, including certain of my formulations. But... under his pen and in his thought, even the meanings he gives to formulations he has borrowed from me are transformed into another, quite different meaning than my own (from Macey, 1993, pp. 196–7).

One of those differences, perhaps the major one, is that Foucault refuses to see 'subjection' to power relations as wholly repressive and negative. It was seen earlier how disease, in order to be 'repressed', first had to be made visible. The overcoming of disease required first that it be given an identity, an independent existence. In other words, disease had to be born before it could be vanquished. The negation of disease required a positive identity for disease first. The same is the case for all of those 'subjects' who are subjected to power relations. They, too, have to be identified before they can be disciplined, although the two are, for Foucault, only aspects of the same power relation.

To see in genealogy and power/knowledge solely a negation, or a repression of subjectivity, is to place power within the juridical model where power is seen as the property of a person. Power cannot be the property of a master because power is not personal. Rather, the personal is one manifestation of a particular network of power relations. Foucault notes, 'it's my hypothesis that the individual is not a pre-given entity which is seized on by the exercise of power. The individual, with his identity and characteristics, is the product of a relation of power exercised over bodies' (1980, pp. 73–4). Only when this 'product' is viewed from the perspective of power as personal property is it viewed, with regard to discipline, wholly negatively. Thus, it could be said that power/subject would enable 'power never to be thought of in other than negative terms: refusal, limitation, obstruction, censorship. Power is what says no' (1980, p. 139). Explaining further, he notes:

> Between every point of a social body, between a man and a woman, between the members of a family, between a master and his pupil, between everyone who knows and everyone who does not, there exist relations of power which are not purely and simply a projection of the sovereign's great power over the individual; they are rather the concrete, changing soil in which the sovereign's power is grounded, the conditions which make it possible for it to function (1980, p. 187).

This genealogical insight points the way to finding that which in power/knowledge is positive. Not just the no-saying of a master/teacher to his slave/pupil, but a yes-saying which identifies, locates and makes visible that which the juridical model keeps hidden. In other words, where Foucault differs from Althusser is in emphasising that repression requires visibility, and that visibility is the positive side of power relations because it is what gives life. Genealogy itself is a form of critique which makes visible that which has remained subjugated by dominant discourses, and in particular that of the law. Freed from the tyranny of universalistic scientific and historical regimes of thought, genealogy is able to ask why this knowledge becomes truth when this other knowledge does not. This Foucault describes as 'the *local* character of criticism' (1980, p. 81), one which investigates at the level of the everyday rather than in accordance with overarching universalist theory. These theories are precisely what are brought into question by local analysis. It investigates those knowledges 'that have been disqualified as inadequate to their task or insufficiently elaborated: naïve knowledges, located low down on the hierarchy, beneath the required level of cognition or scientificity' (1980, p. 82). It is through this 'insurrection of subjugated knowledges' (1980, p. 81) 'that criticism performs its work' (1980, p. 82). Genealogy, in this positive sense of making visible that which is subjugated, is not itself a different form of power to that which it is investigating. Rather, it is a form of analysis which uses struggle, the war, as a critique of dominant theories. It employs the struggle in which subjugated knowledges are the visible result, in the sense that this new visibility, this new power/knowledge, can be used both to reveal the war and to participate in the war against 'the effects of the power of a discourse' (1980, p. 84). This war is being fought against all sciences which proclaim that their domination is not a war. Genealogy seeks to embarrass such claims of non-struggle by asking, 'What types of knowledge do you want to disqualify... which speaking, discoursing subjects... do you then want to "diminish"... which theoretical-political *avant-garde* do you want to enthrone...?' (1980, p. 85). At the heart of genealogy is the struggle to make visible that which scientific discourses make invisible, so that being visible they become strategies in the struggle and in the war which is the reality of the networks of power relations. Speaking about prisons in particular but about genealogy in general, Foucault remarks, 'I wanted to make it intelligible and, therefore, criticisable' (1988, p. 101), and intelligible here means visible.

Power/knowledge therefore has its positive side. In relation to schooling and discipline it encourages an insurrection of those knowledges which, in the power struggle, have remained subjugated, voices which have remained unheard and bodies which have remained invisible. Equally, it seeks to ask why this type of disciplinary education and not another, and what are the effects of this type of education, what truths does it create and which does it repress? Genealogy in schooling explores the local knowledges which struggle for a strategic intervention in the battle but remain invisible within the engagement as it appears at any one moment.

Allied to genealogy as critique, in the sense of making visible, there is a second way in which power/knowledge is positive. Foucault works hard to try and show how power is creative of knowledge and subjects. For example, the identification of each pupil as a field of knowledge, a 'case history', is not simply the determination or repression of the pupil, it is the construction and production of the pupil. The pupil is born, as it were, through power. Power, in its making visible, gives life to that which is the pupil, as it does also to that which is the teacher.

> We must cease once and for all to describe the effects of power in negative terms: it 'excludes', it 'represses', it 'censors', it 'abstracts', it 'masks', it 'conceals'. In fact power produces; it produces reality; it produces domains of objects and rituals of truth. The individual and the knowledge that may be gained of him belong to this production (1977b, p. 194).

What we are, how we know ourselves, our very identities as subjects are not just lost to power relations, they are created by them as well. In the Lost and Found department of individual identity, the juridical model concentrates on these as exclusive states. Yet in Foucauldian genealogy they are not exclusive states belonging (or not) to a subject. Rather the department of lost and found identities is itself a whole manifestation of struggle. It is itself the war where that which is visible is also repressed, and that which is repressed is also visible. To be visible is to be subject, and also to be subjected. The one requires the other, for that is the way the war is fought today. In the *History of Sexuality*, Foucault gives the following example of the positive and the negative aspects of genealogy, of visibility being both subjecting and subjectifying.

> There is no question that the appearance in 19th-century psychiatry, jurisprudence, and literature of a whole series of discourses on the species and subspecies of homosexuality, inversion, pederasty, and 'psychic hermaphrodism' made possible a strong advance of social controls into this area of 'perversity'; but it also made possible the formation of a 'reverse'

88

discourse: homosexuality began to speak in its own behalf, to demand that its legitimacy or 'naturality' be acknowledged, often in the same vocabulary, using the same categories by which it was medically disqualified (1978, p. 101).

The identity which was constructed so that a group could be repressed became, at the same time, the identity within which a group could wage war, could struggle, and in which their subjectivity could become a strategy by which intervention became possible. To subject is at the same time to create a subject. The homosexual, like the teacher, the pupil, or any identified case which is brought to visibility, is part of a discourse which is not merely a distributor of power, but is a creative power. Foucault's later works cite the importance of locating and hearing from the 'dangerous individual' so that his crime can be integrated into his subjectivity, his identity. 'The more clearly visible this integration, the more clearly punishable the subject' (1988, p. 139). Similarly, sexuality could only be repressed once it had been made visible, an identity made possible through confession. Since the 18th century, 'Sex was driven out of hiding and constrained to lead a discursive existence' (1978, p. 33). Only in affirming sex, in telling everything, could sex then be repressed. Visibility in all cases combines identity and repression, repression and identity.

Therefore, and here Foucault appears to offer strategies as a possibility for change, discourse, in making visible, also creates 'a point of resistance and a starting point for an opposing strategy' (1978, p. 101). Summing up the theme that visibility is both negative and positive, repressive and creative, deterministic and oppositional, Foucault writes, 'Discourse transmits and produces power; it reinforces it, but also undermines and exposes it, renders it fragile and makes it possible to thwart it' (1978, p. 101).

No one to teach

For the despairing teacher, then, it could be said that Foucault both deepens the anxiety and yet, at the same time, offers strategies for opposition. On the one hand teachers are determined within the disciplinary structures of schools. They are the vehicles of disciplinary power, they give materiality to surveillance, they give reality to examination, and they create the identity, the case history, which is the student. Teachers are an instrument of power, because to teach is already to be an effect of power. They enter the war as the embodiment of discipline, disciplined themselves and ready to ensure the discipline of others. This they do 'voluntarily', for the beauty of the teacher is that the network of disciplinary power is material in and as the body of the teacher, and is an identity which each has internalised. Discipline *is* the teacher.

On the other hand, in revealing teachers as a result, an effect, and as individual (subjected) bodies of power, the teacher as subject also arises. Here teachers are able to offer themselves as an opposition to their subjugation within discipline. They are made visible as an identity, and as such can begin to enter the struggle as strategies. Being determined within and by discipline becomes also the self- (as) discipline. This self can now be made intelligible, and therefore can be criticised. For Foucault, such critique could not be at a 'personal' level, for that would be to misunderstand genealogy and concentrate only on the subject rather than its subjection to and within the distribution of power. Genealogy is not a question of who has power. If teachers demand power as property rather than remain as effects of power, then this is to repeat the view of the sovereign, and the perspective of power as held by an individual. Just as it would not be 'much better to have the prisoners operating the Panoptic apparatus and sitting in the central tower, instead of the guards' (Foucault, 1980, pp. 164–5), neither would it be so for teachers (or pupils) to 'control' schools. Foucault does not offer an alternative to disciplinary power or, therefore, for the teacher, an alternative to subjection and subjectification.

> If one wants to look for a non-disciplinary form of power, or, rather, to struggle against disciplines and disciplinary power, it is not towards the ancient right of sovereignty that one should turn, but towards the possibility of a new form of right, one which must indeed be anti-disciplinarian, but at the same time liberated from the principle of sovereignty (1980, p. 108).

Resistance to discipline is not embodied in a struggle for legal rights, 'It is simply in the struggle itself and through it that positive conditions emerge' (1988, p. 197).

In the critiques of the teacher examined in Chapter 1, each was seen to be critical of the teacher as 'sovereign', or as the master in whom power is personalised. Yet at the same time, each critic also repeated the personalisation of the sovereign by having knowledge (critique) as property and employing it as justification for his intervention. In such educational critique 'we still have not cut off the head of the king', as Foucault might say (1978, pp. 88–9), for all that happens is that power is claimed by one king after another, having as their authority the critique of the abstract claims to kingship of the preceding ruler. For Foucault, it is an unavoidable contradiction but an outmoded one. He points out that 'Knowledge and power are integrated with one another... It is not possible for power to be exercised without knowledge, it is impossible for knowledge not to engender power' (1980, p. 52). But genealogy does not seek to maintain a separation between knowledge and power, as sovereigns do in order that the law appear egalitarian. Genealogy understands the inseparability of power and knowledge, and its terrain is not law but the battlefield and struggle upon which law is based. For those despairing teachers who finds themselves repeated as master even in their attempts to undermine that mastery, their mistake is to seek to transfer power from master to pupil. Such an attempt is always a repetition of

90

mastery. What genealogy offers teachers is a view of their role in the continuing war which is manifest in the various networks of power relations which mark the body. Only in the comprehension that the teacher's hands are, by being a teacher, already 'saturated in blood', and that 'knowledge is not made for understanding, it is made for cutting' (1991, p. 88) will teachers realise their place in the war, their role as the 'cutters' of their pupils, and their materiality as the body which wields the knife.

However, such an understanding or 'self-cutting' is not likely to remove but rather to deepen the despair of those teachers who find now that even their radical or humanitarian concerns to overcome domination are only a further strategy in the battle. Even worse, the teachers, like the pupil, are made visible and are therefore subjected to the same apparatuses of power which the teacher embodies, or which the teacher is. Under the arrangement of the gaze both are permanently visible, even when no one is looking at them. Both embody and are the materiality of surveillance, they (are) discipline themselves, internalising the principle of surveillance and discipline as their own subjectivity. 'By this very fact, the external power may throw off its physical weight; it tends to the non-corporal... it is a perpetual victory that avoids physical confrontation and which is always decided in advance' (1977b, p. 203).

However, the educational value of Foucault's analysis for the teacher begins precisely where Foucault ends. Whereas previous theorists have personalised enlightenment, knowledge and self-relation as their own property, and have become (i.e. repeated) the teacher, Foucault seeks to point out that any personalising, any assumption of knowledge as property, is in fact knowledge as power. Knowledge cannot be personalised because the person, the 'subject', is already an effect of power and marked as what it is only by its place within the network. What Foucault seeks to reveal is that the personalising of power is only the power of personalising, an effect not of the person but of power itself. It is not the activity of the individual which does the work of negation, because the work of the individual is never an individual task. It is already only the exercise of power itself, an exercising which produces the subject, not the other way round.

Thus there is in Foucault both subject and subjection. They are the same, for the one is at the same time the other. They do not 'belong' to experience, for they are not produced and reproduced in the work of the person. They become clearer in the genealogy of the person, an enquiry which is not experiential but is itself an (immanent) self-realisation of power/knowledge. When genealogy, or power/knowledge, makes visible the process by which persons are themselves constructed as visibility, as subject and subjection, then genealogy is power/ knowledge and an immanent enquiry regarding itself. When power/knowledge makes itself visible, then visibility - the power of power/knowledge - is also made visible to itself - the knowledge of power/knowledge. Here genealogy is power and knowledge as immanent critique or immanent self-reflection. But here, where genealogy ends or knows itself, our experience of it is only beginning (again).

What Foucault has produced is a dialectic of subject and subjugation, but with no substance. It has no substance because it has no experience of self or of loss of self. His critique of the individual involves positing the loss of self as a unity of power and knowledge, i.e. a self-relation which is not a self. But the movement which is loss of self is only determinate, or knowable at all, as and in (negative) self-experience. Without experience there is no movement, and without movement there is no return. In Foucault there is no self, no experience, no movement and no return. Because there is no experience, and no loss of self, there is no substance. The attempt to eradicate dialectic by fixing the opposition of positive and negative into a unity of power/knowledge reproduces a dialectic without substance, a 'dialectic of nihilism' (see Rose, 1984).

The dualism of subject and subjection is only half the story. The subject in Foucault is not the subject for it is subjected to, and repressed by, the material exercise of power in which it finds itself. The subject which finds its self finds both its self and its not-self. For Foucault this is not a dialectic but a unity. Yet it cannot be a unity for it is a broken middle, a self-relation. The nihilism implicit in Foucault is the self which, although identified, is never a self. This, as it stands, is not educational for the self, nor for the teacher, because according to Foucault it learns nothing except that it is, and that what it is, it is not. The substance Foucault imputes to this learning is power, i.e. that power learns about itself. Whereas, therefore, the teachers examined in Chapters 1 and 2 have personalised movement as their own knowledge/property, Foucault seeks to depersonalise movement, seeing it purely as 'power'. The substance of the person, its positive and negative visibility, is posited as power. But a depersonalised power, a posited power, is a power which is not known, not experienced. Therefore the unity of power as positive and negative has to be guessed at, presupposed. Its 'self' (the identity of power/knowledge as genealogy) can only be asserted, which may well be the substance of power *per se*, but it can only ever be asserted. If Foucault is prepared to say that one bare assertion is worth the same as any other because it is the identity of power, or because that is the truth of war, then he has personalised power in the assertion of his teaching. To make such a claim presupposes he has power as his object, and as his own property, one which he can now pass on to us, his pupils. He ceases to be a soldier still engaged in the war and appears now shining for others as the teacher whose knowledge of the war is the result of his victory over it, or, rather, his desertion from it. If, in addition, Foucault argues that his claims about power will be undermined by their own truth, that in their being made visible they are also seen as merely effects of particular networks, then that negation is realised in the work and activity which is our experience of the visibility. If our experience has no part to play then power as negative can never be known, and moreover, nothing which becomes visible is actually seen. This is what is missing in Foucault. For whom is power negative? Who experiences repression? Who has their own visibility as object? Not a sovereign subject (as Foucault would agree), but a person who, in the experience of being subject (positive) and subjected (negative), experiences this as repetition. Foucault sees both. We, however, can only experience both as our inability to see them. The result of the activity of power/knowledge is the further activity of power/knowledge against that result. It does not let itself be known, and that is where (and why) the despairing teacher is forced, always, to begin again without a beginning. It is in the negation of power/knowledge that Foucault's subject is visible to itself. To posit the subject/subjection as positive and negative is to presuppose visibility before it has been seen, and to deny that both are already present in what is visible. What is visible is what is, or what is actual. Without the contradiction of actuality, Foucault cannot see visibility, he can only assert it. His 'enlightenment' with regard to visibility does not achieve its own actuality (as shadow or return), and remains only a movement of darkness within itself. These themes of enlightenment, darkness, shadow and return are explored in more detail in Parts II, III and IV.

The tension between subject and subjection, between positive and negative, is apparent throughout Foucault's work. The early archaeological analysis presented subjection without subject. His response to this was to adopt genealogy from Nietzsche which tried to give a more 'balanced' analysis of subjection as subject. This was attempted in the formula power/knowledge where power is struggle and knowledge is that which is identified by being made visible. The two are posited as being the same; visibility is both negative and positive, both subjection and subject. But in refusing, ultimately, the negation of power/knowledge by itself, Foucault denies us our experience of, and our self-determination within, the illusion of bourgeois property relations. Ultimately, Foucault denies struggle and war altogether. There is a war in bourgeois society, there is a constant struggle with the contradiction that its universality and our particularity, the same principle, are irreconcilable. The sovereign 'I' (the person) is already at war with, in contradiction to, the law which is its own universality. Equally, the 'we', the social relation in which each 'I' is at one and the same time all other 'I's, is at war with the persons for whom that universal is merely a return of the particular to itself. In relation to the law, the person is returned to the independence of the 'I'. In relation to the person, each is returned to the dependence of the 'I' upon the law. This war is already in progress. Bourgeois law is not an imposed peace. It is an abstract imposition on that which knows the universal as a return of the particular and can find no experience of it save that of contradiction. Contradiction is struggle because it is the experience of not being that which we are imposed as being. It is Foucault who resists the struggle by positing the work of struggle as already done. He wants, in his genealogical work, to show how the self is the war, but what he disallows us is to know the war as the self. In Foucault, the struggle is not ours for we are already returned from the war. We actually do no fighting, for we know that we are the (temporary) result of the war. It is a struggle fought without reference to the bourgeois property relations which determine its illusions. It is posited as belonging to no one, whereas ownership (identity) is precisely what the war is about. For Foucault, in a world of private property, the war belongs to no one.

By ignoring the illusions inherent in bourgeois property relations, Foucault's struggle is rendered without relevance or meaning, and devoid of its own actual political and social significance. It is a struggle about nothing except the self-fulfilment of something called power, something of which our own determinate experience is denied. Power gives us life, and then denies us that life. In Foucault's theorising, birth is already death, for without experience there is no life or death, no broken middle, no relation between positive and negative, subject and subjection, and therefore no substance. As Rose puts it succinctly, 'To transcribe experience in terms of the body as Foucault does is to rob persons of experience altogether' (1984, p. 180). Foucault's war for us is the absence of war. Foucault's person is the absence of experience, of contradiction, of movement, and of the person as relation. Foucault's person is presupposed as negative and positive, a presupposition which seeks to make visible or enlighten us regarding the contingency of the sovereign subject once and for all. Yet this sovereignty is itself a presupposition in Foucault, one which avoids the negative lessons of relation. There is no need for Foucault to fight our battles for us. Indeed, to do so is to become the worst kind of teacher, the patronising shepherd who seeks to tend his flock in their own best interests, and to preserve them from the struggle by settling the issue for them.

Even though Foucault's vocabulary 'of "strategy", "tasks", and "techniques" is derived from warfare, its use avoids the risks of war, for, although resources are "deployed", no battle is ever fought, lost or won' (Rose, 1984, p. 178). His pupils are not allowed their experience of negation, of the property and the knowledge relation, for that experience has been had by their teacher, found to be the truth of something else, and pronounced false. Here Foucault becomes the same kind of teacher examined in Chapters 1 and 2. Each presupposed in their own critique a self-relation of enlightenment in and as their practice. Here, Foucault's enlightenment about visibility (self-light) is his presupposed self-relation. This enlightenment is then the basis of his justification for intervening in the education of others. But, whereas for the despairing teacher the contradiction of enlightenment and justification is return and a re-opening of the possibilities of his education, for Foucault, the teacher of visibility, this contradiction of teacher and student, of positive and negative, is no longer formative. The teacher of visibility lifts himself out of the struggle which both is and is not visibility, and out of education altogether. Our negation of him as the teacher is no longer possible, for the teacher is already pronouncing himself visible as non-teacher or non-master. We are thus denied our experience of his domination, and therefore our education. And that denial is a more dangerous mastery than the teacher who refuses to acknowledge their negation and their return, but does not refuse us that experience. The anonymous 'masked philosopher' (i.e. Foucault, see 1988, p. 323) seems to be claiming the same non-truth as Magritte's pipe. But the pipe was not a pipe only when it was an object for us. In its relation to the observer it was its own non-truth. Foucault's refusal to place himself in that relation is to seek to preserve himself from the identity which his name carries with it. But without the name, there is no visibility, without visibility there is no subjection, and without subjection the subject does not exist. Such logic is Foucauldian. Anonymity is only the refusal of the war which is the self. In an interview in 1983, Foucault remarked that his key question was 'at what price can subjects speak the truth about themselves?' (1988, p. 30). The answer is, at the cost of themselves. But that requires risking identity and not merely refusing it.

Foucault is in contradiction of his own formula. In denying himself, or his self, he is trying to remain invisible. But no negation is possible without visibility. As Foucault noted in 1978, in *The Dangerous Individual*, without the man, the subject, the individual, the case, then the 'machine ceases to function' (1988, p. 151). Foucault is not the dangerous individual, for he is not the subject. He tells us he is merely a relation, or a network of relations. This teaching is a denial of the struggle, the contradiction and the risk of being the person and the teacher. It is a refusal of the relation of self. It is empty of substance because it is empty of the relation which, even in Foucault's work, is the negation of self. To find the dangerous individual in education, the teacher who is genuinely 'dynamite', it is necessary to turn to Foucault's inspiration, to Nietzsche (see Chapter 8). But unlike Nietzsche, Foucault, in teaching the war, refused to become the war. He preserved the self by removing the self from the war which is its substance. Only in Zarathustra does the teacher become the war, only in Zarathustra and not in Foucault is the teacher and the relation of genealogy lived out, and, as such, genuinely educational. Only in Zarathustra and not in Foucault is genealogy a yes-saying to what is. Foucault's no-saying to the experience of the subject is our education regarding Foucault, but it is not his own substantive (self-) education, for in Foucault there is actually no one to teach.

Part II
CONTRADICTION OF ENLIGHTENMENT

This section examines the determination of the category of enlightenment. It introduces Hegelian terms and concepts from the *Phenomenology of Spirit* to explore how Hegel charted the development of reason from Stoicism and scepticism in ancient Greek philosophy to the European Enlightenment. This development is placed first within the relation of natural and philosophical consciousness. For Hegel, natural consciousness is that which presents itself immediately. Philosophical consciousness is the ambiguity of a consciousness which has natural consciousness as its own object (self-consciousness) and which knows of that relation as its own (contradictory) self-determination. The instability of this self-relation of natural and philosophical consciousness is traced in Chapter 4. Its despairing voice is heard in Chapter 5 as the dialectic of enlightenment, before that despair is itself explored as the broken middle, or as what is. Chapter 5 ends by seeking to answer the question 'what is enlightenment?' in terms of its own self-relation; that is, in terms of its broken middle as light, dark and shadow.

4 What is enlightenment?

In 1784, in answer to the question 'what is enlightenment?', Kant declared:

> Enlightenment is man's release from his self-incurred tutelage. Tutelage is man's inability to make use of his understanding without direction from another. Self-incurred in this tutelage when its cause lies not in lack of reason but in lack of resolution and courage to use it without direction from another. *Sapere aude*! 'Have courage to use your own reason!' – that is the motto of enlightenment (Kant, 1990, p. 83).

A number of important characteristics of the concept of enlightenment are immediately apparent here. First, enlightenment is the result attained by the use of reason. Reason, aimed at examining itself, will realise and produce enlightenment as (its) result. Second, not to use reason is to remain in a state of tutelage, an immature state in which one person is dependent upon the thinking or otherwise of someone else. It is to have to rely upon the guidance of others rather than to have the courage to think for oneself. Thinking for oneself is the freedom which reason supplies to each individual. Finally, enlightenment and rational activity require courage because independence, thinking for oneself, and refusing to be told what to think, are a risk. To leave behind the immaturity of dependence is to move into the world alone, and is, as Kant records in the expression *sapere aude*, to 'dare to be wise'.

However, for the philosopher Michel Foucault 200 years later, an answer to the question 'what is enlightenment?' has not been achieved either by Kant or by those who have come after him. He says that Kant's own response marks the birth of a question but not its answer, and that since Kant, modern philosophy can be characterised as 'the philosophy that is attempting to answer the question raised so imprudently two centuries ago' (1991, p. 32). Indeed, Foucault sees the question representing a historical crossroads and the point of departure for what 'one might call the attitude of modernity' (1991, p. 38). This attitude for Foucault is the conjoining of enlightenment and critique as a self-activity, each needing and existing within the freedom of the other. Enlightenment for Kant, says Foucault, is the 'moment when humanity is going to put its own reason to use, without subjecting itself to any authority' (1991, p. 38). It is for this reason, to prevent 'illegitimate uses of reason' (1991, p. 38), that critique is necessary, for it alone can determine legitimate knowledge, correct actions, and appropriate hopes. Thus the Enlightenment is the age of critique, and critique is the self-examination of reason by itself, the result of which is enlightenment. Foucault concludes his essay by noting that this 'critical ontology of ourselves' (1991, p. 50), our self-reflective critique, can be thought of as an attitude,

> An ethos, a philosophical life in which the critique of what we are is at one and the same time the historical analysis of the limits that are imposed on us and an experiment with the possibility of going beyond them (1991, p. 50).

Such a description accurately describes the critiques of Rousseau, Marx and Durkheim examined in Chapter 2. However, what they, and Foucault's own description of critique in these terms, do not do is to investigate the constituent moments of the self-reflective attitude. To say that enlightenment is critique and that critique is enlightenment is only to offer tautologies, without investigating further into what it is that critique and enlightenment believe their achievements are, and what in fact they do achieve. In Part I, it was seen that the attempts in those critiques of the person to overcome the limits in which the critique was itself determined, only repeated those limits. To comprehend critique as this failure, and as repetition and return, requires us to dare to be wise about critique itself. It is to risk no longer being satisfied with the immediate self-assertion of reason that it is enlightenment, or that enlightenment is the immanent and therefore legitimate result of critique. But the question 'what is enlightenment?' is so difficult because every answer is forced to assume as its own justification the very concept that is under investigation. How would an answer know that it was an answer unless it presupposed what an enlightenment would look like beforehand? Enlightenment only has itself with which to conduct an enquiry into itself. It is faced, therefore, with the situation that every enlightenment about itself merely repeats an empty tautology: reason knowing itself is an enlightenment, and enlightenment is reason knowing itself. The self-critique of reason has no way of avoiding this repetition, and no way, equally, of doing anything other than offering the tautology as justification. It is the same tautology which characterises the assertions made by critical theorists that their critique is immanent and therefore self-transformative for the practitioner. However, only an investigation which risks not dominating enlightenment, not presupposing it beforehand, is one which is truly ready to learn about itself, and one in which the broken middle of social and educational relations can be known.

Natural and philosophical consciousness

In Hegel's *Phenomenology of Spirit* and *Science of Logic*, the 'philosophical life' of critique is not presented as a tautological assertion of its own truth and identity. On the contrary, in the *Phenomenology*, critique is presented as the experience of contradiction and return, a movement which the critiques of Rousseau, Marx and Durkheim were seen to reproduce for us in Part I. By understanding the constituent moments of critique as it is experienced, that is as contradiction and return, one can also begin to see how the result of critique (or enlightenment) is always a misrecognition by consciousness of its own merely illusory appearance. In this 'critique of critique' an answer to the question 'what is enlightenment?' emerges.

Hegel's *Phenomenology* follows the path of two consciousnesses, natural consciousness and philosophical consciousness. Natural consciousness is the consciousness which takes the world, or itself, to be exactly as it immediately appears. The person is one such appearance of natural consciousness, the teacher is another. Philosophical consciousness is the consciousness in which the first appearance is known as an appearance, or where its negation as an independent identity is experienced. The determination of philosophical consciousness is always the destruction of one of the appearances of natural consciousness. Philosophical consciousness can therefore be seen as the experience in which consciousness learns about its mere appearances or shapes in the world. These experiences constitute the path of consciousness's own education about itself. Since natural consciousness 'directly takes itself to be real knowledge, this path has a negative significance for it, and ... counts for it rather as the loss of its own self' (Hegel, 1977, p. 49). Thus, says Hegel, the experience of natural consciousness by itself in philosophical consciousness counts for it as 'the pathway of *doubt*, or more precisely as the way of despair' (1977, p. 49). The path is 'the conscious insight into the untruth of (its) phenomenal knowledge' (1977, p. 50). The education of philosophical consciousness about the mere appearances of natural consciousness is always the death of natural consciousness in that form. In other Hegelian terms, the immediacy of natural consciousness is mediated in and by its being experienced, and it is this experience which is the determination of philosophical consciousness. A phenomenology, says Rose, is 'the presentation of the contradiction between natural consciousness's definition of itself and its experience' (1981, p. 107). However, it only appears as philosophical consciousness after the completion of the stages described in the *Phenomenology*. The presentation of the contradiction which is the truth of abstract philosophical consciousness, and of its actuality, is presented in the *Science of Logic*, which as Rose points out is also therefore a phenomenology (1981, p. 188).

At first glance, from what we know of the experiences of natural consciousness in its appearances in Part I, it might seem that the education of consciousness only amounts to a vicious circle. Each time philosophical consciousness arrives at the negation of natural consciousness, for example, of the person, that knowledge becomes another merely immediate appearance. It, in turn, is negated, and the circle continues. This circle is examined in various ways in what follows, as the positing of enlightenment, as the dialectic of enlightenment, and as the broken middle of the knowledge relation. For now, it is important to understand that the relationship between natural consciousness and philosophical consciousness is a broken middle, and that its truth lies in what Hegel calls 'determinate negation'. Only then can we begin to understand the development which runs through the *Phenomenology of Spirit*, and from that to follow the development of consciousness up to its own abstract and immediate appearance as reason.

The relation between natural and philosophical consciousness is a broken middle because it is a determinate negation. This is a key concept in Hegelian philosophy. A negation is determinate when the negative activity and the (negative) result of that activity are the 'same'. How a negation can have substance is precisely that which is at stake in what follows. In comprehending the instability of enlightenment it is also recognised that this instability is inherent within and caused by enlightenment itself. Enlightenment therefore, in this and the next chapter, will be seen as a relation which is formed in and as a contradiction. In its determinate negation, activity and result are not only the 'same', they are also different, united with each other yet also separated from each other. It is this contradictory self-relation which is negative substance, a contradiction which is Rose's notion of the broken middle. The Introduction to the *Phenomenology* attempts to set out this broken middle. It shows that to think something is to be related to that object by thought, but also to be separated from that object by thought. The relation which thinking produces is therefore contradictory. In knowing something, consciousness is joined to it but separated from it at the same time. The contradiction is contained in the word 'for', because if an object is for consciousness then it is part of it and apart from it at the same time. Rose notes that 'Consciousness is always this opposition between itself and its object, for to know an object means that it is both "in-itself" and "for us"' (1981, p. 153).

When it comes to examining 'truth', the same problem applies, in that truth is only ever truth as it appears for consciousness, and never as it is purely in itself, unmediated by the knowing consciousness. This separation between consciousness and truth is often taken to mean that the truth cannot be known, and gives rise to (ancient and post-modern) forms of scepticism and relativism. However, to draw such a conclusion is a mere prejudice, a prejudgment upon what is to count as truth before truth has actually appeared. What such views do not comprehend is that scepticism (meaning here the view that there can be no absolute truth) is only another appearance of natural consciousness, another illusory relationship between itself and the absolute based on another misrecognition of itself. Scepticism is another immediate shape of natural consciousness which is negated in the experience of itself, wherein it realises itself in its own loss, rather than presupposing itself in the loss of everything else. It holds itself to be enlightenment regarding the universality of truth as mere appearance, but does not continue its education to see that this, too, is another immediate shape of natural consciousness. Scepticism refuses to recognise its own self-experience as a determinate contradiction, and therefore it offers no education for consciousness, and refuses itself any development. It is here that the circle of thinking becomes vicious. Scepticism represents the half of the broken middle which is separation, but it has no conception of the truth of this appearance as return, nor therefore, of its self-relation. Hegel warns at the beginning of the Introduction to the *Phenomenology* that this mistrust

> takes for granted certain ideas about cognition as an instrument and as a medium, and assumes that there is a difference between ourselves and this cognition. Above all, it presupposes that the Absolute stands on one side and cognition on the other, independent and separated from it (1977, p. 47, emphasis removed).

This, says Hegel, amounts only to a 'fear of the truth' (1977, p. 47).

However, when the object of thought is thinking itself, or when consciousness reflects upon the truth of itself, then in this act of courage which risks even the despair of losing its own scepticism, there is the possibility of further education. What is for consciousness in this case is consciousness itself. It could now be said that although philosophical consciousness is determined in the destruction of natural consciousness, when natural consciousness is for philosophical consciousness in this way, it is the case that consciousness is for itself. When philosophical consciousness knows natural consciousness, then consciousness knows itself, for the negation of itself is by itself, resulting in itself. In this way, the experience of philosophical consciousness is not merely a negation of natural consciousness, but a determinate negation in and of consciousness by itself. It is itself the result of its own negative self-activity. In separating itself into its two moments of immediacy and mediation, it achieves a (self-) relation between the two which is dependent upon that separation. Thinking, therefore, when it is experienced by itself, has its truth as a broken middle in which what is thought, although separated and opposed to consciousness, is only consciousness itself. Its self-opposition is its self-knowledge.

Truth is no longer external to reflection because 'Consciousness (now) provides its own criterion (of truth) from within itself, so that the investigation becomes a comparison of consciousness with itself' (Hegel, 1977, p. 53). It is for this reason, i.e. that the experience of natural consciousness is only an experience of itself, that the *Phenomenology*

> does not consist solely of the presentation of the experiences of natural consciousness, but also of the *science* of that experience. It consists both of a presentation of the contradiction of natural consciousness and a doctrine of that consciousness' (Rose, 1981, p. 150).

The science of the experiences of natural consciousness is known by philosophical consciousness when its own determinate negation and broken middle are known by it as its self. The *Phenomenology of Spirit* presents at one and the same time the experiences of natural consciousness and the education of philosophical consciousness. Hegel advises that in reading the *Phenomenology* 'the essential point to bear in mind throughout the whole investigation is that these two moments... "being-for-another" and "being-in itself" both fall within that knowledge which we are investigating' (1977, p. 53). Their relation is the broken middle of the knowledge relation, or is what knowing is in and for itself.

Three further points can be made in general with regard to Hegel's *Phenomenology of Spirit*. The first is that, in describing the experiences of natural consciousness, it is describing the misrecognition of natural consciousness. How natural consciousness understands itself in those experiences depends upon the stage of its development towards its self-relation in and as philosophical consciousness. As long as that relation, that broken middle, is not comprehended, then the experiences of natural consciousness will reproduce that relation in so many other ways. Each misrecognition is a misrepresentation of the self-relation by itself, determined as a shape in which the relation merely shines or is illusory. Each experience of natural consciousness by itself, therefore, is also an experience of a return to itself from the mere appearance of that relation. The relation is only available to itself in the form of a contradiction. The reasons for this are explored later in Parts II and III. Some of the shapes in which this misrecognition appears are described in the following section.

Secondly, because the *Phenomenology* is tracing the development of scientific (i.e. philosophical) consciousness, it is, in keeping with science as a broken middle, following one consciousness (scientific) as two consciousnesses, and two consciousnesses as one. This means that throughout the *Phenomenology*, while natural consciousness does not comprehend its appearances and experiences, seeing only contradiction and return, scientific consciousness does comprehend it as self-determinative. The philosophical observer can see what natural consciousness misses, that its experience is its own work and its own development and education. We are able to observe how the experiences of natural consciousness are forgotten by natural consciousness in its next appearance, for we are able to understand the whole of the experience, and to recognise its misrecognitions. But this educated perspective does not lie at a point where there are no longer contradictions, or where natural and philosophical consciousness are an immediate unity. On the contrary, the educated viewpoint knows the contradiction as itself, and that both moments are present in this contradictory self-relation. It is from within this relation that the identity of enlightenment can be known without being dominated.

The third point is that the *Phenomenology* necessarily poses a chronological conundrum. The *Phenomenology* can only by written by scientific consciousness, but scientific consciousness requires its own development in the *Phenomenology* before it can appear. The conundrum itself lies in the fact that the Preface and the Introduction to the *Phenomenology* are abstract, and presuppose that the *Phenomenology* has been completed, and that scientific consciousness can state truths about itself. They appear in this sense as if they are mere assertions of a truth which, it asserts, must be developed in experience. However, as Rose points out, it is abstract natural consciousness which comes to read the book, and therefore its beginning is as abstract as ours. In this sense, the Preface and the Introduction are an acknowledgement that what they state is not true. Rose comments,

> The Preface and Introduction are not simply abstract statements denouncing abstract statement. The abstract rejection of abstraction is the only way to induce abstract consciousness to begin to think non-abstractly. This consistency is the Hegelian *system* (1981, p. 151).

Or, she might have added, is the truth of the contradiction which is the broken middle. The same is also the case for the teacher, as will be shown in Chapter 7.

In addition, Rose points out that chronological readings of the events described in the *Phenomenology* invariably lead to the conclusion that the book culminates in a philosophy which has reunited abstract understanding and experience, or natural and philosophical consciousness as immediate self-relation. No such unification is achieved. Absolute knowing is not the reconciliation of difference, it is the truth of difference within the relation which is its being known. Philosophy is the end of the education of consciousness in two senses. Following Rose (1981, p. 209), it is the end of the education of consciousness as telos (i.e. in the sense of its ultimate purpose), in that it is a definitive experience of spirit in and for itself. It is also the end or exhaustion of the education of consciousness as culture, for that education now does no more than (eternally) repeat prevailing social relations in its opposition to that whole. These two ends are the two senses of the causality of fate (see Rose, 1981, pp. 154–9) of philosophical consciousness. It knows itself as a whole, and it knows itself determined as opposed to the whole. These two ends, or fates, or determinations, taken together (i.e. together and apart) are the comprehensive education of philosophical consciousness, its education regarding its continued domination in and by what Rose calls 'the modern, abstract culture of *Verstand*' (1981, p. 154), or by continuing bourgeois social relations. Even as philosophical consciousness, consciousness 'does not receive itself back from the whole, but only part of itself' (Rose, 1981, p. 158). Its return is negative but comprehensive. The educative purpose of the *Phenomenology* is not to complete all experiences, but to present experiences so that their misrecognition in and as the return of natural consciousness to itself can be re-cognised for what they actually are. It was seen in Part I that return was the necessity and fate of the critique of the person, for the theorist who experienced the negation of the person has that truth available to him only personally, or negatively, or in opposition to himself. The experience for us of return and the consequent illusory appearance of

105

critique as result is the same education which Hegel sets for us in the *Phenomenology*, i.e. that we will come to understand that 'our abstract culture of *Verstand* is also necessary' (1981, p. 159) in any comprehensive education or absolute knowing. That contradiction is the truth of the contradiction of scientific consciousness.

Path of despair: from stoicism to reason

Having (abstractly) described the misrecognition of the experiences of natural consciousness by itself, and the re-cognition of this misrecognition by the observing of philosophical consciousness, it is possible now to examine the development of natural consciousness in the *Phenomenology* along its path of despair, up to its appearance as reason and (the) enlightenment.

Self-consciousness, in the *Phenomenology*, appears at first only immediately as the abstract 'I', lacking the moments of differentiation and return which will later characterise it (as spirit). This 'I' is a shape of natural consciousness, a shape which takes itself to be a thinking consciousness, but which, as yet, is merely an abstract negation and lacking substance. Taken in this its immediate appearance, natural consciousness appears as stoicism, whose principle is 'that consciousness is a being that *thinks*' (Hegel, 1977, p. 121). The life of the stoic consciousness, without determinate negation, is therefore a 'lifeless indifference' (1977, p. 121), 'in which nothing is determined' (1977, p. 122). But all thinking is a thought of something and is therefore determinate thinking. The realisation that the stoical freedom of thought is dependent upon a content is a different appearance of natural consciousness. The new consciousness has arisen as a result of the embarrassment suffered by stoicism, that when it was asked for a criterion of its own truth, it was forced into the realisation that it was not the unity of freedom of thought and the truth or universality of thought. In this experience, stoicism is realised as merely negative and insubstantial. The new natural consciousness which appears is the one which has its own truth as that negative consciousness, or as the consciousness which does not have universality within it. This purely negative self-consciousness appears as scepticism. It exhibits a dialectical movement between what it believes to be its own negative universality and the non-identity of all objects. It holds neither them nor itself to be true, but holds that belief as true. The sceptical consciousness:

> Is therefore the unconscious, thoughtless rambling which passes back and forth from the one extreme of self-identical self-consciousness to the other extreme of the contingent consciousness that is both bewildered and bewildering. It does not itself bring these two thoughts of itself together (1977, p. 125).

But the sceptical consciousness, although denying determinate existence, is still determinate for that (new) consciousness which has the sceptical consciousness as its object. Whereas the sceptical consciousness is never able to realise that its two sides are only one consciousness, this is possible for the consciousness which experiences scepticism as a whole. This new appearance of natural consciousness is an 'unhappy consciousness', unhappy because 'it recognises that this contradiction between the universal and contingent exists within itself' (Rose, 1981, p. 161). It knows itself as consisting of two irreconcilable sides, the negation of its own truth, and the negation of truth in the external world. It is 'the consciousness of self as a dual-natured, merely contradictory being' (Hegel, 1977, p. 126). The unhappy consciousness is the appearance as natural consciousness of the contradiction of scepticism; it lives out that contradiction as itself.

The unhappy consciousness is, in a sense, the return of the 'I' to itself in the experience of itself. But whereas, as we will see shortly, critique posits return as a self-relation, here the unhappy consciousness does not have that knowledge of itself. It knows of itself only as divided, not also as related in and by the division.

> The Unhappy Consciousness *is* the gazing of one self-consciousness into another, and itself *is* both and the unity of both is also its essential nature. But it is not as yet explicitly aware that this is its essential nature, or that it is the unity of both (Hegel, 1977, p. 126).

Therefore, in knowing itself as divided but not self-related, it posits one half of its contradictory self as external to it, calls it the 'Unchangeable', and holds it to be independent. It casts this half of the relation out because it takes itself to be self as contradiction. Its instability means for it that stability is to be found as other than itself. This other is only the misrecognition of natural consciousness's own experience of itself, and therefore although the unchangeable becomes a fixed point in the external world, and although the changeable, contradictory unhappy consciousness believes it is separated from the unchangeable, nevertheless, that separation is still a relation. As yet, however, it is a relation which self-consciousness does not know to be its own. That realisation lies ahead, as 'Reason'. For now, divided natural consciousness knows the changeable single individual on the one hand, and the unchangeable essential being on the other. Or again, it has untruth as itself, and truth as other. This living out a life as untruth is what Hegel calls 'the grave of its life' (1977, p. 132), a life in which the individual is not independent, and has no concrete identity except as a yearning for and a devotion to the unchangeable, for whom it works selflessly, and to whom it offers thanks even for its own nothingness. In Chapter 6 the grave of life reappears as the experience of pure being-for-another, and in the teacher/student relationship outlined in Chapter 7 as the pure dependence of the student. For all three – the unhappy consciousness, the master and the slave, and the teacher and the student – it is in the developed form of this experience that each becomes 'capable of finding individuality in its genuine or universal form' (1977, p. 132).

The positing by the unhappy consciousness of the unchangeable as external to itself puts self-consciousness into a state of 'perpetual agony' (Rose, 1981, p. 162), for the relation of the person and the universal is only a constant reminder to the former that its truth is alien to it. The unchangeable appears through the perspective of the person to be the truth which it can never become. 'The Unchangeable that enters into consciousness is through this very fact at the same time affected by individuality, and is only present with the latter' (Hegel, 1977, p. 127). The fact that the universal and the person are related as alien explains why there is no rest from the perpetual agony of the grave of life. When this universal is Roman property law then, says Rose, consciousness as the negative individual is divorced from 'the definition of legal persons and [retreats] to the solitariness of inwardness and the search for an absent God' (1981, p. 163). When the universal is feudal property relations then law is replaced by force, and gives rise to a dualism not of consciousness and law, but consciousness and mere (barbaric, pure) culture (see Rose, 1981, pp. 164–5) where private interest reigns. The Church stepped into the vacuum of the universal and represented law as 'other' than the real world, a law which it mediated on earth. For Rose, as for Hegel, the imposition of 'non-worldly freedom on a lawless society… becomes a positive reinforcement of the prevalent lack of freedom' (Rose, 1981, p. 167), or merely another reinforcement of the perpetual agony of the grave of the life which the unhappy consciousness leads. This relationship between the shape of natural consciousness and the form of the universal highlights the importance in Hegel, drawn attention to by Rose (1981, p. 49), of how the state and religion are both forms of law or universality which arise out of the same shape of natural consciousness. In the phase of the unhappy consciousness, whether law is worldly or non-worldly, it is still determined in and by natural consciousness's misrecognition of itself.

In the grave of life, however, the unhappy consciousness has already experienced its own truth as negative. This truth is not present to the unhappy consciousness, but only to the new shape of natural consciousness which has experienced the grave of life as itself. This is the next development of self-consciousness on its path to reason, and is where the path of despair becomes re-cognised, for the first time, in its wholly negative and educative significance.

The unhappy consciousness has the universal as something which is unattainable, and something for which it yearns and works. This work is a reinforcement of its own non-identity, of its own absolute lack of substance. As long as it yearns and works, it is always separating itself from the universal. The work of the unhappy consciousness is its separation. The only relief which is at hand for the unhappy consciousness is to surrender this work to someone else so that they take on the burden of this grave of life which the person is living. The person finds just such a worker in the form of the priest. The priest has set himself as the middle-man between the insubstantial people who inhabit a lawless world and the absolute which is the law. In surrendering its personal unhappy relation with the universal to the priest, the individual divests the self even of the negation which its work has produced. Now, however, a new consciousness arises which understands the unhappy consciousness very differently. On the one hand the unhappy consciousness was negative or nothing for (or in relation to) the universal. Now that it is no longer in that relation, it has become nothing or negative in itself, a complete surrender to the relation which was its only determination. But this is implicitly a determinate negation of the new consciousness which has arisen in the experience of this absolute negation. It has before it the negativity of the unhappy consciousness as true not only as negative in relation to the absolute, but negated by its own act of self-surrender. What was nothing, now becomes its own truth by its own hand. What has been produced and what has produced it, this new consciousness, is one and the same negative consciousness. This negative self-activity and negative self-result form an absolute self-relation, requiring no input from elsewhere to realise itself. The new self-consciousness, then, is reason. Reason is the expression of that new shape of consciousness which relies upon none other than itself for its own determination. In its surrender of its relation with an alien universal it returns to itself as the truth of the negative consciousness which it always knew itself to be. What was for the unhappy consciousness a lack of substance, is now understood to be the pure substance of the rational consciousness. This new consciousness is the negation of negative consciousness by itself, an activity in which it becomes independent. For us, the philosophical observer, it has been understood as self-work, and in this sense, therefore, the pathway of despair is realised as the pathway of self-education.

Natural consciousness is now reason, and reason therefore is the truth of natural consciousness, or of the particular individuality which has determined itself.

> In grasping the thought that the *single* individual consciousness is *in itself* Absolute Essence, consciousness has returned into itself... In this movement it has also become aware of its *unity* with this universal, a unity which... is present in consciousness as such as its essence (Hegel, 1977, p. 139).

What was for the unhappy consciousness a merely negative relation is also the experience in which that negativity becomes a positive result, and a new shape of natural consciousness. It is no longer the case that consciousness understands itself in relation to the rest of the world (and the non-worldly). Now consciousness understands all worlds in relation to itself. Reason is independent, it is the universal, and therefore it is in relation to itself that everything else exists. The relation of the world to reason is reason's knowledge of the world. The world exists only as it is known for and by the rational individual. He is sovereign, and the world is now dependent:

> as reason, assured of itself... it is certain that it is itself reality, or that everything actual is none other than itself... Apprehending itself in this

way, it is as if the world had for it only now come into being... Reason is the certainty of consciousness that it is all reality (Hegel, 1977, pp. 139–40).

Terror of certainty

It has been seen how reason develops within the logic of determinate negation. What has now to be explored is its own misrecognition of itself as this activity and result. For us, the philosophical observers, we can see the development of consciousness up to this experience, and we can see that its determination is wholly within the sphere of the negative. But for natural consciousness the result of the negation is itself as an individual and independent self, and is therefore positive. The path of despair and the grave of life in which the experience of reason was made possible as negative self and negative work are no longer visible to this new positive natural consciousness. 'The consciousness which is this truth has this path behind it and has forgotten it' (Hegel, 1977, p. 141). Natural consciousness appears immediately and, as always, takes itself at face value. The relation of self-work and self-result, the determinate negation from which it has arisen, is no longer present to it as the contradictory self-relation of the unhappy consciousness. The determinate aspect is visible, but the negation (the work of the contradiction) has vanished. We know its truth to be the broken middle of the relation, but reason does not have both of its moments, separation and relation, present to it as itself. The relation will only appear in the experience of reason as further contradiction, an experience which takes shape in many ways. In Part I it has appeared in and as the repetition of the critique of the person and the teacher. In the next chapter it will appear as the dialectic of enlightenment. In Part III this experience of itself is examined as the educational logic of self-relation. For now, prior to such appearances, reason has no doubts about its own identity and universality, for there is nothing which it cannot know, and nothing therefore which is not within the universality of reason.

However, because natural consciousness is not yet experienced or educated, its certainty is only an immediate appearance. 'Thus it merely *asserts* that it is all reality, but does not itself comprehend this' (Hegel 1977, p. 141). This assertion has three implications, which will be mentioned briefly.

The first is that this abstract sovereign consciousness, the rational subject, enjoys a relation of domination over the world similar to that which persons enjoy over their own property. Reason owns the world because rational knowledge of the world is the will of the rational subject cast over that world as its own object. In this sense knowledge and property are the same victory of will over that which is only a thing. The world falls into the domain of the rational subject, and is owned by its being known, or as being merely for it. The world becomes the property of rational consciousness, whereby the latter exercises its will over the former in the form of knowledge. The contradictions which are implicit in the property relation

110

(see Chapter 6) are the same as those implicit in this knowledge relation (see Chapter 7). Part I has already drawn attention to the way in which this contradiction is active in the critique of the person. The aporia for any critique of bourgeois property relations, and of the person, is that any universality which it claims for itself is already knowledge of the world, and is therefore for it, or is its own property.

The second implication of a merely abstract reason which can only assert its universality is that it becomes a provider of laws, but of laws which reflect its own merely formal certainty. Its justification of its laws becomes a tautological justification of the rational subject. If laws reflect the truth of the person, then they are deemed rational and legitimate. But this too results in contradiction, for the universal and the particular, laws and the rational subject, are in opposition. On the one hand, the universality of law requires that it be known. But knowledge reveals the law as merely for consciousness, and therefore as the 'property' of the particular. The law thus 'contradicts itself by the content being contingent' (Hegel, 1977, p. 254), and can only therefore assert its universality in the form of a commandment. Such an abstract reason cannot provide laws, for its universality is only abstract and has its own justification, the rational subject, in opposition to it.

On the other hand, all that is left to abstract reason, since it cannot justify laws, is to test them to check for their formal universality, or, which is the same thing, that they are not self-contradictory. 'Reason as the giver of laws is reduced to a Reason which merely *critically examines* them' (1977, p. 256). The problem here is that formal universality is not substantial universality, and provided that a law is 'rational', that is, not particular but universal, it does not matter what the content of the law is. Thus 'this testing does not get very far. Just because the criterion is a tautology, and indifferent to the content, one content is just as acceptable to it as its opposite' (1977, p. 257). The nearest abstract reason comes to examining itself critically is in psychology and phrenology, but this too is only a tautological enquiry (see Hegel, 1977, pp. 180–210).

Thirdly, this reason, which is at liberty to choose the content of law arbitrarily, is also at liberty to define that over which it will enjoy domination, even if that means over other rational subjects. Abstract reason employed in the world in this way enjoys its own absolute freedom not only over the world but also over all those 'subjects' who, it deems, are not sufficiently rational for their particular wills to be counted as falling within the absolutely rational will. An example of such absolute freedom, given by Hegel in the *Phenomenology*, is the terror which was practised during the French Revolution. There, says Hegel, 'the world is for it simply its own will, and this is a general will' (1977, pp. 356–7). Reason, as this universal domination, therefore asserts itself as universal truth not just over those subjects whose will it believes itself to be, but as 'the fury of destruction' (Hegel, 1977, p. 359) of all individuals whose purpose is not the general purpose, whose language is not its universal law and whose work is not its universal work (paraphrased from Hegel, 1977, p. 357).

111

What each of these abstract certainties of reason succeeds in producing is the experience of contradiction. Knowledge which enjoys the world as its own property becomes merely personal knowledge, or personal property, and the world which appeared immediately as at one with the rational consciousness is now divided from it. Laws which appeared as the universal expression of the rational subject became just such another knowledge, and are separated from that whose immanent truth they claim to be. Finally, abstract freedom given absolute freedom is purely arbitrary, and each of its determinations, each shape it takes in the world, becomes a domination of itself as a particular will masquerading as a general will. Each form of abstract reason becomes experienced in natural consciousness as self-contradictory. Each certainty which reason asserts generates uncertainty and doubt for the consciousness, which experiences itself only as the loss of its certainty. This experience, by reason of its own contradiction, is also a determinate negation. Whereas reason forgot the path of its own education, this time philosophical consciousness has the path of its own determination present within it. That is why philosophical consciousness is able to comprehend the contradiction of reason as both the truth of itself and the becoming of itself. Philosophical consciousness is the same as reason, in that it is a self-determination. What is produced and by whom are one and the same. The negation of abstract rational certainty, realised in the experience of contradiction, is a negation brought about in and by that experience. Since what is experienced is the same as the consciousness which has the experience, then the result is one consciousness, or what Hegel calls scientific or philosophical consciousness. The self-activity and self-result of philosophical consciousness are presented in Hegel's *Science of Logic*.

However, what Hegel calls the actuality of this one consciousness, although known in and as philosophical consciousness, is still determined in and through its appearance as natural consciousness. The relation of the one consciousness to the other vanishes even in the knowing of this relation, and becomes abstract once again. Philosophical consciousness appears as natural consciousness, and is known only as another immediate appearance, or as, for example, the person, the teacher, or the philosopher. The experience, the contradiction, the education, is present only in the knowledge that what appears as natural consciousness is in fact actual; that is, is already a result and activity of determinate negation, or of the broken middle. What is actual is already a return from the experience to the one-sided appearance of that experience as result, or non-relation. A discussion of actuality appears in the next chapter.

That it is actual is present only in and for the philosophical consciousness which comprehends the whole of the experience. It is in keeping, therefore, with the self-contradictory nature of what is actual, that something known as actual is something known as already negated, and that in that negation the something reappears immediately as natural consciousness. What is actual has the path of its own development present to it in its own separation from it. Natural consciousness known as a determinate negation by philosophical consciousness is actual. Philosophical consciousness, in knowing what is actual, has already fallen into its separated moments of relation and non-relation, confirming its truth as the broken middle of the relation. This circle is now examined in relation to the contradiction of self-reflective critique which was described in Chapter 2. In this way an answer to the question 'what is enlightenment?' begins to appear in the experience of what enlightenment is *not*.

Critique of critique

Critique is held by those who practise and teach it to contain two moments which, together, constitute the whole of enlightenment. Such a view of critique is exemplified by the teachers and theorists examined in Part I. For them, critique as enlightenment brings about, on the one hand, the negation of the independent identity of the civil/bourgeois/individual person, and on the other hand, the realisation of this 'negative non-identity' as critical or reflective consciousness. The negated identity is now for another and this other which it is for, and upon which it is dependent for being known, is its own self-reflective, critical consciousness. The real significance of the relation between the non-person and the critical consciousness is that each is the truth of the other. The negative activity of reflection has the non-person before it as the negative result of reflection. Equally the non-person, the negative identity, understands reflection to be the work in which it is determined. Since the reflecting consciousness and the negated natural consciousness are the same consciousness, their relation is a self-relation. Each appears as the truth of itself, or as its own essence. It is this self-relation which allows critique to claim to be self-transformative (*praxis*).

This self-relation is interpreted in critique as an enlightenment about the self brought about by the self. Essence is taken to be (the result of) critical reflection, for in critical reflection the truth of the person (as negative) is realised. The activity and result of critique are therefore one and the same, negation and negative identity. Critique claims itself as the activity and the result in which each of us realises our true nature, and become self-enlightened.

This notion of enlightenment as reflective self-relation can be illustrated concretely in each of the three practitioners examined in Chapter 2. For Rousseau, consciousness appears in the form of the civil person, an individual who is living a false life based on false needs. In Rousseau's critical reflection, the independence of the person is seen to be a false independence determined by the existence of private property. The civil person is therefore negated in this reflection. For Rousseau this non-civil individual is now a new object, one whose new identity is based in, and is dependent upon, its (natural/rational) relationship with itself. Its illusory social independence is replaced by a genuine (rational) understanding of its (natural) self. This new object is the negation of the old object, a negation achieved when the old object becomes an object of critical reflection. In such reflection the old civil person is negated, and the truth of each

113

individual becomes clear. Since Rousseau takes reflective consciousness to be a natural (i.e. a non-civil) rational (self-) consciousness, then the self-relation required for enlightenment, that what is known is the same as that by which it is known, is present. Assured of the essence of each individual, Rousseau is now justified in educating his pupils in line with this truth. By leaving nature to take its course in the early years, the civil person will be avoided. Therefore, when in more mature years reflective consciousness thinks about itself, it will have its true self already as its object. This self-relation, or enlightened individual, is then the basis of why the general will is rational, because it will be grounded in our essence, our true self, and not merely our false appearance.

In Marx's critical reflection, the person is also the form and appearance which consciousness immediately takes itself to be. This appearance, however, is seen through when the person becomes an object in reflection. There its independence is understood to be merely an illusion produced by private property relations. It now becomes clear in this reflection that a person is in fact one who is dependent upon and constructed within particular economic and historical conditions. The new understanding produced, therefore, is of a non-independent individual, or the non-person, i.e. a member of the class which is also the species. Equally, this non-person, or dependent self, has its truth in and as the reflection in which it has appeared. Not only are such individuals determined within history and social relations, they also know that they are so determined, a knowledge arrived at through the critical reflection in which the independent workers have appeared to themselves. Since the reflective consciousness and the non-person are the same consciousness, then this untruth is revealed to be its essence as the non-person. This self-relation is again what is required for enlightenment. In critical (revolutionary) consciousness workers can be said to have become enlightened about their true selves as species being. Convinced of such self-enlightenment, not only can essence now be stated, it can be worked for through a programme of enlightenment where, through the self-transformative activity of critique and revolutionary activity in the world, workers will come to know themselves as they truly are.

Durkheim's sociology is not often described as a form of critique. Nevertheless the educational aspects of Durkheim's theorising share the same features of reflection, negation and enlightenment that characterise the work of Rousseau, Marx and other more familiar critical thinkers. For Durkheim, reflection upon the individual reveals its identity to be one which is constructed within and by the social whole. In (sociological) reflection, then, the identity of the individual is negated, and a new object appears, one who is now known to be dependent upon the social, and lacking altogether an identity of its own. However, since the untruth of the individual has appeared in reflection, and since the reflecting consciousness is the same consciousness that is being negated, then its untruth has also appeared negatively to itself through its own negative or critical (or sociological) activity. The self-relation required for self-determination is present here, and the reflecting consciousness therefore achieves enlightenment about itself and its true essence. Durkheim's sociology is built around the idea that sociology is just such a reflective enlightenment about our true (social or negative) essence, and his educational programme, like Rousseau's, is designed to ensure that the object which the mature consciousness comes to reflect upon is already the true social being, and not an abnormal individual misrecognition of its true social nature.

There is, however, a problem with all such forms of critique. The self-relation which they presuppose to be immanent, and therefore to be self-enlightenment, falls into an empty tautology. To understand why this is so, it is necessary to examine the illusions which reflection itself is able to manufacture, and how critique, taken as enlightenment, is a repetition of just such illusions. These illusions are brought out in Hegel's section on essence in his *Science of Logic*.

The two sides of reflection, as seen at the beginning of this section, are the appearance of natural consciousness and the reflecting consciousness for which this abstract person appears. In fact, since they are the same consciousness, then the one consciousness is really appearing to itself as a divided self (only this time it is insufficiently unhappy to be able to enjoy its return to self!). It is divided between itself as object, and itself as that for which the object appears, or by which the object is known. The unification of this divided self is what the presupposition of critical reflection as enlightenment is based upon. In fact, however, such a self-relation or enlightenment is only an empty and illusory result, for essence is not only the relation of consciousness and object, it is also their separation, or non-relation. The presupposition of critique as enlightenment does not take this latter fact into account.

The problem for reflection lies in how it becomes determinate, that is, how it comes to know itself. At first, critical reflection achieves only a negation, or no result at all. In the negation of natural consciousness – or, in the *Science of Logic*, the negation of (determinate) being – the reflective consciousness does not know itself. It exists only in so far as it has a negative object before it, and it is, therefore, in and of itself, nothing at all. The relation here, then, which critique takes to be essence or self-enlightenment, is between a negative object and a negative consciousness. The reflecting consciousness has no substance. To the extent that it can be said to 'exist', it exists purely as the result of the disappearance of determinate being. It is the result of a negation, and exists in a relation of dependence to that negation. It is related to nothing, and has nothing as its own determination. Reflection, here, is what Hegel calls 'illusory being'. In relation to enlightenment, illusory being will be interpreted in the next chapter as a *shining for others*, a phrase which tries to capture the sheer nothingness of the reflecting consciousness. For Hegel, illusory being is a reflection which merely '*shines*, or *shows within itself*' (1969, p. 391). It is not a relation, for there is not a relation between nothing and nothing, there is only an empty showing of itself, a mere shining, present only by its absence, but an absence that is indeterminate. Nothing is doing the reflecting, for there is nothing to reflect upon and nothing from which to return. In this its immediate appearance, then, reflection is wholly

115

insubstantial and indeterminate. 'Illusory being is *not*' (Hegel, 1969, p. 395), or, as will be seen later, is merely a shining for others, but not (yet) a shining which is for itself or, therefore, determinate.

The reasons why this idea of illusory being is so difficult but so important are twofold. Firstly, we are, in the sphere of essence, working with the negative and seeing how it comes to determine itself. Whereas determination with regard to natural consciousness or to being is to know it as a something, in the realm of the negative to be determinative is to know something as nothing, and to have negation as a constituent part of that knowing. This contradiction is the substance of the negative, and will reveal itself in Chapter 5 to be the whole of enlightenment. Secondly, in examining reflection it looks as if we, and Hegel, are making a beginning with illusory being. But illusory being, as with all immediate appearances, cannot be a beginning. Everything immediate is always already mediated, for in the mediation it is determinate, substantial and, which is the same, it is known. Illusory being, then, is already known, and its presentation here as the nothingness of reflection is purely abstract. What knows it is still to be explored (and is so in the final section of Chapter 5). Neither of these factors is grasped by critical consciousness. They appear together only in the notion, or in philosophical consciousness which is in and for itself.

Illusory being does have a determination, but it is only, as yet, implicit and not explicit or for itself. In other words, illusory being is reflection, but it is the showing of reflection which does not yet know itself. What shines as illusory being is not the universality of reflection as self-relation, i.e. of the relation between object and consciousness. This universal is present only as an illusion, and here the illusion is that the reflecting consciousness is something.

Reflection 'proper', as it is found in critique, therefore occurs in relation to illusory being or an illusory show or appearance of itself as immediately something. This amounts to the abstract understanding of reflection as self-relation, as return to and from itself. It is abstract because the return is only from illusory being and is therefore insubstantial. The determination of reflection is empty. What is believed to be achieved is in fact only presupposed. The real achievement, determinate negation, is therefore avoided. Reflection is determinate only in its return to itself from illusory being. Consequently 'its reflective movement, is the *movement of nothing to nothing and so back to itself*' (Hegel, 1969, p. 400). Hegel notes that this 'pure absolute reflection that is the movement from nothing to nothing determines itself further' (1969, p. 400), but this is not a development which critical reflection makes. For philosophical consciousness, it is the presupposition of reflection as self-relation which provides the determinate negation in which its education continues. In this way, philosophical consciousness does achieve itself as something from nothing, but something which is contradictory, and will not satisfy a merely testing abstract reason. This next development, of reason as return and of return as the actuality of the broken middle of reflection, is examined further in the next chapter.

Determinate negation, then, is known as self-relation only to the philosophical consciousness which realises the broken middle of determinate negation to be its own contradictory self-determination. This education is not achieved in reflection as essence, it is achieved in the contradiction of essence as this return to itself as the notion. But, for the critical theorists we have examined, this self-relation is believed to have been achieved as essence. This belief or enlightenment is grounded in another important aspect of the determination of essence, that of 'positing', or presupposition.

Critical reflection holds itself to be a self-relation of return, where what is thought and what does the thinking are one and the same. This relation, and therefore the movement of return, is understood as self-enlightenment. The self-relation of return and the enlightenment which critique produces are one and the same thing. However, this self-relation is purely immediate. The return of nothing to nothing does not achieve its determination as a something, because the two moments within it are not self-differentiated. It does achieve determination as another relation, but that is of no interest now to the presupposing critical consciousness. The relation of reflection is therefore not earned through self-work, through self-contradiction; it is posited or presupposed in the absence of that work. The universal self-relation, posited as immediate self-relation, is only the abstraction of the relation from the work which is return. The return which is posited as self-relation is undifferentiated and therefore not really return at all; it is the presupposition of return as essence. Positing avoids the work whose truth it intends to express. The truth of critique as enlightenment is merely the relation of reflection into itself, a mere shining. It is 'essentially the presupposing of that from which it is the return' (Hegel, 1969, p. 401).

It was seen earlier how reason, when it tried to legitimate itself as a universal expression of rational individual consciousness, fell into contradiction, and that the most it could achieve was to test laws for self-contradiction. The case is the same with regard to enlightenment. When reason examines itself in reflection it, too, falls into contradiction. This contradiction of particular and universal, or of determinate being and essence, cannot be stated by abstract reason, and the contradiction is denied a universal expression in and as natural consciousness. Therefore, reason retreats from the difficulty of its own education with regard to the negative, and posits its own identity in the only terms left open to it; that is, in regard to testing itself for non-contradiction. Enlightenment is posited as a self-relation in which the contradiction of the non-person and reflective consciousness is overcome, and overcome here means, precisely, tested for and found not to be self-contradictory. Enlightenment is therefore abstracted from the return of reflection, and is posited as the truth of return. Return, posited or fixed as abstract, is not self-determinate. But since further self-determination is only further (and unnecessary) contradiction and negation, reason takes this non-contradictory enlightenment about itself as a victory of self-determination, self-relation, and self-education.

Positing, therefore, provides only a Pyrrhic victory. It gains for reason the peace and contentment of a non-contradictory self-relation and essence for itself. But the cost is that it is denied access to its own further and higher self-education. The implications of this victory, however, do not just concern the determination of the notion in the *Science of Logic*. This victory is also the shape and form of the certainty of reason that its critical reflective activity is enlightenment, a certainty that underpins both the activity and the result of critical enquiries. The result, as has been seen, is always tautological. But so is the activity. The presupposition of critique as enlightenment allows reason the illusion that it has critique as a method and an instrument which can be applied to all objects in order that rational consciousness may gain enlightenment about them. Employed as this method, critique provides us with enlightenment about ourselves, about nature, about history, about society and about social relations. Even though it is claimed that the enlightenment is immanent, our philosophical consciousness knows that the actual result of critique is contradiction, and the return not of philosophical consciousness to itself, but only of natural consciousness to itself. The positing of the latter return as enlightenment is the avoidance of the risk of learning from the former return. The use of critique as a method simply repeats the presupposition of reflection as self-relation. In both cases it is to know in advance that which is in fact the object of the enquiry, and to use this knowledge then to discover itself as the truth. This empty relation can only ever repeat critique and essence as tautological. Critique as method is always the presupposition of what is to be known before it is known. Hegel's comment in the beginning of the shorter *Logic* with regard to Kant applies both to the presupposition of critique as enlightenment, and of enlightenment as immanent in the critical method, for both are the same presupposition.

> We ought, says Kant, to become acquainted with the instrument before we undertake the work for which it is to be employed... But the examination of knowledge can only be carried out by an act of knowledge. To examine this so-called instrument is the same thing as to know it. But to seek to know before we know is as absurd as the wise resolution of Scholasticus, not to venture into the water until he had learned to swim (1975, p. 14).

The victory of enlightenment as critical reflection is no victory at all, for the positing of enlightenment is only the presupposition of reason's self-relation by and for an abstract consciousness which posits itself as just such a self-relation. The tautology seen before when reason tried to provide laws is repeated here. Reason's answer to the question 'what is enlightenment?' is always a tautology. To know what enlightenment is, is to be enlightened, and to be enlightened is to know what enlightenment is. Or, enlightenment is reason's own self-determinative relation, or reason's own learning about itself is enlightenment. All of these answers are circular, and rest upon a presupposition of reflection as a self-relation, but one which is not substantial, not self-differentiating, and therefore not a comprehensive education. The experience of this tautology, of enlightenment as a self-defeating circle, is examined in the next chapter as it is expressed in the dialectic of enlightenment.

5 Dialectic of enlightenment

Answers to the question 'what is enlightenment?' mostly take the form of
certainties which are themselves little more than assertions and presuppositions.
When such answers are put to the test, the only criterion that reason accepts as a
fair test is that reason be tested to see if it is rational. This empty tautology reveals
the lack of substance that underpins enlightenment, and leaves reason as a
universality unable to produce any self-justification other than its own certainty.
This inability to raise itself above its merely circular self-assertions is not the
result that enlightenment claims. Our experience of reason and enlightenment is
not one of certainty at all. We experience its claims negatively, for we know that
reason, each time it tests universality as non-contradiction, succeeds only in
manufacturing another contradiction. It can test the rational identity of everything
else, but it can do no more that assert its own. It undermines the claims to
universality of everything except itself by having ownership of everything else in
the knowledge of it. Everything is *for* reason, and therefore reason is the universal
of all things. But reason, at the same time, undermines its own claims to
universality because, in its self-justification, it generates the contradiction that it,
too, requires to be known. Reason knowing itself, or enlightenment, does not
provide universality, it only repeats enlightenment as something which is itself
contradictory. Success in becoming enlightened is at the same time also the failure
to become enlightened. The return of reason to itself is posited as enlightenment.
But that return is also of natural consciousness from 'itself' as philosophical
consciousness.

Therefore the positing of enlightenment and our experience of enlightenment
are (at this point) two different things. We experience enlightenment as a circle in
which every justification is also a negation. There appears to be no way out of this
circle, for it appears total. How consciousness responds to this circle depends upon
the kind of presupposition it brings with it. If consciousness presupposes the circle
to be a positive result, then this is another positing of enlightenment as critical
reflection, overlooking the negation of this enlightenment. Such a positing is to be

found in the work of Habermas. If, on the other hand, this circle is posited to be the lack of a positive result, and eternally negative, then this is a positing of negation and contradiction as non-identity or as the impossibility of enlightenment as a substantial result, which is again only a rational presupposition and testing. Such a positing characterises the negative dialectics of Adorno. Overall, this experience of the circle of enlightenment is examined in social and political thought as the dialectic of enlightenment. This chapter now examines the one-sided interpretations of this circle, and argues that it is from the experience of contradiction, and not its presupposition as positive or negative, that the education of our philosophical consciousness is determinative, and is known as what is actual.

Myth and enlightenment

The circle of certainty and uncertainty receives an explicit treatment in *Dialectic of Enlightenment* by Adorno and Horkheimer. 'Enlightenment', they announced 'is totalitarian' (1979, p. 6). Its rationale, in line with its own certainty, is to extinguish all forms of thought, all explanations and all accounts of the world which are not its own. Anything which is not the result of (critical) rational enquiry, and which does not conform to the logic of non-contradiction, is merely myth and can be discarded as the irrational musings of unenlightened subjectivity. Non-contradictory identities are exemplified by number, for what can be quantified can be calculated, and what can be calculated is deemed by reason to be truly known and understood. 'To the enlightenment, that which does not reduce to numbers, and ultimately to the one, becomes illusion; modern positivism writes it off as literature' (1979, p. 7). Reason dominates, therefore, by explaining everything in its own image. The more opposition it encounters, the stronger it becomes. The greater the number of mythical interpretations it can explain (away), the more dominating and all-embracing as a universality it proves itself to be. Indeed, the more content there is for it to explain, the stronger it becomes.

> Every spiritual resistance it [enlightenment)] encounters serves merely to increase its strength… Whatever myths the resistance may appeal to, by virtue of the very fact that they become arguments in the process of opposition, they acknowledge the principle of dissolvent rationality for which they reproach the Enlightenment (1979, p. 6).

However, this totalitarianism is seen by Adorno and Horkheimer as unable to secure its own certainty. This inability forms part of its totalitarian regime. It cannot absolutely justify itself, but that inability is itself a result of its success in overcoming all other forms of thinking. Thus reason performs a circle in which its success and its defeat, its certainty and its uncertainty, are continually reproduced, each overcoming the other. The circle is closed, but its constituent parts are in

122

continual opposition. This is the dialectic of enlightenment, and it is where, as Adorno and Horkheimer express it, 'myth is already enlightenment: and enlightenment reverts to mythology' (1979, p. xvi).

The first half of this formulation, that myth is already enlightenment, is a Nietzschean form of genealogy, uncovering the origins of knowledge as lying in power and domination. Adorno and Horkheimer argue that, for the primitive, terror of the unknown was terror of that which could not be dominated, or that over which the will could not be exerted. Typically, the sacred and the supernatural were beyond such human control. The inability to explain is the inability to possess as knowledge, and such an inability is, for Adorno and Horkheimer, the origin of human fear. Fear is 'the echo of the real supremacy of nature in the weak souls of primitive men' (1979, p. 15). Language is the medium through which this terror controls itself, and through which the unknown is known, overcome or possessed, by its being named. 'Language is required to resign itself to calculation in order to know nature' (1979, p. 18) because a name is a fixed identity and conforms to the domination of reason as non-contradiction. The controller of this language contains the power of the name, a power which has control thereafter over the object. Such controllers are 'priests and sorcerers' who soon learn to expand 'their professional knowledge and their influence' (1979, p. 20). Even the gifts offered in fear of the unknown during rituals are not the lack of power which they appear to be. The overcoming of myth by enlightenment is present even here in its most primitive outpost, because the gift is nothing less than a rational calculation of the amount of gift which this unknown merits. The gift is already a calculation of the unknown.

> If barter is the secular form of sacrifice, the latter already appears as the magical pattern of rational exchange, a device of men by which the gods may be mastered: the gods are overthrown by the very system by which they are honoured (1979, p. 49).

In this half of the formulation of the dialectic of enlightenment, then, sacrifice is control, the unknown is an identity, and myth, therefore, is already enlightenment. The progress towards modern societies can, argue Adorno and Horkheimer, be seen as based upon this formula. 'Man imagines himself free from fear when there is no longer anything unknown' (1979, p. 16). Therefore everything has to be explained, because 'the mere idea of outsideness is the very source of fear' (1979, p. 16). Thus Adorno and Horkheimer conclude that 'Enlightenment behaves towards things as a dictator towards men. He knows them in so far as he can manipulate them' (1979, p. 9). This process of demythologisation reaches its zenith in bourgeois society, which is 'ruled by equivalence' (1979, p. 7) and where the commodification of everything ensures that everything is known, controlled and calculated.

The second half of the formulation of the dialectic of enlightenment states that enlightenment reverts to mythology. It is in this movement that the dialectic of enlightenment is revealed to be eternally circular and self-defeating. 'The principle of immanence... that the Enlightenment upholds against mythic imagination, is the principle of myth itself' (1979, p. 12). Enlightenment is unable to provide a justification of its own universality which can resist the repetition of its becoming something known and therefore also something overcome. The power of reason over everything else is its knowledge of it. It cannot avoid the implication that even its own thought must inevitably become an object for it, separated from itself, and thus another source of terror requiring to be explained. This is reason's own self-contradiction. The instrument which provides it with control over everything else – knowledge – is also the instrument which denies it an unquestioned universality, and repeats it as something which also requires to be explained. It can explain everything, but when it also explains itself, and names itself as enlightenment, then it has simply repeated itself again as a universal myth which requires to be comprehended. Enlightenment always has itself as another question, because its immanent principle is repetition and contradiction. This point was realised in the opening two chapters by the despairing teacher as being precisely the self-defeating dialectic in which enlightenment traps itself. Enlightenment cannot hold out against the all-encompassing logic of non-contradiction which is its own rational instrument. The totality of myth which enlightenment undermines becomes the myth of the totality of enlightenment. It is this repetition which ensures the circular nature of the dialectic of enlightenment, and which is our experience of the enlightenment as a self-contradiction. It is in the dialectic of enlightenment that, as Hegel says, 'reason remains a restless searching and in its very searching declares the satisfaction of *finding* is a sheer impossibility' (1977, p. 145).

The negativity which is therefore implicit in rational critique is a result of the fact that enlightenment cannot move beyond itself as mere repetition. Every assertion of its universality which tries to break out of the dialectic of enlightenment is only another repetition wherein the assertion becomes a myth which now requires to be overcome. The dialectic of enlightenment has not itself been particularly popular as a form of critique, precisely because it seems to get us nowhere, leaving the theorists with only the negative implications of its repetition. Adorno and Horkheimer sum up the lack of potential when they state that:

> It is characteristic of the sickness that even the best-intentioned reformer who uses an impoverished and debased language to recommend renewal, by his adoption of the insidious mode of categorisation of the bad philosophy it conceals, strengthens the very power of the established order he is trying to break (1979, p. xiv).

Nevertheless, Adorno and Horkheimer are not resigned to total failure and a completely negative outcome, nor do they abandon the critical project. They hold out the hope that at the very least, dialectical and negative thinking will enable the more overtly totalitarian and positivistic representations of enlightenment to be subjected to criticism, and thereby lose the power they currently enjoy. The dilemma is summed up by them in the following way: 'There is no longer any available form of linguistic expression which has not tended toward accommodation to dominant currents of thought' (1979, p. xii). Nevertheless, they say, 'We are wholly convinced... that social freedom is inseparable from enlightened thought' (1979, p. xiii). Critique is necessary, because 'if enlightenment does not accommodate reflection on [its] recidivist element... If consideration of the destructive aspect of progress is left to its enemies, [then)] blindly pragmatised thought loses its transcending quality and its relation to truth' (1979, p. xiii).

Adorno and Horkheimer share a belief and a faith in critique that, although its results may be negative, this negative is educational. Enlightenment, they argue, is only a 'half-education' which 'hypostatises limited knowledge as the truth' (1979, p. 196). The result of this half-education is that 'the dutiful child of modern civilisation' (1979, p. xiv) is offered as truth knowledge which calculates and controls, and becomes 'possessed by a fear of departing from the facts' (1979, p. xiv). They add that because this half-education of enlightenment 'declares any negative treatment of the facts or of the dominant forms of thought to be... alien, and therefore taboo, it condemns the spirit to increasing darkness' (1979, p. xiv). It is precisely to lift this darkness that Adorno and Horkheimer offer their analysis of the dialectic of enlightenment. It is intended, they say, 'to prepare the way for a positive notion of enlightenment which will release it from entanglement in blind domination' (1979, p. xvi). The point, they stress, is that even if the results are negative, 'the Enlightenment *must examine itself*' (1979, p. xv).

Adorno's examination is returned to later. The most recent attempt to escape from the negativity of the dialectic of enlightenment can be found in the work of Jurgen Habermas, and in particular in his theory of 'communicative action'. The two halves of the dialectic of enlightenment, (positive) enlightenment and (negative) dialectic, are now examined separately with a view to revealing its truth as the self-relation of the broken middle. It is argued that Habermas and Adorno between them offer the whole of the relation of the dialectic of enlightenment, a whole which appears in the relation of each of them to Hegel and to philosophical consciousness. In the previous chapter the education of reflective consciousness was seen to be indeterminate. The education of that consciousness becomes determinate, now, in the experience of contradiction. It marks the return of philosophical consciousness to itself, or, put another way, the shining of illusory being for others now also becomes its own shining in and for itself. This is a return which does not resolve the contradiction of the broken middle, but knows it to be what is actual.

Habermas: enlightenment without dialectic

Habermas has clearly stated that the purpose which lies behind his work, and particularly his theory of communicative action, is to move beyond the merely negative implications found in the dialectic of enlightenment to a positive outcome on which rational values and actions can be based. For Habermas, the dialectic of enlightenment represents the crisis which is modernity. The Enlightenment brought forward a rational subject which no longer required the past in the form of traditions, dogmas or faiths. The rational subject, says Habermas, gained for itself 'an unexampled power to bring about the formation of subjective freedom and reflection and to undermine religion, which heretofore had appeared as an absolutely unifying force' (1987b, p. 20). But reason does not fully replace religion as an absolutely unifying force. Subjective reasoning as an activity has truth, knowledge and enlightenment as its objectives. This (subjective) activity is therefore separated from the (objective) results which it hopes to achieve, and the power of an immanently unifying force is lost. In the ensuing philosophical discourse of modernity, as Habermas calls it,

> The question arises as to whether the principle of subjectivity and the structure of self-consciousness residing in it suffice as the source of normative orientations – whether they suffice not only for 'providing foundations' for science, morality and art in general but also for stabilising a historical formation that has been let loose from all historical obligations (1987b, p. 20).

Habermas credits Hegel and Adorno for revealing that the principle of subjectivity does not suffice in overcoming the separation of rational activity (subject) from enlightened result (substance). Their contribution, says Habermas, is to show that subjective reasoning in fact only produces and repeats a negative dialectic, one which cannot act as the positive unifying force of subject and substance. Hegel, says Habermas, showed in his negative and circular phenomenology that reflection is always already dependent upon an object which is prior to it, and therefore can only and always repeat their separation. Hegel shows convincingly, says Habermas, that 'critique of knowledge is condemned to being after the fact' (1987a, p. 8). This, he argues, is a rupture and a repetition 'which the Enlightenment cannot overcome by its own power' (1987b, p. 20). The problem is that:

> Modernity's form of knowledge is characterised by the aporia that the cognitive subject, having become self-referential, rises from the ruins of metaphysics to pledge itself, in full awareness of its finite powers, to a project that would demand infinite power (1989, p. 177).

126

Habermas praises Adorno in particular as being the only philosopher 'to develop remorselessly and spell out the paradoxes of... the dialectic of enlightenment that unfolds the whole as the untrue' (Dews, 1992, p. 99). But, Habermas adds, this insight into the fallibility of subjective knowledge 'should be trivial by now' (Dews, 1992, p. 199). His own view is that we have to learn from the dialectic of enlightenment the negativity which Hegel first expressed some 200 years ago, and move on. His own work has therefore been based upon the conviction that 'one cannot live with the paradoxes of a self-negating philosophy' (Dews, 1992, p. 99). To this end he has attempted 'to explicate a concept of communicative reason that can stand out against Adorno's negativism' (Dews, 1992, p. 108), in order to arrive at 'forms of living together in which autonomy and dependency can truly enter into a non-antagonistic relation, that one can walk tall in a collectivity that does not have the dubious quality of backward-looking substantial forms of community' (Dews, 1992, p. 125).

It is Habermas's argument that Hegel, and Adorno after him, produced only an incomplete and one-sided understanding of the dialectic of enlightenment because they presupposed the paradigm of the reflecting subject as absolute. The development of this argument is worth considering briefly, because it reveals how the presupposition by Habermas of critique as enlightenment, and enlightenment as self-relation, enables him to argue that the paradigm of subjective consciousness is overcome in the realisation of the intersubjective lifeworld.

Habermas's own critique of Marx, in *Knowledge and Human Interests*, is based on the idea that Marx was not reflective enough. Whereas Marx concentrated his critique and synthesis of class antagonisms solely in the process of social labour, Habermas argues that it 'conceals the dimension of self-reflection' (1987a, p. 50) in which its activity is to be found. The dialectic of class antagonism, he states, 'is a movement of reflection' (1987a, p. 58), and is a dimension which requires to be added to that of production. He concludes,

> If the idea of the self-constitution of the human species in natural history is to *combine both self-generation through productive activity* and *self-formation through critical revolutionary activity*, then the concept of synthesis must also incorporate a second dimension (1987a, p. 55).

This second dimension is reflective critique.

Habermas then bases his early work on the three knowledge-constitutive interests: the technical which aims at control over objects; the practical, which understands the contingency of knowledge and therefore has practical implications; and the emancipatory, which sees through the ideological appearance of universals like history and society, and therefore frees the reflecting subject from such distortions. Critique is based in this last interest. It is more than mere reflection, it is *praxis*, in which reflection is also transformative, a self-activity which at the same time produces a new (self-) result. It is therefore in the emancipatory knowledge-constitutive interest that Habermas locates critique as the self-relation which is (posited as) enlightenment. It is in this interest, argues Habermas, that result and activity are united, or, as he puts it, 'knowledge and interest are one' (1966, p. 297), and it is itself the production of 'a new stage of self-reflection in the self-formative process of the species' (1987a, p. 213).

Habermas finds this new stage of self-reflection, and the activity by which the emancipatory interest is realised, in language. Critique, he argues, is itself only made possible by and in the consensus of linguistic rules which must presuppose all learning activity. 'In every speech act the *telos* of reaching an understanding is already inherent' (1988, p. 17). Therefore, behind the activity of reaching an understanding there lies the conditions of the possibility of that activity: 'functioning language games, in which speech acts are exchanged, are based on an underlying consensus' (1988, pp. 17–18), and this consensus is realised (known and made real) each time agreement is sought by participants in speech acts. This consensus is the framework within which the search for agreement becomes possible. Thus Habermas describes discourse as 'the condition of the unconditioned' (1988, p. 19), an insight which he then develops into the theory of communicative action and the lifeworld. Communicative action is performed by subjectivities, but at the same time participants will realise that their subjective activity itself depends upon an unconditioned framework of language. What is realised is the same as that which is doing the realising. Put another way, the subject who enters into dialogue has left his independence behind, and left behind also the paradigm of subjective consciousness. He has entered an intersubjective situation. The subject is 'lost' to the intersubjectivity of discourse, and, at the same time, the (non-) subject realises that intersubjectivity is the truth of that loss, or what makes the loss, and the new existence, possible in the first place. This return is of the non-subject to itself as intersubjectivity, and is the return which Habermas posits as the self-relation which is genuine critical enlightenment.

> [The] concept of *communicative rationality* carries with it connotations based ultimately on the central experience of the unconstrained, unifying, consensus-bringing force of argumentative speech, in which different participants overcome their merely subjective views and, owing to the mutuality of rationally motivated conviction, assure themselves of both the unity of the objective world and the intersubjectivity of their lifeworld (1991, p. 10).

That the loss of the subject is enlightenment is emphasised in his stating that 'The concept of *grounding* is interwoven with that of *learning*' (1991, p. 18). But learning, as used here by Habermas, is no more that the positing of illusory being as substantial. The non-subject of which intersubjectivity is the return, and is held to be determinate in, is illusory being. Illusory being in Hegel is a mere appearance or shining for others, but it is not yet a shining for others which is also a shining in and for itself. That determinate negation lies ahead in the experience of return in and as the dialectic of enlightenment. However, for Habermas that negativity has now been left behind, for the view which holds the dialectic of enlightenment, or the loss of the subject, to be merely negative is a view which is still held captive within the paradigm of subjective consciousness, and which has not learned about itself, or become enlightened about its truth as intersubjectivity.

Such a view, for Habermas, is characterised by Adorno and Horkheimer's *Dialectic of Enlightenment*. Their view that reason and enlightenment are now only possible indirectly through continual self-negation is, for Habermas, still dependent upon the paradigm of the philosophy of (subjective) consciousness. It is Habermas's point that they continually fail to realise the unconditioned intersubjectivity upon which their own theorising is dependent. In a lecture in 1982 Habermas pointed out this inconsistency, stating that their own *Dialectic of Enlightenment* is forced to 'make use of the same critique which it has declared false' (1982, p. 22) In failing to learn from the contradiction, their 'suspicion of ideology becomes total', says Habermas, and 'opposes not only the ideological function of the bourgeois ideals, but rationality as such' (1982, p. 22). This 'myopic perspective' (1982, p. 30) prevents them, in his opinion, from fulfilling the task they set for themselves, that the enlightenment must examine itself. If Adorno and Horkheimer 'do not want to give up the goal of an ultimate unmasking and want to carry on their critique, then,' says Habermas, 'they must preserve at least one standard for their explanation of the corruption of all reasonable standards' (1982, p. 28, emphasis removed). What is therefore required to overcome the negative contradictions or aporias of the dialectic of enlightenment is a shift from the paradigm of the philosophy of consciousness, which finally exhausted itself in Adorno and Horkheimer, to the theory of communicative action. This is then to give up:

A subject that represents objects and toils with them – in favour of the paradigm of linguistic philosophy – namely, that of intersubjective understanding or communication – and puts the cognitive-instrumental aspect of reason in its proper place as part of a more encompassing *communicative rationality* (Habermas, 1991, p. 390).

Habermas builds upon the theory of communicative action by showing that as critique it is the immanent self-relation (the work and the result) of the intersubjective lifeworld. This lifeworld, he states, 'stands behind the back of each participant in communication' (Dews, 1992, p. 109) and is therefore not something that can be known in the same way as experiences of the self and the world. The self-relation of intersubjectivity is not available to subjective consciousness in the same way as an ordinary object, because the lifeworld is currently available only through and as its own distorted structures. One of these distortions is of its separation from communicative action, a separation which Habermas sees as caused by the 'uncoupling' of the lifeworld from the social system, of communicative action from the structures which (now do not) embody it. For Habermas, 'The uncoupling of system and lifeworld is experienced in modern society as a particular kind of objectification: the social system definitively bursts out of the horizon of the lifeworld [and] escapes from the intuitive knowledge of everyday communicative practice' (1987c, p. 173). What fill this gap, and appear as determinative factors, are what Habermas calls 'steering media', for example, money and power. These media, after the uncoupling of system and lifeworld, are then able to 'take over the integrative functions which were formerly fulfilled by consensual values and norms' (Dews, 1992, p. 171). This then becomes our domination by non-mutual, merely technical interests, and the object of our (intersubjective) critique. The necessity of the lifeworld always becomes clear in critique, and thus critique is always the realisation of the lifeworld, overcoming its distortions as they appear within the system. Although Habermas believes that he avoids the negativity of the philosophy of consciousness because of this intersubjective grounding of critique, it is nevertheless still a grounding based in a presupposition of learning. He can only assume that 'the analysis of the lifeworld is a self-referential enterprise' (1980, p. 130), because the movement of return from lifeworld to communicative action is posited as the self-relation of enlightenment. In fact, we return from Habermas only with a further contradiction, one which is shown clearly by reading Habermas against Hegel.

There is on the surface little disagreement between Hegel and Habermas on the phenomenological necessities of philosophical enquiry. *Knowledge and Human Interests* begins with praise for Hegel who, says Habermas, 'replaced the enterprise of epistemology with the phenomenological self-reflection of mind' (1987a, p. 7). The problem for a critical philosophy is that, in trying to understand the *a priori* conditions for the possibility of self-validating reason and reliable knowledge, it has at its disposal for this task only that which is the subject of the investigation, namely the faculty of (rational) knowledge. This point was seen at the end of Chapter 4 in relation to the positing of critique as the method of enlightenment. Habermas goes so far as to state that 'Hegel's argument is conclusive... For the circle in which epistemology inevitably ensnares itself is a reminder that the critique of knowledge does not possess the spontaneity of an origin' (1987a, p. 8). Thought always examines itself 'after the fact', as Habermas puts it (1987a, p. 8). The value of Hegelian phenomenology for Habermas is, then, that through these insights it brings into being 'a new learning level' (1979, p. 122) about the inevitability of contingency in critical reflection. This, however, is not an insight or a level of learning that Habermas is able to maintain in his own theorising of communicative action and the lifeworld. This is because, while Hegel, he argues, takes this level of learning to be essentially negative, Habermas can find within it a positive result. The inability of consciousness to exist without presupposition leads to Hegel 'abandoning the critique of knowledge itself' (Habermas, 1987a, p. 9). Habermas concludes that 'The apparent dilemma (Aporie) of knowing *before* knowledge... returns in Hegel's thought as an actual dilemma: namely, that phenomenology must in fact be valid prior to every possible mode of scientific knowledge' (1987a, p. 21). It is this misrecognition of

130

return which characterises the whole course of Habermas's theorising, and is what enables him to presuppose his own enlightenment as 'a new learning level' (1979, p. 122).

It is also a misunderstanding which does not change in his later remarks on Hegel. His more recent *Philosophical Discourse of Modernity* traces the problem of Hegel's presupposition of critique as negative to one of his early essays, *Spirit of Christianity and its Fate*, written between 1798–9. In it, says Habermas, Hegel presupposes an ethical totality, rather than pursue the intersubjective preconditions which lie behind the discursive possibility of such a totality in the first place. By remaining fixed within the philosophy of the subject, Hegel 'fails to achieve the goal essential to the self-grounding of modernity: thinking the positive element in such a way that it can be overcome by the same principle from which it proceeds – precisely by subjectivity' (Habermas, 1987b, pp. 29–30). There are, says Habermas, traces of communicative rationality in this early work which Hegel, driven by his commitment to 'self-consciousness or the reflective relationship of the knowing subject to itself' can only ignore (1987b, p. 29).

The different interpretations of phenomenology in Hegel and Habermas can be summed up as a difference with regard to the understanding of 'learning'. Habermas states that 'It is my conjecture that the fundamental mechanism for social evolution in general is to be found in an automatic inability not to learn' (1976, p. 15). However, he argues that technical rationality and even philosophies of subjective consciousness, have reproduced forms of learning which are merely abstract and, most importantly, have proved unable to learn about the necessary preconditions of learning itself. Such forms of learning raise validity claims which 'are naïvely taken for granted and accepted or rejected without discursive consideration' (1976, p. 15). Habermas identifies as characteristic of modernity 'not *learning*, but *not-learning*' (1976, p. 15), and his own theory of communicative action is his response to this. It is his learning about and from the non-learning of abstract, technical and merely subject-based enquiry.

Just such non-learning, Habermas believes, ultimately exhausts Hegelian phenomenology. In *Knowledge and Human Interests* Habermas cites Hegel's mistrust of mistrust (see Hegel, 1977, p. 47) as a scepticism which aims itself against learning and which prefers, instead, the methodological presuppositions of an unconditioned doubt. This, says Habermas, is in fact the 'modern form of scepticism' (1987a, p. 9) which exhausts all subsequent philosophies of the subject. Hegelian phenomenology marks the high point of such philosophies which, by remaining tied to the paradigm of the subject, refuses to learn from its own activity about the logically necessary, intersubjective communicative rationality on which it depends, and which it reproduces. The result is that Hegelian phenomenology, in highlighting the contingency of all other objects, refuses to apply the insight to itself. Hegel is, for Habermas, 'a master thinker' (1990, p. 5) who assumes for himself an absolute vantage point above learning. It is this absolute scepticism which prevents Hegel from understanding that the negative activity of phenomenology for one consciousness is, in fact, a positive intersubjective result. Subjectivity, for Habermas, is not self-activity, it is only a particular activity of intersubjective communicative rationality.

The notion of learning which grounds communicative action is one which posits itself as the self-relation of critique as enlightenment. Critique, in having the subject reflect upon itself, negates that subject, or sees it vanish as an independent person. The loss of the subject is brought about because critique reveals the dependency of the subject upon pre-existing rules of language. In addition, such a result, or learning, is itself only possible because critique, or reflection, is itself no longer the work of the subject, but is the realisation of that upon which reflective critique is itself made possible. This, as was seen earlier, is embodied in the presupposition that 'the analysis of the lifeworld is a self-referential enterprise' (Habermas, 1980, p. 130). Learning as negation and learning as critique are one and the same learning. They are both the work and result of intersubjectivity. It is this synthesis of activity and result in intersubjectivity which Habermas posits as the positive result of the negation of the subject. The dialectic of enlightenment cannot learn positively of this result because it does not allow itself to comprehend that the loss of the subject is the positive truth of the (non-) subject in intersubjectivity.

This is the same presupposition of enlightenment that has been noted above as characterising critiques of the teacher and teachers of critique. What Habermas has done here is to posit that critique is the immanent self-relation of negation as work and as result, or as the lifeworld and non-subject. On the one hand this self-relation requires to be posited because its unification is empty and indeterminate. There is no experience here in which the return of the negative to itself can become substantive. That experience has to be presupposed by Habermas. It is in this positing of experience that Habermas grounds 'enlightenment' or 'learning'. Thus the relation between the lifeworld and the non-subject is indeterminate and mere appearance; literally for Habermas, nothing is not-learned. Therefore, on the other hand, what Habermas ends up with is a result or a knowledge of self-relation which is itself *not* self-relation. It is Habermas and not Hegel who has removed himself from phenomenology through presupposition. The determinative experience of the negation of negation is contradictory and is what is contained only in what is known as being actual. Habermas, however, removes himself from the experience of contradiction, believing it to be only a refusal to learn about the self-relation of critique. What he claims to have learned in fact only symbolises his own refusal to learn. He lifts himself out of experience once he has posited its truth as self-relation, and is then able to construct a theory of communicative action and of the lifeworld upon that positing. Contradiction is therein resolved for Habermas, and the negative consequences of experience and of the dialectic of enlightenment are avoided.

The dialectic of enlightenment is only overcome by Habermas by his presupposition, in the first place, that the self-relation of enlightenment is not contradictory, that it overcomes the aporia of subjective experience, and that it can be known as an intersubjective result. But this result cannot contain the negation of which it claims to be the truth. Instead it is the presupposition of self-relation as enlightenment, a presupposition which only repeats the shining of illusory being, and therefore repeats the circle of certainty and uncertainty. This is an experience for us of contradiction, for we now have self-relation, our truth, as an object or knowledge for us, and this experience is therefore not one of unification but of separation. To claim unity is, at the same time, to experience unity as an object and therefore as not-unity. The subject is returned to itself from the theory of communicative action; it is not able to rest in the peace of the intersubjective self-relation which Habermas posits. His positing, although claiming to know the truth of experience as learning, only repeats that learning negatively for us. The subject is not the lifeworld, self-relation is not experience, and critique is not intersubjective unification. To propose that they are is to grant 'to the mediated the illusion of immediacy' (Adorno, 1976, p. 204), precisely the criticism Habermas made at the beginning of his career against the positivism of Popper.

Habermas is claiming immunity from the dialectic of enlightenment, but in fact he is returned to it by the negative experience of, or our learning about, the lifeworld as object. He offers us a learning about the dialectic of enlightenment. But this offer is enlightenment without dialectic, or, in terms of learning, it is result without activity, and therefore not the whole of the relation which it claims to be. It is knowledge of the truth of critical self-activity removed from that activity. It is therefore denied the determinative substance which it posits as held within its own enlightenment. Our experience of the theory of communicative action, and of the self-relation of learning upon which it is grounded, is negative, and another contradictory meeting between universal and particular. The dialectic of enlightenment reasserts itself and enlightenment becomes myth. Result is again negated and returned into activity. Having sought to escape the paradoxes of 'self-negating philosophy' (Dews, 1992, p. 99) and to 'stand out against Adorno's negativism' (Dews, 1992, p. 108), Habermas finds himself returned precisely to that negativity by our consciousness, which experiences his positive result as only for us. Written some 40 years before Habermas's theory of communicative action, Adorno and Horkheimer's *Dialectic of Enlightenment* is not a work from which he escapes, but to which he inevitably returns, ensuring the repetition of the circle, not its overcoming. The determinative aspect of this return cannot be explicated in the work of Habermas, for he has already removed from his theory of learning the activity and experience in which learning occurs. What lies ahead is to see how this return to the dialectic of enlightenment, for Habermas and for us, is a substantial education. First, however, the other half of the dialectic of enlightenment, the repetition of return, will be examined in the work of Adorno. Whereas Habermas finds a result and refuses dialectic, Adorno finds dialectic and refuses a result.

Adorno: dialectic without enlightenment

It was seen earlier that Adorno and Horkheimer were fully aware of the totalitarian nature of reason which claimed exclusive rights to explanation, knowledge, understanding and definition. Nevertheless, even given the inescapable totality of this, they still held the view that the negativity implicit in the dialectic of enlightenment did form a weapon against reason, and the law and logic of identity. This law and logic was, as seen in Chapter 4, based upon the testing of all identities according to the principle of non-contradiction. Adorno, in his later work *Negative Dialectics*, notes that such a logic works on the premise of an 'excluded middle' (1973, p. 142, footnotes); that is, that one thing shall not also be able to be something else. The aim of this critique against such 'identity thinking' is to make consciousness aware that identities are not what they appear (or not merely how they shine for others), and that all such rational knowledge, including rational self-knowledge, falls into contradiction and negation when it asserts its universality.

It is a challenge which Adorno takes up. By concentrating on the negativity of the dialectic of enlightenment, its repetition as a constantly undermining but never-ending circle, the critical potential of reflection is kept alive. For Adorno to achieve this required, argued Rose, 'a changed concept of dialectic' (1978, Chapter 4), one which would allow the contradiction of identity to speak for itself without being resolved or subjected to further domination. Rose writes:

> Adorno's philosophical ambition was to redefine the subject and the object, and their relationship, without presupposing their identity, and to show that this can only be accomplished if the subject and the object are understood as social processes, and not as the presuppositions of pure epistemology (1978, p. 56).

To achieve this, Adorno employs an immanent method, aimed at inducing contradictions in thought, and using enlightenment against itself to reveal its own mythological character. Whereas Habermas assumed the result of critique to be the self-relation and identity of enlightenment, Adorno is concerned to preserve the negative activity of critique by undermining all such results, including those which seek to fix its own identity, as Habermas does. The result of such activity may well be no result, but a lack of result is precisely the active and continuing critique of identity thinking. 'Thinking,' says Adorno, 'which teaches itself that part of its own meaning is what, in turn, is not a thought, explodes the logic of non-contradiction' (1976, p. 24).

This method, says Rose, expressed itself as Adorno's style, and she notes that 'it is impossible to understand Adorno's ideas without understanding the ways in which he presents them, that is, his style' (1978, p. 11). 'Criticism and composition in Adorno's works are thus inseparable,' she writes (1978, p. 12). His idea is to write in such a way as to create the movement and experience of contradiction, the dialectic of enlightenment, in the reader, and thereby undermine any fixed identities for concepts, objects or persons. Non-identity is induced by the use of chiasmus where statements are made in an antithetical, logically contradictory fashion such that the identity of A is also claimed to be the identity of B (see Rose, 1978, Chapter 2). This is, therefore, a critique of the excluded middle upon which the domination of identity thinking is based. 'Adorno presents whatever philosophy he is discussing so as to expose its basic antinomies' (Rose, 1978, p. 54), and to return it to the circle of the dialectic of enlightenment, and of non-identity.

Negation, in Adorno, becomes an educational weapon against identity thinking, and in his later work it takes for itself the title of 'negative dialectics', often shortened to just 'dialectics'. Adorno says of dialectics that it is 'the consistent sense of non-identity. It does not begin by taking a standpoint. My thought is driven to it by its own inevitable insufficiency' (1973, p. 5). Thus, Adorno concludes, 'dialectics is the ontology of the wrong state of things' (1973, p. 11), a form of thinking which enables thought to break through 'the appearance of total identity' (1973, p. 5). In contrast to Habermas, although preceding him, Adorno does not hold that dialectics is a method which is itself the result of any enlightenment. Dialectics is the circle, it is not an empty and insubstantial enlightenment about the truth of the circle. 'Totality,' says Adorno, 'is to be opposed by convicting it of non-identity with itself' (1973, p. 147), not by presupposing a totality beforehand. Adorno acknowledges that 'No theory today escapes the market-place' (1973, p. 4) and that includes dialectics. The impact of dialectics is its contradicting of identity, including its own. In this way Adorno hopes to include dialectics within his own work by convicting it of non-identity with itself. This would be the opposite approach to Habermas, who believed he had achieved the identity of critique as intersubjective enlightenment, and thus kept this immune from its own posited truth. Adorno writes that 'It lies in the definition of negative dialectics that it will not come to rest in itself, as if it were total. This is its form of hope' (1973, p. 406). Dialectics cannot be a method, for it is always carried out as and in experience, both prior to any result and then on any result which might appear. No result or identity can stand secure from negation because it is already within the circle which is the dialectic of enlightenment. Precisely because 'objects do not go into their concepts without leaving a remainder' (1973, p. 5), there is always a lack of identity, and therefore always the window of hope in the prison wall. Negative dialectics does not need to be, nor can be, a method of critique, but it can be induced by encouraging thought always and everywhere to know its own contradictions. Dialectics is therefore immanent as the education of consciousness, for it is the work of return which consciousness finds unavoidable. This education is only immanent, however, when it is not dominated, and when it is itself also contradictory. That is why the negative, rejected by Habermas, is embraced by Adorno, for only in gaining no result is critique immanently educational. 'In dialectics,' says Adorno, 'it is not total identification that has the last word, because dialectics lets us recognise the difference that has been spirited away. Dialectics can break the spell of identification without dogmatically, from without, contrasting it with an allegedly realistic thesis' (1973, p. 172).

Seeking the negative as the non-result of critique, and maintaining and encouraging the dialectic of enlightenment is not, for Adorno, the act of resignation or non-learning that Habermas accuses it of being. The refusal of a positive identity for education proves too much for those who, faced by the eternal return of contradiction, cling 'to the idea of something beyond contradiction' (Adorno, 1973, p. 146). Adorno declares that 'Philosophy must do without the consolation that truth cannot be lost' (1973, p. 34). It is therefore not in negativity that resignation is to be found, but in the positing of a result, a self-relation, which avoids negativity and believes itself to have overcome the circle of the dialectic of enlightenment. 'For the individual, life is made easier through capitulation to the collective with which he identifies. He is spared the cognition of his impotence... It is this act – not unconfused thinking – which is resignation' (1978, p. 167). Against such resignation, Adorno offers the hope which the negation of identity can realise. 'The power of the *status quo* puts up the facades into which our consciousness crashes. It must seek to crash through them... Where the thought transcends the bonds it tied in resistance – there is its freedom' (1973, p. 17).

It is in the confrontation with Hegel, however, that negative dialectics appears as less than immanently self-critical or dialectical. While Habermas claimed that Hegel had not learnt from phenomenology that critique is enlightenment, Adorno argues that Hegel has not learnt from phenomenology that critique is not enlightenment, but is in fact only the repetition of its negation. Adorno credits Hegel with being the first to envisage the modern contradiction between experience and object (1973, p. 153), yet he accuses Hegel of failing to remain consistent to this insight. 'Hegel does not carry the dialectics of non-identity to the end' (1973, p. 120), argues Adorno. He does not 'put his trust in dialectics, does not look upon it as the force to cure itself' (1973, pp. 337–8), and resolves it in favour of an identity, a totality, which 'takes ontological precedence' (1973, p. 120). For Adorno, non-identity cannot enclose itself within a system, for the circle is antithetical to closure. Hegel's system is therefore removed from the circle because:

> No matter how dynamically a system may be conceived, if it is in fact to be a closed system, to tolerate nothing outside its domain, it will become a positive infinity – in other words, finite and static. The fact that it sustains itself in this manner, for which Hegel praised his own system, brings it to a standstill. Bluntly put, closed systems are bound to be finished (1973, p. 27).

According to Adorno, then, Hegelian logic escapes the pathway of despair of which it so proudly boasts, by having 'advance assurance of what it offers to prove' (1973, p. 39). Adorno is clear that the negation of the negative cannot produce a result which is itself immune from being an abstract identity and therefore requires further negation to 'crash through' this appearance. 'To equate the negation of negation with positivity is,' says Adorno, 'the quintessence of identification' (1973, p. 158). He adds that the production of such a result, and the construction of a system upon that result, merely goes to prove that 'the negation was not negative enough' (1973, p. 160).

Just as the difference between Hegel and Habermas on the dialectic of enlightenment lay in their respective concepts of 'learning', so, too, does the difference between Hegel and Adorno. For Habermas, enlightenment was possible as result, a result not recognised by Hegel. For Adorno, enlightenment is not possible as result but is presupposed by Hegel to be so. In fact Hegel's system is the one contradiction of which these two 'positions' are its broken middle. But before examining both of these positions together, it is important to see how it is Adorno and not Hegel who is ultimately guilty of identity thinking.

The identity which Adorno presupposes is the negative. His understanding of the negative is placed firmly within the logic of non-contradiction, and it is this identity thinking upon which his critique of Hegel rests. In the assertions seen earlier that the definition of negative dialectics is unrest, and again that negative dialectics is 'unconfused' thinking, it becomes clear that Adorno is using negative dialectics as a consistent and non-contradictory identity. Furthermore, to deny categorically that the negative can be positive, or that the negative can produce a result, is to presuppose that the negative is not contradictory. Whereas everything else is to be convicted of non-identity with itself, the negative is protected from this, and held as purely negative, or as an identity in itself. 'To proceed dialectically,' says Adorno, 'means to think in contradictions... [and to be] suspicious of all identity. Its logic is one of disintegration' (1973, pp. 144–5). Yet the one identity of which Adorno is not suspicious, and protects from disintegration, is the negative. The negative is the one concept which Adorno protects from contradiction, and from its own logic. It is held in immunity, protected from the loss of its own identity. It is Hegel and not Adorno who allows even the negative to appear immanently as itself; that is, as a contradiction, and therefore as negative and positive at the same time. The process by which this achieved, and how it comes to be known, in explored both in the next section of this chapter, and in Chapters 6 and 7. The fact the Hegel does not dominate the negative by protecting it from being understood as a contradiction (i.e. as itself) is interpreted by Adorno to be granting the negative a positive life which cannot be justified. Yet only in this positive appearance is the negative truly contradictory. It is this contradiction, of negativity by itself, which is the truth of the Hegelian system. Adorno wrote that 'The principle of absolute identity is self-contradictory' (1973, p. 318). Intended as a criticism of Hegel, it is, in fact, a precise formulation of the self-determination of the notion.

It is Hegel who avoids dominating the negative and it is Hegel, not Adorno, who is able to draw out the full educational importance of the dialectic of enlightenment. Adorno resists this education by denying the negative its own learning and knowledge as self-activity and self-result, or self-negation. By denying the negative as result, he denies that the negative can learn from itself, about itself. It is to presuppose that negative education is dialectic without enlightenment, activity without result, negation without the return of itself to itself as contradiction. In Habermas, the dialectic of enlightenment is presupposed as (the identity of) the positive, and it relapses into contradiction, or is negated. In Adorno, the dialectic of enlightenment is presupposed as (the identity of) the negative, and also relapses into contradiction; where it becomes itself, it becomes contradiction of self-relation. Only in Hegel are both moments of the dialectic of enlightenment, the positive and the negative, comprehended as the whole which is their self-relation. It is within the Hegelian system that this self-relation is given immanent self-expression, where the contradiction of negation appears as itself. It is in Hegel that the positive and the negative are self-determinate, and it is in Hegel that the dialectic of enlightenment is a self-education of the relation which is philosophical consciousness. Philosophy, says Hegel,

> does not remain content with the purely negative result of Dialectic. The sceptic mistakes the true value of his result, when he supposes it to be no more than a negation pure and simple. For the negative which emerges as the result of dialectic is, because a result, at the same time the positive: it contains what it results from, absorbed into itself, and made part of its own nature (1975, p. 119).

How it contains this is explored in the next section.

It is learning, therefore, which lies at the heart of the dialectic of enlightenment. Critique which takes itself to be enlightenment about dialectic, as in Habermas, prevents itself from learning about return by positing itself as a self-relation. Critique which takes itself to be the negation of all enlightenment, as in Adorno, prevents itself from allowing its own truth to emerge by protecting the negative from itself, and from appearing as itself, or as a self-result. Both are merely one-sided interpretations of the broken middle which is the self-relation of learning, and both are forced to learn from and within the dialectic of enlightenment that their respective presuppositions, although dominating learning, cannot avoid it. These two approaches, the positive which overcomes the negative, and the negative which returns the positive to negation, are the two sides of the broken middle of the education relation. In presenting the two sides through Habermas and Adorno, it is their separation from each other which is highlighted. But a broken middle is separated and joined at the same time. That is the nature of its self-relation. It is not therefore in either Habermas or Adorno that the broken middle of the education relation appears, but in our experience of both of them. Habermas offers enlightenment without dialectic, Adorno offers dialectic without enlightenment. Habermas posits enlightenment as self-relation, but one which is indeterminate and therefore merely a tautological result. Adorno posits dialectics as indeterminate repetition and therefore as an activity which has no result. In

Habermas there is substance without subject, in Adorno there is subject without substance. Habermas's position is undermined by the universality of the dialectic of enlightenment as negative, Adorno's position is realised as result by the same universality. Habermas's theory of communicative action is returned to the dialectic of enlightenment. Adorno fails to identify return as result. This is the circle of the dialectic of enlightenment, and Habermas and Adorno between them constitute the whole of the circle. It is a whole or a circle which can only appear in being experienced or in being thought, an experience in which the truth of the dialectic of enlightenment as the broken middle of the education relation is known, and is actual.

What is

Having examined enlightenment as a presupposed self-relation, it is now possible to offer an alternative answer to the question 'what is enlightenment?' Enlightenment, posited as self-relation by Rousseau, Marx and Durkheim, proved itself not to be a self-relation in their personification of it. To have the self-relation as knowledge is to be related to self-relation as the property owner. To teach the self-relation to others as their truth is to repeat this personification of the self-relation, its negation, as domination. The messenger contradicts the intended message, the teacher contradicts the intended education. This circle is repeated as and within the dialectic of enlightenment. Any attempt to reconcile self-relation with self merely repeats their separation (Habermas), and any attempt to hold them apart is a denial of the actuality of their broken middle (Adorno).

This self-relation, or broken middle, appears therefore in the form of a contradiction, and as an irreparable division between universal and particular. Contradiction is not a substantial result as far as our abstract consciousness is concerned, for it works only with the logic of non-contradiction. It will, in its own image, seek to resolve this broken middle to its own satisfaction, and its favoured method is to presuppose the overcoming of contradiction by having it as knowledge. However, the actuality of self-relation as contradiction speaks louder and longer than its posited resolution in and by abstract reason. When our experience is allowed to speak for itself, then contradiction can be comprehended as activity and result, or the self-relation which is the broken middle. This self-relation appears at the end of the section on essence in Hegel's *Science of Logic*, where positing comes to suffer the contradiction of self-relation or self-knowing.

On the one hand, the illusory being which appears at first to be an essence, or the truth of reflection, is now known as posited. It is known merely as an immediate presupposition which lacks any substance or determinate being. It is known as the mere shining for others and, in itself, to be nothing. The first 'knowledge' of consciousness in regard to positing was the immediate presupposition that reflection is itself. Now, in the relation wherein what is posited (reflection) knows itself as posited, there is a second knowledge, a development of the first knowledge. Positing cannot survive its being known as positing. In being known, its presupposition of immediacy collapses and it becomes mediated knowledge. Now, illusory being is no longer posited as something. On the contrary, now illusory being is posited as nothing for now it is known as being indeterminate. (Posited) illusory being is now posited as illusory being.

That which was presupposed as something, but which is now known as nothing, is replaced by that which is known as nothing, but is therefore something. Both positings are self-contradictory. Immediate positing is contradictory because mere shining is presupposed as determinate. Reflected positing is contradictory because shining is presupposed as indeterminate. It is in the second of these positings, the presupposition that illusory being is indeterminate, which, in fact, not only is a self-relation, but is what Hegel calls 'the absolute relation' (1969, p. 554). The positing of illusory being is a determinate negation in which what is negated is negated by that which is negative. A determinate negation realises itself. This absolute, says Hegel, is 'imperfect' (1969, p. 533) because it is only arrived at, or is 'the absolute in a determinateness' (1969, p. 533). But it can be thought, and therefore is substantial, or substance. Hegel writes 'Substance as this unity of being and reflection is essentially the *reflective movement (Scheinen)* and *positedness* of itself. The reflective movement is the reflective movement that is self-related, and it is thus that it *is*; this being is substance as such' (1969, p. 555). Substance is the negative realising itself through its own self-negating. That is the significance of positing positing itself. It is an illusory being negating its own nothingness, and coming to know itself. It is where shining for others becomes self-light.

It is as this self-relation that the dialectic of enlightenment needs to be comprehended. Rather than employing specialist Hegelian terms, this can be explored through the terms which are integral to enlightenment itself, those of light, dark and shadow. Illusory being, or positing, appears as a self-light (a reflection), or as self-enlightenment in which we come to know ourselves, by ourselves. Who is seen, and by whom, immediately have the appearance of being one and the same. Enlightenment is posited as this self-illumination. It is the presupposition that the light in which the self is visible to itself is the self as its own sun, its own source of light, its own illumination. However, this self-light is precisely what is presupposed or posited. It forgets that the light in which it appears is not its own. (Critical) reflection is carried on in the light of others, i.e. in relation to them. Reflection is not self-light, it is a shining or mere appearance of itself for others. As such, enlightenment is always already negative. It has to presuppose its shining for others to be its own substantial self-relation because it is, in itself, wholly indeterminate. It has as yet no life of its own outside of its being for others. In the light of the other, the posited self is darkness. It is in this darkness, now, that the dialectic of enlightenment becomes its own substantial enlightenment.

The emptiness of shining for others, its mere show of self-light, is revealed when shining for others is examined in relation to itself. When shining for others comes to know itself as a mere shining, then this positing of enlightenment collapses and is now realised as nothing. This is the same activity seen earlier in this section with regard to positing coming to know itself. When the enlightenment presupposed as and in reflection is realised as merely the show of shining for others, and as lacking its own light, its own substance, then this self knows itself now to be not enlightenment, or as darkness. This darkness is the insubstantial and indeterminate self of illusory being. The shining for others is not yet a source of light for itself. Only when darkness is illuminated, when the self is illuminated with regard to its (being) darkness, does darkness, or self, appear in its own light. Enlightenment is this self-relation of light and dark, for this self-relation is the actuality of (i.e. which is) shining for others. The whole of enlightenment is the relation of the relation between shining for others and the realisation of that shining for others, by itself, as darkness or emptiness. The whole of enlightenment, its own comprehensive education, is precisely this process, this determinate negation, wherein it comes to know itself. This comprehensive education cannot be grasped by a merely dualistic model of light and dark, for that expresses only their difference and not their actuality. Darkness, the nothingness of shining for others (i.e. negativity) can be known, it can be seen. Darkness becomes visible as shadow. Equally, therefore, shining for others has its actuality, its self-relation, as shadow, for shadow expresses the self-relation of light and dark in which they are separated and related.

This contradictory and determinate negation expresses the whole of enlightenment, i.e. enlightenment appearing in its own light. The whole of enlightenment is a triadic structure of light, dark and shadow. In the contradiction of the illumination of darkness by itself, there is the contradictory self-relation which is enlightenment. This self-determination of enlightenment is now explained further.

In realising that enlightenment is a mere shining for others, the negative (or the posited illusory being) becomes known. The two responses to this knowledge, that the negative is or is not determinate, have been rehearsed earlier through the dialectics of Habermas and Adorno. For Habermas, this knowledge of the negative is darkness made light. The negative is known and understood. Its illusory appearance as darkness is overcome and is now brought into the light of our (communicative) comprehension. This, for Habermas, is a positive result. For Adorno, it is also the case that the negative is known. Adorno's enlightenment regarding the negative is given away by his presupposition that the negative in fact overcomes all enlightenment about it, and thus that the negative cannot be known. For both Habermas and Adorno darkness, or the negative, or the self-relation of critical (negative) consciousness, can be known. They share the presupposition of what learning is. Where they differ is in regard to what is learnt. It is this presupposition of learning on which they base their judgments that illusory being is or is not fully comprehended, enlightenment is or is not a whole, and that the negative (critical consciousness) is or is not self-determinate.

For neither Habermas nor Adorno is the knowing of darkness, or of the negative, subject and substance, return and overcoming. Habermas and Adorno, in their different ways, both posit a knowledge of positing, repeating the dialectic of enlightenment but not comprehending its whole educational structure, nor the whole of its negative, contradictory nature. They know positing (or the emptiness of shining for others), but positing is not allowed to know (determine) itself. For us, this is a further development. This development is the determinate negation wherein positing is known as positing, or wherein shining for others sheds light on its own emptiness, its own darkness, its own non-light, and appears as the whole of that contradictory self-relation. In this self-relation there is not only light and dark, overcoming or non-overcoming, enlightenment or myth. Now, non-light is now known as non-light by itself, rather than by that which merely posits its own overcoming or non-overcoming of positing. Here posited illusory being, or shining for others, *is* a self-relation, for darkness is posited as the absence of light by itself, i.e. it knows itself. For darkness to be known by itself means that it must be visible to itself, or seen in its own light. Darkness cast in its own light (i.e. as the substantial absence of light), appears for itself as its own shadow. Shadow is the truth of the relation of non-light knowing itself. It is where and how darkness is visible. It is where the negativity of (the dialectic of) enlightenment is known to itself, by itself and as itself. Or again, it is the self-relation of enlightenment's enlightenment regarding itself. This negation of the negation in Hegel is the absolute relation. In terms of enlightenment, it is learning and development as self-determination.

How, then, is enlightenment known? It is not known as light or dark, as enlightenment or dialectic, as positive or negative, for each posits enlightenment as known in advance of its own self-development. Enlightenment can only be known by itself. Its own enlightenment regarding itself falls within the broken middle of self-relation. When its own non-enlightenment is known to itself, then darkness or non-light is visible or actual as the self-relation which is its own shadow. It can be said here, then, that enlightenment 'known' contains two equally contradictory moments. Not only is the light of shining for others negated by being forced into a self-relation with darkness, but darkness enjoys a relation with itself in which its own nothingness becomes determinate, or known. The truth of the latter is equally the truth of the former, and both are the actuality of shining for others. The determinate negation of darkness which is shadow is also the truth of the negation of enlightenment by darkness. To our abstract consciousness, light and dark are merely opposites, and darkness and shadow are indistinguishable. But to our philosophical consciousness the opposite of each is also true. Light cannot avoid its relation to darkness and darkness (indeterminate) can be known (or illuminated) as shadow (determinate). This is the whole of enlightenment coming to know itself, or becoming enlightened about itself. If one asks what is the difference between negation and determinate negation, or

142

darkness and shadow, or the dialectic of enlightenment and actuality, the answer is the same in each case: *we* are the difference, and the difference is the presence of the whole which is our work, our activity and our education.

This absolute relation of enlightenment is, like the absolute itself, imperfect, for shadows do not resolve the opposition of light and dark, they are the knowing of that relation by itself. Shadow is the self-relation of light and darkness in their relation and in their opposition. It is the result of their opposition, and does not exist separately from the activity of their opposition. Like 'recognition' and 'spirit' (see Part III), shadow implies a unity which includes division. 'This unity mediates between the poles of the opposition and is hence triune' (Rose, 1981, p. 71).

It is tempting here to describe this relation as the shadow of enlightenment, or the spirit of enlightenment. But the word 'of' here does a great deal of work, expressing not merely external possession, but internal self-relation as well. This is the difficulty with any speculative statement which contains self-relation as well as self-difference. Its truth as a broken middle is the contradiction which is the whole, not the resolution of that contradiction. Shadow is not merely of enlightenment. Enlightenment is also of itself in and as the shadow of its own darkness, its own illusory being. It is its own contradiction appearing in and for itself and therefore as itself. The phrase 'shadow of enlightenment' cannot help but read initially as if shadow is only the possession of enlightenment. Thus the phrase risks removing precisely the difficulty which it expresses. But the risk is the movement, the experience and the education. Just as the absolute can be thought, so enlightenment can be realised, but in neither case is the thinking or the knowing merely a finishing. On the contrary, movement known to itself is also always the continuation or repetition of that movement. The activity in which enlightenment becomes enlightened about itself is overcome and is not overcome. It is a comprehensive movement. The implications of this comprehensive education are returned to in regard to social and educational relations in Part III and in regard to Zarathustra in Part IV.

By way of a summary of this triune structure of enlightenment, it can be said that in its self-relation - which is already in relation to and a shining for others - enlightenment shines as its own light in the negation of itself. This negation is visible as shadow. Shadow is therefore the actuality of the negation of enlightenment, or its self-determinate negation. When the negativity of enlightenment, its darkness, is cast in its own light and falls to itself as its own shadow, then enlightenment is enlightened about itself. This is how and when shining for others is also shining in itself. In the contradiction of this triune relationship the answer to the question, 'what is enlightenment?', is that it is a self-relation, one in which light and dark, result and activity, wisdom and negation appear together for themselves in their opposition. This opposition and relation is expressed but is not realised within the dialectic of enlightenment. Enlightenment, in its own light, is realised as the contradiction of enlightenment, a movement and result which we are continually positing, performing, risking, losing and returning to. In no other way can enlightenment be realised. In no other form is it determinate as self-negation. In no other shape is it genuinely a self-relation.

The absolute relation can be known, then, in the sense of realised. The negation of the negation (enlightenment as shadow, reason as spirit) appears for us as what is actual. Hegel's most infamous proposition concerning actuality appears in the Preface to the *Philosophy of Right*. There he wrote, 'what is rational is actual and what is actual is rational' (1967, p. 10). This statement has been a favourite source for misinterpretation and is rarely read in the context of Hegel's system of philosophy. He himself states clearly in the same Preface that the *Philosophy of Right* 'rests on the logical spirit [and that] it is also from this point of view above all that I should like my book to be taken and judged' (1967, p. 2). That this was not done so was clear even to Hegel himself, who noted in his shorter *Logic* that 'These simple statements have given rise to expressions of surprise and hostility' (1975, p. 9). Rose remarks that the proposition of the actual and the rational has been read without reference to illusory being, or to positing (1981, p. 81). Equally, therefore, the proposition has been read without reference to the implicitly educational nature of actuality. This discussion will complete the examination of enlightenment in this chapter.

To believe that objects in life appear as they really are is to posit that they, and our knowledge of them, are in immediate self-relation. In fact, our knowledge of an object is always our experience of it. The object is known through something else. 'There is nothing,' says Hegel, 'nothing in heaven or in nature or mind or anywhere else which does not equally contain both immediacy and mediation' (1969, p. 68). It is for this reason that, for example, natural consciousness is distinguished from philosophical consciousness, for philosophical consciousness knows natural consciousness as mediated. Similarly it is necessary to distinguish between mere reality as it immediately appears, and actuality, which is the mediation of 'reality' by its being known in and for consciousness. To know what is actual is to know something after it has been mediated or experienced. What is actual is always in this sense a result, in that what is actual is determinate. To be determinate is to become an object for reason. Reason, therefore, cannot know anything without the negation of the immediate (posited) thing in itself becoming negated and only now a thing for consciousness. Everything known is already mediated by being known. When this mediation is posited as being no result at all, or as the impossibility of knowing the object in itself, then we have the same movements described earlier of illusory being positing itself as illusory being. Reason, which is doing the knowing, knows that it does not know. This is a knowing of itself as not-knowing and therefore is a knowing and a not-knowing, or darkness cast in its own light. That which negates everything else also, now, negates itself. It is this self-relation which is contained in what is actual. That which reason actually knows, or knows to be actual, is known as contradiction. It is known in the knowing which knows that it is not known. It is known negatively, but is still determinate. What is actual, therefore, is reason's own determinate negation of itself. The knowledge of the object is the knowledge of itself (as contradiction) and thus the external (world) and the internal (mind) are now a self-relation.

Here what is actual emerges as true, or as a broken middle, for the internal and the external are apart from each other, and a part of each other. Actuality is just this self-relation, the work of reason whose result is its own shadow cast by the self-illumination of its negativity or darkness. Reason is therefore actual because knowledge is a negative self-relation. What is actual is still rational, for it is still reason's own work, no longer its immediate positing of knowledge, but its truth as the shadow (the relation) of its own light. Unless actuality is comprehended as the relation of light and dark, as the relation of reason's self-illumination, then statements like 'what is rational is actual' and 'what is actual is rational' appear immediately as positing the identity of one another. Actuality is the result of the experience of non-identity. It is testament of how reality is not in an immediate self-relation with reason, and that reason does not have its immediate self-expression as the world. Actuality is the critical element in Hegel's philosophy. It would look more critical to the abstract consciousness if actuality asserted that it and reason were not the same. But that would only be to refuse this knowledge a light of its own, and it too would remain indeterminate. The fact that they are not identical is contained in the statement that 'what is rational is actual' and 'what is actual is rational'. It is a statement of their non-identity which affirms that the non-identity is known and is determinate. The statement expresses the absolute relation. Actuality contains light and dark, for what is actual appears in its self-light and is, therefore, the truth of that relation, known as its own shadow. Actuality is the absolute relation. It is not therefore indeterminate. Thus it must be, and is, contradictory. The absolute can be thought but only as relation. Actuality is this relation.

Actuality is the result of experience and the activity of experience. It is the realisation of negation (shadow) by an act of negation (darkness made visible). For us, this experience can only be known as contradiction. The actual is a self-relation in this experience, for both of its moments are present. We experience reason as negative, but it is the experience itself which negates reason. The work and the result are one and the same experience. How we learn from the experience depends upon the way in which we presuppose learning beforehand. If we believe enlightenment to be positive, then experience is posited as immediate (negative) self-relation, or enlightenment *per se*. Here, as with Habermas, what is rational cannot be actual because experience as self-relation is posited before the experience. The experience is denied its own substance, and also, therefore, its actuality. If we believe enlightenment to be negative, then there is no longer any learning at all. Here, as with Adorno, what is actual cannot also be rational because the 'result' is no-result. Here the negative is posited by itself and is denied its own actual learning, or self-knowledge. We, however, cannot choose to learn in one way or the other, positively or negatively. Our experience of enlightenment as contradiction is already both of those moments, and both of those moments, the relation itself, appears for us as what is. Hegel, again in the Preface to the *Philosophy of Right*, says, 'To comprehend what is, this is the task of philosophy, because what is, is reason' (1967, p. 11). But what is, is not reality, it is actuality. What is, is already mediated and known as the shadow of its being known. For us, what is, is the truth of the broken middle, repeated not only in bourgeois social relations (see Chapter 6), but also in the rational knowledge relation (see Chapter 7).

If the absolute (relation) cannot be thought, then the broken middle cannot be known. That it has to exist as a contradiction is further evidence of its continuing truth. In our reflection upon social relations, and in our critique of the person, we are returned in the experience to our own subjectivity. But our return from this universal is also our relation to it, and it is in this broken middle that (our) return is realised as the shadow which is enlightenment, or the self-movement and result which is determinate negation. To know this experience as the broken middle is to have experience always as risk. Each experience contradicts the self whose experience it is, but only in the risk is the return. To seek sanctity from the negative, and from its actuality in its own light as shadow, is to refuse the difficulty and struggle which the broken middle, as our own truth, sets for us. To refuse the risk of loss is to refuse the broken middle and its truth as return. It is to refuse our own self-light and it is, therefore, to refuse learning. Rose concludes that 'The perceived failure of reason has led straight away to recourse to the most drastic remedy – the abandonment of reason as such' (1993, p. 3). Reason does educate and enlighten, but not in ways that our own abstract consciousness finds satisfactory. It seeks non-contradiction, but is continually returned to the truth of enlightenment as self-contradiction. To refuse the risk of this learning is to remove thought altogether from 'the difficulty of actuality' (Rose, 1993, p. 5). 'Reason that is actual is ready for all kinds of surprises' (1993, p. 5), including the shock and difficulty of learning that 'the authority of reason... [is] risk' (1995, p. 119). This risk is refused by those offering critiques of the teacher examined in Chapter 1, and by those who teach critique, examined in Chapter 2. It is a risk refused by those who express the contradiction of enlightenment by teaching teachers rather than revealing themselves as teachers in the shadow which is their own learning. Part IV of this book explores the life of a teacher who learnt to become a teacher not only of this contradiction, but also as this contradiction. In Zarathustra we find a teacher who comprehends the return of the teacher not merely as shining for others but in the darkness of his own self-light.

Part III
HEGEL AND THE BROKEN MIDDLE

This section brings together aspects of Hegelian philosophy and Rose's interpretation of the broken middle to reveal the interrelationship in both of their works between social and educational relations. Chapter 6 argues that our relation to 'other' requires to be comprehended as a formative yet contradictory self-relation in which self and other are inextricably bound within a circle of misrecognition. This misrecognition determines the relation of each to himself, of each to the other, and the relation between those two relations. To comprehend social relations is to comprehend the determination of misrecognition by itself, a determinate negation which has its own self-relation in this educational activity and result. Similarly, Chapter 7 argues that educational relations, particularly those of knowledge to consciousness and teacher to student, are also bound within the same circle of misrecognition. Educational categories and identities are already formed within the misrecognition which constitutes our social relations. To comprehend educational relations, therefore, is at the same time to comprehend social relations. The separation of social relations from educational relations is already misrecognition. To recognise this misrecognition, and to comprehend the relation between social and educational relations as a broken middle, is a development described later as comprehensive education.

therefore expresses the contradictory truth of what a relation is. The truth of a middle and a relation are contradictory, and are the same contradiction. This contradiction is that a middle or a relation can only appear in and as a self-opposition of unification and separation. To be the middle or a relation is also not to be a middle or a relation. To be the joining of two or more things a relation also has to ensure that those two things are separated. Without separation there is no middle or relation. A middle and a relation can only appear in and as this contradiction.

Just such a middle or relation is enlightenment. It was seen in Parts I and II that enlightenment is offered as the truth of the relation between reason and critique. Reason, investigating itself in critique, produces a self-relation which it mistakenly believes to be (self-) enlightenment. But such a self-relation, like all self-relations, falls into the contradiction of what a relation is. Enlightenment, the name given to the relation between reason and critique, is itself only in its contradictory self-relation. Its posited unity is always already negated. It can be a self-relation not by overcoming its two sides, but only as their contradictory relation to each other. It can be said here of enlightenment, as of any self-relation, that it can be known only as 'the relation of the relation'. If it is known simply as 'the relation' then its extremes have vanished or have been overcome, and have dissolved into it. It is relation of nothing, or it is indeterminate, a merely illusory being, a mere shining for others. Such a relation is always a positing or presupposition of unity. When it is genuinely a relation, then its sides are present, and it is the relation of them to each other. This relation is therefore the relation which is both the opposition of the two sides and their unification. It is not the overcoming of their opposition, it is the actuality of their opposition.

In examining social relations, this logic of relation becomes the 'law' of (our) misrecognition. Reason knew critique to be its own self-activity, for the examination was of itself by itself. An enquiry by philosophical consciousness is posited as a self-enquiry, a unity which has to be negated if the relation of the relation is to appear in its absolute form. But in an examination of social relations it is not unity which is posited but separation. Here it is the separation which has to be negated if the relation of the relation, or subjective substance, is to be known. It is not philosophical consciousness which develops the understanding of social relations through the *Phenomenology of Spirit*, it is natural consciousness. It is true that natural consciousness posits itself as the unity of self-consciousness, but this certainty only reinforces its separation from any external relation or dependence. Only when the investigation by natural consciousness is complete can philosophical consciousness reveal that the social relation was its own self all along. Up to that point, the self-relation of philosophical consciousness appears only in various illusory forms of itself as self-consciousness. As always it is important to stress here that knowing the social relation as the self-relation of subject and substance in philosophical consciousness does not overcome the broken middle of social relations. Rather, it reveals that the middle is broken, and that self-consciousness is determined within and as that relation.

150

Two further points need to be made before engaging fully with the shadowy realms of social relations. The term social relation is, in a sense, already carrying within it its own contradiction as the relation of the relation. Expressing as it does the separation between individuals, and offering itself as their middle or relation, it contains the contradiction that it is both a joining and a separation of individuals. The social relation is the relation of one individual to another, and can only express itself determinately provided that these individuals are differentiated, i.e. are known separately from each other. Therefore the social relation is that which expresses both their separation from each other and their relation to each other. The social relation is the expression of this contradiction, or the relation of the relation.

But, as stated earlier, the social relation, unlike the scientific or philosophical relation, does not appear to be a self-relation at all. It differs from the philosophical relation in that the social relation is not itself a consciousness. It cannot therefore express itself as a unity, only as an object for the consciousness which knows it. This is why (as it first appears) the social relation is characterised by the positing of separation and not by the positing of unity. The social relation expresses a universality which can only be determinate or known in the consciousness which is particular, or by us. The individual has its social relation therefore only negatively, and as an experience from which he returns to himself. It is more accurately a non-social relation which we experience as our own selves and take to be our own personal identity. This misrecognition determines every shape in which self-consciousness appears, and its understanding of that shape. This is what makes the analysis so complicated.

Such a (non-) social experience is negative. But it has positive significance as a personal experience. Philosophical consciousness, as Hegel puts it, has the courage to stare the negative 'in the face', and receive from it the 'power that converts it into being' (1977, p. 19). But natural consciousness, taking itself immediately as it finds itself, 'closes its eyes to the negative, as when we say of something that it is nothing or is false, and then, having done with it, turn away and pass on to something else' (1977, p. 19). When self-consciousness turns away from the negative it closes its eyes to its determination within the social relation. When, therefore, it comes to try and understand itself and its relation to others, it does not see that it is already a result of that relation. This involves a double misunderstanding. Self-consciousness fails to comprehend the social relation, and it fails to comprehend itself, for the social relation (as the broken middle) is both of these moments. Therefore an investigation into the social relation is not as straightforward as appears at face value. The object of the enquiry has already vanished in our negative experience of it. It has left its mark in the form of an individual self-consciousness, but the individual self-consciousness takes itself as a natural consciousness, and does not see the determination which lies behind it. What is being investigated is therefore present only as the investigator, a form which is one of its illusory appearances. The social relation is present as the individual self-consciousness. Thus the enquiry is already self-contradictory,

151

setting out to discover that which is already actual but unrealised as such. Hence the critique of the person can only ever repeat the person. However, viewed as a broken middle, this is exactly the truth of the enquiry.

Hegel sets out the social relation in two ways. Throughout the *Phenomenology of Spirit* he chronicles natural consciousness's contradictory experiences of itself, showing how it repeats its separation of itself from substance, and its misrecognition, in various different ways. Rose says of this that the *Phenomenology* is 'the presentation of the formation of consciousness as a determination of substance and consciousness' misapprehension of that determination... [i.e.] of the inversions of substance into the various forms of misrepresentation' (1981, p. 152). The *Phenomenology* in this sense is the presentation of the relation of the relation in its various appearances as the illusion of the illusion, where both self-consciousness and the social relation repeat their (illusory) non-relation to each other.

But Hegel also presents the social relation in a non-historical form. This he does in the section entitled 'lordship and bondage'. However, this section also demands very careful reading, and is itself divided into three different presentations of the social relation. The first is that of mutual recognition, where Hegel describes the social relation as the totality of a pure self-relation. Secondly, he describes how this relation becomes a broken middle in the life-and-death struggle. Thirdly, he reveals the life of that division in its separation as the master and the slave. Each of these is now examined.

Mutual recognition

Mutual recognition is the event whereby a free and genuine social relation is realised between individuals who do not have the relation as an object for them but as themselves. The recognition that each is also the other is the basis for an equal social relationship. It is the social relation *per se*. The process of the recognition it involves is described by Hegel as one where each individual 'has come *out of itself*' (1977, p. 111), and also returns '*into itself*' (1977, p. 111). It comes out of itself because it has lost the immediate presupposition that it is an all-inclusive identity in coming face to face with another. This other calls into question the self-identity of the first self-consciousness. Faced with this threat to its own identity, self-consciousness sets out to overcome the other, so that in its negation it will again be assured of its own exclusive self: 'it must proceed to supersede the *other* independent being in order thereby to become certain of *itself* as the essential being' (1977, p. 111).

In the encounter where each self-consciousness comes out of itself, it comes to recognise the other as itself. Thus each is returned to itself now knowing what each is. But the self-knowledge has been achieved only in the (social) relation between them. A knows itself because it recognises itself as B, and B likewise knows itself in his return from the recognition of A. The truth of both is the

152

relation wherein each knows itself because 'Each sees the other do the same as it does' (1977, p. 112), and each therefore in seeing the other sees also itself. 'A self-consciousness exists for a self-consciousness. Only so is it in fact self-consciousness; for only in this way does the unity of itself in its otherness become explicit for it' (1977, p. 110). Hegel does not present this experience as belonging to one or other self-consciousness. The experience of return is not a return to each self-consciousness. Rather, the experience of return is from all self-consciousnesses to all other self-consciousnesses. The experience is not particular, it is universal. It is the truth of all self-consciousnesses who come to know themselves only in and as their social relation. The truth of each self-consciousness is therefore the relation itself. It is impossible for our subjective consciousness to comprehend such a relation, for we can only view it as particular self-knowledge. However, as Hegel presents it here, the truth of each particular is its universal existence. It is where the 'I' is the 'we', and the 'we' is the 'I'. There is no distinction between the two, for in mutual recognition all difference has collapsed into the unity of the social relation. This *is* a middle, and not a broken middle. It is a relation existing in and for itself, and it is the relation which Hegel calls mutual recognition.

Each is for the other the middle term, through which each mediates itself with itself and unites with itself; and each is for itself, and for the other, an immediate being on its own account, which at the same time is such only through this mediation. They *recognise* themselves as *mutually recognising* one another (1977, p. 112).

Such a perspective is only possible from the middle, or as the relation. It is described by Hegel, here, as an immediate relation wherein there is no distinction between subject and substance, nor between individual and society. Such an immediate relation was, for Hegel, characterised by the ethical life of ancient Athens. In the pre-Socratic *polis* self-consciousness drew no distinction between itself and substance. Substance was itself as custom, i.e. as it was performed or done by the people. Such a society was 'the absolute spiritual unity of the essence of individuals in their independent actual existence' (i.e. in custom) (1977, p. 212). The *polis* shares the characteristic of mutual recognition that it is an undifferentiated 'universal self-consciousness' (1977, p. 212), or the existence of an immediate ethical unity where 'laws are the thoughts of its own absolute consciousness' (1977, p. 261). Our own subjective consciousness would want to question the origin and legitimacy of custom, for our perspective is not mutual recognition but subjective misrecognition. The fate of such a perspective is that in having the law as a question, the immediate ethical life or social relation has already vanished or been negated. In being the author of such an enquiry into the laws, says Hegel,

I have transcended them; for now it is I who am the universal, and *they* are the conditioned and limited. If they are supposed to be validated by *my* insight, then I have already denied their unshakeable, intrinsic being, and regard them as something which, for me, is perhaps true, but also is perhaps not true (1977, pp. 261–2).

Mutual recognition, then, is Hegel's presentation of the social relation not as a broken middle, but as the middle itself. He explains mutual recognition from the point of view of the middle, a point of view which is not available in its immediacy to our subjective consciousness. In describing mutual recognition, therefore, it is clear even beforehand that the description will not match our experience of mutual recognition. For us the unity described is contradictory and impossible, yet that contradiction plays no part in mutual recognition when it is presented as a middle or as the social relation in itself. In mutual recognition the extremes, of which the relation is the middle, are the middle. Since these extremes are self-consciousness, it is hard for us to imagine how mutual recognition is anything other than a political or Utopian fantasy. What we can say, however, is that our necessary response to the middle as self-contradictory represents the continuing domination of the social relation in its shape under bourgeois property law, and the possibility of our knowing that domination. It is precisely the impossibility of mutual recognition for us, the subject, which is one of the key aspects of Hegel's critique of the bourgeois form of the social relation. When the contradiction between subject and substance, or between the 'I' and the 'we', is known and comprehended as self-determinative misrecognition (or spirit), then the contradiction is itself as the broken middle. This (contradictory) truth is present as what Hegel calls 'ethical life'. Mutual recognition, here, is only the abstract presentation of (purely subjective) spirit, where subject and substance are an immediate unity, an immediate ethical life, but not one which is self-determinate. In its development and self-determination, spirit forces subject and substance apart from each other.

This is, as was seen earlier, why the social relation presents a double difficulty. Not only are subject and substance separated, but each is known only in this separation, and thus as particular and universal respectively. Their opposition to each other becomes our immediately present reality, or is the determination of the world as we find it and ourselves as we find us. 'Spirit that is objective is a person and as such has an actuality of its freedom in property' (Hegel, 1971, p. 21; Rose translation, 1981, p. 183). This is the destruction of immediate ethical life, and it is now not mutual recognition but the mutual misrecognition of subject (person) and substance (property, law). The misrecognition, for Hegel, is that objective reality – how the world appears – is in fact subjective, or is what is actual. But the actuality of subject and substance in and as the positing of property relations is precisely what is missed by natural consciousness. Only when that positing of the person is known by the person as a positing does subject return to substance. This absolute self-relation of spirit has to wait until its reappearance in the *Science of*

Logic, as fully subjective in and for itself and, therefore, as a negatively-determined form of mutual recognition. But since this, too, is an immediate self-relation, we are in a sense only back where we started, with an immediate and abstract presentation of purely subjective spirit, or an immediate middle or a mutual recognition which cannot be an individual self-consciousness. In subjective spirit the universal and the particular are comprehended as one. But subjective spirit as the middle, or the genuine social relation of freedom and non-domination, is a determinate negation. If it is stated abstractly, then the self-relation is once again merely divided into consciousness and object. If it is stated abstractly and used as a political principle, then it becomes another domination of freedom (of itself) and a repetition of our abstract consciousness as misrecognition. Posited as (self-) enlightenment, in critique it becomes a domination of experience and a repetition of the abstract enlightenment of abstract consciousness. This was the fate of the 'middles' offered by Rousseau, Marx and Durkheim. Yet it is equally the case that freedom can only be stated abstractly, or for subjective consciousness. The experience for natural consciousness of freedom as the negation of the subject is the actuality of the subject. In acknowledging actuality, Hegel recognises both the domination of freedom by bourgeois social relations and our own realisation that we, the subject, are not free. Rose notes that in the recognition of actuality 'another indeterminate, non-actuality is not posited' (1981, p. 203). It is in the comprehension of the broken middle of the social relation as what is actual that the repetition of the domination of freedom is not itself dominated.

It is not mutual recognition, and therefore not the realisation of objective freedom on earth, for, as Rose remarks, such a unity 'has never existed in history' (1981, p. 200). But it is the recognition of freedom as a relation, a relation which is known by us, or is actual, in our contradictory experience of it. Hegel's *Science of Logic* acknowledges its own actuality in the way that Hegel begins the *Logic* with an abstract statement about the impossibility of beginning, and ends it with an abstract statement of method. Both are the same abstraction of that which is experienced and mediated in the *Logic* itself. But the whole of the system requires that the moments of immediacy and mediation fall apart, for only in their opposition are they the notion. A *Science of Logic* which did not have an abstract beginning and end would have no broken middle, and would not therefore be subject and substance, or the knowing of freedom. The necessity of abstract consciousness in the self-determination of the absolute is therefore acknowledged, and is not dominated by another posited overcoming or middle. The absolute is allowed to speak for itself, and is therefore contradictory for we who live 'in the experience of lack of freedom' (Rose, 1981, p. 184).

Realising the absence of freedom in what is actual may be another return to abstract consciousness, but it is a return which contains the learning which has been gained in the experience. It is the return gained from the (speculative) risk of the certainties of reason, reality and subjectivity. Such a return, therefore, is always to a different beginning, still abstract, but now knowing that abstraction to be only a part of the whole contradictory movement and result of experience. This recognition, says Rose, 'itself *commends* a different way of transforming that unfreedom' (1981, p. 201). What it commends is our continuing education.

> Self-knowing spirit is a relation and this knowing whether presented in the historical shapes of consciousness or as a science is perpetual and never-ending. Absolute knowing is a path which must be continually traversed, re-collecting the forms of consciousness and the forms of science. This idea of a whole which cannot be grasped in one moment or in one statement for it must be experienced is the idea of the system (1981, p. 182).

This is why comprehending (the broken middle of) the social relation in Hegel becomes an educational issue. The truth of the system is experience, and the truth of experience is our education. The truth of both is the broken middle of the social relation and the education relation. These relations together constitute the truth of the self-determinative experience of self-consciousness, which is now explored.

The life-and-death struggle

Mutual recognition is not for us. That is its truth and its impossibility, its self-developed determinate negation. For us, mutual recognition can only be known as it is experienced. Hegel develops the experience in two ways. First, in the life-and-death struggle, he shows how the encounter with another appears not as the social relation *per se* or the middle, but in the broken middle from the point of view of self-consciousness. The life-and-death struggle is the experience in self-consciousness of the other and the collapse of the middle which is their mutual recognition. Thus the life-and-death struggle is the vanishing or negation of the mutual social relation. In that mutual relation two consciousnesses are unified as one consciousness, and that one consciousness is social. But in the life-and-death struggle this one consciousness is divided into its two constituent moments of being for self and being for another. In mutual recognition, those two aspects are unified and are not separated. In the life-and-death struggle they are separated and the result is a one-sided relation, an anti-social relation, where one self-consciousness is recognised but the other is seen merely as someone who recognises. The former is the master, the latter the slave, and the result is an unequal (social) relation based on domination.

The self-consciousnesses which meet each other are simply independent shapes which know themselves in the sense that they know they are alive. This sense of living is, for them, the whole of their existence, the whole of what they are, a sense which is preserved 'through the exclusion from itself of everything else' (Hegel, 1977, p. 113). Hegel writes, 'For it, its essence and absolute object is "I"; and in this immediacy, or in this [mere] being, of its being-for-self, it is an *individual*' (1977, p. 113).

156

The universality in which it holds itself directly affects how it sees other such individuals. Since it is the whole of itself, then 'What is "other" for it is an unessential, negatively characterised object' (1977, p. 113). We know that each sees the other in the same way. Therefore, what for the living individual is an encounter only with a simple ordinary object, is for us who are looking on an encounter between two such objects. The significance of this only becomes clear after the struggle when the existence of one of them is confirmed as a mere thing, while the other achieves a recognition of its own certainty and living individuality. Before the struggle, the two individuals which face each other are not yet self-consciousnesses in the eyes of the other, nor, yet, in their own eyes either. This is because according to the process of recognition described earlier, a self-consciousness can only achieve a knowledge of itself when what is before it is the same as itself and what it receives back from the other is itself. This is not the case here, because what confronts it is not the same as itself. This confrontation does not achieve the conditions required for mutual recognition, for each individual sees before it only an object, something which is not part of its own living universality. 'Each is indeed certain of its own self, but not of the other' (1977, p. 113).

The view that the individual has of itself determines both its view of the other and its strategy in seeking to secure its own self-certainty. The living universality is defined as such by its 'exclusion from itself of everything else' (1977, p. 113). It is present to itself as an individual which is not in relation to anything like itself, nor in relation to anything which could compromise its own universality. This non-relation must include life itself. If the individual is self-consciousness of life rather than being itself as alive, then it would be in relation to life and would be a merely determinate aspect of life, something which depends upon life for its self. This would make it no different to the other which stands before it. In order, therefore, to assert its own universality it must show itself not to be in relation either to life itself or to the object confronting it. This self-certain universality, or non-relation, will present itself when self-consciousness shows its independence from life and from the other. This presentation, says Hegel,

> Is a twofold action: action on the part of the other, and action on its own part. In so far as it is the action of the other, each seeks the death of the other. But in doing so, the second kind of action, action on its own part, is involved; for the former involves the staking of its own life (1977, p. 113).

Each seeks the death of the other because the vanishing of the other is the objective proof of their non-relation, and non-relation is the proof of the independence and certainty of the individual. But this is not just the struggle of one individual, it is a struggle by both this self-consciousness and the other. Therefore when each seeks the death of the other, each also becomes that which the other wants to kill. What emerges here is a contradiction, and not at all the truth that was intended. The struggle, in which the goal is to prove non-relation,

157

becomes a mutual life and death struggle which therefore is a relation. Each individual is related to each other precisely because each seeks the death of the other; 'the relation of the two self-conscious individuals is such that they prove themselves and each other through a life-and-death struggle' (1977, pp. 113–14).

The result of the life-and-death struggle therefore is a mutual recognition. But it is not a positive mutual recognition and cannot therefore sustain itself. It is a mutual relation because in the mutual action of each individual, each learns two things. First it learns that, in risking its own life, it could die. Its universality is quickly put into perspective here. The assumption that, in its universality, it was not attached to any particular existence is now realised to be clearly wrong. In the experience that it could die, the 'I' is forced to realise that it is not universality, but a finite existence attached to life and which, without that attachment, would be nothing. In the experience of its own mortality it learns 'that there is nothing present in it which could not be regarded as a vanishing moment, that it is only pure *being-for-self*' (1977, p. 114). Its first lesson, then, is that the 'I' is in relation to life, and is only a particular existence.

The second lesson it learns is that what faces it as other is the same as itself. It saw the value of the existence of the other as nothing, as something which was a merely particular living thing lacking its own universality, because it had tried to kill it. But now self-consciousness knows that this is also its own truth. It, too, is just such a particular. Just as self-consciousness staked its own life and learnt that it was not universal, so in seeking the death of the other it shows that it treats the other also as not universal. Therefore, 'its essential being is present to it in the form of an "other"' (1977, p. 114). The death of self-consciousness and the death of the other would be their (positive) mutual self-relation, united in their mutual 'absolute negation' (1977, p. 114).

But, as Hegel points out, absolute negation, the mutual relation of the life-and-death struggle, 'is not for those who survived this struggle' (1977, p. 114). The mutual recognition which would be achieved in death is not the result for that self-consciousness which is left alive. The struggle, in the end, 'does away with the truth which was supposed to issue from it, and so, too, with the certainty of self generally' (1977, p. 114). The truth that was supposed to be the result was the objective presentation of the I's non-relation to anything particular. But the result, in fact, is its awareness that it is in relation both to life and to the other. Life alone is insufficient for self-certainty, for the self-consciousness which is alive now knows that this life is in relation to death. Thus, this independence is without the absolute negativity (death) which would make it truly independent of life. Similarly, it has not found its independence in the other for they have not both died, and therefore the negativity or relation which each shares as their mutual truth, where each is 'present' as the other, is not their actual relation while alive. For mutual recognition to result from the life-and-death struggle, life and death would have to be unified. but they are not. 'For just as life is the *natural* setting of consciousness, independence without absolute negativity, so death is the *natural*

158

negation of consciousness, negation without independence, which thus remains without the required significance of recognition' (1977, p. 114).

The result of the life-and-death struggle therefore is the negative self-determination of mutual recognition. It is not the positive middle of the social relation. On the contrary, for the survivors of the struggle something rather different has happened. They can no longer enjoy the (abstract) presumption of their own universality because now self-consciousness knows that it is not a pure universality, but a determinate and particular self-consciousness. It is a life which knows itself as a life. It is therefore not merely an object, but not absolutely infinite either. It is an individual person. Determined by its experience of death and of the other, it returns to itself as an awareness which is present as this individual. In death it would be all others. In life, therefore, it is only and solely itself. This marks the end of its 'natural existence' (1977, p. 114) and the beginning of its socially determinative existence, although the social here, the relation, is kept separated from the identity which is produced. This is also the end, therefore, of the life-and-death struggle, for no longer does each need to prove its independence through non-relation. Now each self-consciousness is non-relation. Now they are done away with as extremes, needing to prove themselves as separate from each other, for now they know themselves to be separate. The struggle is no longer necessary. Thus, says Hegel, the (social) relation of the struggle is converted, in experience, into a non-struggle and non-relation. 'The middle term collapses into a lifeless unity which is split into lifeless merely immediate, unopposed extremes; and the two do not reciprocally give and receive one another back from each other consciously, but leave each other free only indifferently, like things' (1977, p. 114).

Here the contradiction of relation and non-relation works in reverse to that noted a moment ago. The struggle was contradictory because the goal of non-relation required relation. Now the result of that relation (the struggle) is non-relation. Once self-consciousness stops trying to kill the other, and stops risking its own life, then this self-consciousness has achieved non-relation or independence. The struggle proved the truth of relation to be death, and the truth of non-relation to be life. The self-consciousness that lives has therefore risen above the untruth of relation and knows its living truth to be non-relation or independence. The truth of relation is, for it, only a living death, the truth of being merely for another, a 'life' of absolute negation. The contradiction of the middle, or of the social relation, is present, however, in both. Non-relation is a relation, and relation is its own truth and therefore also non-relation. But because the middle is now a broken middle of life and death, so the social relation is divided into non-relation and relation, and is itself a broken middle. The truth of those two extremes is therefore the relation of their relation, or the broken middle itself. But before that is comprehended as a self-opposition, its self-division will appear in many different shapes. These shapes are the appearance of natural consciousness as non-relation, a non-relation which has its substance in the different forms of property law and work relations which it takes as its own truth.

159

Each form is a misrecognition by the non-relation of its relation, and is a positing of non-relation as its own certainty.

In the case under examination at the moment, the natural consciousness which takes itself as it immediately appears puts the struggle behind it, forgets it has taken place, and does not see that it is the result of the struggle or even admit the struggle in the form of relation. Relation is not the characteristic of this self-consciousness. This self-consciousness is now the independent person. It no longer needs to prove itself in struggle, for its independence and its non-relation are now recognised legally. The legal status of this person is the recognition of its non-relation to others, that it needs no others to prove its independence. The relation has therefore vanished as far as the person is concerned, for it is no longer for anyone except itself. But the relation on which this recognition depends, and of which it is the result, is present in the form of the slave. The slave is the aspect of the struggle which is relation, which the master has now conveniently forgotten. The master's identity has its truth as non-relation. The work of relation, of dependency, of being for another, it leaves to the slave. The whole of mutual recognition is present here, being for self and being for another, but not as it is in and for itself, or as the middle term. Out of the relation of struggle comes the non-relation of the person or the master, and the relation of the slave. The one consciousness which was mutual recognition is now divided into its two moments of relation and non-relation. The result is a recognition which is one-sided and unequal. It sees 'the splitting-up of the middle term into the extremes which, as extremes, are opposed to one another, one being only *recognised*, the other only *recognising*' (1977, pp. 112–13).

Relation of master and slave

The relation between the master and the slave described by Hegel can be taken to illustrate at least three related situations. First, as seen in the previous section, it is the result of the experience of relation and non-relation in the life-and-death struggle. This experience is the loss or the negation of the middle, or the social relation *per se*, and the division of that middle into the two consciousnesses of which it is both. Mutual recognition is being-for-itself and being-for-another. Such a relation was experienced in the life-and-death struggle as absolute negation, and possible only as the mutual risking of life by each in seeking the death of the other. This experience of absolute negation is determinative for those who continue to live. For those who survive, being-for-another (or relation) becomes known as negation without independence, and, conversely, being-for-self becomes life without negation. The experience of mutual recognition therefore results in the separation of mutual relation into being-for-itself and being-for-another. The actuality of this experience is the existence of the master and the slave. When both are visible, then both moments of the experience – relation and non-relation – are present, and the domination of mutual recognition by property relations is clear and transparent.

Secondly, the master/slave relation, as Hegel describes it, illustrates the contradiction of the broken middle of the social relation as a whole. As will now be shown, it explains how the truth of their (social) relation is relation and non-relation, or is the relation of that relation. Taken in a non-historical context, the master/slave relation describes the return of the relation to itself through its own work, to the point where absolute negation achieves a mind of its own. In this sense their relation is another presentation of determinate negation, and presents not just the truth of the broken middle of the social relation, but also, as will be shown in Chapter 7, the broken middle of the education relation.

Third, the master/slave relation not only describes the workings and contradictions of an overt and transparent relation of domination. In bourgeois social relations, where all are legally recognised as masters, the slave vanishes. When the slave vanishes, relation loses its presence and visibility in the world. Equally, then, the domination of mutual recognition by property relations is no longer transparent. In these circumstances, the master/slave relation can be used to illustrate that the slave and the master are now one person, free and not-free, non-relation and relation at one and the same time. In the domination of bourgeois social relations, the master/slave relation is internal within each person as the whole of determinate negation. It is the truth of the self-relation of the person, of the return of the person from its illusory relation as a shining for others. The master/slave relation here becomes the truth of the experience of the person as contradiction, or of subjectivity. When the bourgeois subject achieves a mind of its own, it is as the truth of the broken middle which is now itself. This truth is contradictory; it is actual in the return of the subject, and it is comprehensive in that this experience of return is self-determinative of the relation as a broken middle. The subject, like the slave (and like critique), has its truth present for it only when it is not itself (or when it is its own shadow).

With this in mind, this section now describes the master/slave relation, and the contradiction or broken middle which this relation contains and lives out.

The master is the experience of the social relation which is the separation of each from the other, and of their independent status from each other. It is, in the world, the result of the experience of the life-and-death struggle, a result which is independence or non-relation. Its 'essential nature is to be for itself' (Hegel, 1977, p. 115). The slave is the experience of the social relation in which each is related to another. It is the existence in the world of the mutual activity of each participant in the life-and-death struggle, but an activity which is no longer part of the result of the struggle as far as self-consciousness is concerned. The slave represents the relation of each to the other, a relation which no plays no part in establishing the identity of the master. The slave is 'the dependent consciousness whose essential nature is simply to live or to be for another' (1977, p. 115). In their separation and their relation, the master and the slave together constitute the experience of the broken middle which is the social relation. The master is able to resist any relation to, or mediation by, or dependence upon, the other by doing two things. First, it no longer sees the meeting of itself with the other as a direct confrontation between them. They relate to each other, now, as owners, as persons, as non-relations. They have proved their independence by having their relation only with that which is not the same as they are. In relating to each other through their relation (only) to the slave, they avoid relating directly to anyone else at all. Secondly, therefore, the master views the slave as merely a thing without its own independent existence or status. Since the master is independent, the work of relating is not its own. Relating is something which the master is defined as not doing. Since the master is not relating to others, recognition is a purely one-sided affair, gained in relation to objects and not to other individuals. It knows the slave and the object to be the same living death of those whose existence is purely dependent upon another. They are, therefore, *for* it. This right to relate as owner is the domination which the master enjoys over that which has no independent existence. It is domination guaranteed in the legal status of a person. Indeed, it is what a person is. Thus, says Hegel, the lord 'takes to himself only the dependent aspect of the thing and has the pure enjoyment of it' (1977, p. 116).

The law of ownership is therefore the actuality of the splitting up of the social relation, or the middle. Property rights are the truth of non-relation. They are what non-relation is. Whether visible or hidden, property rights are always a domination of the social relation *per se*. Equally, the shape which the property law takes at any particular time is the actuality of the social relation for us. It determines how we 'relate' to each other, for it is the determination of that relating. It is always the negation of our mutual relation, and we always arrive too late to precede that negation, for only in the negation does the question (or the experience) of social relations arise. What property rights ensure, in fact, is that the mutual relation between individuals is always determined in the form of a relation between objects. This is true both of the non-relation which owners enjoy between each other, and the non-relation which they enjoy in the ownership of their objects. The relation of the non-relation (the person) to objects replaces its relation to others. It becomes what relation is, i.e. ownership.

Thus, while the slave negates itself in relation to the master, and the social relation is transformed into ownership or the absence of mutual relation, the master is free. But in fact the master is not free from relation at all. It needs the slave to do the work, to be the relation, which would otherwise negate the master. What the master is forced to recognise is that its independence is not independence at all, but rather the opposite of itself. The truth of the broken middle of the social relation asserts itself here. Non-relation (the master) is dependent upon relation (the slave) for its own independence. The master is related to the negative. It can only assert its own non-relation or independence in relation to the relation. In this realisation, the master expresses its own self-contradiction. It is no longer certain of its self as non-relation: 'On the contrary, his truth is in reality the unessential consciousness and its unessential action'

(1977, p. 117). The contradiction of the social relation, which is non-relation and relation, is experienced by the master as the loss of self. It is where it experiences itself as a non-relation which is also relation. It has become the opposite of itself – non-master, or non-person. 'The truth of the independent consciousness is accordingly the servile consciousness of the bondsman' (1977, p. 117).

This is, for the master, a purely negative self-experience. That is because, for it, dependence is a purely negative state, a living death, lacking any positive sense of self. However, the contradiction of the social relation works not just not on the master but also on the slave. The master's independence has become dependence, and non-relation has become relation. Similarly, the dependence of the slave will turn into independence, and relation will become the truth of non-relation. 'Just as lordship showed that its essential nature is the reverse of what it wants to be, so too servitude in its consummation will really turn into the opposite of what it immediately is... a truly independent consciousness' (1977, p. 117). The master and slave become the truth of each other, a truth which together is the broken middle of the social relation, or the relation of the relation.

So far, the nature of the slave or of relation has been examined only from the point of view of the master. For the master, the slave is the unessential relation to otherness, a relation which is negated in and as the independent status of the master. The non-identity of the slave, however, has to be reassessed by the master when its independence is seen to be illusory, i.e. in the experience of independence as self-contradictory or also dependent. The slave appears now for itself as the truth of this loss of independence. In the life-and-death struggle, there was the experience of each participant that 'there is nothing present in it which could not be regarded as a vanishing moment' (1977, p. 114). This experience of absolute vanishing is also the truth of the work which the slave performs, work in which it, too, vanishes. It is the truth of the slave because the slave is the consciousness that has no existence of its own, and exists solely in relation to the other. It, the slave, is nothing on its own. Fear of death is the experience of that which would be nothing. Therefore death is the 'absolute lord' (1977, p. 117) and master, or is the identity of the slave. That which exists as nothing has experienced in fear its own true form, pure nothingness, or, in Hegelian terms, pure being-for-self or absolute negativity. But nothingness is not just the truth of the slave merely in principle, it also exists in the life of the slave. In the service which the slave performs for the master, that is, in relating to others so that the master can remain unrelated and independent, the slave 'rids himself of his attachment to natural existence in every single detail; and gets rid of it by working on it' (1977, p. 117). In its life of service, or work that is for-another, the slave has no life of its own. It constantly repeats its own nothingness, and through its own activity, ensures its own negation, and its master's identity.

The master failed to achieve mutual recognition because, from its point of view, 'the aspect of unessential relation to the thing fell to the lot of the bondsman' (1977, p. 118). However, as we have seen, in fact the unessential relation belonged to the master because, in its dependence upon the slave for its own independence, it was it, the master, whose existence became uncertain, unstable and incomplete. 'It lacks the side of objectivity and permanence' (1977, p. 118) because it has negated the other, but not itself. That is why the independence of the master 'is itself only a fleeting one' (1977, p. 118). The whole of the contradiction of the broken middle of the social relation asserts itself here. The service of the slave both ensures and undermines, at one and the same time, the independence of the master. The independent self dissolves into absolute contradiction, which is to say it becomes the truth of the social relation, or the relation of relation and non-relation.

A negative result for the master is a positive result for the slave. The master cannot sustain its own self through its dependence upon another. The slave, however, which appears to have no identity at all, in fact can sustain itself. The slave, in keeping with the contradictory logic of the broken middle of the social relation is, in being the slave, also the master. The slave becomes also the master because the slave is both self-activity and self-result. It does not become independent, or just the master. The identity of the slave is negative, it is one where the truth of independence is seen to be in-dependence. Through the work of the slave, the truth of the slave is brought about. Whereas the master could not realise its self because its independence contradicted itself and collapsed, the slave realises its self, i.e. dependence, in service. Its work is the living out of the negative life which has pure nothingness as its truth. Through what it does, pure relating, it brings about what it is. Negative work and negative identity, or activity and result, are for the slave, its own self. It is a self-negation of the negative, and is therefore a self-determination.

> Through this rediscovery of himself by himself, the bondsman realises that it is precisely in his work wherein he seemed to have only an alienated existence that he acquires a mind of his own (1977, pp. 118–19).

It is itself in the active loss of itself to another, for this is its own negation and return. This, and not the master, is the relation of non-relation and relation. This work is the truth of the master and the slave, a truth which appears only in their separation, and which is itself only as the truth of their opposition. Independence is only itself negatively, or as the result of its own loss in relation to another. An individual is only for-itself and in-itself in being for-another.

The slave therefore achieves, in relation to another, a self-relation which the master cannot. The master is negated in the contradiction of the social relation, but the slave comes to know itself in the contradiction. This is the significance of the master/slave relation for understanding social relations in Hegel. The social relation when it is purely itself is mutual recognition, or a middle in which self and other are indeterminate. But the truth of such a relation or a middle cannot appear in this, its purity. The social relation always appears as a relation between individuals, and therefore can only be known by those individuals as what it is not, or as its division. It is for self-consciousness, here, to take on the work of the

164

slave in relation to the modern form of non-relation, the bourgeois property relation. As the next section will illustrate, this work is the self-work no longer of the slave but of the bourgeois subject, but like the slave, it only achieves self-determination in the loss of itself which is already itself.

The bourgeois form of the social relation

This section explores the broken middle of the social relation in its modern form as bourgeois private property law. To do so is again to discuss the relation and non-relation of the individual person. It was seen earlier how in the life-and-death struggle the two aspects of the social relation were kept apart, and how the relation itself appeared only in the self-contradiction of each aspect. However, in the social relation as it appears in its modern form of the bourgeois property relation, the two aspects of the relation do not appear as clearly separated, for one of them has vanished from view. The slave, the aspect of relating or dependency upon another, is no longer visible. As a result, the domination of relation by non-relation is not visible. This relation of domination is now hidden behind the appearance of the 'free' person. In beginning such an enquiry, then, it is helpful to examine briefly the way in which this free person can be described as a misrecognition of itself.

Rose notes that Hegel, in the Jena lectures of 1803–4 and 1805–6, employed the term recognition rather than intuition because it emphasised the lack of identity in what is seen. Recognition, or better, re-cognition, 'implies an initial experience which is misunderstood, and which has to be re-experienced. It does not imply an immediate, successful vision, but that the immediate vision or experience is incomplete' (Rose, 1981, p. 71). Recognition would therefore be the term to use in describing how the slave achieved a mind of its own. The immediate experience of the slave as existing purely for-another is a misrecognition of itself. This experience is re-cognised, or known in a new and different way, when the slave realises that in the work which it performs, it reproduces the relating which is its pure (non-) self. Thus it comes to recognise that in its activity it is the truth of itself. Misrecognition, its immediate nothingness, is still a part of its identity, and therefore this re-cognition is of misrecognition by itself. If misrecognition were overcome then it would no longer be a re-cognition of the slave by itself. What has happened is that it has come to know itself now as it already was, although previously its own actuality was unclear to it.

Misrecognition is a necessary part of all relations or middles in Hegel. All such relations appear at first as if they have fallen apart into contradictions which are not only unsolvable, but wholly negative. Misrecognition is (i.e. is already) the experience of self as loss, or as negated. Re-cognition is the realisation that loss is a part of the (contradictory) whole, and is necessarily its determinate existence. The loss of the master is the truth of the social relation, and as we will see in the next chapter, the loss of the teacher is the truth of the education relation. Both

165

involve the re-cognition of misrecognition by misrecognition. Both therefore are self-determinative, and self-relation.

As was seen in Chapter 4, the 'instrument' of misrecognition is thought itself. In its immediate appearance as natural consciousness, thought 'knows' itself as a result or non-relation. Behind it, or hidden from it, lies the path by which it came to be a non-relation, a path which it has forgotten. This was the case with the appearance of natural, rational consciousness. It had forgotten its development as surrender and nothingness, and appeared only as the universal certainty of its independence. Reason and the free person are the same appearance of natural consciousness as non-relation. They are the same principle of non-relation which is wholly independent, but now appearing as universality. Knowledge and property are the objective proof of their independence, for through knowledge and property they prove that they are not dependent upon the world or upon others. Through knowledge of the world, and ownership of the object, relation or the aspect of dependency falls to the world and to the object. They exist purely for reason or for the person. This natural consciousness is a misrecognition, because reason and property as non-relations are already in relation to others, but cannot see that they are. They become aware that they are when they experience their universality as a contradiction. Here the relation to others does become clear, and the misrecognition of certainty can be re-cognised. When natural consciousness knows its own determination as misrecognition, then it knows itself to be what is actual. This re-cognition of itself as misrecognition, and as actual, is a comprehensive self-determination. The contradiction of natural consciousness with regard to its misrecognition as person and teacher was examined in Part I. The misrecognition of that contradiction as enlightenment regarding dialectics was examined in Part II. In the next chapter this self-determination will be examined in relation to the education relation as a whole. In this chapter, it is explored now as the dilemma of the subject within the appearance of the social relation as bourgeois private property (non-) relations.

In modern society, characterised by bourgeois property relations, all are masters. Rational consciousness asserts its universality and independence, and shows that there is nothing upon which its sovereignty is dependent. Each consciousness is equally entitled to this recognition, for each rational consciousness is the embodiment of 'the rational principle' (Rose, 1981, p. 88). This recognition is achieved in law, where each self-consciousness is granted equal status under the law as a free person, a sovereign individual.

As described earlier, the very concepts of individuality and independence are themselves the result of the life-and-death struggle in which the social relation is divided into its two moments of non-relation and relation. Independence is the moment of non-relation. The master is independent because it was not dependent upon another, and was not for another. It embodied non-relation. Non-relation is, in pure terms, the freedom of that whose relation to another is purely one-sided. Non-relation has the other for itself only. It is not also for the other. The word 'for' here is firstly possession, and then property. Hegel describes these

166

developments in the *Philosophy of Right*. Freedom is real to begin with in the ability to take possession of the thing in the external world. By taking possession, the will of the individual gains an objective reality in that the object is for him, or is his. Summarising Hegel (1967, p. 42) freedom, here, is the result of my taking possession of an object, of having that object as mine, or for me, as my property, and of seeing in the possession the realisation of (the freedom of) my will. Since it is my independent will or non-relation alone which has been realised, then private property is the objective proof of that independence. The right to own property is the recognition of the domination of non-relation over relation, of owner over object, or, which is the same, of that which is for itself over that which is for another. Property rights therefore define what a person is. I am because I can own. Rose notes that property law establishes personality. A person can appropriate a thing, because that which is only relation, or for another, can have no rights, is not personal. 'It may therefore be appropriated or possessed on an arbitrary and capricious basis. I become the master of what I possess, and it is the embodiment of my "personality"' (1981, p. 85).

Non-relation, therefore, is embodied in the right to own property. Ownership of an object is the recognition in law of the dependency of the object, and of the independence (from relation) of the owner. The object falls purely under the will of its owner. It exercises no control over the owner. The owner can do with it whatever he chooses. In this way, the right to own property is a concrete recognition of the non-relation (the master) as the owner, and relation (the slave) as merely for the owner. The substance of property rights is to distinguish between that which is for itself and that which is purely for another. In bourgeois property relations, all are recognised as enjoying the right to property. It is the expression of the independence of all rational consciousnesses, and the recognition in law that the designation of some as masters and some as slaves is irrational and contrary to the universality of the rational principle. When reason tests the master/slave relation it is found to be self-contradictory. Reason is universal. It therefore follows that to designate only some rational consciousnesses as free and others as not contradicts the principle by which it knows itself. For reason, all self-consciousnesses are free because for reason each self-consciousness is its own certainty and truth. The expression of this universality and freedom is bourgeois property relations, where all are free because none is for another. All are independent. All are non-relation.

What bourgeois freedom achieves, however, is not a change in the division of the social relation *per se* into relation and non-relation. What it changes is how that division now appears to consciousness, and how it is known. In the relation of the master and the slave, the domination of non-relation over relation, or being for self over being for another, of independence over dependence, was clear and transparent. Both sides of the broken middle of the social relation were 'recognised' and were visible in the forms of the master and the slave. But under bourgeois property relations the domination is not visible. It is where freedom only is visible, or non-relation, and where dependency or relation has vanished.

167

The victory of bourgeois freedom is that dependency or non-relation has been overcome. But it is a victory (as Part I has shown) in which each master returns as contradiction. Therefore the bourgeois social relation is still divided into relation and non-relation, but relation is now hidden and no longer has an objective existence in the world. When the slave was overcome, it was the universal victory and ultimate domination of non-relation over the half of itself which it continually denied but to which it was continually returned. In the master/slave relation, the relation of their relation was realised through the contradictory truth of each. The master became dependent, and the slave achieved a mind of its own.

That contradiction still appears in bourgeois property relations. This time, however, it is not a contradiction between the free and the unfree as two separate individuals. Now it is the contradiction of the free individual in and for himself. The domination of the master over the slave in its bourgeois appearance is the domination of the free person over relation itself. The reason that this domination is so hard to see is that the person is now in a self-relation, and its domination is now over itself. That which guarantees its freedom is that which also contradicts it. The victory is of universal non-relation. It is therefore immanently contradictory, for it is at one and the same time the recognition of all that each is independent from all others. This self-contradictory universality is expressed as the law of private property. Its recognition that all are free means that the law both expresses and negates the universality of relation. Each is for no one. But since all are for themselves, and all are equal, no distinction can be drawn between those who are for themselves and those who are for another. Thus, for the universality of one independence to be recognised, it is necessary to recognise the independence of all. This is the same as saying that, in law, the independence of one is for everyone else. Bourgeois property law expresses the contradiction seen earlier in the master/slave relation that independence is in-dependence. Here, personal independence is dependent upon the social relation of which bourgeois property law is the misrecognition.

The contradiction of bourgeois property law is the contradiction of the broken middle of the social relation. Rose describes it as follows:

> Private property is a contradiction, because an individual's private or particular possession can only be guaranteed by the whole society, the universal. The universal is the community. This guarantee makes possession into property. Property means the right to exclude others, and the exclusion of other individuals (particular) is made possible by the communal will (universal). But, if everyone has an equal right to possess, to exclude others, then no one can have any guaranteed possession, or, anyone's possession belongs equally to everyone else (1981, p. 73).

The contradiction, as Rose presents it here, has as its two sides relation and non-relation, and their rational exclusivity of one another. If non-relation is made universal in law, then it is the relation of all non-relations. Here, then, there is

168

absolutely no security of property, for its legality is dependent not upon the will of the individual, but the will of all. Rose writes that the contradiction between the single will and the universal will

> appears to be removed by the communal recognition of possession as property. The security of my property is the security of the property of others: I recognise their right to exclude me from their property in return for my right to exclude them. But the contradiction remains that no one can have any secure property (1981, p. 73).

The contradiction is revealed in the words 'in return', for they signal that independence is only possible in relation, or for others. To know that independence is already in return is to recognise the misrecognition of natural consciousness, and to know the individual as what is actual. This is the significance of Hegel's critique of bourgeois property relations.

Rose notes that the only alternative to the contradiction would be 'for my possession, *qua* possession, to remain in my possession, but, *qua* property, for it no longer to refer solely to me, but to be universal' (1981, p. 73). But this is its own contradiction, for if something is to be thought of as communal property, then relation has been posited in law. This would be a domination over non-relation, for relation is already between things which, in being related, are also separated. The communal (social) relation is another broken middle, for it is not an immediate unity, or middle in itself. Its own contradiction is that in positing itself as relation *per se*, it becomes in itself a non-relation, or the abstract identity of mutual recognition. But, as seen in the life-and-death struggle, such an absolute relation is possible for us only as death. For those who are alive, the immediacy of that relation is already lost, and the individual is returned to itself as not-mutual recognition. Communal relations can therefore only impose themselves on those whose experience of relation is negative, and who know themselves only in opposition to its posited unity. Bourgeois property relations and no property relations are both contradictory. Both oppose the freedom they seek to enshrine. Neither takes account of the actuality of the broken middle, seeking to heal its division without comprehending its determination, even of those attempts themselves, as a repetition of its fracture and the return of the free person.

The freedom which is an implicit and immediate unity in the social relation of mutual recognition is (now) determinate freedom. This means that the idea of freedom is known and negated. Because it is known, it is divided into the constituent moments of all determinate content, i.e. non-relation and relation. Freedom, then, for us, is not-mutual recognition, or the actuality of freedom as the relation between relation and non-relation. Freedom, for us, is a broken middle. It was seen earlier in this chapter that this broken middle determines itself not in one appearance or shape, but in two (master and slave). Both sides of its separated existence, non-relation and relation, are present, but they are only known as present when the particular will (the slave) and the universal will (the master) collide in contradiction. This contradiction returns relation (slave) and non-relation (master) back to themselves, now self-divided (again). As was seen earlier, the master has this experience as its own negation, and its truth becomes the slave. The slave collides with the master and experiences this negation (this service) as its own truth. It is the presence of both of these moments which ensures that return contains the education and the development in which the negative can come to know its own truth. The self-division of relation and non-relation (respectively) enables the moments to appear in and for each other, by which their whole as self-division (of the social relation *per se*) can now be realised. Or, where self-division, faced by itself, is able to comprehend itself for the first time as a broken middle.

To understand this movement in regard to our experience of bourgeois social relations, it is necessary now to follow these two self-divisions in more detail. In this drama (played out by subject and substance), the universal, or independence, or being for self, and the particular, or dependence, or being for another, appear on both sides of the divide. Just as the experience of the master contains independence and dependence, and just as the experience of the slave contains dependence and independence, so in experiencing bourgeois social relations, subject and substance will each be seen to contain both independence and dependence. On the one hand, there is the universal will, the relation (or not) of each to all others. This, for Hegel, is (our experience of) ethical substance. On the other hand, there is our particular will, and its non-relation (or not) to itself. This is not substance but subject. The relation between subject and substance, formed out of the self-relation of each, is the whole which constitutes (our misrecognition of, and its re-cognition of itself as) the whole which is ethical life. Only in subject and substance being divided from each other, and known in and through that division, is freedom or ethical life known and realised as the relation of their relation(s). Freedom is actual, but only in the contradictory experience which is our ethical life. To comprehend the actuality of a society dominated by bourgeois property relations, it is necessary to comprehend ethical life as and in this contradiction. To do so is also to realise how the positing of solutions to the contradiction is already another repetition of the contradiction, and our return again as a free person.

Relations of ethical life

In the *Phenomenology of Spirit*, Hegel describes the division of spirit (subject and substance) in the following way: '*Action* divides it into substance, and consciousness of the substance; and divides the substance as well as consciousness' (1977, p. 266). Viewed abstractly, substance is the side of the broken middle of social relations which might be called the idea of freedom as mutual dependence, or as the truth of not one, but all. It expresses the idea of freedom as mutual dependence recognised in universal law. The subject, on the

170

other hand, viewed abstractly, is the particular freedom and independence of each person, not all, but one. When the two sides, substance and subject, meet in the contradiction of bourgeois property law, then their mutual misrecognition is present again to itself as (the broken middle which is) spirit. What concerns us in this section and the next is to examine the misrecognition of both relation and non-relation in and as both subject and substance, and the recognition of that misrecognition by itself in and as spirit. This is an enquiry, then, carried out by ethical life into itself, and is, in a strictly Hegelian sense, a philosophical enquiry, one containing within it the contradictions and abstract impossibilities of such an enquiry having either a beginning or an end. It is in this spirit of misrecognition that the *Philosophy of Right* and Hegel's other 'philosophies' have to be read.

In the *Philosophy of Right*, relation, or ethical substance, is an immediate unity in the family, a division from itself into non-relation as civil society, and a return to itself as the relation of that non-relation as the state. On the other side, the subject is an immediate identity of the particular will as the person, a division of itself into relation as subjectivity (or in reflection), and a recognition of that relation as relation only for another. Substantial relations and non-relations, and subjective relations and non-relations, are a self-relation only in their opposition to themselves and to each other, an opposition which has to be experienced in order that it can be self-determinative. The *Philosophy of Right* cannot be comprehended unless this educational aspect of its development, and the educational relation between the particular and the universal, is seen as determinative. As such, ethical life is the self-relation of the two extremes which oppose each other, subject and substance, but is only a self-relation because subject and substance are in themselves contradictory. The negation of each is the realisation of ethical life having a mind of its own. Its truth as self-relation (self-opposition) is our determination within the broken middle. It is precisely our subjective experience of substance, i.e. our separation from it, which realises the truth of the self-relation, or broken middle, which is ethical life. This self-divided experience is now examined, although this needs to be prefaced by a few remarks regarding the difficulty of an educational reading of Hegel's *Philosophy of Right*.

Ethical life is the negation of both subject and substance, or the particular and the universal. It is the truth of the dilemma of their opposition. Or, again, ethical life is the totality of relations between individuals, a totality which includes the experience of those relations and the subjective dispositions of those for whom ethical life exists. To comprehend Hegel's idea of ethical life requires us to see how education or experience and return are implicit in this presentation. This is particularly difficult in the *Philosophy of Right*, for in this work the illusions of consciousness which are determined within ethical life are included with little assistance to our philosophical consciousness. It is left up to us to read the work educationally to reveal the broken middle which is our experience of the truth of ethical life. Rose notes that the *Philosophy of Right* is written in the 'severe style' (1981, p. 51) which is 'concerned to give a true representation of its object and makes little concession to the spectator. It is designed solely to do justice to the

171

integrity of the object' (1981, p. 51). The danger with such a presentation is that the negative work of experience is overlooked, and the education upon which the content is based is forgotten and therein often read without it. Hegel does present the contradictions which imply ethical life, but does not impose them, he does not do the work for us. The *Philosophy of Right*, says Rose, *is* a phenomenology; 'the illusions and experiences of moral and political consciousness are presented in an order designed to show how consciousness may progress through them to comprehension of the determination of ethical life' (1981, p. 50). The *Philosophy of Right*, therefore, is a work of education. The text refers to education a great deal in the section on ethical life. This is because education is the self-work of each stage of ethical life, it is how the universal (re)presents itself. However, family and civil education in themselves are also another education, for they prepare the way for their own collapse as universals. It is this (comprehensive) education which is harder to keep in mind in reading the *Philosophy of Right*, but which is essential if the development of ethical substance and the subject is to be understood. This is most difficult when reading the section on the state, for there the education which is the state lies elsewhere, i.e. in the relation of subjectivity which is for an other.

The importance of education will be highlighted in what follows. 'Unfortunately,' remarks Rose, 'the mistakes of natural consciousness which Hegel was exposing have frequently been attributed to him' (1981, p. 50). Such readings miss the educational content upon which the presentation is dependent. They 'forget' the determination of ethical life as self-relation, and therefore do not see the contradictions which are its own self-education and actuality. The educational development of subject and substance is described later, not by separating subject and substance, as in the *Philosophy of Right*, but by reading subject and substance against one another so that their relation to each other is always kept in mind. The preliminary work for this was done in the previous section, where ethical life emerged in and as our experience of bourgeois property relations. We now follow ethical life in its immediate appearance, the family, its self-division into non-relation and relation, civil society and the subject, and their contradiction realised through the negation of the negative subject by itself, whose truth is the state, or the relation of the relation between the private individual and collective interest. In this way the state appears as the return of ethical life to itself, a return realised in the education of the subject, or the re-cognition of itself as misrecognition.

Hegel presents ethical life firstly as the immediate ethical unity of the family. It 'begins' as a contract between two people, but this standpoint is transcended. Two personalities enter into a mutual tie in which the two separate identities are submerged and disappear to become one relationship. In its pure form 'one's frame of mind is to have self-consciousness of one's individuality within this unity as the absolute essence of oneself, with the result that one is in it not as an independent person but as a member' (Hegel, 1967, p. 110). The ethical tie in the family is similar to that of custom, in that there is no differentiation between the family (or law) and its members. Each is and acts as a family member. The family is the law, and the family is the identity of each constituent member. Each is the same as the other. The family is therefore ethical life as the immediate unity of relation and non-relation.

But marriage is a broken middle, for the relationship itself is both a joining and a separation. It is only because the two participants are different and separate that the union is possible at all. Both moments of the broken middle, separation and relation, are present in marriage. The family itself has a real existence in the family property, for property becomes the 'embodiment of the substantial personality of the family' (1967, p. 116). However, the unity of the family, its immediate self-relation, does not appear through its property, for property is only the personal will given reality. It appears through its children.

> In substance marriage is a unity, though only a unity of inwardness or disposition; in outward existence, however, the unity is sundered in the two parties. It is only in the children that the unity itself exists externally, objectively, and explicitly as a unity, because the parents love the children as their love, as the embodiment of their own substance (1967, p. 117).

The immediate ethical relation of the family is reproduced as family education. The relation is itself in its being learnt and known as the universal. Ethical life only is as its own reproduction, which is to say, its self-expression in and as the education of those whose relation it is. In the family a child's education is also immediately ethical. It takes the form of instilling 'ethical principles into him in the form of an immediate feeling... so that... his heart may live its early years in love, trust and obedience' (1967, p. 117). This education, being only an undifferentiated self-relation, also has its negative side, that of 'raising children out of the instinctive, physical, level on which they are originally, to self-subsistence and freedom of personality and so to the level on which they have the power to leave the natural unity of the family' (1967, pp. 117–8). In keeping with the logic of the broken middle, this immediate education contains both the joining of the child within the family and the separation of the child from the family. Family education prepares the way for the dissolution of the family, sowing the seeds, as it does, for the future education of civil society which must replace it. The individual personality which the family develops in each child will soon be recognised as a person outside of the family, and as 'capable of holding free property of their own' (1967, p. 118). As such, his education is no longer a family concern, it now belongs to the sphere of ethical life which is based upon the principle of private needs, a sphere no longer characterised by immediate unity, but by division and separation.

In the sphere of civil society, it is no longer the case that each individual is lost within an all-encompassing ethical totality. Now each is forced to stand alone as a single person, and the principle of civil society, its universality, is the education of each member regarding its own sphere of personal needs, a principle which is given 'the right to develop and launch forth in all directions' (1967, p. 123). The person in civil society is granted freedom from relation altogether. Ethical life appears now in its stage of self-division, the separation of subject and substance, or the division of itself into civil society and the person. It is the sphere of independence, or of non-relation of subject to substance. But, further, it is the ensuing contradiction of non-relation, as rehearsed in the master/slave relation, that enables ethical life then to achieve a mind of its own, as the state. As a stage on the way in the self-education of ethical life, civil society is only its illusory being, an appearance of universality or the truth of all, but one which is simply presupposed, and is not yet for itself. Only in being negated in and by subjective education is ethical life determinate, or for itself, and is the state or the absolute self-relation of ethical life.

Within civil society, the legal status of the person is only an abstract non-relation. However, the education of civil society, in expressing its own totality, is a double education. It is an education about independence, which means it is also an education about the contradiction of independence. Put another way, this is to say that when the subject experiences substance as contradiction, then ethical life is returned to itself.

The person is one principle of civil society, but, says Hegel, 'the particular person is essentially so related to other particular persons that each establishes himself and finds satisfaction by means of the others' (1967, pp. 122–3). However, any co-operation is not based on mutual freedom, but on personal need. Ethical life is not present as freedom but as necessity. The most that such associations can produce is 'formal freedom' (1967, p. 125), because all persons are operating singly, pursuing their own selfish ends according to the necessities which have been imposed. In pursuit of his own ends, civil man is necessarily brought into contact with others, but this contact is established through the work which he performs for his own needs. This is what Hegel calls 'the external state' (1967, p. 123). For example, it becomes clear in his dealings with other persons that his independence from them is called into question when each person interacts with another through the formal status of their identity as property owners. To gain property, each person is required to trade etc. with other persons. There is, therefore, immediately present here a recognition of all other property owners as the 'same' and different. This 'mutuality' of abstract persons is actual in contract.

> Contract is the process in which there is revealed and mediated the contradiction that I am and remain the independent owner of something from which I exclude the will of another only in so far as in identifying my will with the will of another I cease to be an owner (1967, p. 58).

A contract therefore implies that each person 'in accordance with the common will of both, ceases to be an owner and yet is and remains one' (1967, p. 58). In this experience of contradiction, the person ceases to exist abstractly, or merely in

174

itself, and is now also for himself. 'Its personality... it now has for its object' (1967, p. 74), and it becomes a subject. This also means that right and wrong, which were defined only abstractly in relation to the particular will, are now defined in relation to this subject, for this new shape of the will is reflective and knows universality not just as itself, but within itself. It is established 'as explicitly identical with the principle of the will' (1967, p. 75). The subject is now a self-relation, and it is within that universal will that right and wrong are located. The 'reflection of the will into itself and its explicit awareness of its identify makes the person into the subject' (1967, p. 75). Equally, 'a subjectivity become explicit in this way, is the principle of the *moral* standpoint' (1967, p. 74). The subject is that unity which is 'absolutely free in that it knows its freedom, and just this knowledge is its substance and purpose and its sole content' (1977, p. 365). Its self-relation is grounded in reflection, and subjectivity takes itself to be its own essence. The moral standpoint takes shape, says Hegel, 'as the right of the subjective will. In accordance with this right, the will recognises something and is something, only in so far as the thing is its own and as the will is present to itself there as something subjective' (1967, p. 76).

However, subjectivity here is only an empty and insubstantial self-reflection. It is a reflection by that which is merely a shining for others, an illusory being. It is the reflection of the master who takes its independence for granted, not yet realising that this independence, this shining for others, is merely illusory. Subjectivity, here, is a positing or presupposition, not yet determinate. There is the potential now for the subject to know civil society as an empty appearance. But for this, the education of the subject has to develop up to the point where it knows itself as the contradiction of independence or non-relation. The truth of the master is not its own reflection, it is, as was seen earlier, the slave, or its own self-contradiction. This self-contradiction lies ahead for the subject in the realm of morality.

Sovereign subjectivity is the principle of the free will. It is a free will which knows itself as universal because it takes itself to be the essence or self-relation of independence. It is not yet the determination even of critique, for it is not yet the negation of itself. This negation arises in the hypocritical action of the subject.

The universal principle of the free will in the sphere of morality is 'the good'. But every action performed by a subject which has the good as its intention can only repeat its own separation from that universality. A universal which is dependent upon the intentions of a particular is negated as a universal. Thus moral conduct, according to the principle of the free will, becomes self-contradictory. Just as the social relation reminds its determinate existence – the person – of its self-contradiction, so the sphere of morality expresses its determinate substance, the subject, to the same contradiction. Both are only a part of the illusions of the relation of the broken middle. Morality displays an implicit relativism which morality itself cannot overcome. The subject (particular) always has objectivity (universal) as something which, in seeking to identity itself with, it drives further away. They are united 'only by their mutual contradiction' (1967, p.

78), a contradiction which is both the development of consciousness to the sphere of morality and its inevitable negation of that (negative) sphere. This contradictory movement is, as will be seen in a moment, the self-education of ethical life, and its actuality as the state.

The moral or subjective point of view is grounded only in the assertion of 'ought-to-be, or demand' (1967, p. 76). Externally it is the good, or the welfare of all. Internally, it is conscience. 'Conscience is the expression of the absolute title of subjective self-consciousness to know in itself and from within itself what is right and obligatory' (1967, p. 91). However, conscience acts on purely subjective conviction, and 'pure conviction can justify any act' (Rose, 1981, p. 179). When conscience appeals only to itself for a decision in its truth or falsity, 'it is directly at variance with what it wishes to be, namely the rule for a mode of conduct which is rational, absolutely valid and universal' (Hegel, 1967, p. 91). Of morality in general, Hegel remarks that 'the moral world-view is, therefore, in fact nothing other than the elaboration of this fundamental contradiction in its various aspects' (1977, p. 374).

This experience of contradiction between particular and universal is resolved by conscience when it posits itself as the law. But this assertion is again negated when the law of each conscience is forced to confront universality as the law of all consciences. One bare assurance regarding the intentions of an action is as good as any other, and acts as a universal justification for anything. It is this experience, an experience of negation and (eternal) return, which is the true significance of moral education, and of the development of ethical life. The sphere of morality comes about in the experience of the person who, in relation to others, becomes an subject for himself. This is a merely personal education, one which reflects the empty truth of the appearance of ethical life as civil society. Its significance, however, is that this personal education is also a negative education for the person, for the subject is revealed as in contradiction to the universality which it takes to be its own. This is the beginning of its truly social education. The moral consciousness achieves its determination when it is forced to reflect not as itself, but upon itself. In the experience of the contradiction between conscience and the universal, between good and ethical life, it is forced to face the hypocrisy of its assertions. If it still refuses to acknowledge the difference between itself and its actions in the world, it becomes the self-positing of what Hegel calls 'the beautiful soul' (1977, p. 406). Because activity divides it from universality, it refuses all activity. It rests impassively in an empty recognition of its own righteousness and that of other such beautiful souls. However, the consciousness which does acknowledge its hypocrisy has its own negation present before it as object. What lies ahead for it now is the comprehension that this negative result for it is a positive result for ethical life. Now moral consciousness has before it as an object its own work and positing. In relation to the universal other (e.g. welfare), the moral subject appears to himself as he truly is, a merely empty presupposition of universality. In this appearance, in the self-relation of particular to universal other, shining is now of itself, for itself. This is its absolute relation,

176

for its own reflective relation now appears as relation, and in relation. The work and the result are one and the same. It has negated itself in relation to another, and its truth as (self-) relation has appeared for it. Ethical life, here, has achieved a mind of its own. The universal is actual in the negation of the subject, and as the truth of the subject as negative. The illusory appearance of civil society and the person as non-relation, in being known and made objective, are put in (self-) relation. The knowing of independence is the loss of independence, for its universality is self-contradictory. Ethical life appears in this contradiction. The (self-) relation of the subject to the other is the truth of both. In the loss of the subject there is ethical life, where illusory being is known as posited by illusory being.

Ethical life is determinate, for non-relation known as non-relation is now known in and as self-relation. In the contradiction of morality, or of subjective self-relation *per se*, the emptiness of that self-relation becomes clear. It is known as posited. This is the negation of the subject, known now by the subject, and is determinate. It did not know it was a posited unity, it simply was one. When it did become known as posited, then subjectivity was determinate. The education involved here is formative. The particular consciousness comes to know its own indeterminateness in relation to the universal. Conscience comes to know its hypocrisy regarding the good in relation to those whose (universal) good it claims to be. Thus far the subject has been an empty relation. It knows itself, now, to be an empty relation in contrast to the universal. It confronts the universal as a contradiction, but therein realises its own truth. The nothingness of the subject (or empty relation) is now true for it in relation to, or when it is for, others. Its misrecognition is re-cognised or known as misrecognition. Put in terms of relations, the non-relation is now known as posited, and its truth as the opposite of itself now appears. The truth of non-relation appears in relation, the truth of the subject appears in relation to substance, or, again, the truth of the good is realised as the relation of non-relation to relation itself, or as ethical life. What the subject learns here is that its own truth only appears in relation to the universal will, or that ethical life is (the determinate negation of) our shining for others (see Chapter 5).

The education of civil society, then, is not merely that of persons about their own individuality. It is not merely the education regarding the sphere of needs. It is also, implicitly, the education of consciousness about the contradiction of that sphere, and therefore implicitly a higher form of education. Ethical life shows up the principle of civil society to be empty and merely posited when it returns to itself in the form of contradiction. The illusory nature of civil society, as a society of individuals who are unrelated to each other, becomes clear in the increasing relation between non-relations, or persons. The satisfaction of each particular need requires the labour and co-operation of others, and the principle of difference is gradually eroded until the private emerges as a wholly public affair. Public authority now assumes responsibility for the rights and welfare of each person, replacing the immediacy of each family to become, as it were, 'a universal family'

(Hegel, 1967, p. 148). It is civil society which 'tears the individual from his family ties, estranges the members of the family from one another, and recognises them as self-subsistent persons' (1967, p. 148). Civil society accepts all such persons as its own 'sons' (1967, p. 148), and takes upon itself the duties of welfare and education.

> In its character as a universal family, civil society has the right and duty of superintending and influencing education, inasmuch as education bears upon the child's capacity to become a member of society. Society's right here is paramount over the arbitrary and contingent preferences of parents (1967, p. 148).

The public education which Hegel is describing here must not be confused with comprehensive (state) education, for that is a development which emerges out of the contradiction of a universal family which represents each member as independent (this is examined in the next section). The public realm in civil society can only appear in the world as a self-contradiction. This is a higher education again for consciousness. The public realm contradicts the private realm, and the private realm comes to see that it is, in fact, dependent upon the universal will. Here civil society realises that it is illusory in relation to the state. The truth of the state is the realisation that the universality of civil society, a society of free individuals, is a self-contradiction. It universality is merely posited, a positing known in the return of ethical life to itself as the state. The truth of the state is the recognition of civil society as misrecognition by itself. Hegel writes explicitly about the educational importance and significance of civil society in the development of ethical life, and its actuality as the state.

> The final purpose of education, therefore, is liberation and the struggle for a higher education still; education is the absolute transition from an ethical substantiality which is immediate and natural to the one which is intellectual and so both infinitely subjective and lofty enough to have attained universality of form. In the individual subject, this liberation is the hard struggle against pure subjectivity of demeanour, against the immediacy of desire, against the empty subjectivity of feeling and the caprice of inclination. The disfavour showered on education is due in part to its being this hard struggle; but it is through this educational struggle that the subjective will itself attains objectivity... [and] which reveals education as a moment immanent in the Absolute (1967, pp. 125–6).

Ethical life has here emerged as the relation of relation and non-relation. The latter, or civil society, loses itself in relation to relation (or to the public sphere). The truth of particularity, or non-relation, is now realised in relation. This realisation amounts to the experience of ethical life as a contradiction between its own independence and those whose universality it claims to be. The truth of itself as non-relation emerges only when it is in relation. Ethical life is now comprehensive, and has returned to itself, but is itself only in and as the contradiction of the relation of relation and non-relation. Ethical life is a broken middle, separating that which it joins, universal only as the contradiction between universal and particular. We, therefore, cannot experience ethical life except as the truth of ethical life – not as an immediate unity, but as a broken middle. The state is this actuality of ethical life. This means that it is the result of the contradiction and the activity of the contradiction which is ethical life. To see the state either as subsuming or eradicating the particular, or as not universal, is to misrecognise ethical life. The state is already the contradiction of particular and universal. It does not resolve or overcome their differences, it expresses them as its own truth. This is why the state in Hegel has to be comprehended in educational terms, to ensure that its expression of the contradiction of our identity is maintained, and that the state is not turned into another abstract domination of ethical life as either relation or non-relation. The state does not heal or not-heal the broken middle of ethical life. The state is determinative, it is ethical life known or realised. This philosophical work is what the return of ethical life consists of. It is this work, our continuing (negative self-) education, in which the public sphere is realised.

Comprehensive state education

'Social relations contain illusion' (Rose, 1981, p. 81). This has been shown in several ways earlier, where shapes of consciousness take themselves at face value or as their immediate appearance, presupposing this to be the whole. Reason, enlightenment, critique, the person, the master and bourgeois property relations all presuppose themselves to be a complete self-relation and totality. The teacher is another such example, which will be examined in the next chapter. All are only the illusion of self-relation, and are misrecognition. Social relations between these illusions are therefore themselves illusory, for they are the abstract principle of the empty self-relations made into the principle of the whole. They make misrecognition appear natural, and enable theories of social relations to begin with these illusions. As such, social theory also contains illusion, but as something natural, not as something re-cognised. Hegel's *Philosophy of Right* also requires to be read with reference to illusion, but as a work which contains illusion as its own determination and truth. Read without reference to these illusions, and to the formative experience of them as contradiction, and to actuality, the *Philosophy of Right* reads as mere assertion, or worse still as a recipe for what ought to be. Neither of these interpretations comprehends Hegel's work.

Just because social relations contain illusion does not mean that social relations and the illusions cannot be known. On the contrary. But in being known they become determinate, and in becoming determinate they become separated in a

179

broken middle in which illusion is a constituent part and a determinative moment of the absolute relation. It is within this circle of knowing illusion that ethical life has to be approached. Ethical life is the universal self-relation of freedom. But it is determinate or known as the state, and it is actual (and rational) in the contradiction of bourgeois property relations. In this experience of contradiction, ethical life is a self-determined relation of its self to itself, or is itself as the broken middle of a determinate self-relation. But this self-relation is determinate, or known as the state and so the circle continues. Ethical life is not something that could (abstractly) be called absolute freedom; it is determinate freedom, or freedom which is known. Its determination is our experience of its broken middle as freedom and unfreedom. This circle is now briefly described in terms of illusion and education.

Ethical life has emerged from within the contradictions of bourgeois property law. It was seen earlier how the person is defined as non-relation, and has the principle of that independence objectified in property law. It was also seen how non-relation can only experience this relation to or dependence upon the universal will as contradiction. This contradiction was then seen to be a formative or educational experience for the individual. The experience of being an individual for the universal is a negative experience for the individual. He becomes aware of himself, now, as that which he is not. First, he takes this experience of himself as relation as a personal experience, believing that now it has the principle of self-relation as itself, i.e. as the subject. But this is as yet only indeterminate, and exists only as a positing, or as an empty reflection. That which is not appears to have as its essence the whole which is a relation to self. But this relation is illusory, a merely inward shining of that which is itself only a shining for others, and which lacks self-determination. When this subject seeks to assert its certainty of itself in the world, when it practises its own principle as the principle of all, then it finds that its own particularity becomes clear to it in the face of the universal other, or substance. Faced with the public interest, the subjective conscience is found to be not-universal. But this is a formative negation for the subject, which now has its own illusory self-relation for itself. Illusory being is posited as illusory being, and is thus nothing for itself. It becomes what it is.

But this experience cannot be posited as the self-relation of ethical life. It is not a middle. The experience is not a resolution of the opposition of negative and positive, it is an experience of the opposition. To posit this as a collective self-relation is to believe that the experience is for the collective and is of itself. Such a middle, however, cannot be determinate, and cannot therefore be this experience. The difference between ethical life in Hegel and the experience of the collective in those critiques examined in Part I is that, for Hegel, self-relation is determinative and therefore contradictory. To resolve the contradiction is to replace the broken middle in which experience does not begin or end, but returns, with another universal, or law, which is again only another misrecognition of the absolute relation of the broken middle. Illusion is part of ethical life. It is determinative of ethical life. It is our experience of ethical life, known by us in its contradictory self-relation. Ethical life is the relation of non-relation and relation, it is not their overcoming. Rose comments on this process of self-education in the following way.

> Once the shapes of consciousness have been experienced, one thing can be stated. It can be stated that the absolute or substance is negative, which means that it is determined as the knowing and acting self-consciousness which does not know itself to be substance, but which knows itself by denying or negating substance, and is certain of itself in opposition to its objects. This is not an abstract statement about the absolute, but an observation to which we have now attained, by looking at the experiences of a consciousness which knows itself as an antithesis, as negative, and thus 'participates' in this antithesis as its own act (1981, p. 181).

Ethical life, because it is a determinate self-relation, is a broken middle. As such, its appearance in the world is not an immediate unity or middle, but is what is actual. Ethical life, the self-relation of subject (one) and substance (all), if it appeared as an immediate relation, or pure relation *per se*, would be what was described earlier as 'custom', or immediate mutual recognition. 'When individuals are simply identified with the actual order, ethical life appears as their general mode of conduct, i.e. as custom' (Hegel, 1967, p. 108). But ethical life has passed out of that immediate phase by a division of itself. The division is its own determination, i.e. it is that action in which it becomes known to itself. It has passed into civil society, where it has no idea of itself as other than the formal freedom of each person, reproduced in a legal system of rights which ensures 'the means to security of person and property' (1967, p. 110). From there it is returned into itself as the relation of relation and non-relation, or of particular and universal. In this, its self-determination, it is known or has the idea of itself as the state.

The state is the actuality which is the contradiction of ethical life. It is the self-relation of ethical life; that is, the relation of both relation, the public sphere, and non-relation, the private interest. As such, it is not an indeterminate or immediate universal or middle. Because ethical life is determinate, it is divided into the opposition of being-in itself and being-for-itself. It contains this division because that self-determination lies behind it. The actuality of ethical life is that it is a contradictory self-relation. But that self-determination cannot immediately present itself to our particular consciousness. On the contrary, consciousness has its own relation to the state, one in which consciousness knows itself as not the state, and has the state, or ethical substance, as other than itself. But this is precisely the relation which, as was seen earlier, is the self-determination of ethical life. What is actual has its determination behind it, but also ahead of it. Our education in regard to the state will be in regard to its actuality, and therein containing our experience of it. Actuality is this circle, and this circle, as seen in Part II, is the education which *is* self-relation. The truth of ethical life is contained in the

181

actuality which is the state. The state is (self-) determinative ethical life, but it is a truth that can only be repeated by us in our own contradictory experience of it. In that experience we lose ourselves and are returned to ourselves, able now to comprehend that what is actual contains our loss within itself. But what is actual is again something for us, and the work of negation has both been accomplished and lies ahead. Our education is activity and result as this broken middle. As such, we could call ethical life our comprehensive state education. It is where subject and substance, in their opposition, realise their truth to be contained in the broken middle of ethical life. The realisation itself is our education regarding the state as a unification and a separation at the same time. We are never united with ethical life as a middle. Its determination (the state) is our negative experience of the state, of substance as other. The circle of its actuality is our continuing education regarding this broken middle, or our continuing comprehensive state education.

The *Philosophy of Right* is not the end of our experience of ethical life as contradiction, it is itself part of that experience. The contradictions which are the subject and substance of ethical life are not overcome, they are repeated as comprehensive, forcing a return and an education in which the illusions of ethical life are once again determinative. Ethical life is actual in and as our comprehensive state education with regard to the broken middle. The state cannot be comprehended independently of the experiences of misrecognition which bring it about. Comprehensive state education has illusion as part of its determinate content. The state and contradiction have no existence independently of each other. They are the self-determinative activity of ethical life. The state does not resolve the question of identity in bourgeois social relations, rather it is the actuality of that question, and of the formative experience of ourselves as the question. It is the contradictions of ethical life, and the illusions of its broken middle which our experiences repeat, which are the possibility of ethical life for us at all. We cannot known ethical life 'apart from the presentations of the contradictions which imply it' (Rose, 1981, p. 51), or except from within its broken middle.

But, as Rose points out, the illusions which it contains are not always easy to see in the *Philosophy of Right*. The self-relation of ethical life as the relation of relation and non-relation is often hidden within the work because of its severe style.

> The phenomenology of the *Philosophy of Right* is *incomplete* because it is presented in the 'severe' style. The *Philosophy of Right* culminates in the experience of ethical life presented as the will's definition of a series of institutions which are concretely universal. These institutions of the state are normally read as the reconciliation of the contradictions traced, and are thus taken in isolation from subjective disposition and the other contradictions of a society based on bourgeois private property relations

182

which make the analysis of modern society and of absolute ethical life even more complex than the *Philosophy of Right* implies (1981, p. 90).

Those dispositions which Rose talks about have been described earlier as the subjective experiences of contradiction, and the circle of separation and return which constitutes the movement and result of what is actual.

The *Philosophy of Right*, says Rose, has often been read as 'a justification of the *status quo*... [and] as justifying quietism' (1981, p. 79). Such interpretations ignore or do not understand the centrality of education in Hegelian philosophy. A quiescent presentation of social relations, one which justified the *status quo*, would be one in which categories like the person, the subject and the state were treated as if they appeared naturally for consciousness 'as something from which it starts' (Hegel, 1969, p. 403). But, as Hegel pointed out in the Preface to the *Philosophy of Right*, philosophy comes on the scene 'too late' to find such categories occurring naturally in the wild (as it were). Each is already a result of conscious activity, each is known, and each is known by consciousness in a shape which is already determined within the broken middle of social relations. What is found and who finds it are both implicated in a prior relation which is not visible to either. Throughout the *Philosophy of Right*, Hegel 'transposes the categories of idealist natural law into social relations' (Rose, 1981, p. 79). In so doing he is acknowledging their determination. This is a critique of their mere appearance. Rose argues that Hegel, in re-presenting the determination of existing law, is misread if he is seen as justifying that law. She points out that:

> It is natural law theory which takes the illusions or relations of bourgeois private property as the rational principle of the whole society. It is natural law theory which *justifies* bourgeois positive law which it 'derives' from the fictional state of nature. Hegel is precisely drawing attention to the illusions (relations, difference) of bourgeois society. He is warning against an approach which would see illusion as rational, which makes illusion into the absolute principle of the whole (1981, p. 81).

The goal of Hegelian critique is not further illusion. It is not to impose or fix forms of domination and identity upon the broken middle of social relations. It is not to heal the broken middle of the social relation. It is warning us about the inevitability of illusion in all political solutions which believe they can heal the broken middle. Illusion is part of Hegelian critique. That is why his speculative propositions are so difficult to read. Statements such as 'what is rational is actual and what is actual is rational' contain the self-contradiction of relation, and the broken middle of social relations. They contain the illusion of non-relation in and as what is actual. The truth of the statements is developed in our experience of their contradiction, for in our negative experience the whole of the relation is present in the experience of their untruth.

183

Hegel's philosophy is also read as being passive. This too is an uneducational reading. He appears in such readings to offer us no active role by which the domination of reflection and positing can be overcome, and where the unity between people is not negative but positive. Of the *Philosophy of Right* he states that it 'cannot consist in teaching the state what it ought to be: it can only show how the state... is to be understood' (1967, p. 11). This seeming passivity is then further compounded when he admits that philosophy always comes on the scene too late to give any advice to the world about how it ought to be (1967, p. 12). Again, Hegel is concerned here not to impose any new appearances of the social relation, only to expose the existing appearances. He is aware that such a critique will repeat the broken middle of the social relation, and he does not seek to create an illusion that his critique is somehow immune from the process he is describing.

Critique is always already a positing, for it has no place from which to begin the activity which is not already the social relation as misrecognition. Critique is itself a misrecognition when it appears as a tool or a methodology. Such enlightenment does not comprehend its own determination within social relations. Critique is therefore required to begin with itself as a question and not a method, as an uncertainty and a negation, not an enlightenment. In this way, critique yields the political project to be a self-determination, not just positively, but negatively. The critique of social relations therefore falls not just to the teacher of others, but also to the student of self who knows their teaching to be a mere shining for others. It is in the work of the latter that the truth of the critic lies. For the sceptic, such a project yields only an absence of knowledge and result. For us, the experiencing consciousness, what results is the knowledge of no knowledge, the result of the absence of a result. 'The path of despair is not negative, because while natural consciousness may not grasp the necessary connection between its first and subsequent objects, we can grasp it, and hence the experience is formative for us' (Rose, 1981, p. 154). In the critique of social relations, the self learns about its own determination. This is our comprehensive state education. What it learns is that the bourgeois property relation continues the life-and-death struggle. We live, and are non-relations. But in contradiction with universality and substance, we are also negated. In negation we become what we are, a self-relation in relation to others. In the context of the life-and-death struggle, Hegel wrote that 'it is only through staking one's life that freedom is won' (1977, p. 114). For us, that risk continues in our daring to continue our education. The self is only realised in being lost. To be lost it has to be risked, and to be risked is to learn about the contradiction which is identity. To risk this comprehensive education is to dare to lose ourselves and know ourselves. It is, in line with the teachings of Socrates and Kant, to dare to be wise. Education is the risk which freedom demands.

184

7 Educational relations

This chapter explores the broken middle of education as the relation between knowledge and learning. This is the same broken middle of social relations examined in the previous chapter, for in education, knowledge appears as non-relation, i.e. as result or as the teacher, and learning appears as relation, i.e. as activity or the student. Whereas social relations appear for us as property relations, education relations appear for us as knowledge relations. Illusion is contained in both, and has its modern forms as bourgeois property relations and free rational knowledge relations respectively. From within the broken middle of the education relation we can comprehend what education is. This is now presented in terms of phenomenology, of knowledge and activity/learning, and of the spiritual education which is subjective substance. This is followed by an analysis of the teacher/student relationship which shows learning to be the truth of the student, a truth in which he gains a mind of his own and enjoys therein the independence denied to the teacher. In this self-relation of teacher and student, the truth of the teacher is also revealed to be service or work, where service is understood as the substance which is determinate negation. It is in shining for others, the teacher of others as illusion, that there is the return of the teacher to himself, but changed in the return, to know himself as less and more than the teacher of others. This truth of (public) service as determinate negation is the truth which is contained in the contradiction of the teacher. Finally, Hegel's own pedagogy is examined to reveal how it included (the contradiction of) the teacher as part of the content of philosophy. This is in contrast to the way the 'eternal student' refuses to accept the risk and the contradiction of becoming the teacher, or, therefore, the risk of education.

The broken middle of education

The broken middle of educational relations is presented in this section in three ways. First, in Hegelian terms from the Introduction to the *Phenomenology*. Second, in the more familiar educational terms of learning and knowledge, presenting the education relation as the 'life and death' struggle for certainty. Thirdly, by presenting the broken middle as the triune spiritual education which is the Hegelian system, or 'science'.

In the Phenomenology

Education poses the problem of how and where knowing and learning begin. In seeking to know what education is, consciousness is forced to use the result of a previous education. Consciousness, in asking what education is, has nowhere to begin its examination except in relation to or separated from education as knowledge. It is therefore already not examining a middle – education in itself – or an absolute, immediate and undifferentiated unity. It is not examining a whole. The middle – the education relation *per se* – is precisely what is missing from the examination. The middle has divided itself into universal and particular, or into knowledge and the activity which is knowing. Consciousness is the knowing particular, and knowledge, or the result of education, is the abstracted universal. The object under examination, therefore, is already not the object which consciousness hopes to examine. The enquiry is contradictory, for it is the enquiry into education itself which ensures that the universal is never also the middle or the pure self-relation of education. The enquiry is already a division into particular and universal. Illusion is present here, because the division appears to be the place from where the beginning can be made, and is being made. This 'beginning' makes the separation between particular (consciousness) and universal (knowledge) appear 'natural'. This illusion is then posited in many ways. Each positing is an attempt to express the overcoming of the divide in one way or another, but succeeds only in repeating the illusion whose positing it is. If, for example, the particular is seen as something which affects or distorts the universal, then it follows that the universal will appear as itself, objectively, if the role of consciousness is removed. This is the justification for empiricism. If, on the other hand, the particular is seen as something which cannot be removed, and as an ever-present mediation of the universal, then it is argued that the universal can never appear in itself, and can only and always be known subjectively. Both views, however, are the positing of illusion, taking for granted the separation of particular and universal as it appears to consciousness, or as it shines. The fear that the particular is error is a mistrust which, says Hegel, takes a great deal for granted. Should we not, in fact, 'turn round and mistrust this very mistrust?' (1977, p. 47). He continues:

186

Should we not be concerned as to whether this fear of error is not just the error itself? Indeed, this fear takes something – a great deal in fact – for granted as truth... To be specific, it takes for granted certain ideas about cognition as an *instrument* and as a *medium*, and assumes that there is *a difference between ourselves and this cognition*. Above all, it presupposes that the Absolute stands on one side and cognition on the other (1977, p. 47).

The fear of error, therefore, is really only 'fear of the truth' (1977, p. 47), or the fear of doubt and despair. For Hegel, it is in philosophical science that these appearances become determinate, where their 'appearance' is mediated by itself and thus learns of its own determinate self-relation. As was seen in Part I, this learning for the teacher and critic is a path of despair, because it always involves the loss of 'identity' in and to experience. This experience is a self-experience and thus a self-determination, when what is lost is lost to itself. This determinate self-relation of knowledge can be seen in the relation of knowing and of truth as they appear abstractly in consciousness.

The broken middle of the self-relation of education appears to consciousness as the separation of consciousness from itself. In knowing of itself, it has itself as its own object. The relation is also a separation. Its appearance is the 'knowledge relation'.

Consciousness simultaneously distinguishes itself from something, and at the same time relates itself to it, or, as it is said, this something exists for consciousness; and the determinate aspect of this relating, or of the being of something for a consciousness, is knowing (1977, p. 52, emphasis removed).

It is from within the illusion of the knowledge relation that our knowledge of truth is then posited. The relation of knowing and the object is taken to be not the truth. Relation is dependent, contingent, and lacking an identity of its own. Non-relation is independent, self-complete, and therefore an identity in itself. There is, here, the educational struggle of self-relation which repeats the moments of the life-and-death struggle described in the previous chapter. There, the struggle between consciousness and its object was the broken middle of the social relation. Here, that same struggle is the broken middle of the educational relation. There, consciousness and its object fought out the misrecognition of mutual recognition. Here, consciousness and its object fight out the misrecognition of science. In this struggle, consciousness confronts itself. Consciousness and its object are related and separated, for this struggle is consciousness seeking to know itself, or seeking self-certainty. Consciousness and the truth of consciousness are, as it were, adversaries for each other, each seeking to overcome the other in order to realise their own self-certainty. This self-certainty requires that both risk themselves in their relation to the other, and both seek to affirm themselves by destroying the

187

other. Their unification would be achieved in the absolute negation of death. But, as Hegel said earlier regarding mutual recognition, that is not for those who survived this struggle. On the contrary, in their survival, consciousness and truth appear now (immediately and abstractly) as separated from each other or as unrelated. The experience of the life-and-death struggle is already the resolution of the struggle, but only abstractly as the misrecognition of the whole relation (of consciousness) by itself. The one experience survives in being divided into its two parts. Consciousness and truth are now divided into 'immediate, unopposed extremes' (Hegel, 1977, p. 114). Thus, the result of the struggle is the survival of both. But the result is not an equal result for both sides. Rather, the result of the struggle for (self-) certainty is the misrecognition which is the knowledge relation. The result of the relation between consciousness and truth is non-relation, a result which is taken at 'face value'. On the one side, truth is posited as what knowledge is. Truth takes this independence or non-relation for itself, for it is posited as being the result of the struggle. It is what is known. It is what has been learned. Independence is taken, now, as knowing itself. ·

On the other side, in the separation of truth from consciousness the latter is posited as non-result, or as what knowledge is not. Consciousness takes this dependence for itself, as pure relation, for it is posited as being only that part of the struggle which is for another. Learning is seen here to have no result in and for itself, only for another. The work is separated from the result. To the result is granted the status of what is. To the work is granted only the status of what repeatedly is not, or what is lived out as the grave of life, a living death, a living nothing. The purely relating consciousness therefore sees itself as the unessential part of the knowledge relation. In the misrecognition of relation as nothingness, it posits truth as that which is not in relation or dependent. Truth, therefore, becomes non-relation, or that which is not-knowing, and which has an identity as what is known; 'whatever is related to knowledge or knowing is also distinguished from it, and posited as existing outside of this relationship; this *being-in-itself* is called *truth*' (1977, pp. 52–3).

The misrecognition of this relation and non-relation, of consciousness and truth, is developed in the *Phenomenology* as stoicism, scepticism and the unhappy consciousness, to the point where negative and unessential consciousness achieves a mind of its own. This it does through its own determinate negation, where it comes to know itself as reason. As reason, consciousness misrecognises not the separation of itself from truth, but its self-relation as consciousness and truth; a misrecognition which repeats the separation this time as the dialectic of enlightenment. This has been rehearsed earlier in Part II. Later, reason is examined in this its modern form as the free rational knowledge relation.

The knowledge relation which is the result of the life-and-death struggle between consciousness and itself contains illusion. It is a positing of the truth of self-relation in its appearance as division. It is an illusion which achieves misrecognition in and as the knowledge relation, in the same way as the illusion of social relations achieves misrecognition in and as the property relation. This is examined later. Knowledge and the law are the same illusion posited as universality. It accounts also for the aporias which are repeated in the critiques of the person and the teacher. To hold that the negation of the person and the teacher by themselves realises their true mutual dependence is to believe that illusion has been overcome, and has produced a result which is not-itself. This is to mistake both that the examination is carried out by illusion, and that illusion is repeated. The determinate education of critique lies in this return, not in its presupposed beginning or overcoming. The fact that the critiques of the person and the teacher reproduce the person and teacher is evidence not of success or failure, but of the realisation that what is actual is both success *and* failure.

However, when consciousness is presented with an investigation into itself, or into the truth of knowing, what it meets can appear for it only as a contradiction. 'If we enquire into the truth of knowledge, it seems that we are asking what knowledge is *in itself*. Yet in this enquiry knowledge is *our* object, something that exists *for us*' (Hegel, 1977, p. 53). Consciousness is in relation to truth, which means, according to the result of their struggle, that truth cannot appear in itself, and consciousness cannot do anything about it. The 'in itself' that consciousness could know would be only that in itself or truth for us. 'What we asserted to be its essence would be not so much its truth but rather just our knowledge of it' (1977, p. 53); and a particular knowledge of the truth is precisely what consciousness believes it knows to be not the truth in itself. Therefore, 'it seems that consciousness cannot, as it were, get behind the object as it exists for consciousness so as to examine what the object is *in itself*' (1977, p. 54).

However, this appearance of the knowledge relation is only a 'semblance of dissociation' (1977, p. 53). The separation between consciousness and truth is the same separation as that between person and law, and between subject and substance. The semblance is that a beginning is being made here, and that the division is a natural division. The division between consciousness and object is not natural, it is not a beginning; it is, rather, already a result. It has events lying behind it, events in which the universal, or self-relation, in seeking to become what it is, to know itself, divides itself from itself, into a knowing and a being known. Consciousness is the result of that division, and has the division lying before it as if it were the beginning. But our 'beginning' is in the 'middle' of the self-realising education of the universal. Consciousness finds itself in the middle of something which does not appear to be a development at all, nor a middle. The appearance of the knowledge relation therefore is that it is not a broken middle, and that no struggle has taken place beforehand of which this appearance is the result. Consciousness has before it its separation from the truth. It does not see that separation to be its own self-activity and self-result, and thus posits truth in the light of the illusion, or in the light of the illusion which is merely shining for others.

As has been seen (Chapter 5), the light of illusion is only an empty self-relation, a mere positing. Such 'enlightenment' already contains the seeds of its own destruction, and also the means of its own substantial self-light, and of casting itself as its own shadow. This is the case now in the logic of self-relation as it is played out in the broken middle of the education relation. This self-development is described by Hegel in the final pages of the Introduction to the *Phenomenology*. The division of the relation is into truth for consciousness and truth in itself. But because consciousness is examining itself, the logic of self-relation forces the appearance of separation to re-cognise its self-misrecognition. The object, truth, only exists or is determinate because it is known by consciousness. When consciousness knows this, then, to use logical terms employed previously, illusory being is known as posited illusory being. Put another way, when consciousness knows that truth is determinate only for consciousness, this is a determinate negation. It is a negation because 'truth-for-consciousness' becomes for consciousness. Left at this, this is only another non-result, another loss of truth, another cause for mourning the death of the absolute. But the truth that is believed to have died again is now known as merely posited by that which did not comprehend the self-relation of the broken middle. The determinate negation is determinate because the relation between truth and consciousness is now what is known. It is now known that they appear in their truth together, and 'together' means as relation and non-relation. Truth in itself (merely) for consciousness is now the whole of the experience. Now, truth-in-itself-for-consciousness is what is for consciousness. The latter is the whole of the former. This is now the criterion by which to measure the true: no longer according to the presupposition of the true as untrue if it is only known by consciousness, but now to learning from experience (and nothing else) that that was merely a presupposition. What is now learnt is that the true (non-relation) and consciousness of the true (relation) are the two moments in which the true is the true, or is itself. The true is the logic of self-relation, or the relation which is of relation to non-relation. It is only in experience that this truth can appear, for the self-negation of consciousness of truth must appear for itself and become its own object. It is in this experience that activity and result are the same self-relation. Hegel describes the true as determinate self-relation in the following passage.

> Consciousness knows *something*; this object is the essence or the *in-itself*; but it is also for consciousness the in-itself. This is where the ambiguity of this truth enters. We see that consciousness now has two objects: one is the first *in-itself*, the second is the *being-for-consciousness of this in-itself*. The latter appears at first sight to be merely the reflection of consciousness into itself, i.e. what consciousness has in mind is not an object, but only its knowledge of that first object. But... the first object, in being known, is altered for consciousness; it ceases to be the in-itself, and becomes something that is the *in-itself* only *for consciousness*. And this then is the True: the being-for-consciousness of this in-itself... This new object contains the nothingness of the first, it is what experience has made of it (1977, p. 55).

190

Understood in this way, the illusions of the knowledge relation constitute the (self-) determination (self-education) of the absolute not only within the *Phenomenology of Spirit*, but as science itself. The knowledge relation contains illusion. When this is forgotten in the positing of the formal result, then the absolute is not realised, for then the criterion of the true does not fall within experience, but is presupposed as lying somewhere outside. The absolute can only be thought by being a self-determinate self-relation. This means that both moments of the true for consciousness and the true in itself for consciousness are present.

In the risk of education

A second way of describing the education relation is by employing the more recognisably educational terms of knowledge and learning. Knowledge and learning are the extremes of the education relation, which has divided itself from itself as part of its self-determination. Absolute knowledge that would be known re-presents itself as the knowledge relation. This is misrecognition of both itself as universal and of learning as merely particular, and is therefore a spiritual struggle, a triune relationship in which the contradiction of education is actual education.

Knowledge which would be certain of itself faces itself as (another) knowledge. Each side in the encounter requires certainty of the other if its own certainty is to be ensured, for then knowledge would know itself as knowledge, an absolute relation. But this mutual recognition of the education relation as self-knowledge or self-knowing is not the result of their meeting. On the contrary, knowledge holds that it will not be certain of itself if it is dependent upon another knowledge, for then it would only be relative knowledge, or relation. Therefore it must seek to destroy the other. Equally, it must show that it does not hold itself to be a particular knowledge, or just *a* knowledge, for then it would not be truth or knowledge in itself, but only a particular truth. Knowledge therefore seeks the death of that for which it exists, and risks its own death in the process. Both acts are designed to prove its own universality as the true, that it is not attached to another, or to any particular 'I'.

So, in the attempt by knowledge to know itself and be sure of itself, knowledge risks certainty in order to gain it. But this self-division will not provide the certainty it seeks. Rather, the self-division will take on a life of its own. The mutual recognition of self-knowledge would require that both sides of the relation die and lose their particular relation to each other. But death is 'negation without independence' (Hegel, 1977, p. 114) and is therefore not the recognition or certainty that was sought. But neither can knowledge somehow become any sort of natural self-unity. It is too late for that, for now it is determinate in the experience it has just had. This experience teaches knowledge that life is more important to it than the other; indeed, it does not need the other to be alive. Its certainty, then, is no longer seen as a matter of life and death, and the experience of the struggle is forgotten. Seeing that it does not require to be in relation to another to be itself, and that, indeed, it is only preserved precisely because it is not in relation to the other (not dead), knowledge now has itself as an independent existence, a free-standing, independent self-knowledge. The dependent relation from which this independence is the result, in which it becomes known, is now seen as overcome or is forgotten. That relation was not knowledge, but merely knowing, or being for another, a dependence which is now seen as the poor relation, as it were, merely a living death unable to achieve itself as result.

Thus, what results is not the self-certainty of universal (self-) knowledge. What results is the division of self-relation into knowledge, and mere learning about or knowing of another. The form of knowledge which survives this experience of being known becomes knowledge as a result. It does not see itself as the result of experience. Rather, it takes its immediate appearance as a self-truth. This it does because the struggle to know itself now lies behind it. It appears independent, self-sufficient and knowledge in itself. The aspects of dependency, uncertainty, relation to or knowledge of, it leaves to what it sees as mere learning. Learning has no independent existence of its own, for it is always purely in relation, dependent upon something else. Learning is not a result.

The knowledge relation is therefore posited as containing knowledge as a result, and non-knowledge as mere learning or as activity. Their relationship is not equal. Education is not equal. Here education is divided into the misrecognition of knowledge and of learning. The life-and-death struggle of knowledge to know itself has forced its self-constituent moments of education (self-relation) out into the open. Now they know themselves only as separated and mutually incompatible. Knowledge cannot also be not-knowing, or learning, and learning is contrary to knowledge. Each is antithetical to the other. Education, therefore, for us, for our subjective consciousness, is always the experience of this contradiction between learning and knowledge, or particular and universal. It is always a three-sided affair. As will be seen in the next section, in the personified form of teacher and student the truth of each is actually to be found in the other, where the learning of the student achieves a mind of its own, and is the determinate self-relation (student and teacher) of education. It is, however, the case that our idea of education cannot but repeat the contradiction of the knowledge relation. Our views on what education is and how it is to be carried out all fall within the misrecognition of the knowledge relation. It contains illusion, and the illusion is our subjective consciousness. Where we 'begin' our education is already illusion, for it is already a positing of what education is.

Illusion impregnates all educational discussions. As was seen in Part II, it is especially the case in the way reason is posited as education in the form of enlightenment. Reason judges all of its adventures in terms of result. Even Adorno's presupposition of reason as non-result is based within the misrecognition of education as not contradictory. The problem is always that discussions about reason, enlightenment and education all presuppose knowledge as a result, for that is the position in which subjectivity is forced to begin. What is at stake in presupposing that a beginning and an end can be made with knowledge is that it is grounded in the illusion of knowledge as a beginning and an end, or as a result. The education of subjective consciousness enjoys no such privilege. The hardest lesson for us is that all knowledge is a domination of learning, repeating the inequality of the knowledge relation. Reason enjoys the appearance of a 'free' education, but that merely makes its domination of itself all the more difficult to see. As was seen in the case of critique, even in its awareness of its self-domination and its aporias, it still repeats that struggle as the contradiction of its own knowledge. What we learn from the knowledge relation is that education is the struggle of itself by itself. Removed from its life-and-death struggle of knowledge and learning, education is indeterminate. Realised as the struggle it is known, or is determinate, and it is realised that our education is not only of the struggle, but actually is the struggle. Education is not a voluntary risk which some take and some do not. Such a view belongs only to the master who is removed from the struggle and has 'struggle' before as if it were its property. This is not the significance of the risk. The risk is to *lose* education, for that is to *be* the struggle. It is this dilemma which, as will be seen shortly, falls to the teacher.

In and as spiritual education

The third way of examining the broken middle of education is to do so in terms of spiritual education, or as substance which is also subject. The key to spiritual education is that it, too, is a three-sided affair involving the loss of self, the identification with (a) collective and the loss of the collective and the return to self which is the loss of self (again). This is the whole of spiritual education. We are not ourselves and we *are* not-ourselves.

In educational terms the absolute is the relation of relation and non-relation, or of learning and knowledge. Their relation is actual in their opposition, and that opposition is produced in them being thought as contradiction. The experience is the movement and the result which is their relation. For Hegel this experience is actual as spirit, or as the contradiction of the universal in subjective consciousness. Spirit is the reconciliation of activity and result, but this reconciliation is determinate and therefore negative. It is not a reconciliation of the contradiction of spirit for us, for spirit is itself the reconciliation of its opposing sides as their contradictory relation. Spirit only *is*, or is actual, when both sides of itself are in opposition. Spirit is not the disappearance of the subject, or of learning, or of experience. It is the experience of that disappearance, or where subject, learning and experience achieve a mind of their own as substance. The determinate negation requires misrecognition, for it is re-cognition of misrecognition. It requires illusion, for it is the seeing through of illusion by itself. Therefore, spirit is actual as the relation, not in the overcoming of the relation. The subject is still having the experience in which spirit is determinate. Spirit is the actuality of the experience of the subject as misrecognition. Rose notes that it is a 'massive misunderstanding' (1996, p. 72) to see spirit as somehow 'final'.

She writes that 'spirit in the *Phenomenology* means the *drama of misrecognition* which ensues at every stage and transition of the work – a ceaseless comedy, according to which our aims and outcomes constantly mismatch each other, and provoke yet another revised aim, action and discordant outcome' (1996, p. 72). To live in the experience of contradiction is to live in this spiritual education. It is a comprehensive education precisely because it is our experience. The whole which is the true contains this negation or insufficiency as part of its own self-development. Our experience is of spirit, and it is spirit. It is not the absolute vanishing of the subject, it is the having that vanishing as the actuality of what subjectivity is. Our spiritual education is the re-cognition that illusion is a formative part of what we are, but it is both moments, and thus for us is a contradiction, or triune.

This is also our education, therefore, regarding education itself. In our spiritual education we have come to know result (or education) not abstractly, but as what is actual. This is a different kind of educational result than the one posited by our natural consciousness, for now it is a result as self-relation, and as such, as a result, also contains its own self-division. This different kind of result is contained within Rose's notion of the broken middle, for only when it is broken is it a middle, and only as a middle is it broken. The broken middle is the actuality of self-relation, and it is an actuality in which result or education is not only abstract but self-determinate.

In Hegelian terms, just as state education was argued earlier to be the actuality of determinate contradiction of ethical life, so, now, our spiritual education is the actuality of determinate self-relation of the absolute, 'in which the moments just as much *are* as they *are not*' (Hegel, 1977, p. 473). The thinking of this (self-) opposition is spirit. Spirit is the actuality of the whole, and has its actuality as science (see 1977, p. 14). Spirit in this sense is the system thinking itself. It is therefore necessarily misrecognition, for self-determination of self-relation, or the absolute, can only be determinate within the illusion of the knowledge relation.

> Only this self-*restoring* sameness, or this reflection in otherness with itself – not an *original* or *immediate* unity as such – is the True. It is the process of its own becoming, the circle that presupposes its end as its goal, having its end also as its beginning; and only by being worked out to its end, is it actual (1977, p. 10).

For the absolute, to be actual is 'the spontaneous becoming of itself' (1977, p. 11), yet it is also a result. For us, therefore, it is work, division and education. It *is* as the whole which is the broken middle because, for us, it is substance become subject. It does not resolve the question of personal identity, nor of collective identity, it is that question as our education.

Rose has drawn attention to a particularly modern form positing spirit precisely to overcome its impotence as an educational dilemma. Regarding modern 'cultural' spirits, Rose argues that the '"ethnic" communalities, based on "race", religion, language and gender constituencies' (1996, p. 4) all practise 'identity politics' (1996, p. 4). Such politics do not recognise comprehensive spiritual education, nor that such communities are already determined within illusory self-relations, and thus illusory social relations. They are themselves only new codes of ethics, new 'laws', new forms of substance which presuppose the personal identities they are set up to overcome. Their being posited by that which posits itself is the whole of the actuality of spiritual education.

Each return of substance to itself involves and requires our experience of, or our relation to, substance. The law in this sense is always more and less powerful than ourselves. Its unification involves our having that unification as another being for us, for the true is the relation. We cannot escape the necessity of illusion being determinate, or in itself, when it is for another. Actuality is this contradiction, for the contradiction is actuality as 'self-movement' (Hegel, 1977, p. 13). The result cannot stay still as (abstract) knowledge, for it appears only in and as movement. The 'result' of spiritual education, therefore, is not-result, or it is the experience wherein the knowledge relation knows itself. What it gains as result it loses in activity, and what it loses in activity it gains as result. This education is the determinate circle of self-relation. The circle *known* is what is actual, and what is actual is itself only as the circle.

If the circle is known, then it could be asked 'what can be done, now, with this knowledge?' This is a question which itself contains the true but as misrecognition. What consciousness does with the true is to become what it is, both the repetition of misrecognition and the knowledge of that repetition, the doctrine, for us. The 'strenuous effort of the Notion' to which Hegel refers (1977, p. 35) is not the application of abstract truth to persons or situations in a way which only repeats the domination of illusion in its modern property and knowledge forms. On the contrary, it is the negative experience that all such applications are a domination of precisely this negative experience. As such, working with the notion is to risk the education of the actual, or of contradiction. This risk involves the self losing its presupposition of the knowledge relation, losing its presupposition of 'result', losing its presupposition of self. The loss is not 'voluntary', it is the actuality of the experience of contradiction, of the negative experience. It is to realise the circle as the actuality of self and of result. This risk and this education are the loss of the concrete self and its differentiated moments. 'Through this movement the pure thoughts become *Notions*, and are only now what they are in truth, self-movements, circles, spiritual essences, which is what their substance is' (1977, p. 20). Put somewhat polemically, the actuality of spiritual education is not to be found in the question 'what can I do with the true?', but rather in the question 'what is it that the true does with me?'. Such a result may be too passive for the natural consciousness which seeks to have philosophical consciousness as its slave. But such a sentiment is again caught in the illusion of itself as only the master.

Rose employs the idea of comedy to express this movement of the absolute. It will not stay still, it is not satisfactory to our natural consciousness which is both lost and returned to in the comedy. It is ever moving. Consciousness constantly loses itself, fixes the loss in and as universal or law, therein loses the truth of the loss and is returned to itself, which it then loses again... and so on. The comedy, the movement of the absolute, is its self-relation, a self-relation which is always greater and less than the knowledge relation in and as which it (re)appears. Law is always 'the comedy of misrecognition' (Rose, 1996, p. 75) by each person of their self-relation as non-relation to another. In its actuality the absolute means self-relation – for example, law as mutual recognition, spirit as subjective substance or scientific consciousness, the state as ethical life. But the actuality of each requires the self-relation of self-relation to itself, or its own determination. The comedy is that to us who do the relating falls the illusion of non-relation. We who do the work which is required of us are rewarded only with failure, and offered that failure as the measure of our success. But the failure is the re-education of our relation to others, and it teaches us that we are already implicated in misrecognition or comedy, that we are already in the self-relation of relation to self and to others. Our education is this movement and result of the self-relation. For Hegel as for Rose, our education about this comedy implies the person who can become the comedy as himself. Hegel refers to the 'infinite light-heartedness and confidence felt by someone raised altogether above his own inner contradiction and not bitter or miserable in it at all; this is the bliss and ease of a man who, being sure of himself, can bear the frustrations of his aims and achievements' (from Rose, 1996, pp. 63–4).

Hegel offers another version of this absolute movement of education. In the Preface to the *Phenomenology* he writes of it in terms of a 'Bacchanalian revel in which no member is not drunk' (1977, p. 27). The revel requires the activity of drunkenness and its result as the collapse of its participants. The truth of the revel consists in both moments. The members whose revelries make it happen do not survive to its completion. That, however, is the truth of the revel; it is determinate only by being for another, and in the rising and passing away of the others is genuinely itself. Only the whole is the true, and our risk is that we must miss the end, an end which we cannot achieve if we are still conscious (but which is actual in and as the hangover).

The abstract classroom

The other significant relation which the broken middle of the education relation determines is that between teacher and student. The broken middle of social relations reveals its contradictory self-relation not only in terms of the relation between subject and substance in ethical life. To comprehend that relation requires that we also comprehend exactly what such a 'relation' looks like and, as has been seen throughout, each social and political relation returns us inexorably to the relation which is our experience of contradiction, and the self-relation of what is education. So far, we have described the broken middle of education as

196

result and activity, or knowledge and contradiction, and seen how they are the subject and substance of the experience of ethical life. However, result and activity, the education relation, also appear in person within the teaching relationship as the teacher and the student. It is this relationship, in which the actuality of education appears, which is now described.

In all relations there is no beginning. Philosophy has no beginning, for it is always already the activity and result of thinking, or positing. Ethical life has no beginning, because it is always already present as the separation of universal and particular, law and the person. As Hegel reminds us at the 'beginning' of the *Science of Logic*:

> There is nothing, nothing in heaven or in nature or mind or anywhere else which does not equally contain both immediacy and mediation, so that these two determinations reveal themselves to be unseparated and inseparable and the opposition between them to be a nullity (1969, p. 68).

Similarly, education has no beginning because it is always already activity and result. What philosophy, ethical life and education have in common, however, is that this self-relation appears for consciousness in its aspect of self-differentiation. In all three relations, what is visible is the division of itself into separated parts, and what is hidden and available only negatively is the self-work in which differentiation is also a unity. In philosophy what is negative is science, and self-work as the notion. In ethical life what is negative is mutual recognition, and self-work as spirit. In education what is negative is enlightenment, and self-work in and as its own shadow. Each type of self-work is contradictory, for that is the nature of a self-differentiating self-relation. What is actual is the experience in which (negative) subject and negative substance are separated and joined, or subjective spirit. It was seen in the previous chapter how, in ethical life, abstract negations are posited as law. In education, abstract negations are posited as enlightenment. What is actual, however, is our experience and education in which negation and learning are one self-relation.

There is no beginning in education because the separated parts of the education relation are already the determination of the classroom or the lecture-hall, and of the identities of the teacher and the student within them. What is actual in the classroom is not the education which is immediately visible and available in the stated aims, objectives and content of the lesson. It is, rather, the education of philosophical consciousness, an education or experience which negates the appearance of education which is being immediately presented to it.

In the appearance of the classroom, however, to 'begin' with, this education is only visible in and as opposition. Each part of the education relation is already not the whole of the relation. On the one side, the teacher stands as the personification of knowledge or result. He is independent of the student. His identity is self-sufficient and free-standing as the embodiment of previous learning. The teacher is the personification of the education relation as result only. In him, activity or learning has vanished. He is now the result of learning, he is the possessor of the knowledge which has been achieved. His status is independent of learning precisely because he is the teacher and has the result of education as his own identity. Knowledge is his property, and is therefore an external manifestation of his will and identity as a person. This identity is affirmed each time the knowledge which is owned is legitimated as that with which the education of another must begin. There is an implicit violence in this situation, for the teacher imposes himself as this beginning, but into a relation which has already begun. This is both his domination of another and eventually his own downfall or negation.

The student, on the other hand, is merely the particular whose status as a person is incomplete. He is dependent upon the transfer of knowledge from the teacher to the student in order that, when that knowledge becomes the student's property, he too will be an independent and self-sufficient result. The student therefore occupies a negative position in the classroom, as the particular to whom it falls to perform the activity of education, that of learning. While the teacher is complete, the student is incomplete; while the teacher is independent, the student is dependent; while the teacher is universal, the student is as yet only apart from the universal. Their relationship in the classroom, therefore, is not mutual, and is not based on the recognition that 'each sees the other do the same as it does' (Hegel, 1977, p. 112). The teacher teaches, and the student learns. Result is not activity, and activity is not result. This is the abstract and unphilosophical model which currently dominates in teacher/student relationships in the classroom, in the lecture-hall, and particularly in the training of teachers. The experience of this relationship is the education of the philosophical consciousness of teachers and students, an experience which is not encouraged by those who reduce education to a technical training. It is this (philosophical) experience of the teacher/student relationship which is examined in the next section.

In the classroom the education relation appears only abstractly, and offers a petrified picture of itself, devoid of movement. The classroom offers a 'snapshot' of a broken middle, but one in which only the separation of its parts is visible. Its self-relation reappears only in the experience of the way the classroom contradicts its abstracted educational endeavours, and where the education relation appears in its full contradiction. The teacher and the student are merely the constituent parts of that contradiction. The comprehension of that contradiction, or the appearance of the broken middle of the education relation, rests on the experience of the classroom as a whole. What happens in the classroom, the teaching and learning, are educational only in their relation, and this relation is the education of our philosophical consciousness. In ethical life, 'the disfavour showered on education is due in part', says Hegel, 'to its being [a] hard struggle' (1967, p. 125). In the classroom, the same is the case. The actual education which the classroom provides is something other than merely what is taught by the teacher and what is 'learnt' by the teacher. But the hard struggle to comprehend the philosophical nature of the education which the classroom offers is one which is, for the most part, excluded by law (particularly since 1988 in England and Wales). However, even before the domination of 'knowledge' by its abstraction in law, it was still the case that teachers (and students) mostly preferred to hold on to what they are always 'in danger of losing' (Hegel, 1977, p. 51). An education about the classroom, rather than the knowledge which is on offer from within the classroom, is a threat to the abstract identities of teacher and student. An experience of (the notion of) the classroom is negative. It is not the sort of knowledge represented and personified by the teacher, and it is not the sort of knowledge students are encouraged to store and repeat. As Rose points out, 'to natural consciousness this knowledge would appear as a "loss of itself"' (1981, p. 150). What abstract education and its abstract representations as teacher and student do not pursue is how this loss is itself educational. 'A negative experience for natural consciousness is a positive result for us, for natural consciousness has been presented as phenomenal knowledge' (Rose, 1981, p. 150), or, which is to say the same thing, education has been comprehended as self-experience. The hard struggle of education is in part with itself and the despair it produces, and in part with the courage it calls for to travel its 'pathway of doubt, or more precisely... the way of despair' (Hegel, 1977, p. 49). It was seen in Chapter 1 how the classroom repeated the experience of education as contradiction, but how even the emancipatory teacher was already the resolution of contradiction as knowledge or result. It was also seen how rarely teachers, radical or not, were prepared to follow through with the contradiction of their own education as a return, and to pursue this education instead of seeking new forms of domination by and from which to impose ever new beginnings. 'Natural consciousness does not know itself to be knowledge, but it experiences the contradiction between its definition and its real existence' (Rose, 1981, p. 150). This call to further and harder education is refused by teachers (and pupils) who prefer the certainties of abstraction and the burden of hypocrisy to the uncertainties of experience and the burden of negation and absolute knowing. Education 'spoils its own limited satisfaction' (Hegel, 1977, p. 51), but only as a broken middle, returning teacher and student to their separated identities. The refusal to acknowledge this experience, this contradiction, is the refusal of education *per se*.

The classroom, then, is only the appearance of the education relation. Within it, the universal and the particular are re-presented as the misrecognition which is the teacher and the student. The teacher appears as the truth of the student. The knowledge of the teacher is what defines the relation of the one to the other. The teacher is the universal of education, the student merely the particular, or that whose existence is dependent upon the universal. Their relation to each other is therefore purely contradictory. When the teacher is presented in the classroom as the truth of the student, as that which the student is to learn (to become), then this ensures not their unification but only a repetition of their separation. The experience of the student is that of being *not* the teacher, *not* the universal. The student is returned to himself in this negative experience, back to himself as merely particular and lacking any substance. In this negative experience the student does not gain an identity, he repeats his own absence of identity and once again is returned to his pure dependence. The consequences of this negative identity in the classroom are examined later. On the other hand, the teacher is also subject to return. He finds in the classroom that his own independence from the students is continually reinforced and re-emphasised. He does not need them to learn in order for his own identity to be secure, for their relation is not mutual. The teacher is no longer dependent upon learning. Therefore whether the students learn or not, whether they are returned to themselves in a negative experience or are transformed into knowledgeable persons, is not something upon which the identity of the teacher is dependent. The outlook of this independent teacher is 'if they don't what to learn then that is up to them and not my problem'. This inequality from the point of view of the participants is examined in the following section. From the perspective of the broken middle of the relation itself, the classroom is self-contradictory and opposes its own educational task. In teaching, knowledge appears to the students only in the form of a person. The truth of education cannot rely upon the personal will of the teacher, yet that is what is employed in the classroom to assert its universality. Knowledge, in the teacher, is merely personal, and this is what the student experiences.

This is the same experience, described earlier with regard to all relations in which the universal and the particular collide, and is the truth of all bourgeois (free) relations. Just as universal private property law contradicts the freedom of the particular it re-presents, so the teacher contradicts the universal status of the knowledge which he has to pass on to the student. But in having this universal as its own truth, the particular can only experience this truth as contradictory. In both cases the universal is experienced by the particular as not itself, and therefore, which is to say the same thing, the particular knows itself in relation to and therefore as not the universal. Just as private property law is only the appearance of the relation of ethical life, so the classroom is only the appearance of education; an appearance or illusion which is explored in the next section from the point of view of each participant.

It is not difficult to interpret this negative experience of the classroom as a kind of 'life-and-death struggle' between teacher and student. Their opposition in the education relation is highly visible, and few do not have some experience of a manifestation of this opposition. The classroom has always employed discipline in support of its illusion of education, in an attempt to counter the opposition between universal and particular. The teacher has enlisted many and varied forms of domination to turn illusion into painful reality. But each imposition of the universal is another repetition of the experience of the universal as negative. The greater the imposition of the abstract classroom, the more negative is the overall educational experience. There is another kind of discipline in the classroom, however: that of the education relation itself, which imposes itself so as to enable illusions and abstractions to be seen as determinative of the classroom as a whole, including the identities of its participants and what counts as knowledge within it. But that is not the kind of discipline that is being referred to here, the kind which has ensured that, in at least 2,500 years of European schooling, the imposition of abstract universals has been its dominant and dominating characteristic. The opposition between teacher and student in the classroom is the result of the self-differentiation of the education relation. The whole of the relation is not apparent except through this opposition. But the opposition opposes the abstract form of the relation which appears as the truth of the classroom. Therefore, that which is educational is at odds with, and opposes, that which merely appears as education. This is the implicitly critical nature of Hegelian philosophy. To comprehend illusion, and to comprehend the determination of illusion, is to learn regarding the reproduction of abstractions, and the nature of experience as a return. Comprehension is not overcoming and it is not-overcoming. It is the actuality of relation. Our philosophical education is (as T. S. Eliot put it in *The Four Quartets*) our return to the beginning but to know the beginning for the first time.

The teacher/student relation

The truth of the teacher/student relation is the broken middle of the education relation. Each is a part of and apart from the whole, and each requires to be comprehended as and in this broken middle. In the classroom the teacher and the student will experience their relation differently, but it is one experience, or the whole of education. Therefore the teacher/student relation is not only the truth of the broken middle of education as it is self-differentiated in the classroom, it is also the truth of the education relation itself. What follows, therefore, can be read as applying to the relation of education in and for itself, as well as to the relationship of teacher and student, for they are the same relation.

The teacher, like the master, appears as the aspect of the education relation which is for-itself, or result. His identity consists of his being educated. He is the result of learning, and therefore his relationship to learning, to the activity of education, is never one of dependence. His own learning is now result, separated from that educational activity, no longer learning, but now present as knowledge. The teacher, therefore, is separated from and independent of education as activity or learning. As will be seen later, the work of education falls to the student, not to the teacher, and the teacher is related to learning only by having this other do the work for him. He, the teacher, rests as knowledge, as the completion of educational activity. That no further activity is required is the basis of the teacher's identity and independence. Because it is the student who learns and the teacher who knows, the teacher can remain independent in his identity, existing only for himself.

The teacher is related to the student only through knowledge. Knowledge has the characteristic of a thing, it is the property of the teacher and defines his identity. He exists as the personification of that knowledge. It is the fact that the teacher has knowledge, or is educated, which holds a student in subjection to the teacher. The teacher is complete, finished, learned. The student is incomplete, without an identity (a knowledge) of his own, and is only learning. The teacher teaches and the student learns. They are separated, and in that separation a power relation is transparent. In the master/slave relation (examined in Chapter 6) the domination of the master was revealed in the negation of the thing whose existence was to be for-another, and in the fact that the identity of the slave was also this negative existence, equally dependent or being-for-another. The master:

> ...is the power over this thing, for he proved in the struggle that it is something merely negative; since he is the power over this thing and this again is the power over the other (the bondsman), it follows that he holds the other in subjection (Hegel, 1977, p. 115).

In the teacher/student relation the same is the case. In the relation of the broken middle of education, the 'independence' of knowledge is revealed in the experience of the dialectic of enlightenment and return, where the result of education is repeatedly separated from the activity of learning, and where a reconciliation proves logically contradictory. The dialectic of enlightenment is the actuality of the life-and-death struggle of the self-relation of education. On the other hand, as the relation of the broken middle of education is played out in the classroom, the 'independence' of knowledge appears in the form of the teacher himself. In the classroom, as it immediately appears, the life-and-death struggle is behind, and the classroom is already the result of that struggle. There is a struggle in the classroom, as has been mentioned earlier, but it is one whose experience is constantly misrecognised. The re-cognition of that struggle as an educational experience will be examined shortly.

The teacher, then, is master over the student because the teacher has knowledge as property, and is related to the student as owner to non-owner. The domination here is transparent, and is re-presented in many ways, ranging from the layout of the classroom to the use of space within educational establishments, and school architecture. In a Foucauldian sense, schools are the concrete material practice of that domination. The teacher has satisfaction and enjoyment in his status as the owner of knowledge. While the teacher no longer needs to learn, the relation of the student to this knowledge is one of dependence. Whereas the teacher enjoys his own identity as an educated result, the student knows himself to be in a relation of pure dependence to the knowledge. He is only related to it as something which is not his, and something which he must work on, or learn. The teacher can take further comfort from this, as all the educational work which has to be done on the thing falls to the student. This reaffirms his own independence from the student. The teacher is not dependent upon knowledge, he is independent as knowledge. The teacher is therefore not dependent upon the student, for it is the student who must do the work of education. The status of the teacher is not at risk if the student does not learn, for the teacher is already the result of education, a result which is not at risk in the classroom and does not depend upon the work of anyone else. What the teacher has achieved is knowledge as educational result, and the absolute negation of the student and his work, that is, learning. The latter has no knowledge, and thus is not a result. The student has no identity. As far as the teacher is concerned, the student is as yet an incomplete person, one who lacks the recognition due to persons, and one who must seek to have knowledge as his own property if he is to enjoy the recognition which comes with it. In the classroom, however, result and activity, master and slave, knowledge and work, are separated. The former appears as identity, the latter as not-identity or pure negation. 'The outcome is a recognition that is one-sided and unequal' (Hegel, 1977, p. 116).

It is this one-sided nature of the recognition of the teacher which brings into question the certainty of the teacher as educational result. His certainty (his truth) is his knowledge, yet in order to assert his own independence, he has placed the student between himself and the knowledge. His relation to knowledge is therefore not the self-relation that it at first appeared to be. The teacher presented himself in the classroom as the embodiment of the identity of education. Yet part of the identity of education, part of the education relation, is apart from the teacher. He has cut himself off from the student in order to show his independence. But his relation to knowledge is therefore not direct. It is not the master who works on knowledge, it is the student. The teacher has put the student between himself and knowledge so that he will not have to work on that which is already his independent identity. Here the contradiction of the broken middle of the education relation imposes itself. That which is done in order to secure independence and identity is, at the same time, precisely that which also undermines independence and identity. The contradiction of the teacher, therefore, is that in being educated he has separated himself from the educational activity in which he was determined as result or knowledge. What he claims for himself as a self-identity, knowledge *as* education, is now divided into knowledge *of* educational activity. The two parts of the education relation, knowledge and activity, are separated, and the work which the teacher claimed as implicit in his identity now reappears as an other. In the classroom, educational work or activity is for him as the work which is the (non-) identity of the student. To be knowledge requires leaving learning to someone else. But to leave learning to someone else is to relinquish the ownership or independence of knowledge because now he and not the owner is working on the object. Now, as will be seen in the examination of the student, it is the worker and not the owner whose existence becomes objective in knowledge. The teacher has knowledge, but in his placing the student between himself and his property he loses control over that in which he has staked his whole person. This is a total reversal for the teacher, for now he is forced to re-cognise his independence as wholly contradictory. Independence is self-contradictory, for independence from knowing or learning is also dependence upon it. The truth of the teacher is not independence at all, but rather the contradiction of independence, or, which is the same, the truth of self-relation. The teacher cannot work on his property, or, in educational terms, learn what he already knows, for he is already defined as and is a result, i.e. the owner of that knowledge. To re-learn is no longer to be the teacher. In the classroom he is the teacher, and not the student. Abstractly he is knowledge or result, and not learning or activity. Yet as each of these the teacher is separated from that upon which his identity is claimed as a self-relation. The teacher's identity embodies the claim that his knowledge is the result of work, and that therefore he is the truth of that work. Yet, in the classroom, he is again separated from that work, and stands before the students as a merely abstract or indeterminate result. What he stands there as, the truth of learning, now has learning as external to his identity. In his separation from the object (from activity), his dependence upon it for his own independence is revealed.

Put in educational terms, this is the separation of his *being* knowledge from his having knowledge *for him.* This is a separation brought about because the teacher's independence is contradictory. When he defines his relationship within education as result only, then he leaves the work of education (learning) to another. In so doing he separates himself from knowledge and makes his own relationship to it an indirect or inessential one. This is no more than the experience of return where an object known is always an object for us. What has happened in the classroom is that the teacher has been returned, through the contradiction of his own independent identity, to his relation to knowledge. He has been returned to his relation by and within experience, and is now learning that an identity built around the ownership and personification of knowledge cannot sustain itself. In teaching he is forced into a relation with education as activity, for he loses control over his property. The work of the student is his downfall and his return to the education relation. Independence is not the truth of the teacher. Loss of independence is the truth of the teacher, a negativity which, as has already been seen, is also the (non-) identity of the student. As for the master, so for the teacher,

> The object in which the lord has achieved his lordship has in reality turned out to be something quite different from an independent consciousness. What now really confronts him is not an independent consciousness, but a dependent one. He is, therefore, not certain of *being-for-self* as the truth of himself. On the contrary, his truth is in reality the unessential consciousness and its unessential action (Hegel, 1977, pp. 116–17).

Put more succinctly, what we have learned about the teacher, and what the teacher, through the contradictions of his identity, learns for himself, is that 'the truth of the independent consciousness is accordingly the servile consciousness of the bondsman' (1977, p. 117, emphasis removed).

So far learning and educational activity have only been examined in relation to the teacher, to see how the teacher is returned to activity by the contradiction of his independence. It is now possible to try and comprehend what educational activity looks like to itself. This requires an examination of the teacher/student relation from the perspective of the student. Firstly, the student is already pure being-for-self. For the slave, this was the result of the experience in consciousness when, having staked its life, it learnt that 'there is nothing present in it which could not be regarded a vanishing moment' (1977, p. 114). The student, like the slave, is that experience separated from the consciousness which now knows that vanishing, and which takes itself to be not that vanishing. The classroom (already) is the result of that struggle, and is the repetition of that struggle, but now between separate identities whose self-relation is not visible. The student experiences his own nothingness in relation to the independence of the teacher. The teacher is the owner of knowledge, the student, in relation to the teacher, is the non-owner and therefore the non-educational identity. His nothingness is further emphasised when the teacher, in teaching, refuses to allow his own identity to be threatened by returning to the work (learning) of which he is already the result. The identity of the teacher is held to be not dependent upon the work of the student, either as the student appears in the classroom, or as work (activity) in the broken middle of the education relation. In their dealings with the teacher, the students are constantly reminded that, in relation to him, he is knowledge and the identity of education, while they are not-knowledge and therefore yet to achieve independence. The classroom is the constant reminder that the teacher is the person and the students are as yet only non-persons. The students' experience of the classroom therefore, in their relation to the teacher, is constantly one of negation. In his positivity and certainty he is the reminder of their own negativity and uncertainty. For self-consciousness, fear was the experience of absolute negation. For the student, fear is also the experience of absolute negation. The student does not experience the fear of death *per se*, but he does experience fear as the 'certainty' of his own educational non-identity, and his educational non-existence. Fear has proved to be a crucial strategy for teachers to employ, because it is a constant reminder to the students of their own nothingness. It is a reaffirmation to them that, in the classroom, they are not persons. As with the slave, so with the student in the classroom, in the experience of fear, 'it has been quite unmanned, has trembled in every fibre of its being, and everything solid and stable has been shaken to its foundations' (Hegel, 1977, p. 117).

Secondly, however, the negation of the student is not only brought about through the experience of fear. It is also realised in and by the work which the student does. It was seen earlier how the teacher places the student between himself and his property so that he does not have to become dependent upon it by working on it. The student, therefore, is defined in his relation to knowledge. He is not independent of it. He is dependent upon it and has to work on it. That work defines his own identity, or rather, reaffirms his own lack of identity. The student never knows, he only learns. The student is never a result, he is only work or activity upon knowledge. His whole being is negated each time he performs his work, for he dissolves into pure service for another. His will is the will of the object, and in turn the will of the owner of the object. His work is not his own, for it is work carried out for and on behalf of that which is already educational result. The student, in learning, serves education as result, or as master, or, in its personified form, the teacher. Therefore the student is not only negative in principle, through fear, he is also negated by his activity which is always in deference to knowledge. The student has no will of his own, and his work for another is always the reproduction of that lack of self. What the student is, is a non-person. What the student does is not personal. Put in educational terms, what the student is, is a lack of knowledge, and what the student does is to work for knowledge.

Left at this point the classroom is only ever a site of uneducational opposition or empty repetition, as seen in Chapter 1. The teacher and the student, knowledge and activity, oppose one another in their separation and confront one another as a personal threat. The teacher is a threat to the students, for he is their experience as fear. The students are a threat to the teacher, for they may not fully comprehend their status as non-persons, and this may require the teacher to impose this reality upon them in a number of ways. However, the true educational relation in the classroom does not stop at this point. It has been seen earlier how the teacher fell into self-contradiction and discovered that his own truth was more one of learning than of knowledge. It now remains for us to see how the truth of the student is revealed to itself as the in-itself and for-itself, the self-work and result of the education relation. The true education relation of the classroom, and of the teacher/student relation, is the experience of negation, both of the fall of the teacher and of the nothingness of the student. The actuality of the classroom will always be that of separation and opposition, but what is actual is also rational, and the actuality of the classroom is the experience of this opposition, or of the broken middle. Its actual education is therefore of philosophical consciousness.

The identity of the teacher lacked permanence because it was only a one-sided recognition. The recognition of the teacher did not enjoy the mutuality that 'each sees the other do the same as it does' (Hegel, 1977, p. 112), and thus it crumbled into self-contradiction. The student, however, can experience this mutuality, but only negatively. On the one hand, his relation to the object, or knowledge, unlike the teacher's, is permanent. The student cannot exist independently of the object or knowledge, since his identity is precisely always already in relation to the object, and determined only within and by that relation. The student learns from or works on knowledge, and cannot be the student if the learning ceases. If learning ceased, or if the student stopped working on knowledge, then he and knowledge would be separated. But then this would no longer be the student, he would be the non-relation, or contradiction, which characterises the teacher. Therefore the permanent relationship to the object is enjoyed not by the teacher but by the negative student. The negation of the student, his service to the object, is what ensures the permanence of the relation, a permanence denied to the teacher.

In educational terms, the truth of the student is that learning is the permanent relation to knowledge, whereas result (or enlightenment) is only a fleeting one,

206

and one which crumbles into the contradiction of return, and further work. It is in relation to knowledge and not as knowledge, then, that the student gains a permanent existence. This existence is negative, and has its permanence in the nothingness of its own identity compared to the independence of knowledge. Dependence is permanent, while independence is unstable. The permanent self sought by the teacher but denied to him now appears as the negative self which is the student. His dependence

> is at the same time the individuality or pure being-for-self of consciousness which now, in the work outside of it, acquires an element of permanence. It is in this way, therefore, that consciousness, *qua* worker, comes to see in the independent being (of the object) its *own* independence (Hegel, 1977, p. 118).

However, and on the other hand, something else also happens here. The student becomes aware of himself in relation to knowledge. The student knows himself as nothing in the relation, and therefore is a determinate negation, a *something*. In logical terms the student's first attempts at knowing himself , at an identity, are merely illusory being. They are merely a shining or appearance of the universal in the particular, a reflection of knowledge. His permanence, noted earlier, is no more than this empty positing of himself as relation. But the student becomes aware of himself as this empty shining because this is precisely his own self-experience as fear which he has already had regarding his nothingness in the lesson. To experience this nothingness as fear, is the experience of himself as absolute vanishing, absolutely nothing, *pure* being-for-self. But this experience is also not an absolute vanishing. On the contrary, it is the experience of self as that fear. Experience is always substantial, even if the experience is known only as a broken middle and its appearance as a loss of substance. For the student, the experience of fear is the substantial experience of himself , i.e. he experiences what he is. In fear he knows himself as negative, or he knows his own negation. Aware of himself in this way, the student

> posits himself as a negative in the permanent order of things, and thereby becomes for himself, someone existing on his own account. In the lord, the being-for-self is an 'other' for the bondsman, or is only for him (i.e. is not his own); in fear, the being-for-self is present in the bondsman himself; in fashioning the thing, he becomes aware that being-for-self belongs to him, and that he himself exists essentially and actually in his own right (Hegel, 1977, p. 118, emphasis removed).

The student now has for himself two negative moments which turn out to be the same negative moment. The student gains an independence and a permanence in being dependent upon knowledge. The universality of learning is that which is always in relation to knowledge, but is never knowledge in itself or a result.

However, in contradiction to this universality, the student *has* arrived at knowledge, for he knows *himself*. Thus the student enjoys another universality, that through the experience of fear he knows his own negativity, and thus knows his own self-relation. The universality of the student therefore consists of two contradictory states. On the one hand it is pure dependence, pure learning, the complete absence of identity or knowledge. On the other hand it is knowledge of that absence of knowledge as its own truth. The truth of the student is that he knows that he does not know. This truth is a contradiction. But it is a self-determinative contradiction. Its two opposing universalities are both one in and as the student. Learning is produced as the activity of the student, and what is learnt is the truth of the student as activity. Learning is learning about itself. This is the truth of the contradictory self-relation which is the broken middle of education. Only in the separation of learning as activity from learning as result can learning appear in its true form as the contradiction of self-activity and self-result, or as the negation of itself as the negative – the broken middle of the education relation.

The teacher/student relation can now be comprehended in its contradictory truth as self-relation. The truth of the student is also the truth of the teacher. When the independence of the teacher collapses into contradiction, then the experience of the teacher in the classroom is negative. Now, the teacher is ready (again) to learn. He will learn both that his negation is a part of the comprehensive education which takes place in the classroom (or within the system), and he will learn that learning requires his own negation if he is to learn about himself as teacher, or become his own student. He comprehends himself as a part of the whole and apart from the whole of education, when the truth of the student becomes his own truth, or when the teacher/student relation becomes his self-relation. What the student experienced in the classroom as fear, and what the student produced in the classroom through his own work, permanent dependency, are now revealed as the truth also of the teacher who is able to learn from himself, and from his negation as an identity. As a part of the whole of education, the teacher comes to see the importance and unavoidable nature of his own abstract identity. The student educated himself. Yet the truth of that self-education can only appear negatively, and in relation to that upon which it is dependent, the teacher. The student cannot be left in the classroom merely to do his own work, or to educate himself. Education cannot be left to the student, for the truth of his learning depends upon his own negativity. The negative cannot be given an identity as teacher. The truth of the student is as not-teacher. Those pedagogues who force students to become their own teachers are only reinforcing the contradiction. In the negative experience of the classroom, the student is never the teacher, even if he is being told that he should be. Independence itself is a contradiction. Being taught to be independent is that contradiction in action. It is not for the student to become teacher, but for the teacher to realise his own truth as an abstract domination of the activity which is the student. Only negatively does the student become self-taught. And that negation, precisely, is of the teacher. It is in comprehending this that the teacher knows of himself as a part of the whole of education. It is from and within the opposition of teacher and student that the actuality of the whole of this comprehensive education is realised. But where the dependence of the student is imposed either negatively (as subservience) or positively (as emancipation or freedom), both are a refusal of that actuality, and a domination of education. The opposition of teacher and student is the experience in which the whole is realised, a whole in which that opposition is both negative and positive, learning and knowledge.

It is this experience of teacher/student opposition which 'itself commends a different way of transforming that unfreedom' (Rose, 1981, p. 201). This is because knowing that he is a part of the system is not the end of the story for the teacher. It would be easy to say at this point that all that is required is that the teacher perform his abstract role for the whole to be realised. But that 'resignation' to his determination within the system is not the significance of the system for the teacher. On the contrary, for the teacher to learn about his being a part of the whole, or the broken middle of education, he has also to become apart from the whole. Now he has the same relation to the system, or to knowledge, which the student has to the teacher. The teacher is not now the truth which is the system, and is in a relation of dependence upon it for his own truth within it. This relation of dependence is now the same contradictory self-relation for the teacher as it was for the student. The teacher, in being the teacher, is now also his own student. The moments of illusory being, positing, and determinate negation are relevant again here, as the teacher becomes himself as the work or service which are (the truth of) the student. In this work, the truth of the student is now the truth of the teacher, for they are in the teacher (or in the person) now the same self-relation. Indeed, in the classroom the student is only implicitly that self-relation. Only when student and teacher are a contradictory whole, or where dependence and independence collide in subjectivity, is the student also teacher, or does the negative self 'achieve a mind of [its] own' (Hegel, 1977, p. 119).

The truth of the teacher/student relation is their relation, a relation which is the negation of both the teacher of the student, where the student is the truth of the teacher not only philosophically within the system, but actually as the (contradictory) self-relation which is the teacher. The truth of the whole of comprehensive education requires the service of the teacher, and that service is his own continuing self-work as self-relation or broken middle. If he stops learning, he stops working. And if he stops working he ceases to learn that service is his own identity. This is the contradictory truth of the teacher; only in shining for others is he returned to himself as the work which is (already) his determination – indeed, his vocation – within the whole, and his self as relation (see for example the story of Zarathustra in Chapter 8). This relation is hidden from the person in social relations by the freedom of bourgeois property law, and from the teacher in educational relations by the freedom of the rational knowledge relation. The latter is described in the following section.

The (free) rational knowledge relation

A clearer understanding of how illusion dominates education and the identity of the teacher can be gained by exploring the misrecognition of education that is contained within the (free) rational knowledge relation. It repeats the same misrecognition that was described earlier with regard to (free) bourgeois property relations. Both are no longer characterised by the transparency of the relation between independence and dependence. In the master/slave relation and in the teacher/student relation (in the classroom), the domination of non-relation or identity over relation or being for another was clear. In each case, non-relation emerged from the struggle for certainty as independent, leaving the dependent relation to that which lacked self-identity. However, in bourgeois property relations that domination is no longer clear. In a world where all free men have the right to property, and all property owners are free men, none is dependent or merely for another. Here, as has been seen in Chapter 6, mutual recognition appears or shines in and as the relation between persons, or as the law of civil society, the external state. The domination of the universal over the personal appears to have been overcome by the law of free men. Whereas in the master/slave relation the domination of the relation itself by the master was clear, now, in bourgeois social relations, the domination of the non-relation which is the person over our relation to others is hidden behind the illusion of the legal equality of all persons.

The same is the case with the modern rational knowledge relation. In the teacher/student relation manifest in the classroom, domination is clearly visible. The teacher enjoys the status of independent non-relation. He is knowledge as result. He is educated. He has emerged from the struggle for certainty knowing that continually to learn is continually to be nothing. In death this could have achieved its own being in itself, a state of pure learning, but this would have been negation without independence. The survivor of the struggle is a determinate negation. He knows of learning, and he knows himself as the survivor which is that knowledge. He, therefore, is no longer in relation to or dependent upon another for self-certainty, for he has survived the struggle and has emerged from the experience as being for self. He, the teacher, is what knowledge is, and what knowledge is, is non-relation (not death) and independence. To the student falls the lot of relation or mere learning.

In this relation of knowledge and learning, domination is not hidden. It is clear that the teacher dominates the student, for knowledge is what the students are learning. The students are wholly dependent upon the teachers for the students *are* only in relation to the teacher. Or, learning can exist only *for* knowledge. Learning for its own sake, as the saying goes, is indeterminate, here, for learning has no mind of its own.

However, in the modern rational knowledge relation that domination of knowledge over activity has vanished. As was seen in Chapter 4, reason is relation or learning gaining a mind of its own, a mind which it takes to be, now, the certainty of all reality. Reason is learning which is for itself and of itself. Reason, therefore, is self-knowledge. In reason the teacher and the student are no longer separated. Now they appear as one (abstract) educational relation; that is, as rationality. Reason teaches itself about itself and therefore learns from itself. It is its own teacher and student, it is its own knowledge and activity. The experience of this self-relation as contradiction has been examined in Parts I and II. What concerns us here is how reason appears to have overcome the work which is dependency and learning, and therefore how it still misrecognises its own self-relation.

The rational consciousness defines itself as universal because it takes reason to be the truth of all such consciousness. In other words, it takes itself to be the whole of the education relation, i.e. knowledge knowing itself, or knowledge in and for itself. But the universality which rational consciousness takes for itself is merely formal. Consciousness would like to believe that it is no longer merely particular, but this hope is based only in the reflected illusion of the universality with which it is working. The individual consciousness still has to refer to the universal as its own truth. It is still knowledge of the universal, or, as it were, the knowing of knowledge. But it appears that this is not a relation of domination, for it is not a knowing of another, it is a knowing of itself; the certainty of the teacher, or of non-relation. It is this certainty, this apparently pure self-relation, which is the presupposition or positing upon which rationality, enlightenment and critique are all based. Further, it is the presupposition in which ideas of freedom, the person, and of law gain their appearance of self-relation and non-domination. With regard to education, rational knowledge is no longer a tyranny of external force, in whatever guises such force takes (e.g. myth, superstition); now it is a free self-determination.

However, as seen in Chapter 5, such a presupposition of pure self-relation is, in Hegelian philosophy, merely illusion. It is illusion because what appears or shines is in fact only the presupposition itself, or the positing of the free person or the enlightened individual. In shining for others, this independent person or enlightened teacher is reflected back into himself. But this reflection, as yet, is not for himself, not determinate. If it is not for himself, then it is not the pure self-relation it claims to be. This reflection is indeterminate and has no existence except as the empty repetition of its shining for others. Reflection is not yet its own enlightenment. The illusion, precisely, is that in shining for others we do exist and are self-sufficient. What the rational consciousness takes for itself from this illusion is its own rational principle, or the basis of its being rational *per se*. In the sphere of its illusory self-enlightenment, reason believes itself to be the self-contained knowing of knowledge by itself. The activity in which this truth appears is characterised as the knowing of something. Therefore it (mis)takes this activity as the self-relation of knowledge *per se*, or as result, or, again, as what enlightenment is. In the form of result, illusion becomes the rational principle as 'knowledge of'. Rational knowledge is in-itself when it is (posited as) for-itself.

211

Therefore, to be for the rational consciousness is to be within the self-relation which is (or appears to be) knowledge *per se*. We can say here that knowledge as self-relation (as broken middle) is present only as a shining. All rational knowledge merely repeats itself as this result, or knowledge of. It knows that to know is to have knowledge of something, and it knows that this knowledge is of itself. Therefore reason believes it knows that knowledge of itself is the rational principle (its self-knowledge), and that now it simply has to apply this principle to everything else in order to realise the truth of everything else. Thus (rational) knowledge of becomes (the illusion of) the truth of all things. Self-relation, fixed as this result, shines as rational knowledge *per se*, and in which reflection is only an indeterminate repetition.

What this positing or illusion of knowledge (as self-relation) gives rise to, however, is contradiction, instability and return. Knowledge of is not identical with that which it knows. This is the case as much when the object is other as when the object is itself. In both cases, knowledge of is in a state of difference from its object, it is never identical with it. Therefore in knowing anything, and especially in knowing itself, rational knowledge can only ever repeat its own principle as the contradiction that knowledge of something is not a universal self-relation. This has been explored earlier as the negative experience of reason in and as the dialectic of enlightenment.

This rational principle produces the modern form of the free rational knowledge relation. It has the same implicitly contradictory structure as the property relation. Free universal property law and free rational knowledge are the same illusory universal. Ownership of and knowledge of seem to embody the self-relation of universality. They appear to be a self-relation which requires no justification from outside. They appear to be self-contained and therefore self-justifying relations. But private property law and rational knowledge only repeat the contradiction of self-relation or the broken middle which property and knowledge hide. Ownership and knowledge are only shapes of the universal, or self-relation; shapes which contain the universal or self-relation as illusion, shining and mere appearance. The property relation and the knowledge relation have as the key to their security and the cause of their downfall, the word 'of'. 'Of' expresses the contradiction of their relation. It expresses therefore the truth of their relation as a broken middle. To have ownership or knowledge of something is at one and the same time to be related to it, and to be separated from it. Expressed as a universal, 'of' can only be this contradiction. Concepts and institutions which fix and justify this contradictory relation without contradiction repeat and impose an illusory universal. Law and education both do this, and that domination is personified as the person and as the teacher. However, it is also the case that illusion is imposed when contradiction is denied as self-relation, which is the case with the despairing natural consciousness which sees knowledge of as a reason for denying knowledge, the universal or self-relation altogether, allowing itself the luxury of refusing the risk of being the teacher and remaining the eternal student.

212

The eternal student

With regard to the knowledge relation, Rose argues that there is, currently, a new unhappy consciousness (1981 and 1996). Post-modernity represents another negative relation to the world, and is another misrecognition of the self-relation or the broken middle. The argument which Rose advances can be translated into educational terms where post-modernity refuses to accept the risk of the teacher, preferring the luxurious melancholy of remaining the eternal student, the eternal non-self-relation of relation, or of the negative. It is the lot of the eternal student never to learn, never to become the teacher, and always to refuse the difficulty of self-relation, or of teaching and learning.

Rose calls post-modernity the search for a new ethics, or for a new face-to-face relation. She sees it as an attempt to replace or avoid the difficulty of the broken middle. Its difficulty could be overcome if, for example, I could overcome myself and become the 'other', or if I could live my life according to the 'other'. Then the relation of one self-relation to another self-relation, and its misrecognition in and as spirit, would be merely one ethical relation. Rose writes:

> Simply to command me to sacrifice myself, or to command that I pay attention to others makes me intolerant, naïve and miserable. I remain intolerant because the trauma of sacrifice, or the gesture towards the unidentified plurality of others, leaves me terrified of the unknown but effective actuality which forms a large part of myself. I continue to be naïve and miserable, because the insistence on the immediate experience of 'the Other' leaves me with no way to understand my mistakes by attempting to recover the interference of meaning or mediation. This will produce an unhappy consciousness, for the immanence of the self-relation of 'the Other' to my own self-relation will always be discovered (1993, p. 8).

This unhappy consciousness is not the same unhappy consciousness which Hegel describes in the *Phenomenology*. There the unhappy consciousness was unhappy because it existed only as divided and contradictory, containing within itself relation and non-relation. It did not know that it was the unity of both. That unity only comes about as reason. This new unhappy consciousness is unhappy precisely because it does know that both of those moments of relation and non-relation are present within it. This unhappy consciousness knows that it does not know itself, knows of its self-division: 'we are still unhappy in spite of "knowing" ourselves, because we have become our own castigators' (Rose, 1981, p. 163). This is now a highly self-conscious version of life lived as the grave, for it is reason's own unhappy consciousness. The post-modern unhappy consciousness is the despair of the eternal return of the eternal student within the knowledge relation who refuses Zarathustra's greatest risk, to become the sun that shines for others, and therein to become his own teacher.

The unhappiness of post-modernity is that it knows itself, and knows that this knowledge can never be self-grounded, foundational or an absolute self-relation. The loss for it is not only of the absolute, but of knowledge, identity and the subject. Nothing can remain untouched by the immanent negativity of knowledge as return. Therefore, 'This destruction of knowledge is justified by its perpetrators as the only way to escape the Utopian projections and historicist assumptions of dialectic; "eternal repetition of the same" is said to be a harder truth than the false and discredited promise of reconciliation' (1984, p. 1). Yet eternal return is a truth which post-modernity cannot allow itself, for post-modernity still judges truth as result, knowing such a result to be always and everywhere negated, or merely local and contingent. 'Post-modern relativism,' says Rose, 'renounces the modern commitment to reason in view of its negative outcome – the destructive potentiality of science, the persistence of wars and holocausts. It proposes pluralism, localism and reservation as principles, when it has abandoned principles' (1995, p. 126).

Rose describes the post-modern response to the difficulties of reason as 'despairing rationalism without reason' (1996, p. 7). Each part of this formula is significant. Post-modernity is despairing because it is the grave of its own life. It lives out a pure negativity, denying itself as work or activity and therefore denying its own actuality. In the yearning for 'other' which marks 'the new ethics', post-modernity refuses to acknowledge in itself the work which is already the relation. It 'disallows itself any conceptuality or means of comprehension for investigating its own implication and configuration within the broken middle' (Rose, 1992, p. xii). It holds itself as the living death which is pure relation. Its whole negative existence is held as defined by the inevitable and eternal return which is implicit in the word 'for', as it figures in the knowledge relation. Knowledge is always for or of an other. Removed from history, from social relations, from the work and result which is misrecognition, this knowledge relation is purely unstable. This pure instability is the life of post-modernity. Its life is as despair.

Secondly, post-modernity is a despairing rationalism because it is the despair of the knowledge relation knowing itself, or reason's own work. Yet, and thirdly, Rose describes it as without reason because it refuses its own activity, its own work and its own actuality. Rationalism without the work and actuality of self-relation is without reason, and thus returned to itself as despair. The circular nature of the formula 'despairing rationality without reason' is important because it highlights the truth of the relation which post-modernity is but whose actuality it refuses or denies. If it did not despair, then it would not care. It despairs because, like the unhappy consciousness of old, it laments the impossibility of reconciliation. Its refusal to compromise with a reconciliation that is less than completely universal is not only its eternal lament, it is its redeeming feature.

Post-modernism in its renunciation of reason, power and truth identifies itself as a process of endless mourning, lamenting the loss of securities which, on its own argument, were none such. Yet this everlasting

214

melancholia accurately monitors the refusal to let go, which I express in the phrase describing post-modernism as 'despairing rationalism without reason' (Rose, 1996, p. 11).

What Rose is pointing to, and keeping alive, is the learning, the education, which is implicit in mourning, or the grave of life, but refused. She likens this elsewhere to the reaction one friend has towards another who betrays their trust. Speaking of reason and post-modernity, she asks:

> Suppose a friend whom you trusted more than any other, who taught you the meaning of friendship, lets you down suddenly, and then, persistently, ceases to fulfil the expectations which, over the years, you have come to take for granted, and which, without being aware of it, act as the touchstone for all your other friendships (1993, p. 2).

What would you do, asks Rose? You could give up all friendships, abandoning the idea in the light of this disappointment. You could always change the expectations you have of your friends. Or you might seek to investigate further with this friend what friendship actually means. In the first two cases, work is avoided. In the last case the work is formative of the friendship itself. It constitutes work in the spirit or the misrecognition of friendship, and redefines the friendship and the friends. They redefine themselves as they investigate between them their relationship. What they are doing is the relation of their relation and non-relation (to each other); they are doing what friendship is. Rose writes:

> The crisis of friendship results in a changed relationship to oneself as well as to one's friend: a change in my self-identity arising from the change in the friend's self-relation to herself, just as the change in her self-identity arises from the change of my relation to myself. These changes imply a deepening in the notion one holds of friendship (1993, p. 2).

However, this engagement of the friends with the notion of friendship, their 'friendly' work together about friendship, is not, for Rose, the reaction of post-modernists to the crisis of the relationship with reason. In their difficulty with reason they have rejected it altogether. 'The perceived failure of reason has led straight away to recourse to the most drastic remedy – the abandonment of reason as such' (1993, p. 3). To paraphrase Rose, such a response impoverishes the idea of reason and therefore also of ourselves. Working with reason means 'admitting and accepting meanings, emotions and inconsistencies which you do not consciously intend or desire' (1993, p. 3). This means that trust and risk, and not fleeing from unanticipated difficulties, are implicit in rational work. Working in the risk of friendship and reason 'involves recognising our mutual implication in the dynamics of the relationship' (1993, p. 4); that is, it means accepting that the notion of friendship and reason is self-developing, and that its self-development is our relation to self and to others.

It is a risk which, for Rose, post-modernity has been unwilling to accept, particularly in its claim for the end of metaphysics. Removing experience from ethics is the search for 'an uncontaminated ethics' (1996, p. 2), a search which, in the face of an 'unbridgeable distance between thought or language and concrete being' (1995, p. 116), seeks to protect the gap from any form of experience or work which might know the gap in a changed way. In the despair of the grave of life, the work performed aims to prevent the closure, a closure whose impossibility is the source of its despair. The work of post-modernity is to preserve itself as the grave of life, and to prevent at all costs any actuality. 'Terrified of their own inner insecurity at the border between rationality and conflict... they proceed as if to terminate philosophy would be to dissolve the difficulty of acknowledging conflict and of staking oneself within it' (1995, p. 118). It is the case now, then, that reason 'is apparently being forced to abdicate at the combined protests of its unsatisfied petitioners' (1995, pp. 130–1).

For Rose, the mourning which is implicitly post-modernity cannot be work because it does not recognise itself as work. However, she writes that reason 'can complete its mourning' (1996, p. 12). In one sense this completion is to be found in the comedy of the actual described in Chapter 6, a comedy in which completion is its own self-contradiction, and therefore also incomplete. In another sense Rose compares the *aberrated* mourning of post-modernity, a mourning which is displaced from itself and is hardly a mourning at all, with the *inaugurated* mourning of the contradiction of self-relation. The former type of mourning is mere 'melancholia' (1996, p. 64). It fails to work through 'the contradictory emotions aroused by bereavement' (1996, p. 70). The latter, inaugurated mourning, is not the empty despair of the grave of life, but the productive grief which gains itself (and others) as well as losing itself (and others). In terms of the education relation, post-modern mourning is the indeterminate work of the eternal student. A student remains a student only by refusing to acknowledge his own learning, his own education. He takes incompleteness to be a non-learning, and thus refuses to learn about himself as that incompleteness. He can never become his own teacher, in the way that Zarathustra did, for he refuses to learn that risk and failure, contradiction and positing, and law and the subject are all involved in a three-way relationship. As Rose says, 'it takes three to make a relationship between two' (1996, p. 10), but this third, this broken middle, is refused by the eternal student, who prefers the certainty of his posited uncertainty to the education of their self-relation. Post-modern mourning, the eternal student, is the refusal to risk becoming the teacher. It is the refusal to become that which is a positing, an abstract beginning, a domination. It refuses the violence of the struggle which is implicit in all face-to-face encounters, for it refuses to acknowledge the determination of the relation, and of the individual. It remains in the supposed purity of relation *per se*, refusing to risk 'contaminating' this purity with its own self, its own experiences, its own actuality. In holding open the hope

216

of an uncontaminated ethical relation to the other, it refuses the ambivalence and contradiction of relation to others. Such a stance never risks becoming the teacher. Therefore, to return to an analogy used earlier, it never risks the wisdom of education as friendship, for it is not prepared to engage in the work of friendship as the truth of that friendship. To remain in pure relation is to hold out against relation, and therefore against all education.

This mourning of the eternal student would, to quote Rose, 'prevent the process of learning, the corrigability of experience' (1995, p. 119). She notes that the difficulty of reason is precisely whether 'something can happen to it' (1993, p. 8), whether it can learn. Armed only with the presupposition that what it learns is not-learnt, a continual yearning for a satisfactory learning, then the work of education never achieves a mind of its own, and is never the teacher. To become the teacher is to accept the contradiction of education as the determination of the teacher. It is to know the teacher in relation, and not to hold out the empty hope that he will somehow appear as pure relation, or not merely for another but as another. The authority of the teacher, and of reason, is risk. 'Reason, the critical criterion, is forever without ground' (1995, p. 119). There is, says Rose, 'no rationality without *uncertain* grounds, without *relativism* of authority' (1995, p. 129). The uncertainty of the teacher is his authority, for it acknowledges not only the education relation, and his determination within the knowledge relation, but also 'opens reason to new claimants' (1995, p. 130).

The authority of the teacher, the risk of becoming the beginning of education for others, is where the sun which shines for others also shines as itself and becomes its own shadow. This is the comprehensive relation of teacher and student, where each is a self-relation through and in the relation to the self-relation of the other. The risk of the teacher is Rose's inaugurated mourning. It chooses the risk of education over the melancholia of the eternal student. In this sense, reason can complete its mourning, for, as the teacher and the student, reason's mourning becomes what it is – the actuality of despairing rationality. Such a comprehensive education:

> ...reopens the way to conceive learning, growth and knowledge as fallible and precarious, but risk-able. The risk refers to the temporarily constitutive positings of each other which form and reform both selves. This constant risk of positing and failing and positing again I call 'activity beyond activity' to cover the ethical nature of the description (1996, p. 13).

To be teacher and student is not to be the abstract domination of the former, nor the melancholia of the despair of the latter. It is to be both. It is 'to keep your mind in hell and despair not' (1995, p. 98).

The education of the teacher

The contradiction of the classroom, in the repeated failure of radical teachers to overcome their domination of the pupils, is that it is not the students who require to be educated but the teachers. The pupils are already separated from the abstraction of education as knowledge or result. Their negation is assured. More particularly, their experience in and of the classroom is one of return from knowledge to dependency. They do not need teachers teaching them about their negative states, for the teaching itself is just such another reaffirmation of that negativity. The teacher always teaches, and teaching, *per se*, is already the separation of education into those whose identity is knowledge and those whose lack of identity is their absence of knowledge. The misrecognition by the teacher of the student, therefore, is not comprehending that it is the activity of the latter through which a knowledge of education will be revealed. The re-cognition of this misrecognition does not fall to the student, for it is already implicit in the student; it falls to the teacher. It is in the education of the teacher that the truth of the student as self-relation appears.

The education of the students in the classroom aims at their becoming independent persons, ready to take their place in society as their own teachers. The person and the teacher share the same independent status. Despite the truth of the education relation being teacher and student, the goal of education is the abstract result which is the free and equal person. Such an education aims to overcome the student by turning him into an independent master. Becoming this person, or the independent result of education (his own teacher), means that the person is, for the first time, now ready to experience the whole of the relation of education. In the person or the teacher, the education relation is no longer transparent, being now a self-relation but containing illusion. This self-relation of teacher and student separates itself as a broken middle, and is known by us as the illusion which is our shining for others. In the teacher as independent result, the student is overcome, and activity or relation has vanished. The whole of the self-relation is present to the teacher only in his experience of how its two moments, 'itself as an independent object, and this object as a mode of consciousness, and hence its own essential nature – fall apart' (Hegel, 1977, p. 120). This prompts Rose to comments that, in regard to the master/slave relation in the *Phenomenology*, 'The future belongs to the master. For in future societies the master will become master *and* slave. He will know himself as master, but not know that he and others are slaves. They will not be called master and slave for that relationship is transparent. They will be called "persons"' (1981, p. 130). The consciousness which has the falling apart of activity and result as its knowledge, and its identity, is the 'rational' teacher, one who now enjoys (another) self-certainty as an educational result. In him, the education relation is no longer transparent, for his autonomy is the vanishing of the student, of learning. Just as it is the future education of the person that will reveal him to be master and slave, so it is the future education of the teacher that will reveal him to be result and activity. The classroom, for the teacher, is just one arena where the education of this person takes place.

Such an education is the education of ethical life, as was seen earlier. Its presentation now, in the classroom, in no way lessens its substance as comprehensive education. It is in the education of the teacher (and of the person) that comprehensive education is actual, and where the education relation (of teacher and student) becomes a self-relation of knowledge and activity, or abstraction and negation.

Just such a self-education can be illustrated from Hegel's own teaching while Rector of the Nuremberg Gymnasium, a post he held between 1808 and 1816. An examination of his philosophical classroom reveals his own educational relation with his students, a relation in which two complementary contradictions are present. On the one hand, there is the contradiction of the teaching of the negative as a positive content, or as part of the stated curriculum. The students are taught the system abstractly as knowledge, but in the full understanding by the teacher that this is only a secondary education compared to the experience and the negation of that content which is the actual education of the students. The progress that could be made in examining that actuality was, as we will see, limited. The truth of the education of Hegel's pupils is that it was scientifically incomplete, but, and for that very reason, not merely another abstract domination of them. Hegel's experiential classroom is for this reason very different from current ideas regarding experiential learning. While one of the tenets of the latter is the independence of the learner, that abstraction and domination is itself negated in the truth of the learner as in-dependence.

On the other hand, there is the contradiction of the teacher as personally the abstraction of the knowledge of the negative. Given the incompleteness of the students' own learning, and their lack of independence, the teacher in Hegel's classroom is forced into being only a one-sided presentation of the relation, and to face the contradiction of this, his own independence, as self-negation. Both these aspects of Hegel's education relations are now examined in more detail.

As a philosopher, Hegel held contradictory opinions about becoming a teacher, and as a teacher he held seemingly opposing views about students in general. Both sets of opinions are evidence of the importance he attached to the education relation as a broken middle, a relation which, whole only in its separation, truly characterises his time at Nuremberg. He was successful in preventing the closure of the gymnasium, a success which prevented his immediate move to a university post. He stated in his personal correspondence that:

> My personal self-interest and patriotic (duty) to Nuremberg were to be sure in contradiction. I thus had personal experience of the absurdity of the way of the world, for what I myself contributed to generate interest in the institution's future has come to number among the reasons for my own failure to advance (1984, p. 230).

219

However, he was later able to reflect that his time spent as a schoolteacher enabled him to develop both his philosophy and his teaching in a way which a university post might not have done. Of his years in Jena, during which he wrote the *Phenomenology*, he says that he was:

> ...bound to the letter of my notebook. However, eight years' practice in gymnasium instruction at last has helped me gain a freedom in my lecturing that probably can be attained nowhere better than in such a position. It is an equally good way of attaining clarity (1984, p. 331).

In this respect he suggested that being a schoolteacher had been 'more advantageous to me than even a university professorship' (1984, p. 332).

With regard to his views on students, Hegel had a very definite and, on the one hand, seemingly very traditional views on what should be expected from them. He discouraged duelling, fighting and smoking as well as political activity. In his school address of 1810 he stated that, 'From those who attend our school we expect quiet behaviour, the habit of continuous attention, respect and obedience to the teachers and proper and seemly conduct both towards these and towards their fellow pupils' (Mackenzie, 1909, p. 163). He also introduced military drill into the school day, as it helped students to learn quickly and 'to have the presence of mind, to carry out a command on the spot without previous reflection' (1909, p. 165). He cited the pupils of Pythagoras as an example of such discipline, for 'Pythagoras demanded four years' silence of his followers' (Hegel, 1984, p. 293). Surely, adds Hegel, 'the philosopher at least has the right to ask the reader to keep his own thoughts quiet until he has gone through the whole' (1984, p. 293). Such comments give the impression of a dominating teacher, one who did not encourage his pupils to think for themselves nor express their own opinions. His point is that opinions about science are unhelpful, for they emphasise the freedom of the person whereas it is a part of science to comprehend the abstract nature of that freedom and negate the independence of the identity from which those opinions are offered.

> It has become the prejudice not only of philosophical study but also – and indeed even more extensively – of pedagogy that *thinking for oneself* is to be developed and practised in the first place as if *the subject matter were of no importance* (1984, p. 340).

Four years earlier, Hegel had written to Niethammer, then the man who had responsibility for the reorganisation of the Bavarian education system, that 'The unfortunate urge to educate the individual in thinking for himself and being self-productive has cast a shadow over truth' (1984, p. 279).

A more 'liberal' side to his views on students can also be found. Mackenzie notes that he was much liked by his students and that his 'genuine enthusiasm for knowledge' was infectious (1909, p. 32). He could teach most subjects with ease, he encouraged wide reading, and took a personal interest in the students' reading material. He interviewed all students before they left the gymnasium, whether they were proceeding to university or not. His distaste for traditional didactic instruction is clear in his reproach of the District School Councillor, whose:

> ...only concept of educating the young is the misery of endless inculcating, reprimanding, memorising – not even learning by heart but merely the misery of endless repetition, pressure and stupefaction, ceaseless spoon-feeding and stuffing. He cannot comprehend that in learning a young mind must in fact behave independently (Hegel, 1984, p. 199).

This appears to be directly at odds with his view that students should not express their own opinions. What this opposition highlights is the contradiction of independence, i.e. learning about being in-dependence. The student is not acting independently merely by stating opinions, nor merely by thinking for himself. The student is independent when his state of being in-dependence has been raised to its own truth. In the student, dependence is implicit as his self-identity, but it can only be realised by the negation of abstract independence; that is, by the negation of him as a person. The student is not yet a person. To treat him as such is to deny him the truth of his being a student, and to encourage in him the abstraction of education and identity as result. The phrase 'independent learning', currently in vogue in education, is a pure contradiction. Learning can be about independence, but learning itself is in-dependence. Only when learning is a self-relation of result and activity can the learner be said to be independent, but even then its truth is only as the broken middle. The actuality of the 'independent learner' is the self-negation of the independent learner.

The student is only ever implicitly the education relation, and both of his moments, learning as identity and learning as work, lie ahead for him in his experience of negation. As long as the student is dependent upon the teacher, his negation will never be his own work, nor a self-negation. That is the contradictory nature of the teacher, then, to enable the student to become independent so that the contradiction (and truth) of independence will become his own, and not the teacher's. It has to be remembered that the teacher/student relation is the separation of the whole of the education relation, and the separation also of independence and dependence. This relation is implicit in the student, but is only actual or explicit in the comprehensive education of the teacher (or person) who is for himself in being for another. A student therefore learns to think independently in order to become his own explicit contradiction, but this is not the same as expressing opinions, which, in any case, acts as an obstacle to the scientific education of the student. Not expressing fanciful opinions is part of the education to, and in regard of, independence, for it is a part of the discipline which is science. Truth, for Hegel, is not-personal. But to appear as this broken middle requires both person and negation. Hence the necessary ambiguity in Hegel's opinions about his students. The importance of their independence to him is clearly revealed in his comments that teachers should not:

> ...induce in children a feeling of subjection and bondage – to make them obey another's will even in unimportant matters – to demand absolute obedience for obedience' sake, and by severity to obtain what really belongs alone to the feeling of love and reverence... A society of students cannot be regarded as an assemblage of servants, nor should they have the appearance or behaviour of such. Education to independence demands that young people should be accustomed early to consult their own sense of propriety and their own reason (Mackenzie, 1909, p. 175).

Students are not 'servants', for they will become persons. Only as persons is their self-relation of master and slave actual. The contradictory nature of education to (and from) independence is stated by Hegel as follows:

> To regard study as mere receptivity and memory work is to have a most incomplete view of what instruction means. On the other hand, to concentrate attention on the pupil's own original reflections and reasoning is equally one-sided and should be still more carefully guarded against (Mackenzie, 1909, p. 167).

This contradiction is even more apparent in trying to teach science or philosophy as a positive content. The problem is that in science the separation of the positive and the negative is their relation as a broken middle, a relation which is actual in the experience and in the learning of consciousness. In philosophy the content and the activity, as a broken middle, are joined in their separation, a relation which is the work and the result of science itself. 'In learning the content of philosophy one not only learns to philosophise, but indeed really philosophises... The process of coming to know a substantial philosophy is nothing else than learning' (Hegel, 1984, p. 279). Yet, in the classroom and the teacher/student relation, this is precisely the relation whose parts exist only separately; the content is embodied in the person of the teacher, independent of and abstracted from the learning which is the self-activity of that content. The problem posed by the teaching of philosophy, for Hegel, was how to present the broken middle of content and activity, knowledge and experience, in such a way that the experience or work of learning was not dominated by any further abstractions which the teacher might wish to impose. What he found was that, given the incomplete education of the student, the negative could never be experienced by them as self-relation, and that education was always, therefore, in opposition to him as the teacher. The students

222

proved themselves unable to deal with the abstract logical exercises with which Hegel experimented. He quickly abandoned that approach in the realisation that his pupils could more easily comprehend concrete, real, existing content, content which has appeal for 'sense, feeling, figurate conception, and practical interest of any kind' (1969, p. 58). The negative would appear in their experience of this content. He explained the structure of this pedagogy to Niethammer in terms of the outline of the philosophical system itself.

> Philosophical content has in its method and soul three forms: it is 1. abstract, 2. dialectical, and 3. speculative. It is abstract in so far as it takes place generally in the element of thought. Yet as merely abstract it becomes – in contrast to the dialectical and speculative forms – the so-called understanding which holds determinations fast and comes to know them in their fixed distinction. The dialectical is the movement and confusion of such fixed determinateness; it is negative reason. The speculative is positive reason, the spiritual, and it alone is really philosophical (1984, p. 280).

In this particular case the determination which is fixed as an abstract result is philosophical knowledge, both in the curriculum, and in the teacher. Hegel's problem was that the broken middle of educational experience could only be taught abstractly, in the form of knowledge. Rather than begin straight away with logical abstractions, however, he decided to begin with the abstractions which the pupils dealt with on a daily basis, in particular those found in law, morality and religion. By 1822 he had become of the opinion that the teaching of philosophy should not begin with philosophical instruction at all, but rather with 'the study of the ancients' (1984, p. 391). This was because in presenting logical abstractions, he was presenting philosophical content as if it were simply 'shot from a pistol' (1977, p. 16; 1969, p. 67); that is, as if the work of philosophising had been accomplished as result by the teacher, and now all that was required was to give this result to the students. Such a gift robbed the students of the truth of philosophy, for it handed them experience or activity as knowledge or result, something done for them, on their behalf, by another. However, this in itself would be a negation of the content by and in the students' experience of the gift, but it would not be a negation tied to the substance of the content, only to the domination of the teacher. Nevertheless it is part of the contradiction of the education relation that what is taught abstractly at the beginning is not the whole. Any beginning, 'precisely because it is the beginning, is imperfect' (1984, p. 293), and can only be taught as part of the whole of the education relation. The imperfection of all beginnings (and therefore of all teachers) has to be part of the pedagogy, and become a constituent part of the whole which is the educational relation. This is the strategy Hegel adopted in order that his philosophical curriculum would include within it the vanishing relation of negation and actuality. Since the vanishing is known only negatively, the negation requires to be taught for, but not about. It was necessary, anyway, to include 'experience' in the curriculum, if only to comprehend that experience was unavoidable and already the implicit truth of the activity of the student. Students do not need to be taught to think, they require only that the truth of their thinking and experience as negation be recognised, along with the place of negation in the whole which is the education relation.

Hegel's curriculum and pedagogy contain just such an insight. He notes that 'the beginning can only have the form of a fact or – better – of something *immediate*' (1984, p. 293), and that 'thinking is always the negation of what we have immediately before us' (1975, p. 17). Both moments of the education relation are already present here, result and activity, for result is what is experienced as abstract, and the experience, or thinking, is the activity and its negation as result only for-consciousness. It is therefore in the imperfection of all beginnings (and of all teachers) that the relation of education is already present. Once a content is thought, it is already mediated by that activity: 'For to mediate is to take something as a beginning and to go onward to a second thing; so that the existence of this second thing depends on our having reached it from something else contradistinguished from it' (1975, p. 17).

This 'second thing' is the dialectical or negative form of thought, and it has arisen in relation to abstract knowledge. To teach it, as content, would be to turn the activity into result and to abstract the negative from itself. This poses a problem for the scientific teacher. Dialectical thinking is itself dependent upon content which is other than itself, for it arises in the experience of that content. It is not (yet) itself a substantial content and therefore cannot be taught in the same way as other content. In handing students abstract knowledge, experience or negation is not dominated. In handing students the negative, including the content of their own emancipation by the radical teacher, their own experience remains unrecognised, and education then becomes unphilosophical, or merely dominated. Hegel's caution in this regard is clear: 'Dialectical (reason), on the one hand, could only be taught on an occasional basis and, on the other, could be taught more through the deficiency of this or that thought determination than according to its real nature' (1984, p. 264). Teaching about how dialectical reason is dependent, without removing that dependence in so doing, is a contradictory task. To teach it without building in the contradiction as student experience is to resolve those contradictions before they have even appeared. As Hegel had noted in the *Phenomenology*, the system 'must not be regarded as scientific when it is reduced to a lifeless schema, a mere shadow, and when scientific organisation is degraded into a table of terms' (1977, p. 29). Hegel even refused to write an introductory textbook for his students, informing Niethammer that such a compendium 'could not contain the developments necessary for complete insight' (1984, p. 175). A textbook cannot contain experience, it can only abstract it from its dependence in and as the thinking of the student, and therein attempt to rob the student of his own truth in the educational relation.

On a more practical level, the dialectical stage of thinking not only posed the problem of its own negativity as content, but it was itself the negation of all other content. Hegel found it to be the most difficult form of thought for his students. They preferred concrete material to that form of thought which counted as having only a 'negative significance' (1977, p. 49), and which seemed to undermine all that appeared as fixed and positive in the world. To plunge into the dialectical was, for them, to be pulled on to 'the pathway of doubt... the way of despair' (1977, p. 49). Hegel was forced to conclude that this negative stage 'is at once the stage in which the young, eager for material content and sustenance, are least interested' (1984, p. 281).

The third stage of philosophical education is the speculative: 'in so far as what is positive in (negative) dialectical (reason) is apprehended – lies speculative (reason)' (1984, p. 264). However, Hegel was cautious as to the extent to which this stage of reasoning was possible within a gymnasium classroom. It would require the students not only to feel at home in the sphere of the negative, but also to comprehend the substance and subject of a determinate negation. The students, however, were not in a suitable position to experience the full work and result of return, because their dependence upon the teacher in the classroom was already fixed. The broken middle in the classroom is already the separation of the broken middle. Its truth as relation can only appear to the students, therefore, as external. To be their self-relation requires that negation to be produced through their own work, the work which is relation, or dependence, or learning, and a work which is self-relation only as person or teacher. The education of the student is always incomplete, because a beginning has already been made for it, by the teacher, on their behalf. The education of the student is a comprehensive education in its relation to the continuing education of the teacher. This teacher has to recognise his own incompletion in relation to this beginning, a beginning which he both is and is not. Hegel was forced, in his own teaching, to concede that even with regard to those students who appeared to comprehend relation, 'one cannot even really know whether it is apprehended by them' (1984, p. 282). He concluded, therefore, that the aim of philosophy teaching to the young should not be to teach 'the absolute standpoint of philosophy' (1984, p. 264). The necessary incompleteness of a student's education is conceded by Hegel, who informed Niethammer that 'gymnasium instruction is essentially preparatory' (1984, p. 282).

Of perhaps even greater significance in the philosophical classroom is the education of the teacher. It is not only the curriculum and knowledge which appear abstract and fixed, and in opposition to the student. The same is true of the teacher. He, too, in embodying that knowledge, and in appearing as the embodiment or personification of education as result, is also another abstract philosophical content, and also requires to be negated. For Hegel, it is in this negation that the education of the teacher occurs, and wherein education is comprehensive.

225

The teacher has no choice but to accept that he is a domination of the student. The classroom fixes the relation of teacher and student, result and activity, as separated. The work of that separation is implicitly the truth of the students, but they are denied that relation as self-activity and result because their negation is always in relation to the teacher, and never their own work. The relation of the broken middle can only become self-relation to the person (or teacher) who experiences their own negation through that which they bring about by themselves. The classroom or lecture-hall, although explicitly concerned with the education of the student, is implicitly and unavoidably the education of the teacher. It is only from the position of abstract independence that negation is fully experienced as loss of self, an experience which then becomes the substance of that negation, or determinate education. The students have all abstract independence removed from them in the classroom. They are, therefore, never their own (loss of) beginning. For them a beginning in education has already been made, and is embodied in their separation from the teacher. The teacher is inescapably a re-presentation of the violence by which students are denied independence. That violence exists as long as there are classrooms and teachers. It is as a person that the student will gain his abstract independence, but that is only the beginning of his own education with regard to independence and dependence as a self-relation.

As was seen earlier, the aim of education is to raise the students out of the classroom to independence, so that their actual education may then begin. Comprehensive education aims at ensuring students become their own master and slave relation, and do not remain merely dependent upon the teacher. If this is successful, then *this* education marks the return of this master/slave to the classroom, but a classroom which is his own self-relation and self-learning. It may involve a return to a real classroom as either teacher or student. If it is as a student, then this time he accepts, even wills, the violence of the presence of the teacher as a necessary re-presentation of the violence, the struggle, which he is imposing upon himself in and through his own education. This 'higher' education is still a violent separation of teacher and student, but when it is voluntary and not compulsory then the student has been his own beginning, and negated his own independence by himself. The higher education classroom still re-presents violence, but it is a violence which now belongs to and within the student as a person, and is the violence of their own thinking, not merely that of the abstract teacher.

If the return to the classroom is as a teacher, whether the classroom is voluntary or compulsory for students, the position of the teacher as the violent imposition of education as result is inescapable. He cannot help but be another domination in the form of another beginning of education for the students. He is their negation, but their negation is not his, and although he represents their experience for them, he cannot have their experience for them. This contradiction for the teacher is summed up by Hegel as follows:

226

As much as philosophical study is in and for itself self-activity, to that degree also is it learning: the learning of an already present, developed science. This science is a treasure of hard-won, ready-prepared, formed content. This inheritance ready at hand must be earned by the individual, i.e. learned. The teacher possesses this treasure; he pre-thinks it. The pupils re-think it... The original, peculiar views of the young on essential objects are in part still totally deficient and empty, but in part – in infinitely greater part – they are opinion, illusion, half-truth, distortion, and indeterminateness. Through learning, truth takes the place of such imagining (1984, p. 280).

The teacher is the embodiment of science, of the thinking which has already been done and which has earned him the treasure which, now, he seeks to pass on. The path, therefore, is already set out for the student, who is not free to choose his own education. That decision is embodied in and by the treasure which the teacher possesses. Yet part of the treasure is that philosophy is science as experience, and as the work of thought. Since, as Hegel observes, 'no man can think for another, any more than he can eat or drink for him' (1975, p. 36), the teacher holds this treasure only in an abstract form. The thinking which has been done requires to be rethought by the students, for only then will it become also their treasure. The treasure cannot be offered as a gift, even though in the possession of the teacher, and as the embodiment of the teacher, that is how it appears. 'Truth', said Hegel, 'is not a minted coin that can be given and pocketed ready made' (1977, p. 22), it is a relation that requires to be performed and comprehended as work. This, then, is the contradiction of the teacher. What he has to teach cannot be taught in the form in which he possesses it. Put more personally, the teacher is not educational in the immediate and abstract form in which he appears in the classroom. This, however, is his experience, and his education.

The teacher is both that which makes education possible and that which prevents it. This relation, by now, is no stranger to us. This broken middle is relating itself to itself both positively and negatively. The teacher has this broken middle as his own self-relation. It is his own identity which is already a result (and therefore a beginning) of education, yet it is his experience of being such a result which returns him to learning, and where that result becomes merely an object for him. This is not simply a teacher becoming self-conscious in reflection. Such a reflective teacher posits his own subjectivity such that his determinate being is merely illusory being, a shining of the relation which he still fails to comprehend as relation. This teacher takes the view in the classroom that self-relation is his own conscience, and that there is no higher authority for a teacher than that he be true to himself. But what has appeared here as himself is only an empty being. Positing fails to comprehend how its own activity is already within a relation and is work which repeats the separation of the relation. When the negative subject, the reflective teacher, re-cognises what is posited as misrecognition, then it comprehends negation as its work. The education involved here is the education of the reflective and critical teacher regarding his own relation as the philosophical teacher.

This is the education of the teacher within the classroom. He comes to comprehend himself within the relation which is the whole, within the system. He is the abstract result of education and the violence of the beginning of education for his pupils, and he is also not the substance of education, nor the education of his pupils at all. He is both of these moments at the same time, the joining together and the separation of the educational relation. The relation is separated by the positing of the teacher as result, and the relation is joined because the work of positing is done by the teacher, and is his own negation. His experience is that he is not education, and the experience is a negation brought about by his own work. Here, in this experience, he enjoys the truth of the student or the slave, in that his own dependence upon learning, and upon the truth of learning as dependence, are present as his own relation. When the teacher in the classroom is recognised as falling within the contradiction of all abstract content, then the classroom is wholly a philosophical classroom, and the education within it is genuinely comprehensive. In the experience by the teacher that he is separated from education, from the student, from learning, he enjoys the experience of being more and less than this separation.

It is in this contradictory position within the classroom, the contradiction of his education relation, that the teacher becomes the self-education of the broken middle. His own education is his death as the teacher, requiring that the violence perpetrated against the student is now aimed against himself. He is pulled on to the way of despair where he loses all that is certain. This is genuinely a loss of self but is also his continuing education. As a student he can return to the classroom, but for the teacher who now knows himself as contradiction, and as not-education, his actual classroom is now in the school of philosophy. It is in and as philosophical consciousness that education is truly comprehensive, but the actuality of comprehensive education is the philosophical classroom where the truth of the teacher is the broken middle of result and activity, or where he is teacher and student. The teacher is actually educational, is successful, only by having failure and the experience of failure (shining for others) as a key determinative component. This philosophical teacher teaches from within the space in which the contradiction of success and failure, of identity and negation, is both abstract and mediated, or where the contradiction appears in the shadow which is its full light. The education of the teacher does not resolve the contradiction of the teacher; it is the actuality of that contradiction.

Part IV
RETURN OF THE DESPAIRING TEACHER

The developments outlined in Parts I, II and III are personified in the story told by Nietzsche in his book *Thus Spake Zarathustra*. What follows, here, is an interpretation of Zarathustra as the despairing teacher who, in seeking to enlighten the people, is forced to follow his own path of despair. Through Hegel, this pathway has been traced as the comprehensive education of philosophical consciousness, its separation and division, its return to itself, and the actuality of that self-relation or broken middle. The story of Nietzsche's Zarathustra is the story of the same comprehensive education. It includes a change of language, of concepts and of particular events, but the lesson of the broken middle is retained. What in Hegel and Rose is the relation of relation and non-relation is, in *Thus Spake Zarathustra*, the return of the teacher of return.

8 Shining for others: Nietzsche's Zarathustra

Nietzsche's *Thus Spake Zarathustra* is the story of what happens to the radical and despairing teacher of return who becomes the contradiction and, therefore, the truth of the return of the teacher. This return is the circle described earlier in which teaching or shining for others returns as self-negation, and where this negation, in various forms, is then posited as a new shining for others, which in turn returns as another self-negation. As will be seen later, even when Zarathustra believes himself 'enlightened' about this circle as the whole of life and teaches it as the will-to-power, he is still a teacher shining for others. His story, chronicled by Nietzsche, contains the lessons he learns about this eternal return to self, lessons in which his own negation, his own darkness, become increasingly visible as the contradictory whole of his self as the teacher. The importance of light, dark and shadow are critical to comprehending the development of Zarathustra, a development which demands that the book be read as a whole, and as his own comprehensive (philosophical) education.

Book 1: the Prologue

Zarathustra's Prologue is the most abstract part of Zarathustra's story and therefore, like the Preface and Introduction to Hegel's *Phenomenology of Spirit*, induces the reader to experience it as a contradiction. In the Prologue Zarathustra makes pedagogical mistakes in his teaching which form the content of the rest of the book. Books 1 to 4 are his own education regarding the failure of his teaching in the Prologue.

We first meet Zarathustra when he is 30 years old and has been in solitude on his mountain for ten years. During this time his wisdom has grown, in particular with regard to the fact that God is dead and that mankind has no power other than

231

his own by which to explain himself and his values. But with this wisdom comes the need to teach. 'I am weary of my wisdom, like a bee that has gathered too much honey; I need hands outstretched to receive it' (Nietzsche, 1982, p. 122).

In the first section of the Prologue we are introduced to themes which are to play a major part in the rest of the story. First, and perhaps most important, Zarathustra has been accompanied in his solitude by that which enlightens Zarathustra and his mountain, the sun. But, and secondly, the sun has only been able to give its light because Zarathustra has been there to receive it. 'You great star,' says Zarathustra, 'what would your happiness be had you not those for whom you shine?' (1982, p. 121). Already established here in the story are the giver of enlightenment, the receiver of enlightenment, and the relation between the two which makes the gift of enlightenment possible and actual. It is a relation Zarathustra seeks for himself, not only as the receiver but as the giver. He wants to become the sun which shines for others. Like the sun he wants to 'give away and distribute' (1982, p. 122) from 'the cup that wants to overflow' (1982, p. 122). For this to be possible Zarathustra must leave his mountain, and 'go under – go down' (1982, p. 122) to man. The student needs to become the teacher, to shine for others, and for that he needs to leave the mountain wherein he is a relation of student to teacher, and go down to man that he may become a relation of teacher to student. These themes of enlightenment, shining, darkness, the gift, and going down are central to understanding what follows, just as much as are the ideas of will-to-power and eternal return.

In Sections 2 and 3 of the Prologue we learn exactly what it is that Zarathustra seeks to teach to man, and what it is that he has learnt on his mountain over the preceding ten years. His gift to man, the wisdom with which he overflows, is that 'God is dead', and that man is a bridge to the overman, the man who can create his own values. Crossing this bridge, however, is like crossing an abyss. It is dangerous, and is best performed by those 'who do not know how to live, except by going under, for they are those who cross over' (1982, p. 127). This, again, introduces major themes that reappear in all four books which follow the Prologue. With regard to the death of God, we have yet to learn how He dies, how He keeps dying, and who killed Him. Equally, although Zarathustra says he is the advent of the lightening bolt called the overman, we have yet to see the fate and re-education of this messenger by the message itself. Finally, the ideas of going under and going across, and of man being a bridge which, in holding together two sides, is a contradictory self-relation, are not only central to comprehending the re-education of Zarathustra, but are also central negative components of social and educational relations.

Zarathustra teaches the people of God's death, and of the next step which man must take to the overman. But his first teaching ends in failure. The pupils do not attend the master, instead they stand and laugh at him. Zarathustra laments, 'They do not understand me; I am not the mouth for these ears' (1982, p. 128). He believes that what prevents them from learning from him is precisely that they already consider themselves to be educated. It has made them proud and 'that is

232

why they do not like to hear the word "contempt" applied to them' (1982, p. 129). It is only contempt for man, and his consequent going under, that will lead man to the overman. Yet their pride in their own education means that they are full of contempt for the teacher of the overman, but not for man himself. These educated men have become uneducable. They are the 'last men', the last men that it has been possible to educate and the men in whom no further education is possible. Zarathustra argues that for man to give birth to new ideas, and to a new man, 'one must still have chaos in oneself' (1982, p. 129), but that these last men, these educated men, have no chaos left in themselves. Now 'everybody wants the same, everybody is the same' (1982, p. 130), and everybody will remain the same.

This is the end of Zarathustra's first speech. He accuses the people for not understanding what he taught them, but we, in rest of the book, follow Zarathustra's own misunderstanding of, and *naïveté* towards his own teaching. His failure here is the beginning of his re-education, one where he learns not to teach, but to become that which is taught.

As he finishes speaking the crowd call for Zarathustra to give them not the overman but the 'last man', the man who reigns before the time of the overman. At the same time a tightrope walker begins his performance in the market-place. When this artist had reached the middle of the rope, a rope tied between two towers, a jester appeared from a door at one end and followed the tightrope walker to the middle of the rope. After abusing the walker as someone who blocked his path, the jester leapt over the walker and the walker plunged to the ground.

The story illustrates Zarathustra's teaching experience to date. He has taught that man is a rope across an abyss, a rope which leads from man to the overman. Yet in teaching this, he finds man, and particularly the last man, in his way. As the jester speaks to the tightrope walker so might Zarathustra also have said to the people 'What are you doing here between towers? The tower is where you belong. You ought to be locked up; you block the way for one better than yourself' (1982, p. 131). However, Zarathustra fails to learn from what happens next. When the jester leaps over man, man dies. It may look here as if the jester has overcome man, but if man is a rope, as Zarathustra has said, and then man dies, so, too, does the rope and the bridge across to the overman. However, for Book 1 at least, Zarathustra becomes this overleaping jester. Only later will we see the significance of this belief that man can be educated by being sacrificed or overcome.

Zarathustra sees the episode and goes to the fallen tightrope walker saying, 'You have made danger your vocation... Now you perish of your vocation; for that I will bury you with my own hands' (1982, p. 132). It is a nobility which Zarathustra is not yet capable of himself. The walker goes under because he tried to cross, and in trying to cross he went under. He did what he was. What the walker has achieved in action, Zarathustra knows, as yet, only in words. Zarathustra's vocation is, in the Prologue and Book 1, merely theoretical and thus ultimately hypocritical. Zarathustra concludes that his day's teaching has brought in a strange haul. 'Not a man has he caught but a corpse' (1982, p. 132). There could be no finer example of the result of Zarathustra's teaching in the Prologue than this corpse. The people understood immediately that the teacher of the overman appeared as a jester, indeed could only appear as a jester and as one who is claiming that he has leapt over man and beyond him. Appearing as a man, Zarathustra says 'I teach you the next man'. His teaching is self-contradictory. In his own lack of self-contempt as the teacher, in the certainty of his own education, he resembles the last men of whom he speaks. It is his own certainty, his own education, which makes him believe he has leapt over the men who stand in his way. In the very leap, man, who is already halfway across, has the going across taken away from him. The teacher of the overman, as far as the people are concerned, prevents the journey to the overman in the teaching of it. The teaching and the leaping are the same. They produce a corpse. What else could this teacher be, who kills in order to cure, other than a fool?

Zarathustra, however, at this stage does not blame the messenger or the message. It is the people who misunderstand; 'I am not the mouth for these ears' (1982, p. 130). Therefore he resolves to find for himself among the masses a group of followers and companions. It is 'fellow creators, the creator seeks – those who write new values on new tablets... Destroyers they will be called, and despisers of good and evil. But they are the harvesters' (1982, p. 136). The teacher of the overman, in the light of his failure and humiliation, resolves 'Never again shall I speak to the people... To my own goal I will go – on my way; over those who hesitate and lag behind I shall leap ' (1982, p. 136). Thus begins the phase of Zarathustra the jester, the teacher who does not teach man, but seeks to achieve the overman without man, in spite of him, and by leaving him behind. Nothing, in fact, could be more counterproductive, for he is leaving behind and avoiding that which is the rope, and that which goes across. As a teacher, Zarathustra is leaving behind that which his work is for, and that in which his true relation as a teacher is realised. The broken middle of that relation between the teacher and the pupil, between the sun and those for whom it shines, is now set to be one of Zarathustra's hardest lessons in becoming what he is, or in shining in and for himself. But the Zarathustra of Book 1 is not only not himself, neither is he even the sun which he so admires. That sun shines for all; Zarathustra is restricting his gift, now, to the chosen few. 'I found life more dangerous among men than among animals' (1982, p. 137), yet he is now choosing to avoid that danger. The Prologue ends, however, with a sense that even now Zarathustra is reflecting upon the loss of wisdom which his failure in the market-place might represent. In a thought that reverberates throughout his re-education in the rest of the book, he says to his heart 'when my wisdom leaves me one day – alas it loves to fly away – let my pride then fly with my folly' (1982, p. 137). But still the teacher of contempt is proud of the overman. That, in the end, proves to be his repeated downfall.

234

Zarathustra the jester

After the Prologue, the rest of Book 1 consists of Zarathustra's speeches. This is the phase of Zarathustra the jester, of the teacher who seeks to have himself taken seriously, and thus avoids and leaps over those who block the path to his teaching being successful. The main substance of these speeches, the thing which Zarathustra aims to teach his companions, is genealogy, similar to that which has already been examined with regard to Foucault. But, unlike Foucault, the result of teaching genealogy for Zarathustra is the experience of contradiction. Where Foucault sheds blood, it is the blood of a non-subject. Where Zarathustra sheds blood, it is his own.

The speeches begin with the three metamorphoses of the spirit and are an early dramatisation of Zarathustra's education to date regarding will-to-power. The wisdom of the three metamorphoses comes from Zarathustra the solitary who went to the mountain carrying his own ashes, stayed there for ten years, and then returned as the teacher of the overman. It becomes clear in Book 4 that the third metamorphosis into a child is not quite what Zarathustra the jester takes it to be. The camel takes upon itself the heaviest burden, puts upon its own back that which is most difficult, and speeds into the solitude of the desert. In the desert it is the lion who would seek to become master of himself and of his domain. The lion has to vanquish the dragon which preaches 'Thou shalt'; that is, to comprehend the genealogy of morals, and replace those ignoble values with the nobility and self-mastery of 'I will'. But even the genealogist of morals, the lion whose spirit says 'I will', even it cannot create new values. The lion's spirit is essentially *ressentiment*, a reactive no-saying to all that stands in the way of the new freedom to create values. The lion is the truth of the genealogist of morals, for both are beasts of prey and have a history of blood. Both are the spirit of the freedom to create new values, but the lion is not in itself a new value, it is only the embodiment of the spirit to make prey of all old values. For new values, a third metamorphosis is required.

> Why must the preying lion still become a child? The child is innocence and forgetting, a new beginning, a game, a self-propelled wheel, a first movement, a sacred 'Yes'. For the game of creation, my brothers, a sacred 'Yes' is needed: the spirit now wills his own will, and he who had been lost to the world now conquers his own world (1982, p. 139).

What Zarathustra has yet to learn, but does so in Book 4, is that such forgetting and innocence is antithetical to eternal return. There is no child, no third stage of man's education in Zarathustra, which is not also lost and returned. However, by the end of the book, Zarathustra has this truth as his truth of the educational relation, and of the truth of himself as the teacher. Zarathustra's own education throughout the book is of eternal return as the spirit of the camel/lion. The child, like his wisdom, accompanies only his folly.

The speeches which follow tell of Zarathustra's own camel/lion phase on his mountain before the Prologue. Having carried his burden to the mountain, over the next ten years he learnt to say 'no' to God, to the state, to values, to the spirit of gravity; and 'yes' to will-to-power, to war, to the overman, to 'I will' and to new hope. His no-saying is his work as a genealogist on the mountain. With regard to God, Zarathustra acknowledges that he, himself, 'cast my delusion beyond man' (1982, p. 143) and that 'this god whom I created was man-made and madness, like all gods!' (1982, p. 143). The cause of the creation was the body which despised itself. The body waged a war against itself in a spirit of *ressentiment* and negative self-worth. When the body turned against itself to overcome what it was, man created values and gods in this spirit of *ressentiment* and self-war. Man created God so that He might judge man unworthy, in order to save man from the realisation that the value of unworthiness was this self-war. The heavens, and moral Christian values, reflected the view of the enemy of the body. But that enemy was the body itself. God and values were created out of the blood of this self-war, but as long as God and values were seen as a judgment upon man's willing ego, man was spared the ultimate education that even these delusions were a result of the willing ego. God is the manifestation of unwilling ego, the ego that refuses to be itself. What Zarathustra teaches is the willing ego, the will-to-power of a body at war with itself, and that this willing ego is 'the measure and value of things' (1982, p. 144).

> A new pride my ego taught me, and this I teach men: no longer to bury one's head in the sand of heavenly things, but to bear it freely, an earthly head, which creates a meaning for the earth.
> A new will I teach to men: to *will* this way which man has walked blindly, and to affirm it, and no longer to sneak away from it like the sick and decaying (1982, p. 144).

This is the spirit of the lion which has God and values as prey, and which becomes the will-to-power because, in preying, he becomes what he is, a beast of prey. Later in Book 1 Zarathustra attributes all values to this war:

> Men gave themselves all their good and evil. Verily, they did not take it, they did not find it, nor did it come to them as a voice from heaven. Only man placed value in things to preserve himself – he alone created a meaning for things, a human being. Therefore he calls himself 'man', which means: the esteemer (1982, p. 171).

He concludes that 'A tablet of the good hangs over every people. Behold, it is the tablet of their overcomings; behold, it is the voice of their will-to-power' (1982, p. 170).

It is in this genealogical interrogation by Zarathustra, the lion on his mountain in his ten years' solitude, that he overcame himself. He finally understood himself

236

as a self-war, as a self-hater, an unwilling ego, and became himself, i.e. a willing ego. The act of overcoming was itself an act of war. Thus did Zarathustra realise himself as the lion 'I invented a brighter flame for myself. And behold, then this ghost fled from me' (1982, p. 143). Now Zarathustra wants to light this flame in others, to free them from their attachment to the body-haters, to the unwilling, who wage their war by preaching of afterworlds. He would prefer that they listen rather 'to the voice of the healthy body' (1982, p. 145). The healthy body does not merely despise itself, rather it knows itself as doing the despising, that the despising is its creative act, the act which creates God and values. Thus, says Zarathustra, the body is 'a plurality with one sense, a war and a peace, a herd and a shepherd' (1982, p. 146). The self is not what it says it is, it is what it does, and what it does is what it wills. The self is a battle against itself. Despising the body is merely another act of war by the body. 'Behind your thoughts and feelings, my brother, there stands a mighty ruler, an unknown sage – whose name is self. In your body he dwells; he is your body' (1982, p. 146).

But such a genealogical enquiry, which finds at the root of all afterworlds and all values a self which is at war with itself, is an enquiry which reveals struggle and blood and overcoming as what self is. With no one else to blame, the fingers of a deluded spirit can no longer touch the ultimate walls (1982, p. 143) and transport themselves from this despair and destruction. Zarathustra warns that the spirit of the lion genealogist has not proved to be endurable for some, and 'many have gone into the desert and taken their lives because they have wearied of being the battle and the battlefield of virtues' (1982, p. 149). It is here that Zarathustra teaches what is to become the truth of all his teaching and of his self as teacher. The virtues, on the battlefield and as the battle, seek supremacy over each other. 'Each of your virtues covets what is highest: each wants your whole spirit that it might become her herald; each wants your whole strength in wrath, hatred and love' (1982, p. 149). Put into a sentence, this self-war for supremacy leaves us with the genealogical self-truth that 'Man is something that must be overcome' (1982, p. 149). So often read as a sentence which is an instruction from Zarathustra to man, this interpretation robs genealogy, the whole of *Thus Spake Zarathustra*, and Zarathustra himself, of its and his educational substance. Read as an instruction, Zarathustra is no more than the jester who seeks to leap over man to the overman. This is certainly the case at this point in the book.

But, as will be shown, this truth that 'man is something that must be overcome' is not an instruction from Zarathustra, it is a realisation given to Zarathustra by nature itself. It is no more than a statement of the struggle, of the war which is the self. It is expressing the way that the virtues each seek supremacy, and that this supremacy can be achieved only by defeating that which is currently supreme, the virtue which (at that moment) calls itself man. Man, the victory of a virtue which calls itself master, is always that which has overcome (previous man) and that which now stands to be overcome. The sentence therefore contains two meanings in one. Man, the victory, is that which now must be overcome, and man is also that which has done the overcoming and will do it again. But in Zarathustra's speeches in Part 1 of *Thus Spake Zarathustra*, this realisation remains an abstract teaching and is not yet the truth of Zarathustra himself as this contradiction of self-relation.

The genealogical speeches of Zarathustra continue to reveal his loathing of those men who turn against the war and the warrior in acts of self-hatred. The turn against war is still an act of war, but one which seeks revenge against the war itself. These are the worst hypocrites, for these are men who preach peace and contentment and equality and justice, but are never honest enough with themselves to see that such preaching is only another strategy in the war for supremacy. They, too, seek to overcome man. They seek to overcome man the lion, the beast of prey, yet they, too, are part of the battle. What Zarathustra seeks are not those who say 'no' to the struggle, the hypocrites, but those who affirm themselves as the struggle and say 'yes' to what they are. The war of the no-sayers is a war of revenge and *ressentiment* against man. The war of the yes-sayer is a becoming of what man is. Thus Zarathustra says 'Of all that is written I love only what a man has written with his blood. Write with blood, and you will experience that blood is spirit' (1982, p. 152). The lion demands here that man be true to what he is and becomes the struggle, the battle that is man. Wisdom 'loves only a warrior' (1982, p. 153).

It is not enough to know that man is a self-war (or self-relation), man has to be that self-war. Zarathustra meets a youth who complains that even in his own searching beyond good and evil, he finds that he becomes aware of this searching and experiences this awareness as self-contempt. The boy who seeks to become a yes-sayer finds that in his searching he becomes a no-sayer, aware of the desire to fly but therefore also aware that he is not flying. As a result the youth has become envious of Zarathustra, for in having before him that which he aspires to be, the youth can only experience Zarathustra as a negation, that is, as another no-saying by the youth to what he presently is. He complains, 'the higher I climb, the more I despise the climber... It is the envy of you that has destroyed me' (1982, p. 155).

Zarathustra tells the youth: 'You are not yet free, you still search for freedom... To me you are still a prisoner who is plotting his freedom: alas, in such prisoners the soul becomes clever, but also deceitful and bad' (1982, p. 155). Aimed at the youth, the clever Zarathustra, the jester who seeks to have himself taken seriously, has only predicted the lesson which awaits the teacher at the end of his genealogical speeches. He teaches about overcoming as one who knows overcoming, as one who has overcome and has that result, now, available as a gift to others. It is this cleverness which lies at the heart of his speeches, and which he realises, also, to be deceitful. They, too, like the teacher, remain to be overcome.

In another example of that which Zarathustra teaches others but has yet to realise in himself as teacher, he teaches that the war which is the self does not end in peace. 'If your thought be vanquished, then your honesty should still find cause for triumph in that. You should love peace as a means to new wars – and the short peace more than the long... To you I do not recommend peace but victory' (1982, p. 159). Such teaching will later become the teaching of the eternal return of will-

238

to-power. But that wisdom and that spirit lie ahead for Zarathustra. Indeed, what Zarathustra is in Book 1, throughout the genealogical uncovering of the war, is a peace. He did not remain vanquished in the market-place, loving his enemies as the instigators of new wars. Rather, he took to the mountains with a group of disciples, avoiding new wars, teaching them 'Let your work be a struggle' (1982, p. 159), but as a teacher refusing that struggle. His own hypocrisy as a peaceful teacher of war will return to Zarathustra at the end of Book 1.

But, in the speeches, Zarathustra is the personification of self-war and becomes the teacher of yes-saying who, on the mountain with his disciples, has already said 'no' to combat. He is forced, therefore, into contradiction. 'Man,' he says, 'is something that shall be overcome' (1982, p. 160). Yet in the same breath he also says that this 'highest thought... you should receive as a command from me' (1982, p. 160). The teacher who believes that he has overcome falls into the same contradiction of enlightenment which was seen earlier regarding teachers and critics. That which they believe themselves to have achieved as self-relation can only be taught as the destruction of that relation, or as knowledge for others. The teacher who commands self-relation in others contradicts the very truth on which the command is made. The pupil can only receive self-relation in its form as knowledge, or as the property of the teacher. It is already not self-relation, or self-work, it is already merely the command of another. In Book 1 of *Thus Spake Zarathustra*, Zarathustra is merely the personification of the overman, another last man who is educated with regard to the self as war, but whose possession of that knowledge is his own peace, and a war declared only upon others. Zarathustra at this stage has war as object but not as self. The Zarathustra of the speeches is another last man, 'no longer able to despise himself' (1982, p. 129). Zarathustra the teacher of overcoming remains to be overcome, for this Zarathustra, like the jester, refuses the middle of the tightrope where man is, and leaps over him. Like the jester he is not prepared to stay in the middle where man, whose work is the struggle, is to be found. But it is a middle to which he will find himself returned by his own work, by overcoming this education which he has as result, and not as work.

The questions which Zarathustra asks of his disciples in his speeches in Book 1 are questions which will become his own enemies later on. Can his disciples become their own tablets of values? Can they emerge beyond good and evil to become the creators of new values? Can they become 'A first movement? A self-propelled wheel?' (1982, pp. 174–5). Can they become the unification in themselves of the war of values and the value of war? 'Can you give yourself,' he asks, 'your own evil and your own good and hang your own will over yourself as a law? Can you be your own judge and avenger of your law?' (1982, p. 175). Such a unification is Zarathustra's hope for the future, for the next man, the yes-sayers, fellow creators who write 'new values on new tablets' (1982, p. 136). No such unification is achieved throughout *Thus Spake Zarathustra*. Such a unification is not the result of the work which is *Thus Spake Zarathustra*. The Zarathustra of

239

the Prologue and Book 1, the abstract teacher, is concerned with the future. What lies ahead for Zarathustra, however, is not the future, but the past.

At the end of Book 1, the speeches are finished. The disciples present Zarathustra with a gift, a staff on which 'a serpent coiled around the sun' (1982, p. 186). This prompts Zarathustra to think again about the nature of gift-giving. That which has the highest value, he says, is that which 'always gives itself' (1982, p. 186), like gold. This theme is a reminder to Zarathustra of the time before he descended from the mountain for the first time. There, it was the sun which gave of itself. Its light was the gift to those for whom it shone. To become also a gift-giver was the reason that Zarathustra left the mountain. He, too, wished to shine for others, to give them his light, to become the sun for them. Thus, however, did Zarathustra fail in the Prologue, for his sun was not their sun, nor was it his own. Zarathustra, the teacher of the overman, is only ever the pupil of the sun's enlightenment, a shining for others. Thus, also, do Zarathustra's speeches in Book 1 fail. His words are not also those of his disciples. His words shine for them as Zarathustra imparts his gift to them. But the sun becomes itself only in its own light. It does not enable the same self-work in others, for that requires them to become their own sun. Anyone who is to be a giver of light must also give that light to themselves, otherwise they have no self-light to give to anyone. It is how to become the self which is a self as a giving that concerns Zarathustra's education after Book 1. Book 1 itself, and the Prologue, are only his shining for others in such a way that his gift actually prevents that which it would give, self (as) light. Zarathustra the teacher has been giving without working. He has not also received his own light as his self. So much is he the sun for others, he cannot see his own light, nor his own shadow. For this he requires darkness, but that lesson awaits him in Book 2.

However, by the end of Book 1, Zarathustra the teacher is (re)turning into Zarathustra the learner. He is fast doubting his own teaching. 'Back to the body, back to life' (1982, p. 188) he tells his disciples, but is also telling himself. 'Physician, help yourself: thus you help your patient too' (1982, p. 189). His final mention of the new hope plunges him into doubt. When he next speaks, 'the tone of his voice had changed' (1982, p. 190). 'Now I go alone, my disciples. You too go now, alone. Thus I want it... go away from me and resist Zarathustra! And even better: be ashamed of him! Perhaps he deceived you' (1982, p. 190). His own commanding of others now returns to him as a lack of self-commanding, a lack of his own self-war. He is a teacher of war, and in so being is fighting a war against his disciples which, he knows, needs to be their war. He has taught *to* them that which must come *from* them. Zarathustra the jester begins to realise that he has been taken, and has taken himself, too seriously. 'One repays a teacher badly if one always remains nothing but a pupil,' (1982, p. 190) says Zarathustra. But equally, one repays a pupil badly if one remains as their teacher and prevents them from becoming self-taught. Zarathustra becomes aware of the contradiction inherent in his teaching. I taught you yourself, he admits, but 'You had not yet sought yourselves' (1982, p. 190). Therefore, instead of remaining their teacher,

240

'I bid you lose me and find yourselves; and only when you have all denied me will I return to you' (1982, p. 190). So he sends his pupils away to do the self-work which Zarathustra has tried to 'teach' them. What Zarathustra underestimates is that he will also lose himself and return changed: no longer the teacher of will-to-power as genealogy, but the teacher of will-to-power as life itself. Nevertheless, at the end of Book 1 it is still the overman and the future he dreams of, not the teaching of the eternal return of that which is past.

Book 2: life as will-to power

Having delivered his speeches, and then having sent the disciples away to find themselves before they find Zarathustra, Zarathustra himself returns to the mountains and his solitude, and stays there for years. The first lesson he has learnt about being the gift-giver, the teacher, is that one does not only give. 'For this is what is hardest: to close the open hand because one loves' (1982, p. 195). Equally, the gift-giver has to become aware that his shining is not yet that of others, only for others. Indeed, this light may well be so bright, like the sun, that it prevents the light in others from being seen. Thus one has to learn 'to keep a sense of shame as a giver' (1982, p. 195). Zarathustra takes his own light back to the mountain, and awaits the dawning of the light of this disciples, 'like a sower who has scattered his seed' (1982, p. 195).

But still Zarathustra is impatient for the future, and when his disciples do not appear after many years, he assumes that his enemies have distorted his teaching, and so he sets off for the blessed isles to find his companions and speak to them. Again the solitary feels the need to become the gift-giver. After all, what is light without those for whom it shines? What is the gift without those to whom it is to be given? Says Zarathustra, 'a lake is within me, solitary and self-sufficient; but the river of my love carries it along, down to the sea' (1982, p. 196). Love's work has moved him again to teach.

Upon the blessed isles, Zarathustra again begins to teach his friends. He reminds them that 'God is a conjecture' (1982, p. 197), but that he has taught them 'to say: overman' (1982, p. 197). His disciples, if they were properly to 'eat' the ripe teachings falling from Zarathustra, 'could well create the overman' (1982, p. 197). Creation is willing; 'that is the great redemption from suffering, and life's growing light' (1982, p. 199). 'Willing liberates: that is the true teaching of will and liberty' (1982, p. 199). Zarathustra explains his return to the disciples in terms of the joy of his own willing and creating. His return to them has again enabled him to become the gift-giver. His will (to create the overman) 'always comes to me as my liberator and joy-bringer... my fervent will to create impels me ever again toward man' (1982, p. 199); and this from a Zarathustra who, at the end of the Prologue, swore 'never again shall I speak to the people' (1982, p. 136). However, this return in Book 2, even though it is not really to the people in the market-place, but only to his disciples, is still only the return of Zarathustra to

241

others. It is not yet the eternal return of Zarathustra the teacher to himself. Even in Book 2, Zarathustra the teacher of the eternal return of will-to-power does not appear as or in this (self-) light.

He continues to teach the same genealogical insights as before, describing himself as a plough which will unearth 'the secrets of your foundation' (1982, p. 206). He teaches again that virtue is only the battlefield of the virtues, and that, therefore, the self is only a particular victory in this war. Those who preach equality are the most vengeful, for they carry on the war in secret. Their war is against the war itself, driven by the desire for revenge against man. It is the purest form of no-saying. In the souls of these 'tarantulas' sits poison, a poison always aimed against man and, therefore, against itself. This self-revolt is the genealogy of all morals, all values and even of the self. Says Zarathustra, 'that man may be delivered from revenge, that is for me the bridge to the highest hope...' (1982, p. 211).

In the critique of the preachers of equality Zarathustra observes that the war of the virtues, in which the revengeful are full and active players, is never-ending. The first hint of eternal return appears here, when Zarathustra says, 'Good and evil, and rich and poor, and high and low, and all the names of values – arms shall they be and clattering signs that life must overcome itself again and again' (1982, p. 213). And at the same time, the contradiction of the eternal return of will-to-power is also revealed.

> Life wants to build itself up into the heights with pillars and steps; it wants to look into vast distances and out toward stirring beauties: therefore it requires height. And because it requires height, it requires steps and contradiction among the steps and the climbers. Life wants to climb and to overcome itself climbing (1982, p. 213).

This is the first time that Zarathustra begins to explore the implications of his genealogy. This is the beginning of his self-education. What lies ahead for Zarathustra are the hard lessons that the war which is the self does not end, that his teaching has been and continues to be an act of war, that will-to-power and therefore the self are contradictory because in doing what it is, it always seeks to overcome itself, and that the true expression of the self and the teacher is eternal return.

The first of these hard lessons comes to Zarathustra in Book 2, not at high noon in the light of the sun, but at night, without the sun and in darkness. At night, in blackness, things always seem to be louder. It is Zarathustra's soul which he hears now more loudly than before. He is therefore forced to recognise that 'Something unstilled, unstillable is within me; it wants to be voiced' (1982, p. 217). It is his own self speaking to him, an act of self-war, his will-to-power seeking to overcome its present form of victory; that is, to overcome the Zarathustra who has become stilled or fixed as the teacher.

In his self-conversation, his will-to-power, Zarathustra becomes aware that he is now shining. His own light has become visible in this darkness; 'ah, that I were night!' he laments. 'But this is my loneliness that I am girt with light' (1982, p. 217). Now, in the darkness, he sees himself as he has been teaching others to see themselves. The war which has been Zarathustra's shining for others now, at night, becomes that which shines as and for itself. Now, in the darkness, Zarathustra is the shadow cast by his own light. Now he sees himself in the contradiction of the will-to-power, or life which must overcome itself.

In the darkness the giver realises that he only gives to others. 'I do not know the happiness of those who receive... This is my poverty, that my hand never rests from giving' (1982, p. 218). Thus far, Zarathustra has taught the people in the market-place and his disciples. He has not yet taught himself about being the teacher, and therefore has not yet become the teacher. He gives but receives nothing, he teaches but learns nothing. In the absence of this education, in what he calls the 'cleft between giving and receiving' (1982, p. 128), he comes to resent those who merely take but give nothing in return. Zarathustra, not yet realising that what is in return from the gift-giver is himself, admits 'I should like to hurt those for whom I shine... [because] My happiness in giving died in giving; my virtue tired of itself in its overflow' (1982, p. 218). But this is inevitable for the teacher who is the sun shining for others. There is no gift which they possess. That is why they are not the teacher but the pupil. The only return which can be gained from teaching is the teacher himself. In the light, the teacher who has given of himself to others is only an illusory being, lacking any determination or substance. In the darkness, when the light is no longer for others, then there is return, the return of the light to the giver, and thus determination and substance. In the recognition of the absence of return, in that darkness (and enlightenment), there is return, there is life, there is will-to-power. 'The danger of those who always give is that they lose their sense of shame' (1982, p. 218), says Zarathustra's soul, reminding him that it was his shame at being the light which made him send the disciples away at the end of Book 1. In the darkness, Zarathustra recovers his shame at being the giver, for at night he again closes his hand and withdraws it. It is here, in returning the gift, that Zarathustra experiences 'the loneliness of all givers' (1982, p. 218) and 'the enmity of the light against what shines' (1982, p. 218).

But in the darkness, Zarathustra has begun to sing. 'Night has come: alas that I must be light... now my craving breaks out of me like a well... now all fountains speak more loudly. And my soul too is a fountain' (1982, p. 219).

Deepening this insight in the darkness, Zarathustra talks to life, to the will-to-power. It was life which pulled Zarathustra up when he was sinking, but also it is life which Zarathustra finds 'unfathomable' (1982, p. 220). That is because, life tells him, he brings his own (genealogical) assumptions rather than accept life as it is. 'You men call me profound, faithful, eternal and mysterious. But you men always present us with your own virtues' (1982, p. 220). Rather, says life to Zarathustra, you praise life because 'You will, you want, you love' (1982, p. 220).

243

In other words, man tries to understand life without realising that, at the same time and in the act of understanding, they are doing life, that is, trying to overcome life. Therefore to 'fathom' life is to understand life as self and self as life, or to comprehend what is as will-to-power. Zarathustra finds the same problem with wisdom. 'One thirsts after her and is never satisfied' (1982, p. 221). Wisdom, like life, is at its most 'seductive' when it speaks ill of itself, observes Zarathustra. It takes life to point out to Zarathustra that it is in overcoming itself that life does what life is. This wisdom *is* life – as life points out to Zarathustra. When you talk of wisdom, she says, no doubt you are talking of me. Zarathustra has taught others that wisdom is will-to-power and that the self is life, for that has been his genealogical insight. Now life reminds him that he too is also that which must overcome itself. He, too, is at his most wise when he speaks ill of himself.

With this, Zarathustra is plunged into self-pity at being returned by life to the seduction of the unfathomable. 'Is it not folly still to be alive?' (1982, p222) he asks. This pitying is what remains in this night, now, for Zarathustra to overcome. This occurs in the next section, as 'The Tomb Song'.

Once again Zarathustra, in his meeting with life, has been closest to life, and to wisdom, in his lack of fulfilment. But this is still a wisdom he does not have as self, only as knowledge. Now this knowledge of another unsuccessful attempt to comprehend life, this return to 'the unfathomable' (1982, p. 220), plunges Zarathustra into self-pity at yet another failure. Where, he laments, have vanished the 'visions and apparitions of my youth?' (1982, p. 222). How quickly those 'divine moments' (1982, p. 222) died. Now they are available to him only as dead friends, he and they having been equally disloyal to each other. To his enemies who sought to kill Zarathustra by murdering these 'tender eternities' (1982, p. 222), he notes that their 'arrow was shot at my most vulnerable possession' (1982, p. 223), putting an end to 'the visions and dearest wonders of my youth' (1982, p. 223).

Yet even in this lament there is will-to-power. Even in the death of Zarathustra's ecstasy, even in the tombs of his highest hopes and greatest faiths which surround him, Zarathustra himself has not died. The tomb song which he sings is of death but it is not death. It is already an overcoming of death as a tomb song. It is a song of death. In this new understanding of the tomb song as will-to-power, there is the resurrection of Zarathustra from failure and self pity. Again he has risen from his ashes, this time out of abject despair at the failure of the teacher of the overman. The tomb song is nearer to the self and to life as will-to-power than the teacher of the overman, for in the tomb song what is overcome, what is done, is self as life.

Zarathustra asks himself how he endured the death of his friends. 'How did my soul arise again out of such tombs?' (1982, p. 224). And his own will-to-power becomes visible to him. At night it is by his own light that he is able to see himself, to become his own shadow in the darkness, for then his relation is not to a sun that shines for others, but to the source of light which is in relation to its own self. In the light of the tomb song, Zarathustra begins to become the teacher

244

as self, and not the pupil of the sun. In Book 3 this is understood as eternal return. For now, it is visible only as self-overcoming. Zarathustra realises within him that:

> There is something invulnerable and unburiable, something that explodes rock: that is my will... You are still alive and your old self, most patient one. You have still broken out of every tomb. What in my youth was unredeemed lives on in you; and as life and youth you sit there, full of hope, on yellow ruins of tombs.
> Indeed, for me, you are still the shatterer of all tombs. Hail to thee, my will! And only where there are tombs are there resurrections (1982, pp. 224–5).

Zarathustra will have other deaths and other convalescences. This convalescing is Zarathustra's insight into will-to-power as self-overcoming. What lies ahead for him is to recover from (being) its eternal return. For now Zarathustra has overcome pity by having pity as his will-to-power over death and by becoming that pity. He has learnt, and continues to learn, that even pity is will-to-power and therefore the self-work which is life. Will-to-power is not only a creator, it is also an annihilator. It is one in achieving the other. The death of Zarathustra's visions are, for Zarathustra, already his work when he laments or plots revenge, or sinks into melancholy. It is already in his resurrection. In having death as object, Zarathustra is not death. Thus his will-to-power, which in the action of the teacher has shone to the extent that it has overpowered the light in others, now, at night, shines for itself to learn its own lesson. The will of those who would make 'all being thinkable' (1982, p. 225), including the teacher of the overman, is 'a will-to-power' (1982, p. 226), or 'the unexhausted procreative will of life' (1982, p. 226).

Now, in the resurrection, in the life of Zarathustra who has experienced the destructive and the creative power of will, and of the contradictory work of life as self-overcoming, the expression of life itself becomes possible. What lives, says Zarathustra, also obeys, and what cannot obey is commanded. It matters not to life whether what lives obeys or commands, for they are the same. Life obeys itself when life is, also, its own command. Life as will-to-power is self-obedience and self-commanding. It is a (contradictory) self-relation. It is master and slave of itself, but the people are not yet master and slave of themselves. The people obey life when they seek to overcome. Even the priests in their revenge against this self-war obey life, for their revenge is also an act of war. But the people do not command as life, for the priests in their victory of good and evil have made the people join the war of no-sayers. Only the self-commanders are the yes-sayers. When he first came down from the mountain, Zarathustra believed the commander of self to be the overman. But life has returned from the death of the overman to teach the yes-sayer not as the overman, but as the self-overcoming man, the yes-and-no-sayer who says 'yes' to himself as the no-sayer. This is the self-commander, the commander who obeys himself. Thus, says Zarathustra, who is now the teacher of will-to-power as self-overcoming, 'I have crawled into the very heart of life and into the very roots of its heart. Where I found the living, there I found will-to-power; and even in the will of those who serve I found the will to be master' (1982, p. 226).

Zarathustra is a new teacher. No longer a teacher of a future overman, no longer teaching a result of education. Now Zarathustra is the teacher of life's own education about itself. Its first lesson is that the teacher of the overman is the murderer of the overman, for life does itself. The giver, who has deceived those who are to receive, and destroyed the gift itself, now has to receive his own gift. The giver, in the loneliness of giving, now becomes the receiver. In closing his hand, he opened his heart. 'And life confided this secret to me: "Behold," it said, "I am *that which must always overcome itself*... I must be struggle and a becoming and an end and an opposition to ends – alas, whoever guesses what is my will should also guess on what *crooked* paths it must proceed"' (1982, p. 227).

The new teacher now has himself as object, cast in his own light, and before him, and in him, as commander and obeyer, annihilator and creator, no-sayer and yes-sayer. 'Whatever I create,' says Zarathustra, and he speaks also of himself and his own teaching, 'and however much I love it – soon I must oppose it and my love; thus my will wills it... Only where there is life is there also will: not the will to life but – thus I teach you – will-to-power' (1982, p. 227). The teacher of the overman has been overcome. That self-relation is now the whole which Zarathustra begins to teach, but is yet to become.

Obeying and commanding (will-to-power) as self-critique

Zarathustra is now able to offer a self-critique of the teacher of the overman. In all that is esteemed in life, including the overman by Zarathustra, 'out of the esteeming itself speaks the will-to-power' (1982, p. 228). The overman, like all that is esteemed, cannot survive that which creates it, for life wants 'to overcome itself' (1982, p. 213). Zarathustra reflects on his own depths in which he believes swim monsters. Today he saw in himself one who was sublime, an ugly hunter for knowledge who decks himself out after each foray with 'ugly truths' (1982, p. 228). He saw a hunter who returned depressed from the woods of knowledge, one who had not yet 'learned laughter or beauty' (1982, p. 229). Zarathustra, the teacher of will-to-power, is now able to offer these reflections as a self-critique of the teacher of the overman whose light was not his own, but a trophy carried from previous expeditions. Only when such a sublime teacher grows tired of himself, 'only then would his beauty commence... And only when he turns away from himself, will he jump over his shadow – and verily, into his sun' (1982, p. 229). Such a teacher has subdued monsters and solved riddles, but these deeds of overcoming have not themselves been overcome. Such a teacher, therefore, 'must still redeem his own monsters and riddles' (1982, p. 230), for the one 'who wants

246

to create beyond himself has the purest will' (1982, p. 235), and this even includes the teachers of such creation. In such self-critique, in such reflections on the teacher of will-to-power by the teacher of will-to-power, Zarathustra is able to say 'I have moved from the house of the scholars, and I even banged the door behind me. My soul sat hungry at their table too long' (1982, pp. 236–7). In a rebuke to all whose teaching is abstract, to all teachers who are merely a personification of educational relations, and to all scholars whose knowledge is posited and held apart from risk, to all who teach for or against self-overcoming but who do not comprehend both 'positions' as already will-to-power, Zarathustra distinguishes the true teacher. 'I am not... like them,' he says, for such teachers and scholars and educated men are 'trained to pursue knowledge as if it were nutcracking' (1982, p. 237). He continues, 'in everything they want to be mere spectators... [to] wait and gape at thoughts that others have thought' (1982, p. 237).

Again, in this spirit of self-critique Zarathustra is including his old self, the teacher of the overman, among those who are to be condemned. Like other poets, Zarathustra placed his highest idea in the clouds and not among men: 'upon these we place our motley bastards and call them gods and overmen' (1982, p. 240). But for the teacher of will-to-power such poetry is only another form of nutcracking, another way of fixing will-to-power in a victorious identity, rather than remaining in the darkest hour when the light of will-to-power overcomes even itself, even the event or the 'nut' called the overman. 'How weary I am,' says Zarathustra, 'of all the imperfection which must at all costs become event' (1982, p. 240), including the event of the Prologue, the event of the overman, and the event called the teacher of the overman. Those events fix life in their attempts to fathom it, and are themselves overcome precisely by such a fixing. All events are lies which cannot sustain the life which they pretend to understand or know. 'Event' itself is only life commanding and obeying itself. The teacher of will-to-power, and of life as self-overcoming, has grown weary of all such events, for he has 'seen truth naked' (1982, p. 242), or rather, life confided its secret to him: 'Whatever I create and however much I love it – soon I must oppose it and my love; thus my will wills it' (1982, p. 227). Zarathustra has outgrown any belief in events, for all such enlightenments and their teachers are merely more nuts to be cracked. It is, rather, in the stillness of night, and in the blackness of the tomb song, that the greatest events are to be heard – precisely because they are inaudible. Overcoming in the Prologue is lightening and storm, a volcano which is no more than 'the earth's ventriloquist' (1982, p. 243). Now, however, overcoming is self-death, visible only at times when the light is from life's own self-creative will-to-power. The greatest events, self-overcoming and the commanding and obeying of life as will-to-power, 'are not our loudest but our stillest hours' (1982, p. 243). Therefore Zarathustra is no longer teaching the overman, no longer this event. Now Zarathustra is teaching the night song and the tomb song: 'let yourselves be overthrown – so that you may return to life, and virtue return to you' (1982, p. 244).

247

Thus speaks the teacher of will-to-power who, as a student of life, learned its secrets from itself. But the teacher of will-to-power is still the teacher of an event. There are no ears, even, for this mouth, for even though thus spake Zarathustra, 'his disciples barely listened' (1982, p. 245).

The re-education of Zarathustra again

Throughout the whole of the book, at the times when Zarathustra is in greatest despair, and when his teachings have failed, something or someone comes along to teach him, and to return him to what he is actually, rather than what he has become as an event. Zarathustra's self-education is always in relation to an other. In the Prologue, he was returned to himself by the non-ears of the people, in Book 1 he was returned to himself as a deceiver by the faith of his disciples, in Book 2 he was returned to himself by life. Now, at the end of Book 2, the teacher of will-to power, who again is not heard, is given the ultimate lesson for a teacher, that of self-return itself, by the soothsayer.

Zarathustra hears the soothsayer tell him: 'All is empty, all is the same, all has been!' (1982, p. 245). This is to become Zarathustra's next lesson, for it expresses the truth of will-to-power as self, where self is life, or, we might say, is the relation of (or the broken middle of) self-overcoming and event. The teaching of the soothsayer 'touched his heart and changed him' (1982, p. 246), and the teacher of will-to-power felt sad, and then fell into a deep sleep. His disciples stayed around him waiting for him to recover from his melancholy. But Zarathustra's dream is not of recovery, rather it is a dream of that which has been, a dream therefore of himself. What lies ahead for Zarathustra is to will this past, but for the moment the dream, when it is described, is of a teacher who has repeatedly failed in his teachings, such that for this teacher all is empty, all is the same again, all has been and keeps repeating itself.

In his dream, Zarathustra the teacher appears as the no-sayer to will-to-power. 'I had turned my back on all life... I had become a nightwatchman and a guardian of tombs upon the lonely mountain castle of death. Up there I guarded his coffins' (1982, p. 246). This guardian of death is the no-sayer to life, to resurrection and to creation. He is the protector of death as an event, and not of its return as a self-overcoming. Zarathustra stands forthright against self-overcoming, his triumph being 'life that had been overcome' (1982, p. 246), and which now looked up at him out of glass coffins. Yet the guardian sits in the 'brightness of midnight' (1982, p. 246), in the self-light which is loneliness. He has the keys to open all gates, and he knows how to use them. But as he uses them he is frightened by the noise of their opening, and in refusing to use them the silence grows more terrible. Finally, the wind tears open the gates and throws up a black coffin before the guardian. The coffin bursts open, and life spews forth from it, laughing, in the form of children, angels, owls, fools and butterflies.

248

Having described this dream in which life overcomes the guardian of death, Zarathustra tells his disciples that he is, as yet, unsure about how to interpret the dream. His favourite disciple offers Zarathustra an interpretation in which Zarathustra is the wind that releases life from the coffins. Zarathustra, he says, enters 'all death chambers, laughing at all the nightwatchmen and guardians of tombs... You will frighten and prostrate them with your laughter' (1982, p. 248). The dream, says the disciple, reveals Zarathustra as 'advocate of life' (1982, p. 248). But Zarathustra knows this to be an interpretation based upon a misunderstanding of life, but a misunderstanding which he himself has created and fixed as an 'event'. Such failure is precisely why he appears as that which has overcome life. The teacher, in teaching life, also opposes life, and deceives the pupils into believing that he is what he says he is. The teaching contradicts itself. Zarathustra teaches life but protects his pupils from will-to-power by appearing as their light. His victory is their defeat, and the role of the guardian, the teacher, is to protect that victory from life. The success of the teacher is 'life that had been overcome' (1982, p. 246). The dream is not, as the disciple believes, Zarathustra as life. The dream is Zarathustra the teacher as guardian against life. It is life itself, will-to-power, which finally overcomes the guardian, releasing life from his grip and freeing it. Zarathustra has yet to become the overcoming of the event. He has yet to be the wind which in the dream is life's self-creation. For Zarathustra at this point all is empty when all is the same. The lesson of eternal return lies ahead for Zarathustra, but with the dream he is aware, now, no longer to prevent life from overcoming the teacher. As a result, he no longer recognises his disciples, those he has created in the image of his own event. Now he wishes to dine with the soothsayer, the man who has begun the re-education of Zarathustra again.

Zarathustra now realises that as a teacher he has been a healer. But precisely in trying to heal, he had robbed his students of the chance to heal themselves. 'When one takes away the hump from the hunchback one takes away his spirit,' (1982, p. 249) Zarathustra tells the hunchback. To take away from man that which in man is to be overcome is to take away from man life itself. Thus does the healer/teacher become the destroyer of life and guardian of death. It is no longer to heal others that Zarathustra must be concerned, now, it is to heal himself from the need to destroy in others that which he teaches as the deepest meaning of their existence. How can the teacher of the gift cure himself of the fact that, in giving the gift, in teaching the overman, or now will-to-power, he shines for others, negating their light in the brightness of his own? The teacher of war brings peace. Thus has the war of education, the struggle of the teacher, now become (again) a self-war. It is to himself that the teacher, in teaching, is returned.

In this return, education for Zarathustra now becomes self-education. The education that is revealed now is the education of self as return. Zarathustra is not only a creator of the future, he is also 'a cripple at this bridge' (1982, p. 251). He cannot cross the bridge as a cripple, yet without that which must be overcome there is no bridge. The spirit which is the bridge is the same spirit which prevents the bridge from being crossed. To go across is also to be returned (or reminded) of the inability to cross, and is therefore a going under. But equally, going under is also the return of the spirit which is the bridge, and therefore another going across. Return is this contradiction. Across, return and going under are key themes in *Thus Spake Zarathustra*. They are the truth of life as will-to-power, and they are the truth of the teacher. That which is taught negates itself and prevents itself from being realised. But the failure is the truth of the whole which creates and destroys, obeys and commands, and is itself in both.

Thus Zarathustra is able to begin to become what he already is, the teacher of eternal return. It remains for Zarathustra in Books 3 and 4 to become the teacher who is eternal return. For now, after the dream prompted by the soothsayer, Zarathustra is able to teach as a stage on the way of his life towards becoming the teacher of eternal return. He is not yet able to teach eternal return, but he is now able to teach redemption for the man who wills his own inability to achieve peace. Redemption for Zarathustra is to be found by those who, rather than seeking revenge and punishment against the self and who wish they could will differently, understand that they are the war, that the war is themselves, and that it is a war which they have willed. He expresses this in the following teaching.

> To redeem those who lived in the past and to recreate all 'it was' into a 'thus I willed it' – that alone should I call redemption. Will – that is the name of the liberator and joy-bringer; thus I taught you, my friends. But now learn this too: the will itself is still a prisoner. Willing liberates; but what is it that puts even the liberator himself in fetters? 'It was' – that is the name of the will's gnashing of teeth and most secret melancholy. Powerless against what has been done, he is an angry spectator of all that is past. The will cannot will backwards; and that he cannot break time and time's covetousness, that is the will's loneliest melancholy (1982, p. 251).

In Book 1, Zarathustra the genealogist taught of the war which created the valuation of all values. Then, in Book 2, Zarathustra taught that the war was life itself, the will-to-power, and that the self was only ever the work of life obeying and commanding itself. The greatest secret of all is now unfolding for Zarathustra. There can be no rest from this war, or from will-to-power, because life is that which must overcome, and therefore it must overcome itself. All events which are the result of a victory become, at the same time, that which now exists for will-to-power as something to be overcome. This is the contradiction of will-to-power that Zarathustra is now teaching. When will-to-power does itself, when it wages war on all that is before it, it is really waging war on all that is behind it. Whatever is, be it values, or gods, or teachers, is only the result, already, of will-to-power. Each victory is self-defeating, for it is, at the same time, a continuation of the war. Now it is the victory, or all 'it was', which has to be overcome by overcoming itself.

Zarathustra is teaching the victory of will-to-power as 'it was'. What now exists as past, as done, as result, is what will-to-power has produced. Each 'it was' is an overcoming of a previous 'it was'. But 'it was' is not now, and not ever, a satisfaction for will-to-power. 'It was' is not 'thus I willed it' because, even though it was willed, in being willed, and in overcoming, it ceases to be life and becomes death. Life is that which must overcome. 'It was' is that which has overcome and is something now which provokes life into further action. Zarathustra is now, for the first time, exploring the truth of life as will-to-power as a circle, as a self-defeating activity, one which has no control over, nor satisfaction with, the result of its own action. Life can never end the war, it can only repeat it.

It still lies ahead for Zarathustra to comprehend the self of the teacher as the circle, and as return. For now, he is expressing the eternal contradiction of will-to-power: that in its activity it creates a past which is immediately lost, a loss which returns will-to-power back to itself to repeat its activity again. Powerless against this loss of its activity to a result, of will to an event, and of overcoming to 'it was', this is the will's greatest misery. Life knows no rest, and can gain no respite from itself as the repetition of an unsatisfiable self. Willing liberates, says Zarathustra, but in so doing, willing traps itself within the circle from which it cannot escape. 'It was' becomes not only its victory but also its defeat, a defeat which forces it to declare war once again, this time on that which calls itself a victory, and exists as 'it was'. 'That time does not run backwards, that is his wrath; "that which was" is the name of the stone he cannot move' (1982, p. 251). It is this inability to achieve a final victory which so angers life that it tears against itself and seeks revenge against itself for being what it is. Life, rather than display the noble attitude of a yes-sayer, the attitude of a life that is fully, unreservedly and confidently itself, revolts against itself in an act of revenge. It is this self-hatred, this no-saying to life by life, which then results in life not doing itself, but hating itself for being that which does itself. The result of this is punishment, morality, values and truth. All are an avenging of life against itself, all seek to wreak revenge on it for being what it is. All are a judgment by life against itself, a judgment and a punishment which seek their justification by creating the good conscience. But conscience is itself already created out of the spirit of revenge, revenge against life's inability to exist as other than itself, revenge against life's inability to rest as 'it was', revenge against life's inability to change 'it was' into 'thus I willed it'. 'This, indeed this alone, is what *revenge* is: the will's ill will against time and its "it was"' (1982, p. 252).

Still, however, Zarathustra is not fully aware of the contradiction of will-to-power as eternal return. The dream has awoken in him the awareness that life overcomes all death. Even the teaching of the overman lay in a black coffin which life had to come and set free. Zarathustra's own teachings had become 'it was' and therefore not a victory but a defeat, one which returned life to itself and had this 'teaching', now, as that which must be overcome. This dream has become, for Zarathustra, the teaching that the will is a contradiction, liberating and imprisoning itself in the one activity of overcoming, and that the will resents this contradiction, this circle, and punishes itself for producing it by trying to make it

251

accept 'it was' as itself. Punishment is in the spirit of death, an attempt to force completion and rest on that which is only ever itself in its return to incompletion and unrest. The conclusion that Zarathustra draws here is that redemption is not available until the creative will says to 'it was', 'thus I will it; thus shall I will it' (1982, p. 253). But even here Zarathustra seems to be saying that it still lies ahead, at some point, for life to overcome 'it was' and for 'it was' and 'thus I will it' to be unified. Yet the logic and contradiction of life which Zarathustra has already taught prove otherwise. To overcome is only to require, again, another overcoming. It is only in Book 3 that this contradiction of will-to-power becomes the self of Zarathustra the teacher. At this stage it is still only a teaching, another 'it was'. To seek unification of 'it was' and 'thus I will it' is itself born from the spirit of revenge. What lies ahead for Zarathustra is to will the contradiction of will-to-power. That is where 'it was' and 'thus I will it' are unified, in the contradiction of the teacher, not in the overcoming of the contradiction.

At this point, towards the end of Book 2, such thoughts begin to claim Zarathustra. In asking how a unification of 'it was' and will-to-power is possible, Zarathustra becomes aware in his mind of how the one is also the other, and of how 'it was' and 'thus I will it' are only the same obeying and commanding of will-to-power. It is this awareness which will become Zarathustra's most abysmal thought. For now, we must assume that the idea has taken root in Zarathustra, but is yet to blossom in its full horror. 'At this point in his speech it happened that Zarathustra suddenly stopped and looked altogether like one who has received a severe shock' (1982, p. 253). The hunchback asks him 'why does Zarathustra speak otherwise to his pupils than to himself?' (1982, p. 254). The question goes to the heart of the final lessons which are ahead for Zarathustra. Why does he teach will-to-power, obeying and commanding, as the inseparable war which is the self, to his pupils, but not to himself as his own truth? Why can he not become that which he teaches? Why is he preserving himself in death from the life and the contradiction which is the teacher? Zarathustra confesses that he is torn by his own will between man and the overman. He looks up to the overman and down at man. He flies to the former, yet clings to the latter. It is this struggle itself, a struggle Zarathustra describes as produced by a 'double will' (1982, p. 254), which is only the single will divided from itself by itself (or a broken middle). Zarathustra has already taught that man is a rope tied between beast and overman, a rope over an abyss. The 'double will' is only what lies at each end of the rope, kept apart by man, by the rope, by the bridge itself. The victory and defeat which are two wills are only the work of one will, the one will which repeats their separation but is, at the same time, their self-relation.

This gruesome truth, that will-to-power and the self are related in the eternal return of the self-relation (broken middle) of unity (rope) and division (beast and overman) will now become Zarathustra's own truth. He knows he must return to his solitude and accept the truth about himself that life, in the stillest hour, has taught him. In the self-light which appears only at the darkest and stillest hour, Zarathustra has heard his own light speak to him of the idea which he must now face up to as the truth of the teacher. The voice accuses the teacher of *ressentiment* and revenge against that which is the teacher, will-to-power. 'You know it, Zarathustra, but you do not say it.' Zarathustra answers, 'Yes, I know it, but I do not want to say it… Let me off from this! It is beyond my strength' (1982, p. 257). Such defiance, however, is the defiance of the last man, the man who is too proud to unlearn, or to relearn. The last man is the educated man who protects his identity from death, from risk, and therefore also from life. The silence chides Zarathustra the last man, and commands him, 'speak your word and break' (1982, p. 258).

The voice of Zarathustra's own life turns against itself in Zarathustra's self-overcoming of the teacher of the overman. 'You are one who has forgotten how to obey: now you shall command… This is what is most unforgivable in you: you have the power and you do not want to rule' (1982, p. 258). Faced with himself as life that returns in self-overcoming, Zarathustra answers, 'I lack the lion's voice for commanding' (1982, p. 258). The camel has gone into the desert, but the lion has searched for the child, for the self-propelling wheel, elsewhere than in his own struggle. The hope that there is another yet to come who will create new values is merely a self-protection. The lion overcomes all 'Thou shalt'. But in doing so it does not overcome 'thou shalt overcome', it only repeats it. This is the lion's obeying and commanding life as its self. It is a repetition from which Zarathustra seeks relief. The silence speaks to Zarathustra one last time in this regard. 'O Zarathustra, your fruit is ripe, but you are not ripe for your fruit. Thus you must return to your solitude again' (1982, p. 259). Zarathustra is still not yet the eternal return of life as self-overcoming. It is what he is doing in his teaching, and it is what is being done to him in his darkest stillest hours. But it still not what he has become. In fear that he will become what he is, Zarathustra weeps, and, at midnight, when the self-light is brightest, he sets off to leave the blessed isles of his disciples.

Book 3: the teacher who begins to become what he is

At the beginning of Book 3, Zarathustra is on the verge of his most abysmal education. It is in Book 3 that the teacher of the overman, and the teacher of will-to-power, are finally comprehended as the truth of the lion, as the contradiction that overcoming also overcomes itself. This self, in which victory is also defeat, is returned to itself by itself. It has been happening to Zarathustra ever since he first taught in the market-place. It remains ahead for him to learn this as his self-truth. The teacher of the overman and of will-to-power becomes, in Book 3, the truth of the teacher of the overman and of will-to-power; that is, the teacher of eternal return. But even that is not the end of the story, for the teacher of eternal return has, in Book 4, to experience himself and his teaching as victory and defeat, or as return.

By now Zarathustra is becoming ever more ripe for the wisdom of his own fruit. His attempts to emulate the sun and be a light for others have returned him to the darkness where the only light is his own, and which casts the teacher as his own shadow. Finally now, he acknowledges, 'one experiences only oneself. The time is gone when mere accidents could still happen to me; and what could still come to me now that was not mine already? What returns, what finally comes to me, is my own self' (1982, p. 264). Zarathustra begins to understand that he can no longer blame ears that do not hear, nor disciples that have faith instead of self-light, nor, even, his own weakness in moments of revenge. They are all his struggle. They are all his responsibility. They are all the return of Zarathustra to himself. It is his failures in teaching which provide his stillest hours, failures which return his light for others on to himself and illuminate his own self in the activity and the work. Zarathustra, at the beginning of the Prologue, believed that the sun shone for others. Now Zarathustra is beginning to comprehend the true relation of illumination or enlightenment. In shining for others the light returns also to illuminate the one who gives but does not receive, and who is in darkness. In so doing, the darkness is cast as a shadow in its own light. In this return is the triune self-relation of enlightenment, not merely as a shining for others but also as a shining for and as itself.

It is a truth for which Zarathustra must now prepare, knowing in his heart that victory and defeat are the same relation. 'I stand before my final peak now,' he says, 'and before that which has been saved up for me the longest. Alas, now I must face my hardest path!... whoever is of my kind cannot escape such an hour – the hour which says to him... "Peak and abyss – they are now joined together"' (1982, p. 264), joined together as the circle which is, when it overcomes itself eternally. 'Now my ultimate loneliness has begun' (1982, p. 266).

Zarathustra boards a boat away from the blessed isles, and explains the riddle of his vision of 'the loneliest' (1982, p. 268) to the sailors. This is the first time his teaching has replaced the 'thus I will it' which wants its victory over 'it was', with 'thus I will it' as the failure to become at one with 'it was'. Zarathustra is no longer seeking redemption from life which only fails in overcoming itself, now he is saying 'thus I will it' to that failure, and not in a spirit of revenge, but in a spirit that understands the failure also to be the work itself.

At the beginning of the vision, Zarathustra is fighting against a dwarf who, in the spirit of gravity, is trying to drag Zarathustra down towards the abyss. This is the Zarathustra who will not become the contradiction of will-to-power, but only fight against it, resenting its inability to will backwards. However, in the vision, Zarathustra faces up to this *ressentiment*, and faces the continued inability to will backwards with the courage to accept life, and will-to-power, as it is. In this courage he finds not the guardian of the coffins, but the slayer of death, for this courage says, 'Was that life? Well then! Once more!' (1982, p. 269).

Finally, Zarathustra has uttered his most abysmal thought, that instead of the revenge of the no-sayer, there is, for the man who is brave enough to accept life, the courage to will life as a yes-sayer, accepting the painful contradiction of its

254

self-truth as victory and defeat, defeat and victory. He is able, in the vision, to express this as the meeting of two contradictory paths, one leading back to the past, one leading forward to the future. They only come together as the gateway of the present, a gateway in the vision which is called 'moment'. The path leading back is 'it was'. The will has no power over that path, for it is already at the gateway called 'moment', or now. It cannot retrace its steps. The path which is past is too late, always, for the will which has it behind it. The path leading forward is a future which the will seeks to control, a future which the will wills. However, the path which stretches out before it is not merely a path to the future. If the will has a path which it can see, then that path is already a path, already something to be overcome. The will can only have the future as the result of itself, but therefore separated from itself, as something that has already been and which exists before it as the defeat of itself. The two paths, future and past, are both the result of will-to-power. Both are a victory but, in that both are present to will-to-power, they are also yet another defeat and something, now, to be overcome. They are, for will-to-power, a reminder of its own powerlessness against itself. The will now stands at the gateway as the result of paths which it has created and walked. In coming to know itself and the paths as the self-work of will-to-power, then the will also comes to understand its own circular nature. 'Must not whatever *can* walk have walked on this lane before... must not all of us have been there before?' (1982, p. 270). The will is only present to itself as the result of its own activity, as the gateway between what it has done and what it would do. And yet each moment is already another result, each result is already another path. The will arrives at the moment too late to grasp itself as creator, only always as created. It is this circle, the work which in doing itself never allows itself to appear as that work, but only as result, the work which is itself as self-overcoming, which Zarathustra now describes as eternal return: 'must we not eternally return?' (1982, p. 270), he says, speaking softly, 'for I was afraid of my own thoughts' (1982, p. 270).

The vision changes. The dwarf, the paths and the gateway have vanished. Now Zarathustra has not merely a vision of eternal return, but a vision of the teacher of eternal return who must become that which he teaches. Zarathustra sees a young shepherd with a black snake hanging out of his mouth. He urges the shepherd to bite the head off the snake, an urging which is an outpouring of all of Zarathustra's revenge at his most abysmal idea, the eternal return of will-to-power. He asks the sailors who is the shepherd into whose throat the snake crawls. But as he is asking, the shepherd bites off the snake's head, and jumps up jubilant: 'No longer shepherd, no longer human – one changed, radiant, laughing' (1982, p. 272). Zarathustra ends his retelling of the vision in despair. He, too, seeks such laughter.

When he is four days away from the blessed isles, Zarathustra has overcome all his pain. This recovery only precedes the worse which is yet to come. All of Zarathustra's recoveries are illusory and return to overcome themselves. For the moment he again rests content with the new self-knowledge he has of himself, and is able to offer a summary of his education so far. He remembers how, when he first came down from the mountain in search of fellow creators, he found none – only a corpse – and that his first task, therefore, was to create such companions. Thus he is able to conclude 'I am in the middle of my work, going to my children and returning from them' (1982, p. 273), each time having failed to create those whom he seeks. From the failures, Zarathustra drew the conclusion that he must perfect himself before his teaching could be truly creative and effective, and therefore it became time for him to leave his disciples. But the teacher finds it hard to leave those for whom he shines. Zarathustra did not realise that his own light was preventing their self-light, their shining. It is only in his darkest hour, where no sun shines for Zarathustra and the only light is self-light, that he faces the abyss of failure which is part of being the teacher. In the stillest hour, 'My past burst its tombs' (1982, p. 274), and 'many a pain that had been buried alive awoke' (1982, p. 274). Zarathustra's self-understanding of the teacher as failure is only personalised by him when it becomes the most abysmal thought of the circle, in which will-to-power is self-destructive and arrives on the scene only and always as the result of overcoming, never as life itself. The circle is determinative when Zarathustra realises that the victory of will-to-power is also the death of the teacher of will-to-power and the teacher of the overman. Life is that which must overcome itself, including those who would claim it as their own property. Saying 'yes', therefore, to education is also saying 'yes' to the failure of the teacher to create without also destroying. Saying 'yes' to being the teacher is saying 'was that life? Well then! Once more!' (1982, p. 269) as the teacher is again overcome by the truth of his own teaching. Zarathustra is at the point, now, of resisting his own total loss of self within the circle which is the truth of self. 'I did not hear, until at last my abyss stirred and my thought bit me. Alas, abysmal thought... As yet I have never dared to summon you; it was enough that I carried you with me... but one day I shall yet find the strength and the lion's voice to summon you' (1982, p. 274). But, as he finds later that night, waiting for this unhappiness is futile. It has to be done, and for Zarathustra the teacher it will be done as and in the self-light which is his teaching.

His waiting, rather than his doing, is again his tarrying with tombs rather than with life. He is still a teacher who shines for others and, likewise, expects his own education to come from the illumination of the sun. It is the cloudless heavens that Zarathustra expects to find, and waits for this illumination which is, he believes, 'the light for my fire' (1982, p. 276). 'I am one who can bless and say Yes, if only you are about me, pure and light, you abyss of light; then I carry the blessings of my Yes into all abysses' (1982, p. 277).

The implications of this refusal, still, to become his own teacher in the form of the circle, leads to the most resentful set of teachings Zarathustra has yet produced. What follows, before he finally returns to his cave, his animals, and to eternal return, are the teachings of a man refusing, ultimately, to accept himself as will-to-power and passing 'responsibility' for life and self on to chance and accident. This is a reversal, even, of the clarity Zarathustra attained earlier when

256

he spoke of redemption. There, he taught that 'it was' appeared as chance or accident, but such an appearance was misleading. Chance and accident are a no-saying, a refusal. 'Thus I will it' is a yes-saying, no longer hiding behind chance or accident. But now his teaching is a return to no-saying, for it reflects, still, his relationship with the sun – the relationship of the student to the teacher – and not the self-relationship which is the teacher and the student. He is still awaiting his final illumination from beyond, lacking the lion's courage to overcome this last master, and repeating, again, the impossibility of educating the last man. 'It is a blessing and not a blasphemy when I teach: "Over all things stand the heaven Accident, the heaven Innocence, the heaven Chance, the heaven Prankishness." "By Chance" – that is the most ancient nobility of the world, and this I restored to all things: I delivered them from their bondage under Purpose... "In everything one thing is impossible: rationality"' (1982, p. 278).

The teacher is now furthest away from himself as the teacher of life. Zarathustra is at his most sceptical, and is in his most profoundly deep phase of no-saying to will-to-power. Chance, irrationality, prankishness, the 'divine table for divine dice and dice players' (1982, p. 278), are his last and most desperate attempt to lay the blame for what is somewhere other than at his own door. This ultimate no-saying will return to choke him later in Book 3. For now, he leaves the boat and wanders around from town to town again, teaching in this spirit of *ressentiment* and blaming man for being what he is. It is Zarathustra's most bitter period and precedes his most illuminating, precious and joyous education. He accuses the people of resenting him because he is the clear sky and the sun. Why can they not let him shine for them as his sun shines for him? Why can they not become good students instead of damning him with their praise? (1982, p. 280). They are hypocrites who pretend to serve (1982, p. 281), their virtues have made them tame and unable to create new values for themselves. Why can they not be more like the brave and resolute Zarathustra, who accepts even the hardships of winter with honour, and mocks and overcomes its coldness by taking cold baths? (1982, p. 285). In these wanderings, Zarathustra becomes the victim of everything except himself, except will-to-power. Everything is accident, therefore nothing is self. He flees from the difficulty of his most abysmal thought, but, inevitably, it must return.

Zarathustra is only two days or so from his cave when he meets 'a foaming fool' who some people had called 'Zarathustra's ape' (1982, p. 287). The fool asks Zarathustra why he bothers any longer to come to the city to seek to educate those who refuse his wisdom? 'Rather,' says the fool, 'spit on the city gate and turn back. Here is a hell for a hermit's thoughts' (1982, p. 288). The fool foams further about the decaying souls of the city, until Zarathustra stops him and accuses the fool of having become that which he is describing, and of being driven by revenge for not receiving sufficient flattery from the people. He has borrowed Zarathustra's words in his dealings with the people, says Zarathustra, and even if my words were right, 'still you would always do wrong with my words' (1982, p. 290).

However, the fool's revenge is no less than the revenge which is driving Zarathustra's teaching at this time. Zarathustra is still able to claim to the fool that his own despising will arise only out of love and not out of revenge, and that the place 'where one can no longer love, there one should pass by' (1982, p. 290), pass by, instead of lingering and becoming resentful. But Zarathustra looks at the city, realises he, like the fool, is nauseated by it, and passes by both it and the fool. This is a sceptical, revengeful and unloving Zarathustra for whom life is not will-to-power but chance, a Zarathustra who can blame others for his lack of love. This is the Zarathustra who waited for his happiness at night but only found happiness in the rising of the sun that shone for him. This is the Zarathustra who refuses to become himself as teacher. Such a Zarathustra, then, is able to pass by the city and the fool, for such a Zarathustra does not despise himself for his inability to love, he despises those in the city who will not accept his gift, as he accepts the gift of the sun.

He further despises his own disciples, for they have become pious and have been seen by Zarathustra 'crawling back to the cross' (1982, p. 291). To this resentful Zarathustra, all but a few have become 'cowards' (1982, p. 291), a 'light-shunning kind who cannot rest where there is light' (1982, p. 292). The disciples stand at the gateway where God stretches out as one path and the death of God as another. It does not matter which is past and which is future, for they are the same result of will-to-power. Their return to the cross will be also a victory over the cross. But this no-saying has declared war on will-to-power, preferring the gateway to be chance rather than the circle of the eternal return of will-to-power. This resentful Zarathustra has returned to the certainties of the genealogical man who creates his own values. He has crawled back to the overman again, and cannot see that this victory now sets itself against the whole circle of obeying and commanding. For him, at the gateway of chance and resignation, the war is not his own. But this monumental act of *ressentiment* is the last refusal by will-to-power of itself before it destroys itself as such a refusal. Zarathustra's resentful peace-mongering is the prelude to his forthcoming battle for sovereignty, which is now immanent. It is the final self-negation necessary before he says 'yes' to and becomes that self-relation (of war) as his own (contradictory) self. For the revengeful Zarathustra, God is still a rival to the overman for the attention of his pupils. God died, he argues, when He issued the word 'there is one God. Thou shalt have no other God before me' (1982, p. 294). The teacher of the overman, the last genealogical man, is overcome for the same reason. God and the death of God, and teachers of the overman and of eternal return, are the same will-to-power, as Zarathustra is now about to learn for himself, and as himself.

Anticipating redemption

At the end of this period of sceptical and revengeful teaching, Zarathustra was only two days away from his cave and his animals. He had arrived back at the

258

town called the Motley Cow, the same town to which he had given the gift of his Prologue, and which had listened but not heard his gift of the overman. The return to the town prompts also a return to the voice of solitude, a voice which now begins to remind Zarathustra of the lack of peace and the experiences which he suffered on his travels. He remembers, in particular, how in the stillest hour the silence spoke to him without voice, saying 'What do you matter, Zarathustra? Speak your word and break' (1982, pp. 257–8). That was, for Zarathustra, a moment when he was totally forsaken. But now, bitter and resentful, he has returned to his solitude and his mountain, where he need no longer vex his soul among those who misunderstand, and those who do not have ears for him. Up here on the mountain, the air is clear and the silence is joyful. Down there in the city, 'everyone talks and no one listens... no one knows how to understand any more... everything is talked to pieces' (1982, pp. 296–7). But Zarathustra has passed this by, he has refused to 'speak and break', seeing it as futile, and has left his pupils and the city behind. Now he can recover his peace of mind and his clarity without them infecting him with their gods and their values. 'My greatest danger lies behind me,' he announces (1982, p. 297) in an outpouring of self-pity at what he has had to endure while giving his gift to the all-too-human. He has, he thinks, shown them too much consideration; 'Disguised I sat among them, ready to mistake myself that I might endure them' (1982, p. 297). 'To conceal myself and my wealth, that I learned down there; for I have found everyone poor in spirit' (1982, p. 298). His conclusion is a complete reversal of the optimism with which he set off from the mountain in the Prologue. There, overflowing with wisdom to share, he went to teach. Now, having had his teaching find only fools, corpses and devoted followers, he has returned to the mountain determined to give up teaching altogether. 'One should not stir up the morass. One should live on mountains. With happy nostrils I again breathe mountain freedom. At last my nose is delivered from the smell of everything human' (1982, p. 298).

On his mountain, safe from his disciples, Zarathustra has no choice in the solitude but again to become his own shadow, a self-light and no longer a light for others. The return to solitude is always a return to self. This return, however, will result in self as return. In a dream, Zarathustra weighed the three most evil things on the scales of humanity. They are sex, the lust to rule and selfishness. What they have in common, and what the dream is again returning Zarathustra to, is will-to-power and its contradiction. The lust to rule is what requires the teacher to leave the mountain. It is the gift-giving virtue which first prompted Zarathustra to leave his cave. Will-to-power is not the selflessness preached by the 'world-weary cowards' (1982, p. 303); it is the selfishness of that which is itself when it does itself. It is in this spirit that the heights cannot remain lonely and self-sufficient eternally. Will-to-power is not self-sufficient unless it is doing itself. But each time it overcomes, it returns to itself as that which must now overcome again. Finally, it turns upon itself to overcome even its own doing. In this act it is the circle of the self which, in overcoming, is then to be overcome. This selfishness of the lust to rule does not spare itself. It, too, must be overcome. Zarathustra, having been the teacher of the circle, is now that which must be overcome by the circle and, indeed, by the same truth which he is teaching. This is the truth of the teacher which Zarathustra must now not only learn, but learn to love 'with a wholesome and healthy love, so that one can bear to be with oneself and need not roam' (1982, p. 305). But Zarathustra acknowledges that such learning is the result of his teaching it as the truth of self for others. Only when it is taught as the truth of self for self is that which 'is well concealed from the owner' brought out into self-light. 'Man is hard to discover – hardest of all for himself' (1982, p. 306).

To become this self-teacher, and to love man as what he is, the eternal return of will-to-power, is possible only when the lust to rule becomes self as the circle in which life repeats the self as the victory and defeat of its own doing. The process is bloody and uncompromising, but it will not become itself as those who wait, or who dislike the battle which is the self. In an insight of enormous significance for all that has gone before, Zarathustra now realises that he too has learned to wait, 'but only to wait for myself' (1982, p. 307). The teacher who taught flying was not himself a flyer. He had first to learn to 'stand and walk and run and jump and climb and dance: one cannot fly into flying' (1982, p. 307). Thus, in many ways and through many failures, has Zarathustra reached the success of this insight into himself as teacher. His education has been not *the* way, but *his* way. It remains for him still to become that which, throughout his travels, he has already been becoming. But gradually now he is becoming ever more ripe for his own fruit, ever more open to himself, and ever more his own student rather than a seeker of students. Now, he says, I tell myself 'myself' and, still waiting, he is able to offer a still more insightful summary of the way which is his self. Surrounded by old and new tablets, old and new values, Zarathustra looks back and remembers how, when he first came to man, what he taught them was the genealogy of their morals. Good and evil were seen as a human creation, and formed as the result of blood and war. Often, surrounded by the conceit of the academics and the preachers, Zarathustra remembers that he used to fly away 'into distant futures which no dream had yet seen... Where all time seemed to me a happy mockery of moments [and] where necessity was freedom itself' (1982, p. 309). It was in this future, he notes, 'that I picked up the word "overman"' (1982, p. 310), and the idea that man is that which must be overcome. It was a future seen from the perspective of the pupil of the sun, in the hope of 'the great noon' (1982, p. 310) where man, 'a bridge and no end' (1982, p. 310), will be overcome.

Yet, surrounded by old and new values, Zarathustra is the sage and prophet waiting one last time to go down to the people to give them his wisdom and his new values. He runs through the new tablets which he has created. There is the new value called redemption which occurs when the past is understood as the circle of 'Thus I willed it! Thus I shall will it!' (1982, p. 310). There are the new values of not loving your neighbour but overcoming your love of the neighbour and thereby overcoming yourself; of becoming joyous by seeking guilt and suffering; of knowing life as it is, as noble, and not preaching life as if it were death; of knowing that there are gods, but no God; of becoming father to the new children of this nobility; of learning to will, 'for to will is to create' (1982, p. 318); of learning to pass by the masses and the unworthy 'in order to save oneself for the worthier enemy' (1982, p. 321); to break not only the last man, but also the good man and the just man for 'they crucify all man's future' (1982, p. 325); and finally, to learn that the noble are hard, for only the hard can cut through to the new future.

Equally, Zarathustra lists the old values, the old tablets which must be broken. They include the love of knowledge, the values and preaching of the no-sayers, the wisdom of the vain, the pious and the conscientious, and the false assurances of the good. Finally, Zarathustra makes clear that those who wish to break old values and create new ones will be hated and persecuted by those who seek to protect them. 'For the good are unable to create; they are always the beginning of the end: they crucify him who writes new values on new tablets' (1982, pp. 324–5). It is the case, always, that 'the good must crucify him who invents his own virtue' (1982, p. 324).

However, the Zarathustra who is sitting among the old and new tablets is a particular Zarathustra, a teacher still on his way to becoming what he is. These new tablets represent will-to-power cast in stone. But they are cast in stone by a teacher who is still seeking a way by which to teach will-to-power to the people which will be successful. The fate of Zarathustra's teaching to date has been that either no one has listened, or those that have, his disciples, had sought Zarathustra before they sought themselves (1982, p. 190). Either way, his message that man is something which must be overcome has come across as an instruction and not as the self-necessity of will-to-power. The harder the teacher of will-to-power tries, the more counterproductive it becomes for he, too, is that which must be overcome. He, too, is just another sovereign. Where will-to-power has been more than an instruction for others is when Zarathustra has returned to himself in his darkest hours. There, the one who gives instructions to others has become commander and obeyer of himself. Now the instructor is also the instructed, and is the truth of the contradiction that man is something that must overcome himself. Yet after each of these moments of self-light, Zarathustra has always sought to return to the classroom to teach again, each time believing that now he understands more clearly. The teacher of genealogy became the teacher of will-to-power, who became the teacher of the contradiction of will-to-power and of self-overcoming, who became most recently the teacher of the most abysmal thought, eternal return. It is the certainty of this teacher which has cast in stone the new values of wisdom and is ready now to return to man, one last time, to give his latest gift. What is happening to Zarathustra is the eternal return of will-to-power where the teacher, in self-overcoming, repeats himself again as that which must be overcome. But Zarathustra has yet to become this cycle in himself. Still, after each return, he sees himself as the teacher whose vocation it is to give his gift. The return of Zarathustra the teacher is the return of Zarathustra to the people, which is the return for the people of the teacher who is himself something that must be overcome. Their refusal to be instructed is a failure for the Zarathustra who is still trying to be their sun. The teacher of the new tablets is no different. Sitting amidst the old and new tablets, Zarathustra still sees the teacher as one who shines for others by teaching them to shine for themselves. The contradiction is now about to impose itself personally upon Zarathustra as eternal return, but, at this moment, sitting on top of his mountain, he is still ready to repeat his journey across their sky one more time.

> Now I wait for my own redemption – that I may go to them for the last time. For I want to go to men once more; under their eyes I want to go under; dying, I want to give them my richest gift. From the sun I learned this: when he goes down, overrich; he pours gold into the sea out of inexhaustible riches, so that even the poorest fisherman still rows with golden oars (1982, p. 310).

This time he believes that his return will be self-sacrificial. With the new values now cast in stone, that will be Zarathustra's final gift. His own going down will remove the light in which others are forced to reflect, but will leave behind a beautiful golden afterglow in which, as the light fades, the self-light of his students will grow ever brighter. The Zarathustra who has preached life but found life unteachable, now finally in his despair, his scepticism and his bitterness, attempts one final act of gift-giving, that of giving himself so that others may live. From teaching by overcoming others, now he will teach by overcoming himself. But he will return from this also. Neither are options, for life and death are both overcome and repeated in will-to-power. Indeed, it is a final journey across the sky that Zarathustra never makes, for his own star in such despair is burning most brightly now, so brightly that it commands a self-obeying which is not merely a sacrifice. Will-to-power is always itself in risking itself, but only an act of total and pure revenge would have its truth as absolute self-sacrifice. The final act of revenge against the circle is to end it. But it is not the truth of the circle, nor of life, nor of will-to-power. It is that truth, now, which overcomes Zarathustra the sacrificer, and ends his anticipation of redemption.

The illness of eternal return

In the section called 'The Convalescent', Zarathustra experiences the truth of himself in a way which he can no longer overlook or forget. For a long time he has known of will-to-power and of its truth as contradiction lived out as eternal return. But as the guardian of the tombs it was still an idea that forced its own return upon him. In the stillest hour he is a step closer: 'Yes, I know it, but I do not want to say it' (1982, p. 257). In the dream which he relates on the boat from the blessed isles, he is still not certain 'who is the shepherd into whose throat the snake crawled' (1982, p. 272). Now, however, not long after the return to the cave from his wanderings and his most sceptical, despairing and revengeful teachings, he is finally faced with that which has accompanied him all along. In a voice which frightens his animals he cries, 'Up, abysmal thought, out of my depth... For I want to hear you... speak to me' (1982, p. 327). He is now prepared to meet the truth of himself, the truth of will-to-power and of the teacher of will-to-power. 'Zarathustra, the advocate of life, the advocate of suffering, the advocate of the circle; I summon you, my most abysmal thought' (1982, p. 328). He is open, now, to the experience not just of being the student of the sun and the teacher of the sun. Now he is open to the risk of becoming student and teacher as the same sun, of becoming the contradiction which is the truth and self-relation of enlightenment; no longer merely shining for others, now face-to-face with self-light, and cast in and as his own shadow. 'My abyss speaks. I have turned my ultimate depth inside out into the light' (1982, p. 328). Having spoken thus, Zarathustra falls down as if dead, but regains his senses only to remain lying there for seven days. On the seventh day his animals approached him and asked if there was some new knowledge which had come to him. He tells them,

> Everything goes, everything comes back; eternally rolls the wheel of being. Everything dies, everything blossoms again; eternally runs the year of being. Everything breaks, everything is joined anew; eternally the same house of being is built. Everything parts, everything greets every other thing again; eternally the ring of being remains faithful to itself (1982, p. 329).

Zarathustra has awoken from his earlier collapse able to speak his most abysmal thought. Having summoned it from the depths of his own being, it now speaks through him as the truth of his own being. Zarathustra has spoken, and thus breaks himself as he was commanded to do in his stillest hour (1982, p. 258). No longer is he clinging to ideas of the overman, no longer is genealogy a method of overcoming that which man has willed, no longer is will a commanding but not an obeying. Now Zarathustra is that which overcomes itself eternally. Now Zarathustra is a self-willing. Now Zarathustra is a commanding and an obeying. The lessons which form Books 1, 2 and 3 of *Thus Spake Zarathustra* culminate, now, in Zarathustra being able to will them as 'thus I willed it'. The work (the education) in the earlier books now becomes what it always was, Zarathustra's own willing. No longer is Zarathustra the teacher of *ressentiment*, for now even *ressentiment* is part of Zarathustra's 'thus I willed it'. Zarathustra is now himself in and as the 'ring of being' which remains faithful to itself. The ring is the circular nature of will-to-power which in doing what it is, and securing its own victory, is returned to itself as that which must now destroy the victory. Each time Zarathustra the teacher of will-to-power has scored a victory over man's denial of will-to-power, he has personified that victory either as himself or as the overman, or objectified it as genealogy. But each time the truth of his own teaching has contradicted itself by separating its being willed from what results from the willing. The result of will-to-power is never itself when it is solely a victory. This result must assert itself as will-to-power again, which it does in its return to activity, where it has itself as result and as something which must be overcome. It now sets out to destroy the form of itself which exists as an impersonator. The culmination of this education is that will-to-power is returned to itself even in overcoming the teacher of will-to-power. The teacher cannot be allowed to impersonate will-to-power either, for then the teacher rests as a victory, one which must, again, be overcome. Zarathustra, now, is no longer the teacher of will-to-power. Now Zarathustra is the teacher as will-to-power, and therefore as the circle of being. 'Now, being begins,' he says: 'round every Here rolls the sphere There. The centre is everywhere' (1982, p. 330). Zarathustra is now the circle itself. He is in the middle of the bridge, or the tightrope, for he is the rope and the tightrope walker. No longer does he seek to leap over man, for now he is the movement and result of will-to-power, not its impersonator. The most abysmal thought crawled into his throat, but he 'bit off its head and spewed it out' (1982, p. 330).

But even now his disciples are ready to separate the result of Zarathustra's education from Zarathustra himself. They are ready to separate the suffering of the contradiction of will-to-power from the person in whom that suffering and contradiction are the circle which is the self. It is those who seek the gift that are now the greatest danger to Zarathustra, for while it has been he who has prevented himself from becoming himself so far, now it is his disciples who wish him to be other than the light which shines for itself. This relationship between self-light and students is further explored in Book 4.

For now, Zarathustra is able to reflect on how his own will-to-power, that something inside him which was 'invulnerable and unburiable, something that explodes rock' (1982, p. 224), has now exploded himself. Only when his own will-to-power turned against its own inability to have victory without defeat and return did it become the circle of what it is; that is, life that must overcome itself again, and again and again.

His animals, however, bid him go out into the world and 'cure your soul with new songs' (1982, p. 332). They tell him, 'you are the teacher of the eternal recurrence – that is your destiny... we know what you teach' (1982, p. 332). But Zarathustra, now wise to the impersonation by the teacher of will-to-power, by knowledge of the circle, understands their words to be of eternal return but not the circle of eternal return itself. 'We know what you teach,' they say, 'that all things recur eternally and we ourselves too' (1982, p. 332). The animals cling to another victory, but without its defeat. They urge Zarathustra to return to teaching, 'to speak again the word of the great noon of earth and man, to proclaim the overman again to man' (1982, p. 333). Finally, they tell him, 'The hour has now come when he who goes under should bless himself. Thus ends Zarathustra's going under' (1982, p. 333). They might have added 'and thus does it begin again and return eternally', but they are seeing only victory, and not the circle of victory and defeat. Zarathustra, having chastised them for turning the circle into 'a hurdy gurdy song' (1982, p. 332), into something which can be repeated mechanically but is not self as will-to-power, ceases to hear them, and they slip away.

At the end of Book 3, which was originally intended as the end of Zarathustra's story, Zarathustra is conversing with his soul. 'O my soul, I gave you all, and I have emptied all my hands to you' (1982, p. 335). The gift-giver, who sought to be the sun for others and give them his fruit, has now received his own gift. The gift he gives himself is self as will-to-power. The gift is given in return; it is received in the victory of will-to-power over itself. The gift which the circle gives to the giver is self as receiver also, and to the receiver, the gift is also himself as the giver. Will-to-power gives and receives itself. It is in its own light, illuminated by itself, a self-relation visible in the darkness of midnight as itself. The gift-giver is now commander and obeyer. The whole is 'thus I willed it', a whole without rest, for the movement of will, its eternal return, is the whole. Thus Zarathustra is able to conclude, 'Is not giving a need? Is not receiving mercy?' (1982, p. 335). Are not both, to the teacher of will-to-power, one and the same in the teacher?

Book 3 ends with the return of Zarathustra's dancing song. The first dancing song was in Book 2, and formed part of Zarathustra's experience at night with the overcoming of the tombs by life. This dancing song is another resurrection; the same, but different. It marks a return to life for Zarathustra, but a new Zarathustra changed in the return to himself, for he has become what he is, the contradictory circle of will-to-power as self-overcoming. In the previous dancing song he looked life in the eyes and saw that it was most seductive when it spoke ill of itself, denying itself as wisdom or as understandable. Now, in the second dancing song, Zarathustra knows that life teaches best 'with crooked glances' (1982, p. 337). 'I leaped toward you, but you fled back from my leap' (1982, p. 336). But the Zarathustra who sought to know the circle of life, now is the circle of life. 'I dance after you, I follow wherever your traces linger,' (1982, p. 337) says Zarathustra.

Life, however, has met such joy in Zarathustra before, and known it to be only a pretence. Life does not trust Zarathustra to be now what he says he is. 'O Zarathustra, you are not faithful enough to me. You do not love me nearly as much as you say; I know you are thinking of leaving me soon' (1982, p. 338). However, this time Zarathustra has his answer for life ready, for now he knows that there is no leaving, for every leaving is also and inevitably an immediate returning. Life is the whole. Zarathustra reveals to life that he knows her secret as himself, to which life replies, 'You *know* that, O Zarathustra? Nobody knows that' (1982, p. 339). And Zarathustra, ending Book 3, performs the song of the yes-sayer and amen, the 'thus I willed it' song. 'How should I not lust after eternity and after the nuptial ring of rings, the ring of recurrence?' (1982, p. 341). 'I love you, O eternity' (1982, p. 341). With these words of affirmation for the circle, Book 3 comes to an end.

But this could not be the end for Zarathustra. There must be another return, there must be more work, more victory in defeat, more teaching for he whose truth is as the teacher. As life so cleverly warned above, to know return is impossible, for all knowledge is the result of will-to-power. Zarathustra cannot know will-to-power as his own property; he can only know himself as the contradiction which is will-to-power, or as the shadow which is this broken middle of self-light. Nobody knows will-to-power, says life, one can only be will-to-power, even in its being known. Book 4 is not Zarathustra merely teaching the circle, it is about Zarathustra being the circle as he teaches. Book 4 is the overcoming of the dancing song because it is not the saying of amen to will-to-power, it is the doing of it as the self, and as the work which is the teacher, and which is the truth of the teacher. It is the continuing education of Zarathustra by the circle about the teacher, and therefore by himself about himself. In Book 4 education is no longer something done to others; it is something which, in being done to others, is now self-work.

Book 4: the return of the soothsayer

At the beginning of Book 4, years have passed since Zarathustra collapsed and returned to himself from his most abysmal thought. This is no longer a Zarathustra who teaches the overman, or the future. This is now a Zarathustra who is concerned with the present. 'I have long ceased to be concerned with happiness; I am concerned with my work' (1982, p. 349). Just as at the beginning of the Prologue, Zarathustra has his veins full of honey, but now he does not seek merely to give his honey, his wisdom, to mankind as a gift. Now he knows the circle of eternal return where the gift is not his to give, it is rather his to receive in the work of will-to-power which is the self. He climbs a mountain, telling his animals that he intends to sacrifice this gift, but on reaching the summit admits that such is not his intention at all. 'I squander what is given to me,' (1982, p. 350) he admits, remembering how the teaching of his wisdom consistently failed as the shining for others. But now this 'squanderer with a thousand hands' (1982, p. 350), who needed 'hands outstretched to receive' (1982, p. 122), has changed his method of teaching. No longer does he leave the mountain seeking those hands and shining for them. Now he leaves mankind in the dark, awaiting their stillest hour and their self-light to lead them to him. No longer will he impose his gift, he will only give it and receive it when it asked for: 'they must come up to *my* height... men may now come *up* to me' (1982, p. 351). Having repeated the circle of descent, failure and return many times, Zarathustra now waits on his mountain for the sign that the time is right for descent. He will find, however, by the end of Book 4 that the circle of descent, failure and return is the truth of the teacher, and to protect himself from that, by waiting on his mountain and not teaching, is not work, and is to deny himself. This last lesson for Zarathustra is the same lesson – become who you are (1982, p. 351) – as in the rest of the book, but it is the one which finally enables Zarathustra to realise descent and failure, or teaching, as the truth of (the return of) the teacher. Zarathustra's mountain refuge, his 'eternal ground' (1982, p. 352), is safe from further education because it has no students.

266

In Book 4 the truth of Zarathustra's first words in the Prologue – 'what would your happiness be had you not those for whom you shine?' (1982, p. 121) – are about to become his own truth. The teacher cannot rest on the mountain, the teacher has to teach. Only in shining for others is the teacher of will-to-power returned to the self whose truth is return, or the shadow which is self-light. The sun to which Zarathustra first spoke appeared merely to shine for him, to be his light. It is not until the illness of Book 3 that Zarathustra realises that the sun is not just light for others, but its own self-light. In its giving it is returned to itself. It becomes what it is. In Book 4 Zarathustra realises the truth of the relation of return as requiring that from which it is returned. Zarathustra is about to become teacher again, but not until he has stopped protecting himself from relation and self-relation, and not until he ceases to pity those who do not sit where he does, on the eternal ground of his high mountain. The teacher who says 'amen' and 'yes' to the circle, to the ring of recurrence, has become petrified, fixed and immobile. He is now merely a personification of the whole circle, and requires again to shine for others, to teach, in order to be returned to and as himself. That is his work, and that is why, in the end, or the beginning, he again understands the need to descend from the mountain.

As always, at times of impending education and greatest despair, the soothsayer returns to Zarathustra to provoke him into new thoughts and new work. The Zarathustra which waits on the mountain doing no work has 'squandered the old honey down to the last drop' (1982, p. 353). He has nothing to teach because he has no one to teach. And if he has no one to teach, he does not have himself, for the teacher is the relation of the relation. Thus the soothsayer appears and, despite Zarathustra's friendly greetings, informs him that he will not remain on the mountain for much longer. There is a cry of distress coming from below the mountain, a cry which the soothsayer predicts will climb up the mountain and carry Zarathustra away. Zarathustra believes himself immune from this cry. He listens to it as it is thrown to and fro by the abysses to each other 'for none wanted to keep it: so evil did it sound' (1982, p. 354). Zarathustra knows this cry to be the cry of man, but says to the soothsayer 'what is human distress to me?' (1982, p. 354).

The cry, says the soothsayer, is that of the higher man crying for Zarathustra. Zarathustra does not see himself as one of these higher men, even though his position on the mountain is the highest of all men. Nor does he see that the cry which comes from the abyss is also a cry from within himself, and is the cry, again, of the will-to-power which, to become itself, must seek out and destroy the higher man who sits victorious on his mountain waiting for the sign of that victory to come to him. He does not realise yet that the suffering of those below the mountain is the same suffering which he now has himself. Zarathustra, in having no one for whom to shine, like them, is not his own self-light. Zarathustra pities those who are in distress. This pity is also self-pity, and is the final obstacle preventing the further education of even this highest man. The soothsayer, as always, knows of the problem and of its inevitable self-overcoming as will-to-power. Indeed, he has come to seduce Zarathustra the highest man to his 'final sin' (1982, p. 354), that of pity. For now, the soothsayer does merely enough to return Zarathustra to himself as the shadow which appears in the self-light of doubt about his own identity. Zarathustra, he says,

> You are not standing there as one made giddy by his happiness... no one could say to me 'Behold, here dances the last gay man!' Anybody coming to this height, looking for that man, would come in vain: caves he would find, and caves behind caves, hiding places for those addicted to hiding, but no mines of happiness or treasure rooms or new gold veins of happiness – Happiness – how should one find happiness among hermits and those buried like this? (1982, p. 355).

But such an education is too soon for this Zarathustra, who is still protecting himself as the circle of eternal return and therefore from it. So Zarathustra sets out to find the higher men who seek him, and to educate them, only this time not by going down, but by having them come up to his kingdom. The education of the higher man which follows is at one and the same time the self-relation and therefore the self-education of the teacher, whose truth is not merely the knowledge of work, but the circle of victory and defeat which is the work. Zarathustra, again, is about to become what he is, and the soothsayer will be waiting for him one last time.

The seven veils of the higher man

Zarathustra goes walking around his kingdom searching for the higher men whose cry he had heard while with the soothsayer. He is about to meet seven forms of the higher man, some of which are his own shadow, and to invite them all back to his cave. The first appearance is of the two kings, who are no longer revered by a mob which has grown 'false and foul' (1982, p. 357). However, it is still demanded of the kings that they represent the mob, and they point out, 'it is this deception that has come to disgust and nauseate us' (1982, p. 357). Zarathustra makes himself known to them, for he is attracted by the plight of such kings who have gone under and now seek the man who is even higher than they. They reveal to Zarathustra that they 'must hear him who teaches' (1982, p. 359). Zarathustra is delighted to hear the wisdom of the kings: 'man's fate knows no harsher misfortune than when those who have power on earth are not also the first men' (1982, p. 358). Here is a plight with which Zarathustra can identity most strongly, for even the teacher of this power has been rejected by those whose truth he speaks. The first form of the higher man that Zarathustra meets, then, is the form in which power has deteriorated into showpiece occasions and a grand deception. Those who flee such hypocrisy seek Zarathustra for he, too, has taught that power and war is hallowed and to be pursued, not rendered impotent. This

268

path has led them to Zarathustra, and now they are invited to his cave to await his return.

The second form of higher man Zarathustra comes across, by stepping on him, is the conscientious in spirit who lies beside a swamp so that leeches may feed off his blood. He has learnt from Zarathustra that 'Spirit is the life that itself cuts into life' (1982, p. 363), but rather than perform life itself, the man obeys life as if it were an other and, in an act of self-deceptive revenge, seeks the brain of the leech as if it were doing the cutting. The man is not commanding himself as life, thus he requires the leech to draw his own blood. Zarathustra also invites this man to be his guest in the cave.

The third form of the higher man who Zarathustra meets is the magician who appeared first as 'like one abandoned and forsaken by all the world' (1982, p. 364), throwing himself around in convulsions and contortions, and moaning about the cruelty of God's love, and the greater torture of its disappearance. Zarathustra cannot bear such unbridled *ressentiment* and starts to beat the man with his stick. But this brings about a change in the man, who loves those gods most which inflict most pain. 'Don't strike any more, Zarathustra!' says the man, 'I did all this only as a game' (1982, p. 367). Zarathustra asks the magician who he was pretending to be, and he replies, 'the ascetic of the spirit' (1982, p. 368), that man whom Zarathustra himself knows who 'turns his spirit against himself' (1982, p. 368). When Zarathustra was such a guardian of death, in revolt against life as will-to-power, then it took the soothsayer and dreams and life to shake Zarathustra out of this *ressentiment*. But life has always guarded itself against Zarathustra's enlightenments, warning him, 'you are not faithful enough to me' (1982, p. 338). Now, as the circle of life itself, Zarathustra is able to speak to the magician as life has spoken previously to Zarathustra: 'what you have now confessed, that too was not nearly true enough or false enough to suit me' (1982, p. 368). By pretending it was a game, the magician has not been honest enough to admit his own asceticism. The game is another form of lie, another self-punishment for being merely self. Zarathustra, who has himself been caught game-playing by life, and by the soothsayer, is now able to solve this riddle of deception and see through to the very core of what is left of a man who hides behind games: 'your magic has enchanted everybody, but no lie or cunning is left to you to use against yourself: you are disenchanted for yourself. You have harvested nausea as your one truth' (1982, p. 368). The magician agrees, confessing that 'everything about me is a lie' (1982, p. 369), except the fact that he is breaking under the weight of the deception. This breaking is no lie, and thus he seeks the one who understands such breaking to be genuine – Zarathustra. Hearing this, hearing himself described as genuine, Zarathustra is again plunged into the stillness of a long silence, perhaps remembering his own breaking, after which he chastises the magician for searching for a great human being, but invites him to the cave nevertheless, to join the others.

The fourth form of higher man is a seeker who has lost his way while seeking the last pious man, the hermit who had not yet heard that God is dead. This seeker, himself, is the last pope and he 'served that old God until his last hour. But now I am retired, without a master, and yet not free' (1982, p. 371). The last pope has found that the hermit too is dead, and now seeks 'the most pious of all those who do not believe in God' (1982, p. 372), namely Zarathustra. The last pope tells Zarathustra that, of the two of them, God's death hits him harder than it hits Zarathustra. Zarathustra tells the pope to let go of God, accept the death, 'rather make destiny on one's own, rather be a fool, rather be a god oneself' (1982, p. 374). The last pope finds in Zarathustra a devotion and an observance fit for the most pious believer. Zarathustra is pious in his disbelief in God to the extent that, and with such a strength that, 'Some god in you must have converted you to your godlessness' (1982, p. 374). Moreover, implies the last pope, is it not this devotion to the commanding and obeying of will-to-power which 'no longer lets you believe in a god?' (1982, p. 374). The pope acknowledges that he has met a man whose 'overgreat honesty' (1982, p. 374) will lead him even beyond good and evil. Zarathustra has previously taught that 'is not just this godlike that there are gods but no God?' (1982, p. 294). *That* God is thoroughly dead. Yet even the death of that God at the hands of life itself, as a victim of the war which is will-to-power, is still the return of gods that would be God, and of those who would seek to command all past and future as the 'moment' or 'event' of themselves. All such commands are created as *ressentiment* against past and future. All such commands are already defeated by that which they (now) seek to become. As the last pope has identified in Zarathustra, God and godlessness are the same will-to-power, the same war of commanding and obeying. Zarathustra predicts that the old pope's God will not rise again. He is wrong, for later on, in the cave, the old God will return again in the pity and self-pity of those who, as will-to-power, are both the death and the return of the war of commanding and obeying.

The fifth form of higher man is the ugliest man. Whereas the last pope sought Zarathustra as a witness to the self after the death of God, the ugliest man is he who killed God because God was always already a witness to the self (i.e. to the war). 'You are the murderer of God,' says Zarathustra. 'You could not bear him who saw you – who always saw you through and through, you ugliest man! You took revenge on this witness!' (1982, p. 376). In the self-relation of will-to-power the last pope has witnessed the death of God, but the ugliest man has attempted to kill even the (eternal) witness of this (eternal) struggle, to end, once and for all, eternal return, so that even in the stillest and darkest hours self-relation (or, for the ugliest man, self-pity) could be eternally avoided. The ugliest man reminds Zarathustra that he, too, knows how it feels to murder in this way, a reference to the form of the higher man which Zarathustra became when he refused his most abysmal thought. Zarathustra does not pity the ugliest man, as do all those who, out of *ressentiment*, also murder the (eternal) witness. Rather, he passes by this ugliest man, but, in so doing, blushes out of self-recognition. In passing him by, Zarathustra has honoured the ugliest man, for he repeated his sense of shame and did not try to overcome all that was left to the ugliest man. Zarathustra taught a long time ago that what is hardest is 'to close the open hand because one loves'

270

(1982, p. 195). Now the ugliest man, too, has learnt that 'to be unwilling to help can be nobler than that virtue which jumps to help' (1982, p. 377). Both are will-to-power, but while help (pity) is revenge against the condition, embarrassment in the courage of self-recognition is love as the condition. This, for the teacher, is the hardest lesson of all, for it requires always to be the teacher of return by return.

The ugliest man admits that he killed God because God became just such an overpitying burden. He was always too ready to crawl into man's depths and seek to save man from his condition. 'His pity knew no shame: he crawled into my dirtiest nooks. This most curious, overobtrusive, overpitying one had to die... Man cannot bear it that such a witness should live' (1982, pp. 378–9). Zarathustra invites this 'self-exiled exile' (1982, p. 379) to his cave, seeing in the ugliest man one of the greatest of human despisers, yet at the same time one who also loved himself. Zarathustra asks whether this man might be the higher man whose cry he heard earlier, but reminds himself that all men, even the higher man, are something that must be overcome.

The sixth form of higher man Zarathustra meets is the voluntary beggar whom he comes across preaching to a herd of cows. The man informs Zarathustra that the only way to overcome man's great melancholy and nausea at himself is to be like the cows and learn to chew the cud. Such rumination is itself a circle, where what goes in is repeated but in a different form. Yet when the voluntary beggar realises he has met Zarathustra, he greets him as 'the man who overcame this great nausea' (1982, p. 381).

Zarathustra recognises the voluntary beggar as the man who, ashamed of his own wealth, gave it away and fled to the poor, but was not accepted by them. Thus, says Zarathustra, did the voluntary beggar learn 'how right giving is harder than right receiving, and that to give presents well is an art and the ultimate and most cunning master-art of graciousness' (1982, p. 382). It is a lesson Zarathustra understands well, for his own gift has been returned to him on each occasion he has given it. But he has not been particularly open, either, to receive his own gift. The art of giving is to know how to receive, and that it is in receiving and not giving that the grace and humility of the act are to be found. The graciousness of the gift is in its return to the giver. To see this as rejection, as both Zarathustra and the voluntary beggar have done, is to have missed the eternal return of the gift of itself to itself which is will-to-power, or life.

Zarathustra, refusing to accept the compliments which the voluntary beggar wishes to give him, sends him up to his cave to await his return.

Finally, Zarathustra meets the seventh form of the higher man, his own shadow. Just as Zarathustra is becoming annoyed about all the intruders on his mountain, asking himself 'Where has my solitude gone?' (1982, p. 384), so he is joined in this self-awareness by his own shadow. Seeking to be alone, and not to shine as his own shadow, he begins the futile attempt to run away from it until, laughing at the futility, he stops and begins to talk to his shadow. The shadow has followed Zarathustra's adventures always at his heels, but always following, never having a goal or destination of his own. His life is that of the wanderer who lacks his own

271

shadow, who commands but never obeys. Now Zarathustra's shadow, that which obeys him as will-to-power, is no longer satisfied merely to obey. Now he seeks to command himself, to have his own goal and find his home. For the shadow, the eternal is without meaning, for it is not his self; it is therefore in vain. On the mountain, on Zarathustra's eternal ground, even Zarathustra is ceasing to create himself as his own meaning and losing therefore his constant companion, the shadow who obeys as will-to-power commands.

Thus are the seven veils of the higher man revealed and removed. That which is revered as highest, the kings, are no longer revered and the power of the highest has become an empty form. It is the necessity of this deception which drives the kings up to Zarathustra. The conscientious in spirit offers himself to life but is unable to make life his own responsibility. It is this deception which brings him into Zarathustra's domain. The magician knows of his deception and confesses to Zarathustra, but even this confession is only another deceit and thus he too belongs in Zarathustra's kingdom. The last pope is without deceit for he is without a master, a master that he has served faithfully. He finds in Zarathustra someone even more pious than himself and invites himself to Zarathustra's cave. The ugliest man has overcome deception by killing the god that eternally intervened out of pity. This man has put an end to return; this is his deception. The voluntary beggar is he who has learnt to receive rather than to give, although his deception is apparent when he showers praise upon Zarathustra. Finally, Zarathustra's own shadow appears as the spirit that can no longer merely obey, but must command. Each form of the higher man represents a different face of deception and of *ressentiment*, and each is a face that Zarathustra has known as his own on previous occasions. Zarathustra has been, respectively, an dishonoured teacher, a conscientious teacher, a confessional teacher, a pious teacher, a revengeful teacher, the gift-giver, and the obeying teacher. Yet he has also been an honest student of the eternal return of will-to-power, self-taught and commanding. The latter, however, has not survived its own victory in its own kingdom upon the mountain, and the cry of distress has again been heard. Zarathustra's education in Book 4 is that he is resisted by each form of the higher man which he has overcome, in order to show him that such overcoming is not only victory, but defeat. Now, in his cave, the eternal return of will-to-power, of that which must overcome itself, again sits waiting for Zarathustra.

The laughter of self-sufficiency

At noon, Zarathustra finds himself alone again, and he lies down on the ground to sleep. Doubts about his kingdom come to him in a semi-dream which leaves his eyes open and his soul awake. No complete sleep is possible, just as no final higher man is possible even in his own kingdom. Unlike this half-sleep, the problem for Zarathustra on his mountain is that his own life is too 'perfect' (1982, p. 388). The kingdom was built on the truth of the self-war of will-to-power, yet

272

the mountain represents only victory. The defeats have come when Zarathustra has become self-light and shadow away from his mountain and in the failure of his teaching relationship with the people and his disciples. His return to the mountain has each time been his failure, in the market-place or on the blessed isles, to have his gift accepted. In his return he has found happiness but little or no work, while away from the mountains he has found work but little or no happiness. Now, faced again by the need to teach, his own kingdom appears too perfect, and his soul cries out for the work which is return. Zarathustra wonders now if his soul has 'already roamed happily among good and ripe things too long?... Too much that is good has she tasted' (1982, p. 388). Thus this happiness, too, is spoken and breaks. 'What is happening to me?' he asks, 'I have been stung... in the heart... break, heart, after such happiness' (1982, p. 389).

With this awareness that the ring of eternity has become too perfect, too still, Zarathustra wakes again to himself and, not without resistance, realises that the time of innocence, of the child on his mountain, is over and that the time of the labour of the camel and the courage of the lion has come again. The man who, at the beginning Book 4 asked what mattered happiness, he was concerned with his work (1982, p. 349), has now awoken from the slumber of that piety to become the commanding and obeying which is the work. The truth of the self-taught at the end of Book 3 is now, again, the truth of the self-taught as teaching and learning, a commanding and an obeying. The will-to-power has returned to Zarathustra in the forms of the higher men who have again forced him to face himself.

Zarathustra returns to his cave and realises that his guests comprise the higher man and that it was their cry of distress which he had earlier heard. Their despair fills him with good humour and not a little *schadenfreude*. He offers them his hospitality for the evening.

The king begins to speak in praise of Zarathustra. The cry of distress of these higher men is no more. They have found Zarathustra, knowing that in a life which is in vain, without gods, then the only life left is to live with Zarathustra. Many people down the mountains are feeling the same. They may have heard Zarathustra when he taught, and refused the gift. But now, increasingly, their despair is forcing them to seek the teacher again. 'Your tree here, O Zarathustra,' says the king, 'refreshes even the gloomy ones, the failures; your sight reassures and heals the heart even of the restless. And verily, toward your mountain and tree many eyes are directed today; a great longing has arisen, and many have learned to ask, "Who is Zarathustra?"' (1982, p. 393). Many of those who did not listen are now asking why the overman has not returned to them, and some have concluded that perhaps it is they who are to go to him. 'Now the waves are climbing and climbing around your mountain,' (1982, p. 393) says the king, echoing the words of the soothsayer earlier in Book 4. 'And however high your height may be, many must come up to you' (1982, p. 393), including those in great despair and nausea, those who wish to learn from Zarathustra how to hope again. Zarathustra, having refused to take his work back down the mountain, now

273

finds that it is being returned to him by his students. The self-relation of the teacher which had become still on the mountain is being moved again, this time by the relation which is its truth in the world for others. He cannot escape from the work which is his failure and from the failure which is his work, even high up on a mountain. Still, the relation follows him. But what lies ahead for Zarathustra is even now a new lesson, that his truth of self-relation as victory and defeat is also the truth of the relation between teacher and student. At the end of this lesson Zarathustra is again ready to become the truth of the self-relation or broken middle which is the teacher.

But first Zarathustra speaks to the guests in his cave as to those who are a threat to the Zarathustra they seek. In seeking him, they force him to become something which he is not. They seek Zarathustra the overman, the victor, whereas Zarathustra knows himself to be victor in defeat (even though it is a defeat he is lacking in his own kingdom). He will not, therefore, show them consideration, for that would be against the spirit of war which has driven them to him. 'I show my warriors no consideration' (1982, p. 394), he says to his guests, and informs them that it is not for them, nor for those suffering despair and nausea who follow them, that he has waited on the mountain. Indeed, these people would only spoil his victory by showering praise upon him. Their gifts would return the victory of will-to-power to itself, and thus ensure further defeat, further work. Zarathustra in his kingdom is not seeking such work. Rather, he is seeking those who do *not* need him, those who are already their own self-relation. Their gift will not be to Zarathustra as their teacher, for their gift is already given and received by themselves. Zarathustra awaits free spirits who will know his kingdom as their own, he seeks friends and companions, not students. 'It is for others that I wait here in these mountains, and I will not lift my feet from here without them; it is for those who are higher, stronger, more triumphant, and more cheerful... laughing lions must come' (1982, p. 395). Zarathustra questions his guests as to why they do not tell him stories of such people, why the seed which he has sown on his blessed isles has not blossomed into the children who are the 'life-trees of my will and my highest hope?' (1982, p. 395).

The soothsayer breaks into the ensuing silence, reminding Zarathustra that they have been invited for supper but have so far received no food, only speeches. Thus begins the supper at which the topic of conversation is the higher man and the desire for the overman. Zarathustra tells his guests how he first spoke to the mob in the market-place but gained only corpses for companions. The mob preached equality before God, but now that God has died, and the higher man, the unequal man, has been resurrected. Thus 'now we want the overman to live' (1982, p. 399). Man is no longer something that must be preserved, but is now something that must be overcome. The small man who seeks to preserve himself is now the overman's greatest danger. Zarathustra's hope for the overman therefore lies not in those who would surrender to the will for preservation but who would wage war on such a revengeful spirit, even to the extent of despairing when alternative futures do not appear. 'I love you for not knowing how to live today, you higher

274

men! For thus you live best' (1982, p. 400). The higher men are lost, not preserved. Even the higher man has therefore changed from the start of the book, for these men do not consider themselves to have finished with education. Zarathustra, however, again teaches them the overman. He does not see that perhaps his seed has given birth to these new men, not to the overman, but to people like himself, fighting the war of will-to-power as a self-relation which knows no rest and finds no peace. It is these children who now threaten the illusory peace that Zarathustra has created for himself on the mountain. These students are about to remind him of who he is, and what he must do in order to be himself. They are about to ensure that the teacher of the overman overcomes this self-pitying self-relation which refuses its relation to and return from others. These men know the fear of self-relation, a fear Zarathustra has forgotten, for he no longer shines. They have the courage to defeat themselves. Zarathustra must again find the same courage.

But such students as are assembled in the cave are those who have still sought the higher man in someone other than themselves. Zarathustra knows this because it is the truth of his own journey. In the Prologue and Books 1 and 2, Zarathustra taught the overman as someone who was to come. But each time his teaching was returned to him and the giver of the gift received the gift. Finally, in Book 3, Zarathustra learned that the truth of the overman was returned to him as his own relation, as his own work. Overcoming was present only in its relation to its self or as contradiction. When Zarathustra learns of himself as eternal return, as the circle, then he is no longer suffering from the illusion of self-relation as the overman, but from the truth of life itself, a truth in which the overman and overcoming are overcome and not overcome, suffering, that is, from the eternal return of will-to-power. It is this education which enables Zarathustra now to tell his guests that they 'do not yet suffer enough to suit me. For you suffer from yourselves, you have not yet suffered *from man*... You all do not suffer from what I have suffered' (1982, p. 401), namely from the truth of man as his own contradictory self-relation or broken middle.

If these higher man are to learn that overcoming is return then they must not seek light from others, only from themselves. Until their gift is to themselves, of themselves, they will suffer only as man, but not from the truth of mankind which is life. 'If you would go high, use your own legs. Do not let yourself be carried up; do not sit on the backs and heads of others' (1982, p. 402). The teacher is now telling his guests that he has learnt the truth of man by being man, and becoming what man is. He has climbed his own mountain using his own legs, doing what he is. These higher men must become their own teachers and climb their own mountains. However, it still lies ahead for Zarathustra to learn that the teacher is not victory and defeat on his mountain and that he, too, must return to that which is life. He tells his guests, 'solitude is inadvisable for many' (1982, p. 404), but for Zarathustra the teacher, the self-teacher, solitude is proving insufficient for the working life which has been, is, and will be his self-truth. There is no return in solitude. For the teacher there is only the solitude which is return, the solitude in which shining for others is also a shining for self, as self. Return, or education, is in relation to the teacher, and the teacher is also in relation to those he teaches, for education, or self-light, is only the relation of the relation. That, precisely, is why and how it is self-work. This is Zarathustra's final lesson, but is still to come.

Zarathustra's message to his guests is that they must learn to laugh at their failures to overcome, for in that way they will become what they are. They must learn to dance 'as one must dance – dancing away over yourselves. What does it matter that you are failures? How much is still possible. So learn to laugh away over yourselves' (1982, p. 407). The speech ends with Zarathustra's entreaty to his guests to 'learn to laugh' (1982, p. 408). But Zarathustra does not find much humour, and slips out of the cave for some fresh air and some silence. While Zarathustra is away, the magician admits that, even though he loves Zarathustra, his old melancholy caused by the death of God returns to him. He picks up the harp and sings to the others of his own melancholia at being 'banished from all truth' (1982, p. 412). It is the conscientious in spirit who tries to fend off this melancholy devil, reminding the magician that this is the sort of thinking which would 'lure us back into prisons' (1982, p. 413). But in looking around, he can already see that the other guests are beginning to return to the joy of the defeated, and separating themselves again from the despair of the victorious: 'you free souls,' the conscientious man asks them, 'where is your freedom gone?' (1982, p. 413). The conscientious in spirit reveals his own fear of freedom to the guests, but Zarathustra returns and reminds them all that fear is not a characteristic of those who have found their way to Zarathustra's kingdom. It was man who learnt courage from the animals, and then it was this courage 'finally refined, spiritualised, spiritual, this courage with eagles' wings and serpents' wisdom' (1982, p. 415) which is now called, and his guests reply with one voice, 'Zarathustra' (1982, p. 415). The melancholy again vanishes amid great laughter, but still Zarathustra feels uncomfortable and seeks to slip outside for some clean air. However, he is prevented from doing so by his shadow who pleads 'Stay with us. Else our old musty depression might seize us again' (1982, p. 416). The shadow, who has only ever obeyed and never commanded, is now afraid that his new-found spirit of freedom will disappear if Zarathustra is not present to ensure that the air remains clear and pure and free from pity. Zarathustra has now become the witness to the free selves of these higher men, a witness whom they need and are dependent upon, says the shadow, and without whom 'the evil routine would resume... the evil routine of our own howling and cries of distress' (1982, p. 416). It remains to be seen whether the guests will also have to murder this witness, or whether the teacher will withdraw his hand from them once again and return to the solitude of the mountain, or whether something else will result from this meeting.

The shadow sings his song and the cave is filled with noise and laughter, which Zarathustra takes to be 'a sign of convalescence' (1982, p. 422). Perhaps his guests have finally learned of themselves as return, as life, as will-to-power, and have returned to themselves able to laugh in and as the circle. 'Where is their

276

distress now?' (1982, p. 422), asks Zarathustra. Even if their laughing is still not quite his laughing, nevertheless 'This day represents a triumph: he is even now retreating, he is fleeing, the spirit of gravity, my old archenemy' (1982, p. 422). Such developments are the way to the most abysmal thought, and Zarathustra is able to offer himself a little credit for this development. 'They are biting, my bait is working... Even now they have learned to laugh at themselves' (1982, p. 423). The teacher who has become the fisherman, casting his hook from the mountain instead of wielding it indiscriminately in the market-place, has hooked some worthy pupils. Under his tutelage, and by this new method of teaching, 'Nausea is retreating from these higher men. Well then! That is my triumph. In my realm they feel safe, all stupid shame runs away, they unburden themselves... They are convalescing' (1982, p. 423). However, pride, as they say, comes before a fall.

Suddenly the noise from the cave becomes a silence, and Zarathustra finds that all his guests have fallen to their knees in worship of the ass that accompanied the kings up the mountain. 'They have all become pious again, they are praying, they are mad' (1982, p. 424). Those of whom Zarathustra had such high hopes, and those in whom he was taking some pride as the result of his own work, are now worshipping the ass as he who 'carries our burden, he took upon himself the form of a servant, he is patient of heart and never says No' (1982, p. 424). The higher men whom Zarathustra believed to be recovering from merely obeying, and who were beginning to command, have returned again to those whose spirit is not of life but against life. Again they are full of *ressentiment* and revenge against what man is.

Zarathustra jumps into the middle of this strange ceremony and challenges their foolishness. He challenges the old pope directly as to how he can adore an ass as a god. The pope replies, 'Better to adore God in this form than in no form at all' (1982, p. 426). The shadow tells Zarathustra that 'The old god lives again' (1982, p. 426). Even though the ugliest man killed him, 'in the case of gods death is always a mere prejudice' (1982, p. 426). The conscientious man tells Zarathustra that 'God seems relatively most credible to me in this form' and he warns Zarathustra that 'overabundance and wisdom could easily turn you too into an ass' (1982, p. 427). Finally, Zarathustra asks the ugliest man, the murderer of God, why he has awakened Him again. Who knows whether he is awake or not, is the reply, but of one thing the ugliest man is certain, and he has learned it from Zarathustra: 'Not by wrath does one kill, but by laughter' (1982, p. 427). God cannot survive laughter because laughter is will-to-power as self-sufficiency, a sovereignty personified by the enlightened sage on his mountain in his solitude. The final lesson ahead for Zarathustra is that he is not laughing on his mountain; far from it, he has become a self-pitying figure cut off from the work which is his truth. His self-sufficient laughter has killed God, but God has returned to his mountain with these higher men as the failure implicit in their own work, their own attempts at self-overcoming. Zarathustra's laughter appears self-sufficient. But this is only the final act of wrath and revenge against life by Zarathustra, who seeks to protect the circle. God survives this act of revenge because it is a revengeful act. But it has taken more teaching and a lack of isolation to bring Zarathustra to the point, now immanent, where he realises this.

The pride of the enlightened and isolated sage is still to the fore and enables Zarathustra to interpret the ass festival as something which child-convalescents do. 'It seems to me such flowers as you require new festivals... This you invented when you were with me and I take that for a good sign: such things are invented only by convalescents' (1982, pp. 428–9).

Return of the teacher

Zarathustra's confidence in his guests is the confidence of the teacher that his pupils have truly learnt his lesson. The proof of this will appear at midnight, when his pupils will reflect, in their self-light, that they have returned to themselves, that they now do their own work, and that the gift which Zarathustra gives is of self-return. But his confidence is misplaced and untimely. He has found his guests inventing a ritual to an ass as a devoted servant, but he has interpreted it as a sign that they have recovered from the most abysmal thought, and are celebrating that recovery. Filled with feelings of success, the teacher and his guests move out of the cave and into the night, where midnight – the stillest hour – approaches. Further evidence of convalescence and of their becoming eternal return as self is provided by the ugliest man, who says that, on this day, 'I am for the first time satisfied that I have lived my whole life... one day, one festival with Zarathustra, taught me to love the earth' (1982, p. 429). The final and overwhelming endorsement comes when he then says, 'Was *that* life... Well then! Once more' (1982, p. 430).

But this midnight revel of self-light is not quite as it appears. The return of which the ugliest man speaks is not self-relation at all. When Zarathustra, at the end of Book 3, embraced the circle, it was as a gift to himself, his own will-to-power as the war which is the self. But here, for the ugliest man, the gift is not returned as his own will-to-power, but still as that of his teacher. When he asks, 'was that life?' he makes clear that it is 'For *Zarathustra's* sake! Well then! Once more!' (1982, p. 430, my emphasis). Self-consciously blasphemous or not, return is still from the teacher, the lesson is accepted on behalf of the teacher, and for his sake. This is not self-relation, it is the illusion of self-relation. The light in which the guests are standing, at midnight, is not their own, it is still Zarathustra's. He is still the sun shining for others, even at midnight. Even in the stillest hour his pupils do not receive themselves, because they do not give themselves. The scene here, at midnight on the mountain, is still one of revenge. The pupils refuse to become what they are, relying on Zarathustra as will-to-power for the truth of themselves, and Zarathustra is still seeking to overcome his pupils for them, out of pity for these higher men. He is forced into becoming the god of will-to-power for them, and the more they worship him, the less of himself he becomes.

When the ugliest man speaks of return, all the higher men 'at once became conscious of how they had changed and convalesced and to whom they owed this: then they jumped toward Zarathustra to thank, revere, caress him, and kiss his hands' (1982, p. 430). Such revenge against return, manifested as adoration of the teacher, returns Zarathustra again to himself, for yet again his gift is returned, yet again his gift has been visible only in the personification of it as the teacher. His pupils have only been involved in overcoming as obeying, not as commanding. Thus is the commander, now, again the obstacle to the self-education of the pupils. His personification is already the defeat and victory of will-to-power over itself, yet, as always, it is also the return of will-to-power which must now overcome that personification. It is this relation as the truth of education which Zarathustra understands, now, at the end of Book 4.

Surrounded by adoring pupils Zarathustra becomes dizzy and dumb, and is forced to ward off 'the throng of the revering' (1982, p. 431). As midnight approaches it becomes clear to Zarathustra, for the first time since the end of Book 3, that the self-light of eternal return has returned to him through his recognition that the shining for others of the teacher is not a gift, it is a domination. Shining for them means shining instead of them. The midnight which approaches is a further self-clarity of his relation as will-to-power. Zarathustra has always been returned to himself in the midnight hour from his work and as his work as the teacher. Now, again, eternal return returns as his own truth, and once again puts him clearly in the relation of self-light. He is about to become return again, he is about to become that which he already is.

As midnight approaches, Zarathustra warns the higher men that in the stillness and the quiet of midnight, 'Here things are heard that by day may not become loud' (1982, p. 431). He asks his guests, 'Do you not hear how it speaks secretly, terribly, cordially to you – the old deep, deep midnight?' (1982, p. 432). Knowing of old the pain and depth of the midnight hour, and knowing the return of return to be the greatest illness and abyss, Zarathustra admits 'Sooner would I die, die rather than tell you what my midnight heart thinks now' (1982, p. 432). It is in the true revelation of midnight, when there is no sun, that the self becomes visible. It could be mistaken for drunkenness when 'the tombs stammer "Redeem the dead"'(1982, p. 432), but this drunkenness is the movement and work of will-to-power on itself, as itself; it is no longer a work done for the master of light. The sun is an illusory master. 'Is not the midnight brighter?' (1982, p. 433), he asks.

Returned to himself not as God but as will-to-power, Zarathustra again deepens his self-relation to eternal return. On earth, as sun, and on his mountain, in a spirit of pity for the higher man, he has sought offspring other than himself. Throughout the book, Zarathustra has wanted pupils, children and disciples, and only in the failure of each attempt has he been returned to himself. Now the new convalescent recovers from his attempt to create children in his own kingdom rather than theirs. His recovery is his return to himself. At midnight, in the joy of defeat which is will-to-power as self-education, Zarathustra knows that joy 'does not want heirs, or children – joy wants itself, wants eternity, wants recurrence, wants everything eternally the same' (1982, p. 434). Zarathustra's education to his guests is no longer to come to his cave to receive the gift of his kingdom. Now, in the clarity of midnight, Zarathustra is able to speak the truth of return and break. The higher men have come in search of the personification of will-to-power. This search has prevented their own return to what they already are, and has further objectified and made static the teacher and his kingdom. All sought to be other than themselves, the higher men by fleeing themselves, the teacher by securing himself. Only together did they perform the work which is the truth of their relation. Now Zarathustra teaches the truth of the contradiction which is eternal return, and therefore of the teacher and of the guests. In contradiction, in work, in the refusal of self to become the refusal, there, 'Just now [the] world became perfect; midnight too is noon; pain too is a joy; curses too are a blessing; night too is a sun' (1982, p. 435). If his guests are able to become that which they already are then they will embrace these opposites, they will embrace victory and defeat as one and the same movement and result. To everything which returns us to self-light, which deepens our self-relation, and which returns us from the sun to midnight, say 'well then, once more'. Such movement will not be our successes or completions, for the circle is never complete except as itself, as return. 'All eternal joy longs for failures. For all joy wants itself, hence it also wants agony... You higher men, do learn this, joy wants eternity. Joy wants the eternity of all things, wants deep, wants deep eternity' (1982, p. 436). Zarathustra invites the higher men to join in his new song of recurrence, to sing it to him. This is his last act of pity for the higher men. This is his last attempt to save them from that which they must become – themselves, through their own work, and in their own self-light at midnight.

In the morning, the end of Book 4 and the beginning of the Prologue form the truth of the circle. Zarathustra awakes and says to the sun, 'what would your happiness be had you not those for whom you shine?' (1982, p. 436). At this moment the whole book could begin again, unchanged, with Zarathustra setting off down the mountain to become the sun that shines for others, the teacher of the overman. But this is not the same Zarathustra with whom the book begins. This Zarathustra has learnt that shining for others is merely a going across, which is already the result of a going down and a going under. It is the going down which enables the work to become the truth of the relation which he teaches. In the sky, the sun shines for others, and is itself not merely as the sun but as the sun that shines. But at midnight the sun shines for itself only, in the darkness. It is in darkness that the sun is its own self-relation, a self-shining. It would not be returned to itself if it did not also have those for whom it shines. Thus as day leads to night, so the teacher, in relation to students, becomes the relation of teacher *and* student. After midnight, and the return of the teacher of relation to (self-) relation, so a new day, a new lesson begins, different because of the night before, but the same because it is the repetition of will-to-power as eternal return. As the sun shines, so those for whom it shines are also returned to themselves at midnight, and thus do students also become teachers. Zarathustra has dreamt of

280

the overman, and of a future where all men are suns and moons, days and nights, teachers and students. But the work which is will-to-power has overcome even dreams of the overman The overman dies and returns, but is not the truth of dying and returning. The truth of dying and returning is will-to-power, and will-to-power will always overcome anything which stands opposed to it, including the teacher. It is this which Zarathustra will now teach. This teacher shines for others in opposition to himself. Opposition is the substance or essence of will-to-power, where any success is also defeat, and where the truth of will-to-power is the broken middle of self-work, self-relation, and self-light.

This is his work for *this* morning. He no longer gives us the overman, now he gives us the teacher of the overman. What he teaches is himself. His present (now) is the circle of past and future of which he is the eternal return of the 'moment'. The present is not a gift which can be given without being returned. Thus he gives the present in order to receive it. What he gets in return is himself, but no longer as the sun which shines for others. Now he is the sun which shines for itself in its relation to others.

What the teacher gives now, in the morning, he receives back as the educational revolution of the day and night. In the return of the present, the revolution is comprehensive. This morning, Zarathustra's gift is no longer pity for those who are not themselves. Self-pity is a *ressentiment* by the teacher against what has been and what will be again. It is the teacher as moment, clinging to his present, refusing to risk it as the gift which can only be received in return. Thus, this morning, at the end of one day and the beginning of another, Zarathustra speaks thus; 'Pity for the higher man... *that* has had its time! My suffering and my pity for suffering – what does it matter? Am I concerned with *happiness*? I am concerned with my *work*' (1982, p, 439). In the truth of eternal return, this morning Zarathustra descends the mountain, embarking upon another day, glowing as the morning sun, in search of those from whom he will receive himself. Now his own hands are outstretched to receive from them the gift which (yesterday) he believed to be his own.

281

The gift of the conclusion

By the close of day man has erected a building constructed from his own inner Sun; and when in the evening he contemplates this, he esteems it more highly than the original external Sun. For now he stands in a conscious relation to his Spirit, and therefore in a free relation. If we hold this image fast in our mind, we shall find it symbolising the course of History, the great Day's work of Spirit (Hegel, 1956, p. 103).

'At daybreak, Zarathustra is shining for others, "glowing as strong as a morning sun that comes out of dark mountains"' (1982, p. 439).

But morning becomes the law. Morning is the teacher who 'promises beginnings of the day' (Rose, 1996, p. 42) for others.

Noon is the zenith of morning. It is where the world becomes perfect, in the full light of itself, its complete self-expression as daylight.

In the afternoon, however, 'I, Zarathustra... summon you, my most abysmal thought' (1982, p. 328). The sun and the teacher begin to go down and to go under.

In the fading light, with the falling of dusk, 'the owl of Minerva spreads its wings' (Hegel, 1967, p. 13), to 'reflect on the remains of the day, the ruins of the morning's hope, the actuality of its broken middle' (Rose, 1996, p. 42).

With dusk, 'the secrecy of the night came closer' (Nietzsche, 1982, p. 429), where 'things are heard that by day may not become loud' (1982, p. 431). 'Gone! Gone! O youth! O noon! O afternoon! Now evening has come and night and midnight' (1982, p. 434). 'Alas that I must be light' (1982, p. 219).

'The danger of those who give [who teach] is that they lose their sense of shame' (1982, p. 218). 'You know it, Zarathustra, but you do not say it!' (1982, p. 257) 'Speak your word and break' (1982, p. 258). Speaking the word is the event of the teacher. The educator is the victory and the defeat of education. He has overcome and he must be overcome. He possesses what he must lose. To teach the circle is the work of the victory and defeat of overcoming himself.

Breaking the event of the teacher is teaching that he is already this circle. He is his own content. He has walked this path before to become what he is and he is already walking it again and losing what he is. His teaching is an overcoming of event, yet it is also the event of overcoming. Must not the teacher have been here before? Must not whatever can be taught have already been taught? Is not the teacher repeating himself?

'The world is deep, deeper than the day had been aware' (1982, p. 439). 'Is not the midnight brighter?' (1982, p. 433). 'The owl of Minerva has spread her wings... we may now be readied for comprehension' (Rose, 1992, p. xi).

But this teacher arrives on the scene this morning too late to enjoy a beginning. For the moment, this teacher is 'already slightly later in the day' (Rose, 1996, p. 62).

However, this teacher no longer merely shines for others. This teacher shamefully gives in order to receive; his gift is given in return for itself. It is the gift of himself, given to others so that he may receive it in return and by return. It is a comprehensive gift and a comprehensive education. As such, it is a contradiction which 'does not need to be superceded... [but] the danger of its experience needs to be exposed. And the same danger will be the means of its exposition. Otherwise we remain at the beginning of the day' (Rose, 1996, p. 58).

Within the contradiction of enlightenment, no longer concerned with happiness, 'now I am concerned with my work' (Nietzsche, 1982, p. 439). It is a call to the vocation of the teacher by the teacher of vocation.

Bibliography

Adorno, T. (1973), *Negative Dialectics*, London: RKP.

Adorno, T. (1976), *The Positivist Dispute in German Sociology*, Aldershot: Avebury, (reprint 1994).

Adorno, T. (1978), 'Resignation', Telos, 35, pp. 165–8.

Adorno, T. and Horkheimer, M. (1979), *Dialectic of Enlightenment*, London: Verso, trans. J. Cumming.

Althusser, L. (1984), *Essays on Ideology*, London: Verso.

Bourdieu, P. and Passeron, J.C. (1977), *Reproduction in Education, Society and Culture*, London: Sage.

Bourdieu, P. (1984), *Homo Academicus*, Cambridge: Polity Press.

Bourdieu, P. (1990), *The Logic of Practice*, Cambridge: Polity Press.

Carr, W. and Kemmis, S. (1986), *Becoming Critical: Education, Knowledge and Action Research*, London: Falmer Press.

Dews, P. (1992), *Autonomy and Solidarity*, London: Verso.

Durkheim, E. (1956), *Education and Sociology*, New York: The Free Press.

Durkheim, E. (1961), *Moral Education*, New York: The Free Press.

Durkheim, E. (1974), *Sociology and Philosophy*, New York: The Free Press.

Durkheim, E. (1977), *The Evolution of Educational Thought*, London: RKP.

Durkheim, E. (1982), *The Rules of Sociological Method*, London: Macmillan.

Durkheim, E. (1984), *The Division of Labour in Society*, London: Macmillan.

Foucault, M. (1970), *The Order of Things*, London: Tavistock.

Foucault, M. (1972), *The Archaeology of Knowledge*, London: Tavistock.

Foucault, M. (1973), *The Birth of the Clinic*, London: Tavistock.

Foucault, M. (1977a), *Language, Counter-Memory, Practice*, New York: Cornell University Press.

Foucault, M. (1977b), *Discipline and Punish: The Birth of the Prison*, Harmondsworth: Penguin.

Foucault, M. (1978), *The History of Sexuality Volume 1*, Harmondsworth: Penguin.

285

Foucault, M. (1980), *Power/Knowledge*, London: Harvester Wheatsheaf.

Foucault, M. (1983), *This is not a Pipe*, Berkeley: University of California Press.

Foucault, M. (1988), *Politics, Philosophy and Culture*, London: Routledge.

Foucault, M. (1991), *The Foucault Reader*, Harmondsworth: Penguin.

Freire, P. (1972), *Pedagogy of the Oppressed*, Harmondsworth: Penguin.

Freire, P. (1974), *Education for Critical Consciousness*, London: Sheed and Ward.

Freire, P. (1995), *Paulo Freire at the Institute*, London: University of London, Institute of Education.

Giroux, H.A. (1983), *Theory and Resistance in Education: A Pedagogy for the Opposition*, London: Heinemann.

Giroux, H.A. (1989), *Schooling for Democracy*, London: Routledge.

Giroux, H.A. (1992), *Border Crossings*, London: Routledge.

Giroux, H.A. (1994), *Disturbing Pleasures*, London: Routledge.

Habermas, J. (1966), 'Knowledge and Interest', *Inquiry*, Vol. ix, pp. 285–300.

Habermas, J. (1976), *Legitimation Crisis*, London: Heinemann.

Habermas, J. (1979), *Communication and the Evolution of Society*, London: Heinemann.

Habermas, J. (1980), 'On the German-Jewish Heritage', *Telos*, 44.

Habermas, J. (1982), 'The Entwinement of Myth and Enlightenment: Re-reading the *Dialectic of Enlightenment*', *New German Critique*, 26.

Habermas, J. (1987a), *Knowledge and Human Interests*, Cambridge: Polity Press.

Habermas, J. (1987b), *The Philosophical Discourse of Modernity*, Cambridge: Polity Press.

Habermas, J. (1987c), *The Theory of Communicative Action, Volume 2: The Critique of Functionalist Reason*, Cambridge: Polity Press.

Habermas, J. (1988), *Theory and Practice*, Cambridge: Polity Press.

Habermas, J. (1989), *The New Conservatism*, Cambridge: Polity Press.

Habermas, J. (1990), *Moral Consciousness and Communicative Action*, Cambridge: Polity Press.

Habermas, J. (1991), *The Theory of Communicative Action, Volume 1: Reason and the Rationalisation of Society*, Cambridge: Polity Press.

Hegel, G.W.F. (1956), *The Philosophy of History*, New York: Dover Publications.

Hegel, G.W.F. (1967), *Philosophy of Right*, Oxford: Oxford University Press.

Hegel, G.W.F. (1969), *Science of Logic*, London: George, Allen and Unwin, trans. A.V. Miller.

Hegel, G.W.F. (1971), *Philosophy of Mind*, Oxford: Oxford University Press.

Hegel, G.W.F. (1975), *Hegel's Logic: Part I of the Encyclopaedia of the Philosophical Sciences*, Oxford: Oxford University Press, trans., W. Wallace.

Hegel, G.W.F., (1977), *Phenomenology of Spirit*, Oxford: Oxford University Press, trans. A.V. Miller.

Hegel, G.W.F. (1984), *Hegel: The Letters*, Bloomington: Indiana University Press, trans. C. Butler and C. Seiler.

Kant, I. (1990), *Foundations of the Metaphysics of Morals*, New York: Macmillan.

Macey, D. (1993), *The Lives of Michel Foucault*, London: Vintage.

Mackenzie, M. (1909), *Hegel's Educational Theory and Practice*, London: Swann Sonnenschein.

Marx, K. and Engels, F. (1967), *The Communist Manifesto*, Harmondsworth: Penguin.

Marx, K. (1970), *The German Ideology*, London: Lawrence and Wishart.

Marx, K. (1973), *Grundrisse*, Harmondsworth: Penguin.

Marx, K. (1975), *Early Writings*, Harmondsworth: Penguin.

Marx, K. (1976), *Capital Volume 1*, Harmondsworth: Penguin.

Michaelis, E. and Keatley Moore, H. (1915), *Autobiography of Friedrich Froebel*, London: George, Allen and Unwin.

Neill, A.S. (1961), *Summerhill*, Harmondsworth: Penguin.

Neill, A.S. (1992), *The New Summerhill*, Harmondsworth: Penguin.

Nietzsche, F. (1968), *Basic Writings of Nietzsche*, New York: Modern Library, trans. W. Kaufmann.

Nietzsche, F. (1982), *The Portable Nietzsche*, Harmondsworth: Penguin, trans. W. Kaufmann.

Roche, S. (1987), *Icon Bent Booklet 1*, Brighton: Icon Bennett.

Rose, G. (1978), *The Melancholy Science: An Introduction to the Thought of Theodor. W. Adorno*, London: Macmillan.

Rose, G. (1981), *Hegel Contra Sociology*, London: Athlone.

Rose, G. (1984), *Dialectic of Nihilism*, Oxford: Blackwell.

Rose, G. (1992), *The Broken Middle*, Oxford: Blackwell.

Rose, G. (1993), *Judaism and Modernity*, Oxford: Blackwell.

Rose, G. (1995), *Love's Work*, London: Chatto and Windus.

Rose, G. (1996), *Mourning Becomes the Law*, Cambridge: Cambridge University Press.

Rousseau, J.J. (1973), *The Social Contract and Discourses*, London: Everyman.

Rousseau, J.J. (1974), *Emile*, London: Everyman.

Sharp, R. (1980), *Knowledge, Ideology and the Politics of Schooling: Towards a Marxist Analysis of Education*, London: RKP.

Young, R. (1989), *A Critical Theory of Education: Habermas and our Children's Future*, London: Harvester Wheatsheaf.

Index

289